# BOY WONDER
## *of*
# WALL STREET

# BOY WONDER *of* WALL STREET

## The Life & Times of Financier Eddie Gilbert

RICHARD WHITTINGHAM

TEXERE

New York · London

Published in 2003 by TEXERE LLC
55 East 52nd Street, New York, NY 10055
T: +1 (212) 317 5106   F: +1 (212) 317 5178   www.etexere.com

In the U.K. by TEXERE Publishing Limited
71–77 Leadenhall Street, London EC3A 3DE
T: +44 (0) 20 7204 3644   F: +44 (0) 20 7208 6701   www.etexere.co.uk

This book was designed and produced by Meadows Design Office Incorporated, Washington, D.C. www.mdomedia.com

Project Director and Producer: *Peter N. Heydon*
Creative Director and Designer: *Marc Alain Meadows*
Image Researcher: *Amy Frenkil Meadows*
Manuscript Editor and Indexer: *Caroline Taylor*
Production Assistants: *Nancy Bratton, Ching Huang Ooi*

LIBRARY OF CONGRESS CATALOGING-IN-PUBLICATION DATA

Whittingham, Richard.
Boy wonder of Wall Street : the life & times of financier Eddie Gilbert / Richard
Whittingham.
    p.  cm.
Includes index.
ISBN 1-58799-174-8
1. Gilbert, Eddie.  2. Capitalists and financiers — United States — Biography.  I. Title.
HG172.G55W48 2003
332'. 092—dc21
[B]                                                                          2002042984

PRINTED AND BOUND IN CANADA

07  06  05  04  03   5  4  3  2  1

FOR CHUCK WHITTINGHAM

#  CONTENTS

♦

# *Acknowledgments*

The author wishes to express his gratitude to Peter Heydon, director of THE MOSAIC FOUNDATION, whose support throughout the five years it took to research and write this book never wavered and whose enthusiasm was a continuing source of motivation. In addition, his editorial contributions were equally generous. His time, effort, and literary talent provided a most valuable addition to the final product.

The author also expresses his appreciation to Eddie Gilbert, who co-operated fully, while agreeing to the stipulation that he would have no voice in the editorial content of the manuscript nor see any part of the book until it was published. The many face-to-face interviews and long hours on the telephone were as essential as they were illuminating.

Special thanks are extended to attorney Gene Wolkoff for his legal guidance and advice throughout the creation of the book and to Eddie's sister Enid Smiley and her husband Leonard for their many contributions.

Dozens of interviews were conducted during the course of research; hundreds of hours were recorded on tape. To those who provided their time and insights, friends and detractors of Eddie Gilbert alike, the author also expresses his thanks. Of special note are attorneys Tom Field, Peter Fleming, Herald Fahringer, and Jeffrey Livingston; Eddie's close friends in England, the late John Aspinall and Richard Parkes; those having important professional, business, and personal dealings, among them Jerry Stern, Robert Linton, Red Chandor, Hugo Gelardin, Ludwig Cserhat, Larry Kaufman, Gordon Dick, Gavin MacLeod, Ed McGowin, Claudia DeMonte, Hy Gordon, Andy Feltz, Richard Beatty, Fred Papert, John Houseman, Paul Gerwin, and Robin Smith; and especially his two business partners in BGK, Fred Kolber, and Ed Berman.

The author offers special thanks to Eddie's wife of seventeen years, Peaches Gilbert, for her cooperation and enthusiasm in the project. Two former wives, Turid Holton and Linda Watkins, also contributed meaningfully. And for his guidance and persistence in making the book available to publishers, Tom Wallace of T. C. WALLACE, LIMITED has the deep appreciation of everyone associated with this project.

The author is additionally indebted to the late journalist Tony Stratton Smith, whose journal was of great help in illuminating Eddie Gilbert's life in exile in Brazil in 1962.

In addition, the author sincerely thanks the Chicago Public Library, the New York Public Library, the British Library in London, and the Evanston, Illinois, Public Library for their services and resources. For research, Amy Whittingham, and for transcription and secretarial services, Teresa Koltzenburg, both also have the author's gratitude.

# *Prologue*

The sky above New York City was low and gunmetal gray the morning of Tuesday, June, 12, 1962. Blending with the heavy, waterlogged air left over from the previous day's summer rain, the still cloudy sky created a kind of Hemingwayesque aura of doom and gloom. No one should have seen the coincidence between the somber atmosphere and his fate that day so much as Eddie Gilbert, who rose early that morning in the Gramercy Park apartment on 23rd Street belonging to his girlfriend, Turid Holtan, to shower, shave, and go face what was surely to be one of the worst days of his life.

Distracted, he skipped breakfast and shared no more than a few words with the attractive young woman who quietly watched him go about his business in her apartment. He ignored the *New York Times* on the table in the foyer whose stories that day were about as upbeat as the weather outside. Had he glanced at the *Times*, he would have seen the headline story of President John F. Kennedy's commencement address the afternoon before at Yale in which he solicited a reconciliation with America's business community after the stock market crash two weeks earlier, the worst since 1929. Attempting nothing more than to strike a "truce" between big business and labor is all some Wall Street observers saw in Kennedy's remarks, but nevertheless the president was struggling to bring some kind of resolution to the nation's urgent economic woes. Elsewhere Secretary of Health, Education, and Welfare Abraham Ribicoff was trying to reach a compromise with Congress over medical care legislation for the aged, but was making little progress. Prince Souvanna Phouma had been named to head a neutralist coalition government in Laos, in an area of the world where names like Ngo Dinh Diem, Madame Nhu, and Ho Chi Minh were just beginning to reach the radar screen of consciousness in the average American. In Italy, Premier Amintore Fanfani and his Christian Democratic Party appeared to be losing power in a country where only a scant 17 years earlier another head of state, the fascist Benito Mussolini, had last been seen hanging head downward in Milan's Piazza Loreto.

In sports, there was bad news for New York fans, too. The reigning world-champion Yankees, a roster aglitter with such stars as Roger Maris (who had broken Babe Ruth's record the year before when he hit 61 home runs but was far off pace in 1962), Micky Mantle (injured), Whitey Ford (struggling), Elston Howard (slumping), and Yogi Berra (over the hill) had been knocked out of first place in the American League by the Baltimore Orioles at Yankee Stadium the night before. In another ballpark, Willie Mays was leading the major leagues with 21 home runs, prompting speculation by some of a challenge to Maris's new record. "Say, Hey" Willie, however, was doing it now for a Giants team that had relocated some 2,500 miles west of the elysian green field that had been Harlem's Polo Grounds.

The theater section duly noted what could be construed *the* irony of Eddie's day: the biggest hit on Broadway was Frank Loesser's musical "How to Succeed in Business Without Really Trying."

In the real-life world of business, the financial pages reported that steel production had dropped again for the tenth consecutive week, and the U. S. Agriculture Department forecast that the 1962 wheat crop would be down about 14 percent from the year before and 6 percent below the previous ten-year average. But the biggest news consisted of the dismal reports still coming from Jericho-like Wall Street. And that was why this was to be a day Eddie Gilbert and a host of his colleagues and friends were destined to remember forever.

When he stepped outside into the steamy, sullen air that morning, Eddie Gilbert's mind was far too preoccupied, however, to notice the oppresive weather. He had a board of directors' meeting to attend, and it did not promise to be pleasant. Heading over to Park Avenue to flag a taxi, despite the agitated state of his mind, Gilbert still had the brisk, assertive stride of a man carrying an impressive portfolio.

At 39, he was a self-made success story. Not a Horatio Alger perhaps because there were no rags associated with his upbringing in the privileged middle class of New York: none in the house with the governess in

Flushing; nor at the summer home on Long Island Sound; nor at the exclusive Horace Mann Prep School in the Bronx where he had been a classmate and close friend of Jack Kerouac; nor later at the Ivy League's Cornell where he matriculated in the 1940s. But in a relatively short period of time, Gilbert had ascended from a $7,500-a-year salesman in his father's modest lumber company to the presidency of the E. L. Bruce Company, the nation's foremost manufacturer of hardwood flooring. From that corporate position and his aggressive dealings on Wall Street, Eddie Gilbert had built a personal fortune estimated by *Business Week* at more than $10 million, (which by later assessment proved to have reached somewhere around $25 million). Neither sum was hardly of insignificance in the early 1960s when a fully equipped Mercedes Benz sedan carried a price tag in the $5,000 range, and an opulent Park Avenue duplex could be bought for about $200,000.

The swiftness of Gilbert's rise in the New York business world, however, was only part of the story. His masterfully orchestrated takeover of the E. L.Bruce Company four years earlier, in which he quietly went about acquiring Bruce stock on the open market, was considered the first "corner" on Wall Street since the 1920s. That stroke of stock-market virtuosity, which brought about the merger of the much larger corporation with his father's lumber company, Empire Millwork Corporation (with annual sales of about $8 million in 1958), and his ascendancy to the position of chief executive officer of the new company, led *Time* magazine to characterize him as "one of Wall Street's boy wonders."

In a 1962 *New York Times* article, McCandlish Phillips aptly described Eddie in terms of his "energy, versatility and vaulting ambition," as "short and baldish with ice-blue eyes and a round yet rugged countenance"; a gambler with "an inner compulsion to compete, to drive to the very top, to win, win, win, at almost any cost of energy and time."

Eddie certainly had been driving along well above the speed limit during the half-decade before the stock market disaster of 1962. Wealthy, socially prominent, he had acquired all the customary accoutrements: a tenroom Fifth Avenue apartment overlooking Central Park; an elegant five-story townhouse on 70th Street just west of Park Avenue; a sprawling villa at Cap Martin on the French Riviera, neighbor to that of the Kennedys; a large art collection that included a Rembrandt, a Fragonard, and a Monet; a chauffeur-driven Rolls-Royce and a box at the Metropolitan Opera; an enormous line of credit at the casino in Monte Carlo; instant recognition at the jewelers Cartier and Harry Winston and at such fashionable watering-holes as El Morocco and "21"; and appearances with metronomic regularity in the social columns of New York's newspapers.

When he finally settled into the backseat of the taxicab taking him to the Bruce company headquarters at Madison Avenue and 60th, Gilbert's eyes, while always expressive and penetrating, today appeared troubled. But there was nothing else detectable in his demeanor to suggest that in the past two weeks he had personally lost millions of dollars and now was going to face his board of directors to deal with the nearly $2 million he had withdrawn from the company's coffers without their approval. Gilbert, as CEO of the Bruce company, had transferred the funds to pay off margin calls on stock in the Celotex Corporation (a large manufacturer of building and roofing materials with annual sales of approximately $62 million) purchased in his own name as part of the strategy to acquire and merge Celotex with Bruce.

So, along with all those other things whirling in his mind on this early day in June 1962, Eddie Gilbert was carrying a substantial burden: its weight would exact a terrible toll. Before the day would end, both his business career and personal life would undergo a cataclysmic reversal.

Eddie Gilbert is the first to admit he remembers very little of the details of what happened that morning. "I wasn't thinking clearly, that I know," he explains. "I don't know what came over me because I'm ordinarily a pretty clear-thinking guy, and I can usually figure things out. But I guess there were too many forces at work on me that day because I *couldn't* figure things out. I *didn't*, that's for sure, that's a matter of record." As his actions later that day proved, he was not the same young man who had so deftly orchestrated the movements, plans, and expectations for the Bruce company some weeks earlier.

By 1962 the world of finance and business had become Eddie Gilbert's proverbial cracker. He was as comfortable in it as Casey Stengel was in his New York dugout, as committed to it as John F. Kennedy was to his New Frontier. He moved about in that world with an incongruous mixture of precision and calculation on one hand, a helter-skelter ambition and a gambler's penchant for risk-taking on the other. He was characterized in a 1962 *Times'* article by Murray Rossant, as a "free-spending millionaire," a "fast-talking industrialist" who was also introspective, ingenious, and especially persuasive. Eddie may have been tagged with the moniker "boy wonder," but on Wall Street and in various corporate boardrooms there was nothing to suggest juvenility in his actions or his reputation. Brash, yes. Reckless, a little. Controversial, without a doubt. Yet Eddie Gilbert had emerged a recognized force, one to be reckoned with in New York's financial circles.

Up to that time Eddie's success in the business world as well as in his personal life could only be described as that of an uninterrupted and quite delirious ascent. Since he had taken over Bruce, the company had experienced a solid, steady growth to record earnings, with annual sales having increased in his first three years from $28 million to more than $42 million. Building Bruce was only part of the Gilbert agenda, however; his vision was to forge an empire, with the acquisition of Celotex as simply the next logical step in that aspiration. It should be noted in passing that, while still in pursuit of Celotex, Eddie had already targeted the still larger Georgia-Pacific Corporation as his next acquisiton. With just the absorption of Celotex, however, he would have had control of a $100 million corporation— a considerable jump from the $8 million Empire Millwork base he had worked from four years earlier. With such an increase in capital and a newfound strength in the marketplace, the merger, it seemed, was in the best interests of all concerned: the Bruce company, Celotex, and certainly its impressario Eddie Gilbert.

Eddie reached the threshold of pulling off the Celotex acquisition in the spring of 1962 by buying up the company's stock on the open market in his own name and in the Bruce company name, as well as by marshalling his friends and associates to invest and hold the stock until he could claim a controlling interest in Celotex for the Bruce company—in much the same way he had engineered the Bruce takeover in 1958. By April 1962, Eddie himself owned in excess of 100,000 shares of Celotex (with a book value of $45 a share), which constituted slightly more than 10 percent of the more than 1 million outstanding Celotex shares. He received the Bruce board's authorization to purchase an initial $400,000 of Celotex common stock and shortly thereafter an additional $1 million worth of shares for the company's account.

Then the bearish stock market of 1962, which had been in a state of sharp decline for weeks, crashed on May 28 (a day later dubbed "Blue Monday"—the first such day-designate since the ignominious "Black Tuesday" of 1929). No one felt its disastrous effects more than Eddie Gilbert, who was precariously overextended by his quest to acquire Celotex. Eddie's glorious ascent was officially over on Blue Monday, and the roller-coaster ride his life was beginning hurtled into its first terrible plummet.

In his personal life, Eddie had been living a style matching that of the royalty he entertained at his villa on the Mediterranean and the socially significant New York set so often seen in his Manhattan homes. Behind closed doors, things were not so glamorous, however. In the preceding months, Gilbert had fallen out of love with Rhoda, his wife of 10 years. They were now estranged, although Rhoda was still living in his art-filled apartment on Fifth Avenue. Eddie had fallen in love with a Pan American Airways flight attendant from Norway named Turid Holtan.

In May, while he was maneuvering to gain control of Celotex, Eddie decided to move temporarily to Nevada and to establish residence there in order to qualify for a divorce from Rhoda. In the still conservative 1960s, Nevada was the only state relatively hospitable to those wishing a speedy divorce, but there was nonetheless a six-week residency requirement.

Eddie found it extremely demanding and perplexing to conduct business for Bruce, and simultaneously to work Wall Street in his pursuit of Celotex, from an outpost in Nevada. As he suggested later to Murray Rossant of the *Times*, that was "my major blunder"; and still later he acknowledged that "it was perhaps the first real evidence that I wasn't thinking very clearly at the time."

The divorce itself was a trying situation. The Gilberts had two adopted daughters, Robin and Alexandra, seven and five years old in 1962, who were deeply affected by the state of affairs at home. And, during this time, Rhoda had ordered $732,000 worth of diamonds and other jewelry from Cartier, which she would not return and which Eddie refused to pay for. The situation was resolved only after Cartier brought suit against the Gilberts (which all the New York gossip columns picked up) to force the return of the jewelry.

There was still another major complication: Turid was pregnant. This came as a tremendous surprise to Eddie in that he had believed that he was unable to father a child because he had lost a testicle in an injury sustained during World War II. While he was thrilled at the prospect of having a child of his own, he was also frantic over Turid's repeated threats to have an abortion if they were not soon married.

Having to deal with all this from Nevada, Eddie was beginning to feel like a man abandoned in the desert without a camel or a canteen. With each passing day, things were slipping more and more out of his control, a feeling he had never experienced in his meteoric business career. Although he still had plenty of energy to scramble around in search of a way out, now creeping in was the grim awareness of just how vast the desert was and how his resources were suddenly dwindling.

Eddie made several one-day trips back to New York during the Nevada sojourn (under Nevada law, one could not be absent from the state for an entire calendar day during the required six-week residence period), but the trips were ineffectual. He also went once to Celotex headquarters in Chicago at the invitation of Henry W. Collins, the president and CEO of the company that Gilbert so wanted to acquire. Collins, by this point had pretty much accepted the inevitability of the merger with Bruce and wanted to discuss it and to offer Gilbert a seat on the Celotex board. As heartening as this prospect was to him, Eddie knew only too well that it was offset by the considerable drop in value of the huge Celotex holdings he had bought on margins as high as 50 percent. "I was desperate," Eddie remembers. "I wanted Celotex so badly. And now when I was so near achieving that goal, the market began failing, and the margin calls were coming in from every direction." Finally, out of sheer frustration, he gave up on the Nevada divorce, flew back to New York, and checked into a suite in the Waldorf Astoria the evening of Memorial Day, May 30.

In the days after Blue Monday and before the board meeting, with the Celotex merger no more now than a shattered dream he couldn't hold together, Eddie met with his attorneys at Shearman and Sterling, the large and respected New York law firm. They explained the seriousness of his appropriation of Bruce moneys to meet margin calls; and insisted that he sign personal promissory notes guaranteeing with his own assets the $1,953,000 that he had withdrawn from the company without his board's prior authorization. Eddie promptly had them draw up the notes and signed them.

With the prospective merger no longer feasibile, during the week before the board meeting, Gilbert had, in desperation, begun thinking in terms of a bailout. He had initiated discussions with the Ruberoid Company, another building materials firm, which had earlier shown an interest in acquiring Celotex. Eddie hoped to persuade them to buy up the stock in Celotex that he had purchased in his own name, as well as shares bought by his friends and associates and those bought by the Bruce company. He figured it would rescue their positions and enable him to repay the company funds he had authorized to be transferred from the Bruce treasury (or at least a major portion of it). Although not a solution that Eddie could find pleasure in because it meant losing Celotex, it did offer a way to extricate himself from the terrible financial squeeze he was in and the Bruce company from its uncomfortable situation. "I [would still be] in trouble, but at least my friends and others would get out whole," he said at the time.

Eddie's contact for this desperate resolution was Paul Millstein, a friend and sometime business associate who was the brother of Ruberoid executive vice president Seymour Millstein. Paul agreed to intercede for Eddie and the Bruce company with his brother. Ruberoid officials responded quickly and favorably, considering a proposed purchase of as many as 350,000 shares of Celotex. So it appeared that an escape route from Eddie's days in the desert had been opened. Seymour Millstein said he would take the proposal directly to the Ruberoid board of directors and would call Gilbert back shortly with their decision.

But by Monday evening, and with the Bruce board meeting the following day, Eddie had not heard from anyone at Ruberoid about the proposed stock purchase. As he lazed in the hot water of the bathtub in Turid's apartment, with a sense of foreboding—a premonition, he would later call it—he decided to phone Paul Millstein, and asked Turid to bring him a telephone. "I got Paul on the line and said to him something like 'I wish you would follow through on this. I haven't heard anything from your brother.' And he said something like, 'Well, I think there's some problems,' beating around the bush." When Gilbert asked what the problems might be, Paul Millstein said he didn't know exactly what they were. Under Eddie's persistent questioning, however, Paul finally acknowledged, as Eddie remembers, "I think maybe he's having some second thoughts about it. Maybe he's changing his mind."

Gilbert asked him to talk with his brother again that night. "See if you can convince him to do this. It's in everybody's best interests … at this point." Millstein said he would try. But after hanging up, Eddie felt even more profoundly his premonition of yet another misfortune; as he pulled the plug in the tub and watched the water whirlpool into the drain, the symbolic significance of it was not lost on him.

Between horrendous losses on the stock market and the roar of the margin calls, thoughts of the ominous consequences of his actions at Bruce in the aftermath, and the soap-opera situation of his private life, Eddie Gilbert indeed had reasons for not thinking clearly that bleak, overcast Tuesday morning as he sat in the backseat of a taxi on his way uptown to the Bruce offices.

The board of directors' meeting was scheduled for 10:30, but Eddie was at his office before nine. "I really don't remember anything before we sat down in the conference room, other than talking to my father," Eddie explains. "I'm sure I talked with some other officers of the company but I can't remember what about. I was just not acting normally. I usually had everything in hand, knew exactly what I was going to do the next moment, but suddenly everything was out of my control and I didn't know what to expect, which way it was going to go. I do know I was not terribly optimistic."

Harry Gilbert, Eddie's father and chairman of the Bruce company's executive committee, resolutely maintained an optimistic voice when he talked with his son; Eddie, however, could not bring himself to find any plausible reassurance in it. Too many things had been going wrong lately for Eddie to shake the feeling of angst that had been with him ever since he had spoken with Paul Millstein the night before.

The question of the $1.953 million that Gilbert had used for checks written on the E. L. Bruce Company account to meet his margin calls was no surprise at all to the directors convened at the company's New York headquarters that morning. Harry Gilbert had personally contacted each of the other directors at Eddie's request (and on the counsel of Shearman and Sterling attorneys) to inform them about the exact situation they would be dealing with at this momentous board meeting.

The meeting began on a note of cordial formality, and Eddie did not sense any noticeable hostility from the members of his board; in fact, several were outspoken in their positive support. After introductory remarks, Harry Gilbert indicated that he wanted to call a vote on authorizing the withdrawals Eddie had made so as to get that unpleasantry out of the way. But it was not to be.

Because of the plunge in stock prices with the crash two weeks earlier and the margin calls, it was understood that Eddie did not have the cash liquidity immediately to replace the money. Although it would be disclosed at the meeting that Eddie had met with his attorneys and signed promissory notes guaranteeing his personal assets to cover the $1.953 million taken from Bruce, this technicality would largely be ignored in the tumult that erupted in the conference room that morning. "Overlooked," is the way Gilbert describes it with a shrug years later. "The way I let that get away from their attention shows you the way I was thinking at the time!" The significant personal assets he had pledged, including an art collection valued at several million dollars, a world-class stamp collection, and the villa in the south of France, were more than sufficient to cover the check amounts written from the Bruce treasury.

The discussion volleyed back and forth, with some comments favorable to Gilbert and others expressing discontent at what had happened. Using the Bruce money without board authorization had not only been outside his authority, it was illegal, Gilbert's attorneys admitted. On the other hand, the merger of Celotex with Bruce was certainly in the best interests of the Bruce company. Gilbert, as CEO, had been acting in a manner consistent with insuring that, the attorneys argued.

Eddie took the floor and told the directors of the pending deal with the Ruberoid Company, about which he was expecting to hear final word at any moment. He did not, however, share his premonition of doom with the board.

Harry Gilbert continued to press for a vote of confidence for his son. Which direction the board would take, however, Eddie Gilbert had no way of knowing. He was assured of the backing of several members — his father and a personal friend or two– and he felt that E. L. Bruce, Jr., the company's chairman of the board, and perhaps the other Bruce officers who held seats on the board, would stand by him. There were others who were hostile, he sensed, and still others whose positions were clearly an enigma.

After about an hour, the meeting was interrupted by word of a telephone call from Ruberoid. Its substance fulfilled Eddie Gilbert's morbid premonition: He announced to to an already grim-faced board that Ruberoid had backed out of the hoped-for stock purchase deal and that the bailout was officially dead.

After this announcement, as was later reported in the *New York Times*, "Some board members wanted to take immediate action, getting Mr. Gilbert to resign and issuing a [public] statement revealing his withdrawals.

Others felt it might be more prudent to wait until the market closed. Mr. Gilbert, who usually dominated Bruce's board meetings, listened to the arguments raging around him." And while he listened he was considering his alternatives, one of which—the most desperate—he had been toying with since the previous Friday. The next event of the morning would lead him inevitably to that fateful choice.

Henry Loeb, senior partner in the prestigious Loeb-Rhoades investment company who had become a Bruce director at Eddie's request, had brought along his own lawyer, John Cahill, a founding partner of the New York law firm of Cahill, Gordon, Reindel and Ohl, which specialized in corporate and investment law. Even though Loeb was considered a friend, in this situation he was an uncertain ally in Eddie's mind. Following the Ruberoid announcement and the increasingly heated discussion among board members over Eddie's withdrawals, John Cahill asked for and got the floor.

A highly respected attorney, Cahill, at 60 was an imposing figure, well over six feet tall and heavyset, with a round face and a pleasant smile that he could deploy deftly when needed. He was soft-spoken and unintimidating in his manner, yet no one ever questioned the authority with which he spoke. Cahill looked about the boardroom, then settled his eyes on Eddie, "You know, I'm not pleased about what I have to say here today, but I must," shaking his head sympathetically as he spoke. Then he began a reserved but intense refutation of Gilbert's actions. Cahill explained that the misappropriation of funds by Gilbert was an unmitigated breach of trust, not to mention a felonious act, and that if the directors went along with it they, as individuals, could very well be held personally liable. The board members could, he explained, become defendants themselves in litigation brought by stockholders; they could under the law be held responsible for the nearly $2 million now owed to the Bruce company by Eddie Gilbert. In addition, they would be held up to the scrutiny, the judgment, and inevitably the condemnation of the New York financial community. Cahill closed by telling the board that if they voted to ratify the withdrawals, each member was laying himself open to the possibility of personal ruin.

When Cahill's scathing appraisal ended, Eddie Gilbert looked around the room at the faces of the directors and felt it was all over for him As if to confirm that fact, Henry Loeb leaned over to Gilbert and said, "If this is brought to a vote and somehow accepted, I will have to resign from your board."

Then Harry Gilbert regained the floor, his faith and optimism still intact. "This will not happen," he said in response to Cahill's remarks. "Let's just give Eddie a vote of confidence now and get on with the rest of our business."

Looking up at his father, Eddie said, "Forget it. We're not going to vote." There was an awkward silence. Then Eddie said softly to his father, "Sit down."

Eddie proposed that the board recess for lunch and reconsider the matter later in the afternoon. The visibly shaken directors agreed, and then Eddie left abruptly, heading down the hall to his office.

The alternative that Eddie had been toying with, the choice he had entertained in some of the darker moments of the past few days, had now been made. And it would prove to be, unequivocally, the very worst course of action he could have taken. He stopped at his secretary's desk and said to her: "Book a reservation for me on the first flight you can to Rio de Janeiro."

*Money is the easiest thing in the world to make.*

EDDIE GILBERT

FROM AN "EYEWITNESS REPORTS" SPECIAL, CBS-TV, 1962

*Moonlight on the lawn, J. D. Salinger middleclass livingrooms with the lights out, futile teenage doubledate smooching in the dark, poor Eddie and I appeared at that queer era in 20th Century America just before the girls started to chase the boys down the street...*

*When Wall Street's Walter Gutman told me about two years ago that Eddie had become a "financial wizard" I wasn't surprised—We'd both decided to become wizards at something or other as we giggled in the halls of Horace Mann among all the other wizards of that class...*

*But Eddie's style in the halls of the school is what I think of; Eddie used to come breezing and bouncing down the hall by himself with a wicked little pale grin and rush by as everybody yelled at him to stop: he was too busy... he was always rushing and serious faced.*

*He rushed down the hall all the way.*

JACK KEROUAC, LIFE MAGAZINE, JUNE 29, 1962

From the very beginning it was evident that Eddie Gilbert's life would be driven by deep and demanding aspirations.

As a little boy, he was quickly drawn to sports—tennis, track, swimming and diving, soccer, mostly—and, with an inbred fervor, determined to be the best in whichever one he was competing at a given moment. When he began collecting stamps at eight years old, Eddie dreamt of a world-class collection. When his governess taught him to play chess at about the same age, he was immediately absorbed by the complexity of the game; soon he was reading books about the game, copying the strategies of chess masters, and gleefully defeating all those with the temerity to challenge him. Faced with a figurative mountain, Eddie Gilbert never wondered *if* he could climb it, only what he would need and how long it would take to reach the top.

So, by his early 30s, it was to no one's great surprise that Eddie had made a millionaire of himself. It was the 1950s, and it was a time when a million dollars was considered something very special.

In America, the Fifties was a decade with its own peculiar character, a strange mixture of serenity and violence. There was domestic simplicity and stability—the romanceful Leave It to Beaver / Father Knows Best values—countered by dreadful Cold War fears of the communist menace and nuclear annihilation. The decade began on a turbulent note with the frightening revelation that the Soviet Union had developed and tested successfully an atomic bomb; then the more urgent reckoning of a very real war being waged with American soldiers fighting and dying in Korea; and finally lapsing into what would later be perceived as a relatively prosperous and socially conservative period of the nation's history under the laid-back, two-term presidency of the avuncular Dwight D. Eisenhower. As David Halberstam explained in his definitive history of the decade, *The Fifties*, it was an age "captured in black and white, most often by still photographers . . . [of] people who dressed carefully: men in suits, ties, and—when outdoors—hats, the women with their hair in modified page-boys, pert and upbeat and a youth that seemed, more than anything else, 'square' and largely accepting of the given social covenants." It was, he concludes, an "era of good will and expanding affluence [in which] few Americans doubted the essential goodness of their society." It was a quirky decade remembered also for its bomb shelters and beatniks, 3-D movies, coonskin caps, hula hoops, television's coming of age, and the birth of rock'n'roll and populated with personalities as diverse as Bridey Murphy, Marilyn Monroe, Senator Joe McCarthy, James Dean, Rosa Parks, Grace Metalious, Charles Van Doren, and Elvis Presley.

During the decade, Eddie Gilbert discovered Wall Street and, to his delight, its endless opportunites; but he also found a corporate America replete with its various challenges and bountiful rewards. He was neither conservative nor conventional. He looked at the worlds of big business and high finance with the excitement and anticipation of a gambler, and he began to calculate how he could use both to his significant advantage. Eddie Gilbert was an anomaly in the docile decade of the Fifties that David Halberstam describes.

For Eddie, that decade proved to be one prolonged ascent. As it continued, his horizons broadened in concert. Once into the worlds of business and finance, he found the equation was relatively simple: He needed money to buy stock, he needed stock to gain and maintain control of a company, he needed a company as a base from which to operate and expand. "Money," as he later observed, "is the easiest thing in the world to make." For him, anyway. And so he made it, parlayed it, and used it with his own personalized finesse.

By the end of the 1950s, Eddie qualified as a legitimate multimillionaire. At 37 years of age in 1960, he had amassed a fortune on paper in the neighborhood of $20 to $30 million—the first of three separate fortunes that he would earn in his roller-coaster business life. It marked the first apogee on a breathtaking ride, reaching highs and lows experienced by only a few of the world's remarkable individuals. From corporate boardrooms to prison, from Wall Street to prison again, from wealth and prestige to deep debt and dishonor, Eddie would eventually come to a reconciliation with his trials and failures and ultimately a personal redemption.

Eddie Gilbert's stormy career in the business world began quietly enough just after he returned from World War II. In 1946, he was 23 years old, having served more than a three-year tour of duty in the Army Air Corps that took him in and out of combat in North Africa, Italy, and Greece.

When he returned to the United States and civilian life, Eddie had no intention of following the now fabled piece of advice Horace Greeley had offered in 1855, the one so many returning World War II veterans took to heart a century after Greeley wrote it: "If you have . . . no prospect open to you... turn your face to the great West, and there build up a home and fortune." Eddie needed to look no further than his own family and the hometown he had known all his prewar life — New York — in order to begin his own personal quest for fortune.

After resettling into the family's home in Flushing in the borough of Queens, Eddie went to work in a relatively low-level capacity for his father's company, Empire Millwork Corporation, a manufacturer of millwork, doors, sash, frames, mouldings, cabinets, and flooring. He worked at Empire until the autumn of 1946 when he returned to Cornell University in Ithaca, New York, where he had spent two years prior to going off to war in late 1942.

But Eddie was too restless for university life following the years during which he had grown accustomed to wandering in war-torn but still cosmopolitan European cities like Rome, Naples, Athens, even London and Paris. He dropped out of Cornell to return to New York. Although intent on launching a business career, at the time Eddie had no idea in what business or even in which capacity he wanted eventually to work. What he did know was that it wouldn't be something small, something routine, something mundane. Although he did not think about it a lot in those first few months back in New York, it was inherent in Eddie's nature to be looking beyond the present to the various alternatives that lay ahead of him. Conceivably, what he brought to the business world accounted for why he became such an accomplished chess player, a game that entailed the same kind of foresight, planning, strategy, and dogged assault — traits that were so much a part of Eddie Gilbert's nature. Still, he had to start work somewhere; and with no college degree, no specialized training, and no practical experience, the best place seemed to be right in his own backyard. It was certainly the easiest place for him to land a job.

Empire Millwork had been founded in the early 20th century by Eddie's grandfather, Hyman Ginsberg, who had come to America in 1890 from Vilnius, the capital and largest city of Lithuania. At the time of Ginsberg's emigration, Lithuania had been under Russian rule for nearly a century, and Vilnius served as the seat of the Russian governor-general. Hyman Ginsberg was one of approximately 75,000 Jews constituting about 40 percent of Vilnius' population before the turn of the last decade of the 19th century. Vilnius was also the most recognized center of rabbinic learning as well as Hasidism in Eastern Europe at the time.

The Ginsberg family name — at least on Eddie's side of the family — was officially changed to Gilbert by Eddie's father, Harry, in the early 1930s. Although not something of much consequence in the family (in fact Harry had been comfortable with the name Ginsberg and found it neither an encumbrance in the business or social circles in which he mingled), it was the children who wanted it changed. As Eddie's mother, Yolan, remembered. "It just came up one day. The children didn't like the name Ginsberg. They were young, still in elementary school, I believe. One day they asked if we could change it. I believe it was Enid [Eddie's older sister and only sibling]. Something happened at school. It had to do with another child who said something about the association of [their] being Jewish and being wealthy, and it bothered Enid. Eddie and Enid were not brought up Jewish, not raised religiously. And the boy who said it was Jewish himself, as I remember. It wasn't anything important. But they asked about changing our name, insistent I might say, and I mentioned it to Harry. He was perfectly agreeable. So I thought about a name that wasn't too different from Ginsberg, and came up with Gilbert. And everyone was happy with it. So it was changed. That's all there was to it."

In fact, the family name had originally been "Kamaiko." But, according to Eddie's sister Enid, when Hyman arrived at Ellis Island in 1890 the clerk processing the new immigrants couldn't understand Hyman's gutteral pronunciation of his name. So, as the story has been passed down, he said, "Here, just take this," and wrote "Ginsberg" on Hyman's papers. Thus Hyman Kamaiko of Vilnius became Hyman Ginsberg in New York.

The first job Hyman Ginsberg found in the United States was scaling fish at the South Street Market area in New York's bustling lower east side. It was not long, however, before he dropped that unattractive job to resurrect the skills he had developed as a glazier in Lithuania. He outfitted himself with a pushcart and some tools and began plying his trade of replacing broken windows on the streets of lower Manhattan. A short while later, he met Dora Greenwald in New York and, in what was presumed to have been an "arranged" marriage, wedded her in 1896. Dora was his second wife (his first had died), a fact Dora did not discover until after the wedding when she moved into Hyman's house where, to her great surprise, his three teenage children awaited the newlyweds.

The Ginsberg family history is cloudy at best: Eddie's sister Enid, who has a devoted interest in the family's genealogy, points out: "You must remember that immigrant families in those days were embarrassed about their past and told their children very little about it. Those from the Eastern Europe countries, especially the Jews, were ashamed, it seemed, about *not* being American. Anyone who spoke with an accent was looked down upon, and they had no pride in their roots like there is today. So they didn't talk about it; and if the children asked, as I sometimes did, they were told nothing. So much of their story was lost." The feelings of inadequacy among immigrants and the subsequent discomforts they felt, and their children experienced as well, finds corroboration from another New Yorker who grew up in the same years as Enid and Eddie Gilbert. Novelist Joseph Heller, best known for the modern classic, *Catch 22*, spent his childhood in the 1920s and early 30s in a blue-collar neighborhood on the periphery of the amusement park at Coney Island in Brooklyn, less than 15 miles from where the Gilberts lived in Flushing, and remembers in his autobiography, *Now and Then*, "I was never in real trouble in school. The few times a parent was demanded, my sister came. My mother would have been frightened, and I would have felt disgraced by her broken English."

The children from Hyman's first marriage moved on shortly after Dora moved in, and eventually Hyman and Dora had three children of their own: two sons, Harry and Morris, and a daughter, Sara. Hyman taught the two boys the trades of cutting glass and installing the panes in windows while they were teenagers, and soon both began working fulltime for their father in the family glazing business. Sara had no interest in the fledgling business and later married a dentist who developed his practice in New York City. Sara, or "Sech" as she was called, had two children, and her husband's dental practice proved successful enough eventually to enable the family to live on New York's Park Avenue.

For Hyman and his sons, glazing provided an adequate living, but it took one of the nation's most infamous crimes and trials to catapult them into what could be called a full-fledged "business." In May 1920, Nicola Sacco and Bartolomeo Vanzetti, two professed anarchists, were arrested for the murder of two men during the payroll robbery at a shoe factory in South Braintree, Massachusetts. Both of the accused were Italian immigrants who barely spoke English and were known to have avoided military service in World War I by claiming conscientious objector status. Portrayed as foreign radicals and draft dodgers, they went to trial in the summer of 1920 and were summarily convicted of murder and armed robbery and sentenced to death. To some, Sacco and Vanzetti were victims, sacrificed to raw prejudice because of their ancestry and political beliefs, their trial nothing more than a sham. After the verdict was announced, there were cries of injustice in several of America's major cities. In New York rioting broke out and, as a result, there were several bombings in lower Manhattan. At that time, much less violence occurred than would occur when the two men were executed seven years later (the verdict and sentence were upheld in 1927 despite a convict's confession in the intervening years that he and others in a local gang had staged the robbery and murders for which Sacco and Vanzetti had been found guilty). In the 1920 riots, however, enough windows were broken to keep the Ginsberg glaziers frantically busy for weeks afterward, thus bringing a financial windfall that enabled them to launch a now-capitalized business to replace what had been nothing more than a pushcart operation.

But Hyman's young sons Harry and Morris had even loftier ambitions. They soon expanded the business, known as "D. Ginsberg and Sons"—the "D" standing for Dora—into a company that not only provided windows but also sashes, mouldings, and other related wood products. The company name was changed to Empire Millwork shortly after the two sons took over active control of the business. Harry and Morris Ginsberg divided the administrative tasks and responsibilities and hired new help for their fast-growing firm. The company became a thriving enterprise by the time of the roaring and prosperous 1920s.

Eddie's father, Harry, had been born on Christmas day 1899, and he was 20 years old when he married Yolan Czorba in the summer of 1920. Yolan, called "Toots" or "Tootsie," was a year older than Harry: she had been born in Hungary, the youngest of four children, two boys and two girls (Albert was the eldest, followed by Louis, Serena, and Yolan) who emigrated with their parents from Budapest just after the turn of the century. A fifth child, Bill, was born to the Czorbas in the United States.

The Czorba family had been of lesser nobility in Hungary, tracing its lineage back to the 13th Century. Alloys, the father, held claim to the title of baron and was a Roman Catholic of high-standing in Hungary. In Budapest he had married Frances Hirschbein, better known as "Franny," a non-practicing Jew who converted to Catholicism after the marriage. The Czorba children were all raised in the Roman Catholic faith but, as Yolan later admitted, "[It] never worked with me; as far back as I can remember,

I didn't care to be Catholic." Alloys was a certified physician in Hungary when he decided to bring his family to America, but in the United States he was unable to obtain a license to practice medicine and so worked as a pharmacist in New York. Only a few years following his arrival in the new world, however, Alloys Czorba contracted influenza during an epidemic and died as a result of it, leaving his five children to be raised by their mother Franny.

Franny Czorba was a dynamic and driven woman who, it is said, was as tactless and outspoken as she was effervescent and successful. After her husband's death, she opened a lingerie factory in the garment district of New York and nurtured it into a business that eventually employed as many as 80 young women, all East European immigrants themselves, and thus provided a fine living for the Czorba family.

The Czorbas settled into a commodious brownstone on East 68th Street. A staff of servants comprising Hungarian peasant girls did the cooking, cleaning, and other household chores. The job of managing the household and overseeing the help fell to Yolan, the youngest, which she handled deftly while her mother was busy directing the operations of the factory on New York's west side. Franny Czorba was a character in the truest sense of the term, with verve and boundless energy. On weekends she hosted poker games, often played for sizeable stakes, in the family's 68th Street residence. These games ordinarily began when she returned from the factory on Friday night. People from the "Hungarian group," as Enid remembers them being called, included family and close friends. The earliest to arrive were seated at the large gaming table; but when a player got up to visit the bathroom, one of the others would usurp the seat. In the kitchen, the servant girls would begin working in the morning to make the homemade paprika-laced noodles and the strudels to feed the transient stream of weekend partygoers and poker players. The group was raucous and ebullient, with the party on some weekends being said to last from Friday night to Monday morning. Franny was the mainstay at the gaming table; and her brother, Sandor (pronounced "Shan-dor"), a character himself, was often in attendance at the poker games — if only for part of the time. It seems Uncle Sandor, as Eddie and Enid called him, had an extraordinary obsession for beautiful women and managed to surround himself with them, even though, according to Enid, "he looked like a little frog." Although Sandor's means of support were unknown ("Nobody knew what he did for a living," says Enid, "except have a good time"), he was chauffered around town in his own limousine by a tall, striking blond young woman. When he died, three of his former mistresses came to the funeral and, as Enid remembers, "got into an awful fight among themselves."

Eddie remembers finagling a seat at the poker game from time to time, even though he was just a little boy, but apparently only when the stakes were lowered. It was his first introduction to the world of gambling, and he fell in love with it immediately. He played for dimes and quarters at these poker parties, with the money he used coming from his father. These games were as exciting for him then as they would be 30 years later when he gambled for thousands of dollars at Monte Carlo's famous casino or the tables in Las Vegas.

Harry and Yolan Ginsberg had their first child, Enid, in 1921; and a year and a half later Eddie came along, born December 28, 1922. At the start, the family lived with Harry's parents in a spacious house in Corona in Queens, until 1925 when Harry bought a large home of his own in nearby Flushing. Empire Millwork was growing at a very rapid pace during the early 1920s, and the entire Ginsberg family—Hyman and Dora, Harry and Yolan, and Morris and his wife Ethel—moved smoothly and gracefully into what could be called upper middle-class American comfort by mid-decade. By the time Enid and Eddie went off to P.S. 32, the elementary school in Flushing, the family employed a butler and maid for their house, and the two children had a governess to look after them.

Eddie was very active in sports from the earliest days: "a fierce competitor," his sister remembers. "He was always playing one game or another, in the house or outside," according to Enid, "always busy, and he hated to lose." His mother, with typical maternal exuberance, preferred to describe him in softer terms: "a most gorgeous child [with] flaxen hair and big, mischevious blue eyes," she recalled. "He loved people, and they could sense that and they loved him back for it. He was always bringing other children home to our house. And later he would bring them to our summer home on Long Island for weekend parties. He had so many friends."

Several stories Yolan Gilbert liked to tell offer some good insights into who Eddie Gilbert is: "When he was five years old, in kindergarten, the teachers all loved him. And he was brilliant. One day he came home and said, 'Mother, the teacher likes me!'

"How do you know? I asked.

"'She sent a note to the teacher across the hall. It said: Look at him. Isn't he a cute kid?'

"How do you know it said that? I asked.

"'I read it,' Eddie told me."

Another story from Yolan about the days before kindergarten is also informative: "He was always very practical. We had a governess for Eddie and Enid who we called Little Sister Catherine. She was as cute as she was tiny. When he was little, Eddie would not drink his milk, but we were trying to get him to do it. We told Little Catherine that he must. So, when she insisted—and Eddie suffered about this, her insistence—he worked it out. He would say to her, 'Little Sister Catherine, you go and sit on the steps over there,' which was around the corner, 'and when I finish the whole thing [the glass of milk], I'll call over and tell you.' Well, she would do that. He was so clever. And when she did, he would tiptoe over to the pantry and dispose of the milk. Then he would go back to the table and sit down and call her, 'READY, NOW!' he would say, and she would come back. She never knew what he'd been up to. We caught him after a while and made it known we were unhappy and that was the end of his little game. But then, just like Eddie always was, he was worried about his governess being in trouble, and he came to us on her behalf because he told us he didn't want her to lose her job."

Yolan herself was not beyond being manipulated. "We had a beautiful life at home. My husband had a wonderful sense of humor, and he was a fine family man, too. But Eddie, even when he was very little, knew he could get around his father. I was very strict! I had to be. But then, for example, Eddie would ask me if he could go out after dinner and play. And I'd say no, you have homework to do. So Eddie would go into the other room and say to his father in his sad way, 'Daddy, momma won't let me go out.' And his father would always give in to him. Quietly, I might say. But Eddie would end up going out, if that's what he wanted."

Yolan Gilbert also added a rather poignant, if somewhat abstract, observation, the meaning of which may go far beyond what this maternal and exuberant mother thought she'd said: "Eddie never [felt he] had enough. Eddie never has enough."

Although Enid was more than a year older, it became quite clear to everyone by this time that Eddie had become the family focus. Harry

Gilbert had wanted a son, and Eddie quickly became the apple of his eye. "Eddie was the *absolute* idol of his life," Enid remembers. Whatever Eddie did was met not just with approval but a certain cultivated fanfare. Enid quietly slid into the background as Eddie easily accepted his role as the center of attention.

Eddie was the focal point not just because he was a good-looking child, which was part of it, but more as a result of his driven, dominating personality and that inbred mastery of manipulation. He liked people, those his own age as well as adults, and constantly sought their approval and acceptance. At the same time, his overriding passion was to be the one in control. From the very earliest he was, as Enid concedes, "a star . . . always a star in everything. We had a lot of children on the block [in Flushing] to play with, but Eddie was always in charge . . . he just took charge."

One story of hers reinforces that observation: "When we were very young—Eddie was just seven or eight, I believe—we went to Europe. It was 1929, and the great depression was just starting. My father said to my mother one day, 'Look, I'm having a lot of trouble with the business, with money; take the children and go to Europe, leave me alone for a while so I can concentrate here and get things straightened out.' So our mother did. We went on a Dutch ship, I remember, and she told us we were going to be going to a school in Switzerland, Saint George's was the name, in Montreux.

"Anyway, on board the ship, the first thing Eddie did was find himself a girlfriend. Not just anyone, either. A beautiful girl, Maybe sixteen years old. Tall, blonde . . . and he—I remember it so well—he brought her on deck one day to where our mother and I were sitting.

"'Mother, this is my girlfriend,' he said and then introduced her by name. Then Eddie took the girl into the bar for a drink. It was his own idea, and, you have to remember, Eddie was only about half the girl's age. Ginger ale, they ordered. And when the bartender asked him to pay for it, Eddie was astounded. He came back and said to my mother, 'I didn't know you had to pay for this,' looking at her all the time with those blue eyes of his. 'What am I going to do?' he asked—as if he didn't know. Our mother paid. The girl was happy. What can I tell you, that was Eddie, eight years old . . . at most."

Eddie and Enid took different paths following elementary school. Enid went to the public high school in Manhasset, Long Island, and would later go on to Rawlins College in Winter Park, Florida, and after that to the drama school at Yale. Eddie went away to boarding school at the prominent Horace Mann School in the Riverdale section of the Bronx.

The Horace Mann School was named for the Massachusetts educator, politician, and humanitarian, who became one of the most prominent Americans of the 19th century and is considered "the father of American public education" (although he had nothing to do with the founding of what was to become Eddie Gilbert's high school alma mater). Horace Mann was, and is today, a private college preparatory school for the privileged, with the highest of academic standards. The school, which takes a special pride in its reputation for catering to gifted students, was founded in 1887 and claims an illustrious roster of graduates over the years, including such American luminaries as Arthur Hays Sulzberger (class of 1909), publisher of the *New York Times* from 1935 to 1961; poets William Carlos Williams (1903) and Peter Viereck (1933); CIA Director and Secretary of Defense James Schlesinger (1946); economist Robert L. Heilbroner (1936) author and historian Robert Caro (1953); U.S. Congressman and political activist Allard K. Lowenstein (1945); novelist Ira Levin (1946); financier John L. Loeb (1920); and oilman and movie mogul Marvin Davis (1943).

Among Eddie's classmates at Horace Mann was a young man destined to become perhaps even more renowned than any alumni named above, the quintessential beatnik, the so-called oracle of that nonconformist sect known as the Beat Generation, Jack Kerouac.

Kerouac came to Horace Mann in 1939, joining Eddie Gilbert in the junior class that year. They graduated together in 1940. Kerouac went on to college at Columbia University, attending on a football scholarship, although he dropped out in the fall of 1941, his sophomore year, when Columbia's famed coach Lou Little refused to include him in the starting varsity lineup. Eddie matriculated to another Ivy League school, Cornell University, which he, too, would leave before graduating. And that is where the similarities in the lives of these two good friends would end.

Kerouac chose a path in life that would have been unimaginable to Eddie Gilbert. After two stints in the Merchant Marine, sandwiched around a short one in the U.S. Navy during World War II (he was cashiered out of the navy with an honorable discharge but with the notation that he possessed an "indifferent character" after a naval psychiatrist diagnosed him as schizophrenic), Kerouac settled into life in New York City. He insinuated himself into a kind of underground movement that was burgeoning then in Greenwich Village and that would some years later consolidate in San Francisco. Those who became involved were described by *Time* magazine as "a group of American-bred Bohemians... disillusioned with the old American dream of prosperity and conformity." Besides Kerouac, the most famous members of the Beat Generation and his most notorious sidekicks through that era were poets Allen Ginsberg, Gregory Corso, Lawrence Ferlinghetti (the owner of the City Lights bookstore in San Francisco, the unofficial headquarters of the Beat Generation) and Kenneth Rexroth, and novelist William Burroughs. *Time* further described them as "an easily recongnizable breed... The men favored beards... khaki pants, a sweater and sandals [actually, of the most famous of the beatniks, mentioned above, only Ginsberg sported a beard].... The girls wore black leotards and no lipstick, but so much eyeshadow that people joked about their 'raccoon eyes.'" The beatniks, as they became universally known (a term coined from the melding of "Beat" and "Sputnik," both of which were said to be in orbits of their own in the latter part of the 1950s), were most often associated with dimly lit coffeehouses where offbeat poetry was read, folk music and progressive jazz was played, and their devotion to Zen Buddhism, free love, and iconoclasm were practiced.

In the years after the war and his stay in New York, Kerouac took to drifting aimlessly about the country with various of his newfound friends. From his wanderings with that troupe of disenchanted souls came his most famous book, *On the Road*, actually his second published work, written in 1951 but not released until 1957, which immediately became the gospel of beatniks everywhere. He completed it in a three-week writing binge, story has it. As David Sterritt, writing for the *New York Times* in 1999 recorded: "He wrote on a typewriter using sheets of drawing paper taped into a long roll so that absolutely nothing would interrupt the mercurial flow of what he later called his 'spontaneous bop prosody.'" One critic labeled it as nothing more than "a saga of footloose Bohemians who crisscrossed the country having visions and seducing girls," while author Truman Capote dispatched it with the now-famous recrimination: "It isn't writing at all—it's typing!" Still, it was a national best-seller, registering sales of more than 500,000 copies during its first two years in print; and it made Kerouac's name a household word in 1950s America.

In a later novel, a *roman à clef* piece entitled *Vanity of Duluoz*, published in 1967, Kerouac drew upon several of his youthful friends for the characters. Eddie Gilbert, Kerouac later admitted, provided the persona for the character named Jimmy Winchell.

In 1939 and 1940, Kerouac, the son of French-Canadian parents who then resided in Lowell, Massachusetts, was living in Brooklyn so that he could take advantage of the football scholarship that the Horace Mann school had afforded him. According to one of his biographers, Barry Miles, in *Jack Kerouac, King of the Beats, A Portrait*, he had to "ride the rattling subway all the way from his step-grandmother's house in Brooklyn, up through Manhattan to the Bronx to 242nd Street and Broadway, a journey of about 20 miles.... The trip took over two hours." This was in rather stark contrast to: "Many of the students [who] would arrive each morning in chauffeur-driven limousines, bringing delicious packed lunches with them, prepared by the family cook." Gilbert insists he was not one of those pampered souls who arrived in such high style; he boarded at the school and therefore had just a short walk from his dorm to the classrooms.

If anyone could have ridden to school in style, however, it was Eddie Gilbert. His father had become a serious collector of antique cars, which were garaged at the family's summer home on Long Island and kept in spotless, smooth-running condition. Harry Gilbert's collection would grow to include a 1915 six-cylinder Rolls Royce convertible, a 1900 two-cylinder Schact, a 1902 one-cylinder Orient, a 1905 two-cylinder Brush, a 1912 two-cylinder Renault, a Nagant from 1906 and a 1912 Minerva, both Belgian-made, a 1904 four-cylinder Mercedes (which, according to Harry Gilbert's notes, had actually been made in New York by the Steinway Piano Company with parts brought over from Germany), a one-cylinder 1905 Cadillac, a six-cylinder 1931 Pierce Arrow, and even a six-cylinder 1926 La France fire engine, which once belonged to the firefighters of Goshen, New York.

Kerouac was neither awed nor disconcerted by the wealth around him at Horace Mann, nor was he yet dabbling with the unconventional lifestyle that would later become his juggernaut. Then, he was just a rambunctious, slightly rebellious teenager with an eager, creative, literary mind that pretty much went unchallenged by formal education, in much the same way that Eddie Gilbert's fertile, mathematical mind remained unfulfilled and for the most part untapped at the Horace Mann School.

The two young men found an immediate common ground that included a kind of mixture of intellect and competition and the patching together of a good time while in pursuit of both. They remained good friends for many years despite having taken significantly different paths in life. Their individual talents were quite different, which only helped in their relationship. "I used to do his math homework for him," Eddie recalls. And Kerouac remembered in a profile of Gilbert he composed for *LIFE* magazine in 1962, "I wrote English term papers for Eddie at $2 a throw,"

The piece Jack Kerouac wrote for *LIFE* magazine in the aftermath of Eddie's downfall in the Bruce/Celotex failed merger and his subsequent flight to Brazil offered several insights into Eddie Gilbert the high school student. "Among the fantastic wits of the Horace Mann School for Boys in 1939-40," Kerouac wrote, "Eddie Gilbert ranked practically number one — I was just an innocent New England athlete boy suddenly thrown into what amounted to an Academy of incunabular Milton Berles hundreds of them wisecracking and ad libbing on all sides. We were all in stitches... but when mention of Gilbert was made there fell a kind of stricken convulsion just at the thought of him — he was insanely witty."

Jack Kerouac was only one of many friends Eddie had during those years at the Horace Mann School. There was also Jack Sonnenblick, his roommate, and Phil Greilsamer, Rudy Henning, Morton Thalheimer, Herb Zaslove, Matt Sherman, Fred Rose, Harry Allison, Ivy King, and others. Eddie would bring some of them home on weekends to the house in Flushing. This was the Eddie who liked people, who sought their approval and their acceptance. All of these classmate-pals went on to success in one field or another, and many became very wealthy New Yorkers.

Both Eddie and Jack Kerouac were fine athletes. Kerouac's sport of choice was football, and he excelled at it, regularly being recognized for his exploits on the field for Horace Mann in the sports pages of New York's newpapers, all of which, including the *New York Times,* covered high school football in those days. Eddie concentrated on the less publicized sports of swimming and diving, tennis and soccer. The two joined forces, however, to lead the Horace Mann chess team. It is one of Eddie's fonder memories of the days at that school: "We were very good, and I don't exaggerate. It was just the two of us, I remember, and we went to play against this two-man team from another private school, Fieldston, in New

York, for some championship or other. One of their players was a boy named Capablanca, whose first name I can't remember. His father was one of the most famous chess players in the world [the father was José Raul Capablanca of Cuba who held the chess title of World Champion from 1921 to 1927]. Well, they were expected to win. But they didn't. We beat them. We beat every team around, Jack and I."

High school was a good time for Eddie. He did well, for the most part, although he set no academic records nor came close to performing at the level he was capable of, but he had a good time. As Jack Kerouac remembered: "In the 1940 Horace Mann yearbook 'The Horace Mannikin' Eddie is described as a 'speedy, clever' varsity soccer player at the inside position. You see a picture of him with curly hair grinning with the soccer team. He is also described as the number two varsity tennis player, but I think he was actually number one later in the season ... there's also a picture of him playing the violin and a mention of the fact that he was the best jazz dancer, or 'shagger' in the class at the time. The 'SENIOR OPINIONS' in the Yearbook list as follows:

BEST DANCER, *Ed Gilbert*
DONE H.M. [homework] FOR MOST, *Ed Gilbert*
HARDEST SHIRKER, *Ed Gilbert*
THINKS HE'S MOST SOPHISTICATED, *Ed Gilbert*

... signs of his very great intrinsic popularity, considering the other categories for nomination such as MOST RESPECTED, LEAST APPRECIATED...."

Eddie Gilbert graduated from the Horace Mann School in June 1940. But for all the help they extended to each other, both Gilbert and Kerouac missed the formal graduation. Kerouac, according to biographer Barry Miles, was not in attendance because "he could not afford to buy the formal white suit" that was required for the ceremony. Gilbert missed it because he still had to retake his final exam in English: this because when he had taken it at the end of the semester, seated across the aisle from Kerouac, the teacher, who had for some time suspected that there was some sort of unhealthy collusion between the two youths in his English class, believed something funny carried over into the final examination. Although no accusation was ever formally made, Eddie was required to retake the exam, this time seated alone, and there had not been enough time to reschedule the makeup exam before graduation. So, it turned out,

Kerouac, as Barry Miles recorded in his book, "listened to the ceremony from the lawn near the gym, lying on the grass, glancing through Walt Whitman, as the speeches mingled with the birdsong in the clear blue sky, and another chapter of his life came to an end." Gilbert spent graduation day at the family summer home on Long Island, presumably on a verdant lawn of his own with the ocean's crashing surf for a background accompaniment, with no sense of either deprivation or injustice; in fact, he would later admit, he did not give a damn about the formal ceremony at all.

Both later received their diplomas and assumed their rightful places as two of the most famous—and, in their case, notorious—alumni of the Horace Mann Class of 1940.

Eddie Gilbert pretty much had his choice of any college in United States. His family could easily afford to send him anywhere, although his less than sterling academic performance in high school might have been a negative factor with some of the more prestigious institutions. On the other hand, he had stunning academic potential (his IQ was later measured at 163).

In his junior year of high school, Eddie had begun to apply for admission to college. There were about six universities in which he had expressed an interest at that time, and only four that he went so far as to apply to for admission: three in the Ivy League—Harvard, Cornell, and Pennsylvania—and the University of North Carolina at Chapel Hill. Only Harvard declined to offer him admission. He liked North Carolina because of its outstanding tennis team. He had heard some good things from friends about the University of Pennsylvania in Philadelphia, especially the social life. But pragmatism won out. For reasons Eddie couldn't quite explain, he was interested in the law, at least while he was a junior in high school. So when he was accepted for admission by the three universities of his choice, he decided on Cornell principally because of its law school's reputation. By the time he matriculated there in the fall of 1940, however, he had lost all interest in the law, and enrolled instead in the school of civil engineering.

Cornell remains one of the nation's premier universities. The Ivy League school's beautiful campus is set amid the rolling hills of western New York in Ithaca on the southernmost shore of one of New York's Finger Lakes (Lake Cayuga), and has a history dating back to its founding in 1865 by Ezra Cornell and Andrew Dickson White. Over the years, the university has claimed as its notable graduates a number of famous scholars and celebrities, including Nobel Prize winners Pearl Buck (literature, 1938) and George W. Beadle (medicine, 1958); eponymous corporation chiefs Adolph Coors (Coors Brewing Company) and Herbert F. Johnson (Johnson's Wax); Supreme Court Justice Ruth Bader Ginsburg; Dr. Henry Heimlich, popularizer of The Heimlich Maneuver; psychologist Dr. Joyce Brothers; author and critic E. B. White; novelist Thomas Pynchon; sports commentator Dick Schaap; actor Christopher Reeve; and even Candid Camera's Allen Funt.

Eddie Gilbert, however, was not destined to be among these heralded graduates. His college experience, as it turned out, would not persist as one of his fond memories. He did adjust to campus life without difficulty, especially in the first semester. The introductory courses Eddie was required to take in the engineering school included those where he would be most comfortable, such as mathematics, introductory architecture, and engineering; and he received good grades in all of them. He joined the tennis team and was a standout as a freshman; he was a diver on the swimming team and loved that experience; he signed up to participate in the school's drama club because he liked theater, although he never became very active in it at Cornell. But he really did not like college life in general, nor did he feel particularly challenged by its curriculum, as tough as it was at a school the caliber of Cornell. He was just generally and simply not interested. During his second semester, the ennui that Eddie experienced became so overwhelming that he began to skip classes and ignore assignments. Just before that term was to end, he was suspended. He returned in January of the following year and, although his heart was still not in it, worked hard enough throughout the second semester of 1942 to record grades as good as those he had earned during his first semester the year before.

If there were any "throwaway years" in the life of Eddie Gilbert, it would have to have been those two at Cornell, from September of 1940 to June of 1942. Perhaps only during this period in his life did he seem not to have a desire to rise to the challenge; certainly it was only during this period that it could be said that apathy was his prevailing mood.

When Eddie finished the 1941-42 school year, he returned for the summer to the Gilbert's splendid home in Huntington Harbor on the shore of Long Island Sound, unsure whether he ever wanted to return to Cornell.

*The "we" generation of World War II
(as in "We are all in this together") was a special breed of
men and women who did great things for America and
the world. When the GIs sailed for Europe, they were coming
to the continent not as conquerors, but liberators. . . .
They accomplished that mission.*

STEPHEN AMBROSE, CITIZEN SOLDIERS, 1997

America's engagement in World War II was nine months' old when Eddie Gilbert returned to Cornell in September 1942 to begin his sophomore year. Because a number of acquaintances from his freshman year had been drafted or had enlisted in one of the armed services, Eddie felt guilty and out of place being in college when many of his friends were directly involved with the world at war.

Back in Ithaca, he watched the events of the war unfold as best he could from the campus, just as he had during his summer on Long Island. American combat at the time was relegated to the Pacific Theater of Operations, most notably the Midway naval battle and the Marines' invasion of Guadalcanal. The United States had yet to field an army or fire a single weapon in the battles that raged in Europe and North Africa. In fact, America's first recognized shot fired in the European Theater of Operations would not come until November 11th, more than 11 months following the U. S. declaration of war on Germany. That first shot was, coincidentally, fired by a field artillery battery of the 34th National Guard Division (Minnesota) on a German tank in Tunisia, an area in North Africa not far from where Gilbert would soon find himself wandering around in a U. S. military uniform. The newspapers, of course, were filled with the dramatic events of the war against the Axis Powers in mid to late 1942: the devastating wolf-pack attacks in the Atlantic by German U-boats; the brutal combat between German and Russian forces on the eastern front; the British offensive and the battle of El Alamein in North Africa; the incessant bombing of London, Liverpool, Manchester, and other industrial centers in England.

With all the history-making turbulence in the world, Gilbert found college life even more boring than before. He was regularly distracted, he remembers, and knew it was just a matter of time before he would himself join the American forces. He was a healthy 19-year-old, and even though the Selective Service System had not yet reached his number, he knew it would before long.

With the semester nearly half over, an Army Air Corps recruiter came to the Ithaca campus, and Eddie went to listen to his presentation. What the recruiter said was compelling, and joining up to be a pilot, Eddie decided, seemed much better than waiting around to be drafted as a dogface infantryman. What most intrigued Gilbert, however, was the excitement of becoming a fighter pilot: the challenge, the romance, the glamor, which had been so artfully painted by the recruiter.

After he volunteered and had taken and easily passed the necessary tests, Eddie was told he had qualified for pilot training. So by December 1942 he had signed the necessary papers, quit Cornell, and returned to New York to surprise his parents with the news. An unwelcome surprise, it turned out. His father was quite upset with Eddie's decision, and his mother cried upon hearing it. Both tried to talk him out of it. His father, Eddie remembers, had some pretty forceful arguments, but they did not matter to Eddie, because his decision had already been made, the commitment sealed by his signature on the enlistment papers filed in the Army Air Corps recruiting office. With no choice, his parents reluctantly accepted Eddie's decision and offered him their support. Like millions of American parents at the time, they watched anxiously and fearfully as he packed his bag and left for basic training.

In January 1943, after Gilbert had just turned 20 years old, he reported to Atlantic City, New Jersey, a town almost entirely transormed into a military base. Recruits were housed in hotels along the boardwalk, with much of the basic training exercises conducted on the beaches. After completing two months' training, he shipped out to Williamsport, Pennsylvania, for primary flight training. AAC cadets received their initial flight training in Piper Cubs then (a far cry from the screaming fighter planes Gilbert had envisioned). Still an adventure, it was not without its risks and perils as Eddie painfully discovered after having logged about 12 hours' flight time. He was flying a Piper Cub in a routine training exercise to practice how to handle a spin-out. As he struggled to keep control of his plane as it went into a spin, his parachute belt got twisted and and jerked tight into his groin. In great pain, he managed to land the plane, but had to be taken from it and rushed to a hospital. One testicle, it turned out, was crushed. Eddie spent the next two weeks in the Williamsport hospital. But the injury did not prevent him from returning to training; he moved next to the AAC facility later to be known as Maxwell Air Force Base near Montgomery, Alabama.

From there Gilbert was transferred to an AAC base in northwest Tennessee for the final phase of training. It was there that, in air force parlance, he "washed out" of pilot training.

"It wasn't because of any problem with my flying," Eddie explains. "I was as good as any pilot they had in the place. It had to do with my attitude. I had a good attitude, I thought. But they just didn't think so." There was also "a situation." As a part-time duty at the base, Eddie had been assigned to edit the post newspaper. One day he wrote a probing and finger-pointing editorial about "a slush fund" that all the cadets contributed to, which was administered by some of the officers on post. Eddie's headline read: "What Happens To All Our Money?"

He never learned the answer to that provocative question, but discovered that his career as a newspaper editor, at least at that base, had come to a sudden halt. Shortly thereafter, he found that his hopes of becoming a fighter pilot were similarly dashed.

Gilbert was then transferred to Biloxi, Mississippi, where he was to continue flight training, but now as a navigator, gunner, or bombadier. He informed his commanding officer that he did not want any of those flight assignments; he had enlisted to be a pilot, and if that was not to be, "the hell with it," he said. The Army Air Corps took him at his word, and Eddie was soon on a troop ship headed for the war in Europe and North Africa as a ground-crew private.

The transatlantic voyages during World War II took almost a month because convoys had to zig-zag across the Atlantic to avoid the marauding German U-boats. There were more than 5,000 combat-bound troops on board with Gilbert. It was a most uncomfortable journey.

By the spring of 1944, the battle of North Africa had been won. The U.S. and British armies were now moving up the leg of Italy but encountering fierce resistance from the German forces in the northern part of that country. The Allies had control of southern Italy, having captured the important ports of Naples and Salerno as well as the island of Sicily by the time Eddie Gilbert's troop ship finally steamed into the Bay of Naples.

His taste of the war was almost immediate. The troops had barely got off the ship—most were still on the docks—when an air raid siren suddenly wailed, followed quickly by a swarm of German Stukas swooping out of the sky to attack the port. The air was suddenly filled with the ear-shattering noises of the American anti-aircraft barrage and the machine-gun fire and exploding bombs from the attacking German planes. It happened so suddenly and with such awesome violence that it seemed unreal to Gilbert, its pyrotechnical brilliance so removed yet so affective that the only word he could later find to describe his reaction was simply "fascination." He did remember one thing from his basic training, however: A soldier's chance to survive in combat is much better if he is wearing a helmet. Not wearing one at the time of the attack, Eddie rushed to his gear, which was still sitting on the dock, and reached for the helmet. But as he did, the sense of unreality and his "fascination" with the attack quickly evaporated. Bending over, he remembers, he heard a nearby explosion followed by a searing pain in his buttocks. "Shot in the ass, my first day there," he recalled ruefully years later. "It was more embarrassing than anything else, other guys asking, 'which way were you running,' that sort of thing." As it turned out, his injury was not serious, the shrapnel lodged in his derrière being mostly superficial. It was removed by a medic, and the wounds were then cleaned up and bandaged without Gilbert having to be hospitalized. Other than experiencing some discomfort whenever he sat down during the next few days, Eddie survived his initial scrape with combat with firsthand knowledge that war was indeed "a pain in the ass."

The following day he was on another vessel, smaller than the troop ship that had carried him across the Atlantic, this one bound for North Africa.

Out in the middle of the Mediterranean, alarms on board suddenly went off, and the ship erupted with activity. None of the transported troops knew what was going on, but the crew rushed to various stations and duties. The ship ceased cruising along and began to take sharp evasive maneuvers. The troops were huddled in their quarters below deck, but Eddie decided to go topside. It was not because he wanted to see what was going on — fascination had been left on the dock in Naples — but, as he explained later, "I figured if something happened to the ship, I'd be better off on deck. It'd certainly be safer there than trapped below."

The threat this time, however, did not come from the sky above but from the sea below. As he emerged on deck, he saw the ship's crew launch depth charges and felt a shudder as they exploded somewhere beneath the sea. After a short while, the explosions simply stopped. No crippled submarine surfaced, no oil slick defaced the blue Mediterranean, no flotsam or jetsam appeared bobbing on the surface; the ship simply resumed a steady, smooth course with the crew returning to their ordinary sea duties. However, the reality of war — that no soldier was safe anywhere — had by now staked a very real claim in Eddie Gilbert's mind.

The following day the ship landed in Algiers, and the troops disembarked, told they were soon to leave for Oran, another Algerian port city about 200 miles to the east. Algeria, nestled between Morocco to the west and Tunisia to the east on the southern coast of the Mediterranean, had earlier been a major battleground in the desert war fought between Germany's Afrika Korps (under the famed General Erwin Rommel) and the armies of the British (first commanded by General Claude Auchinleck and subsequently by General Bernard Montgomery), and the U.S. army (under the supreme command of General Dwight D. Eisehower with its Western Task Force led by General George S. Patton). When Gilbert arrived there in the summer of 1944, Algiers was, and had been since November 1942, the headquarters of the Allied forces in North Africa.

The troop train waiting for the Army Air Corps men headed for Oran. If Eddie Gilbert's Atlantic voyage on a crowded troop ship had left something to be desired, he would soon find that it seemed like first class compared to travel in a railroad boxcar in the heat of an African desert. As the train headed across the northernmost stretch of the Sahara that night, the trip became almost unbearable. "It must have been used for shipping cattle before because it stunk of excrement, and there were turds all over, and even with the door slid open it was unbelievably hot," Eddie recalls. "So three of us decided to climb up on top of the train, which was moving at only about fifteen miles an hour, and ride up there where the smell and the heat wouldn't be so bad."

At some point, as they were riding atop the slow-moving boxcar under a star-filled night sky, Eddie stood up to stretch. The next thing he knew, he was lying in the sand under a broiling desert sun, hearing voices, but unable to focus on who was speaking and not understanding what they were saying. "We must have come to a tunnel or some kind of overhang or something because I was knocked off the train and I didn't come to until the next day." The Arab voices he heard belonged to some local youths who had found him lying in the sand alongside the tracks. They were trying to help him, he could understand that much, but he kept sliding in and out of consciousness. Somehow they managed to take him to a U. S. army field hospital—or found someone to transport him there—because that is where he finally regained his bearings. He had suffered an obvious concussion and was sick from it. He also had a bad gash on the side of his head. The army doctors kept him there for more than a week to recover and to observe him for any after-effects from his concussion. When they felt he was fairly well recuperated, they told him to rejoin his unit in Oran, about 60 miles away. After walking several miles on the only main road, he hitched a ride on a passing army truck. About ten miles outside of Oran, however, the driver stopped at an oasis and said that this was as far as he could take him.

At the little inn-like establishment at the oasis, the two decided to get something to drink before parting company. When they came out, however, a pack of Arab boys were swarming around the truck. Gilbert's pack in the truck contained all the money he had and, for that matter, every other personal possession he had in the world. As he shouted and ran toward them, one of the older boys separated from his pals and, wielding a knife, met Gilbert head-on and slashed him on the side of the face. Eddie got his pistol unholstered and began firing into the air above the youths, and they quickly scattered back into the desert. The cut was not a deep one, but it would leave a scar. Eddie retrieved his pack, with the money still in it, and, with a bandaged face now, set out again for Oran. Gilbert walked the rest of the way alone which, as he later recalled, "seemed like the longest ten miles ever measured in this world."

By the time he got to Oran, the desert sun and heat as well as the lingering effects of his concussion, his slashed face, and little food (he had been unable to keep anything down) had taken their toll. He was on the verge of delirium, but still managed to hook up with his unit. Once there, however, he passed out and was taken to another army tent hospital where he remained for the next two weeks. He was then reassigned back to Naples, the trip across the Mediterranean this time by airplane.

The city of Naples, *Napoli* as it is known in song and lore, with its famous bay and the fabled Isle of Capri just off the coast, lies in the shadow of Mount Vesuvius, the city's "terror and its pride," the volcano that buried the nearby towns of Pompeii and Herculaneum in its first-century eruptions. During World War II, Naples was the third largest city in Italy, after Rome and Milan. Much of it had been destroyed in the war, and it was a city pretty much in ruins by the time Eddie Gilbert arrived there in 1944.

He was assigned to the post exchange at Capodichino Air Force Base (today Naples' main airport, the *Aeroporte di Capodichino*), reporting directly to the colonel in charge of running that operation. The autumn of 1944 was a relatively placid time in Naples. Fascist dictator Benito Mussolini and his government had been driven from power more than a year before, and the Allies controlled all of the surrounding area from Italy's boot-tip to Rome, that grand city having fallen to the Allied forces in June 1944. The Germans had retreated to the north, so air raids became less frequent, with Hitler's forces focusing their attention on the vast Allied armies that had landed in France on D-Day and on the collapsing eastern-front combat with Russia.

Because of his mathematical wizardry, Gilbert, despite his lowly rank of private, was soon put in charge of running the large PX on the base. "The colonel was not good with numbers," Eddie said later. "He kept screwing up the books. He found out I could add and subtract, so he told me take over. I got them straightened out, and he was delighted and told me just to run the whole damn thing." As a consequence, Eddie was able to finagle an almost unheard of wartime luxury, a small apartment in the old section of Naples. He also had a jeep at his disposal. Outside his daily duties at the PX, Eddie's time was pretty much his own, a freedom not enjoyed by many World War II privates.

During those trouble-free hours he developed a love for opera that would remain with him for the rest of his life. Near his downtown Naples apartment was the Teatro San Carlo opera house, Italy's most famous after La Scala in Milan. Opera works had been staged there since 1737 and included the premieres of some of the world's most beloved operas, such as Donizetti's *Lucia di Lammermoor* and Bellini's *La Sonnambula*. Italy's most revered tenor (and Naples native) Enrico Caruso had made his operatic debut at the Teatro San Carlo in 1894. Even the raging war could not douse the Italians' fervid love for opera, so performances continued regularly in 1944. The magnificent hall, with its near-perfect acoustics, its Ionic columns and ornate bas-reliefs on the outside and frescoed ceiling inside, could accommodate 3,000 patrons. But Gilbert rarely occupied one of the velvet-upholstered seats, preferring, for reasons of simple economics, to stand in the gallery at the back. From his very first exposure, however, he was enraptured with the music and the spectacle, although his Italian was not yet accomplished enough to understand the librettos of the many operas he heard at the Teatro San Carlo. By the time he became a devoted opera buff, having his own box at the Metropolitan Opera in New York a decade later, however, he would understand the Italian dialogue fully, having mastered the language thanks mostly to his wartime Italian stay.

There was still a war going on, however, and Naples was in many ways a lawless, dangerous city. Gilbert was reminded of that the hard way as he was walking down a narrow street near his apartment one day. A shot rang out. The bullet creased him behind the ear and tore away a chunk of flesh. He lay in the street until four middle-aged women came to help. They got him up, but he could not stand on his own; so they carried him upstairs to their apartment. They cleaned his wound, bandaged him, and cared for him over the next few days until he was again ambulatory. The four were sisters, all spinsters, with the surname DiNicola. Gilbert later learned that they had come from moderate wealth but were now quite poor. Eddie never forgot them and after the war regularly sent them cash to help with their rent and other necessities, stopping only after the death of the last sister in 1978.

Nothing is permanent in war, however, especially in a soldier's life, and so Eddie's relatively pleasant interlude in Naples came to an end in November 1944. Papers came through ordering him to Greece as part of a small contingent of about 60 or 70 Army Air Corps soldiers assembled as a unit identified as the Air Transport Command (ATC) to serve in Athens as a support group for the American air base recently activated there. According to Gordon Dick, a sergeant assigned to the same unit who became Gilbert's friend, these overwhelmingly noncombatant troops referred to ATC as the "Army of Terrified Civilians."

Athens sounded like another soft assignment to Gilbert. The Germans had left, and so the country should have been basking in peace. But it wasn't, and, much to his surprise, Eddie got a true taste in Greece of what war in the combat zone was like. The situation was an ironic one because the vicious fighting was not connected to World War II, and Allied forces were not directly involved in it.

Germany had attacked Greece in April 1941 and quickly occupied it until October 1943. This was a time described by one modern Greek historian as "marked by appalling suffering and great heroism." There had been resistance to the Axis conquerors—guerrilla bands formed and hid out in the hills, attacking and making the occupying Germans' life both a hazardous and routinely unhappy one—and peace still did not come even after the German forces withdrew. A power struggle ensued when a coalition of guerrilla forces headed by Georgios Papandreou (a socialist opposed to the exiled Greek monarch King George II) broke apart, separating into communist and noncommunist factions. A bitter civil war ensued, with fierce fighting erupting in Athens in early December 1944.

Neither Eddie Gilbert, nor anyone else in his small unit, had any idea what the Greeks were fighting about, only that there was a bloody civil war going on. "But we sure knew it was a serious thing," Eddie's pal Gordon Dick remembered many years later. "It was a regular war, a lot of shooting and artillery; and neither side cared who we were or where we were. If we got in the way, we'd get killed. So most of us tried to stay out of the way."

Upon their arrival, the "Army of Terrified Civilians" were billeted in hotels on Omonia Square in central Athens, which also happened to be a hotbed of the civil war combat. "It was a big, prominent square," Gilbert remembers of the historic plaza, which was then and remains today the hub of the Athens subway system. "We couldn't go into the square because if we did we'd end up getting shot at or blown up by the Greeks who were killing each other and anyone who got in the way. The British were there too, housed in another hotel on the same square. They were an army unit, a combat outfit, with rifles and machine guns and jeeps and mortars. We had nothing like that. We had guns but little ammunition. We were an Air Corps outfit, supposed to take care of the PX and things like that around the air base."

December 3, 1944 — a Sunday — marked the day fighting actually broke out in Athens. Eddie's hotel was empty except for the American soldiers housed there, though only five of the men from his unit were assigned to this particular hotel, and each had his own room. Eddie's overlooked the square with a balcony surrounded by a wrought-iron balustrade. "A couple of us were in my room when we heard all this noise coming from down in the square," Eddie tells the story later. "We went to the window and opened these huge shutters a little and looked out. There were thousands of people in the square, jammed in down there and milling about and there was a lot of shouting. We didn't know what was going on, and we were just kind of amused by it at first."

Eddie got an idea, "Watch this," he said as he threw open the shutters and stepped out onto the balcony. Some of the crowd looked up, some started pointing at him. He raised his arms, hands high like he was signaling a football touchdown, and shouted: "Welcome!"

"I felt like Mussolini, all those people gathered down there, looking up. It was a joke, the other guys in the room were laughing, but then suddenly all hell broke loose. Somebody started firing guns from somewhere, rifles and machine guns, and people in the square were falling down and others were panicking and running to get out of the square. I remember seeing one guy on the roof of another building, about a three-story building across the way, and he was standing there, and he was shot; and I watched as he toppled over the edge and down into the square. It was like in a movie.

"In a few minutes the square was empty, and there were about 30 or 40 people lying dead on the ground. There was a jeep down there, and suddenly I saw three English soldiers running for it. They jumped into it and just as they did a mortar hit it and the thing exploded. All three were blasted into the air, maybe 20 feet. Killed instantly. It was horrible. We didn't know it at the time, but *that* was the start of the Greek civil war that we would live through for the next couple of weeks."

Intense and incessant fighting would continue for nearly two more weeks until the British intervened to force an uneasy truce, signed on December 16. But combat picked up again in a few days, although more sporadic than during the first two weeks, which lasted until January 11, 1945, when a formal armistice resulted in the two Greek factions finally laying down their arms.

For Eddie Gilbert and his fellow Army Air Corpsmen, December 1944 was the sort of ordeal none of them had ever experienced. They were, in effect, prisoners in their hotel. Although they were not under attack, they were warned they would be vulnerable if they ventured into the square or the streets around it. One street, however, was controlled by the British, but to get to it they had to cross the square, which they did not openly dare to do. Instead they slipped into the subway from an entrance just outside the hotel and emerged from another at the opposite side of the square. Eddie had been assigned to run the PX, which was not operating under these conditions, and had a jeep at his disposal, (although he had no plans to go wheeling about in the dangerous streets outside unless it was absolutely necessary).

After several days of isolation, however, the Yanks in the hotel were running low on food, and nothing was being sent in to them. One of Gilbert's compatriots was a Greek by the name of Peter Bratsos, an American GI who had been stationed in Athens even before the civil war erupted. He spoke Greek fluently and could get around the city pretty well. He knew of a large bakery operation a few blocks away, he told the others, but it was unfortunately right in the middle of where pitched battles were regularly being waged.

"We decided to go anyway," Eddie recalls. "I had the jeep for the PX and I thought we could get through. You see, at the time, I figured I wasn't going to get shot. They weren't going to shoot *me*. Maybe I was stupid, but I really felt that way." This is the same carefree attitude of invulnerability that had been nurtured back in Flushing by the doting Harry Gilbert, the same that would come to the fore throughout his later years. *Bad things won't happen to me.* But bad things *would* happen to him, during the war... and later in the business world.

Peter Bratsos was reluctant to go. Beyond the immediate danger posed by guns and bombs, he also knew well the emotions and the abandon of the Greeks who were engaged in the violence. Bratsos was content simply to ride it out within the safety of the hotel. But Eddie and the others disagreed and persuaded him to go along because his presence on the mission was essential, given his fluency in Greek and his knowledge of the streets of Athens. The mission was going to be carried out, and he *had* to be a part of it.

So Eddie and Pete Bratsos went outside and got into the jeep. They drove out of the square without incident, but they found that the street to the bakery was barricaded with barbed wire. The two got out and began to dismantle the tangled mess. "There were places where you could pull it apart to make a way to drive through," Eddie explained, "but you had to get it open or you couldn't get through." As they finished and were heading back to the jeep (Eddie undoubtedly musing, "See, they aren't going to shoot *me*"), gunfire from the surrounding buildings sprayed the area, and it was indeed aimed at them. Bratsos hit the floor of the jeep and Eddie, hunched down and heart pounding, threw it into gear and careened through the hole in the barbed wire down the narrow street, bouncing recklessly off curbs until they were out of range of those shooting at them.

From his fetal position on the floor of the jeep, Bratsos shouted directions. They reached the bakery safely. It was a large building, with a long hall off the back where a room housed several large baking kilns and storage bins. Eddie stopped the jeep at the front door and the two clambered out; but shooting immediately began again, with bullets richocheting off the ground and the wall of the bakery. Both men dropped down behind the jeep until there was a lull in the gunfire. Then Eddie nodded toward the bakery and the two broke for the door, flung it open and raced down the hall, with renewed shots ringing out behind them.

Several bakers were at work in the room at the back, but they stopped as the two Americans burst in. The bakers started shouting, but Bratsos yelled back in Greek, "Stop...we're Americans." One of the bakers recognized him and he raised a hand to stop the others who were moving menacingly toward Gilbert and Bratsos. "Pete" the baker bellowed, and came over to give Bratsos a big, Zorba-the-Greek-style hug.

Gilbert told the man the American soldiers needed bread. After some negotiation, the bakers filled four large wicker baskets with about ten or twelve loaves each. By now it was late afternoon, the December sun heading quickly toward the horizon. Bratsos wanted to remain inside where there was no shooting, but Eddie wanted to leave, telling Bratsos, "If we don't get out of here before dark, we're going to get ourselves killed. I want to be able to see where I'm driving." Bratsos did not want to go. So

Gilbert grabbed one of the baskets of bread. "I'm going without you," Gilbert shouted. "You explain why you stayed when you get back...if you get back."

Bratsos acquiesced. They decided to take just one basket at a time up to the front door because they were so cumbersome. "I'll take the first," Eddie said, "then you follow with another after I'm there."

But as soon as he reached the front door a loud, long fusillade commenced, and Gilbert hit the floor just inside the door. He waited there for Bratsos. But Bratsos never came. At a break in the barrage, Eddie ran back to Bratsos who explained that he just couldn't do it, he couldn't run up that hall with all the shooting. Rather than argue, Eddie grabbed another basket and headed to the front door, then raced back. He did the same thing again. As he moved out into the corridor with the final basket, shots were suddenly fired down the hall and he lunged back. He felt something in his right arm he could only describe as "strange . . . it didn't hurt, but it felt hot and like something had been pulled away from my arm. I was in some kind of shock, I guess, and yelled, 'I've been hit.' I was standing next to Bratsos and said to him, 'My God, Pete, I think I've been hit in the arm. You look at it, I can't.'"

Bratsos took one look and fainted. "Oh, Jesus," Eddie shouted. The bakers went to Bratsos and slapped him a few times to bring him around. Eddie then turned slowly to look at his arm, thinking the worst, but there was no blood, just two bullet holes in the loose part of the sleeve of his shirt with thin wisps of smoke rising from the burnt fabric. As Eddie relaxed and Bratsos regained consciousness, the shooting finally stopped. So the two then scrambled up the corridor to the front door. They got the four baskets of bread into the back of the jeep. Bratsos hunkered down on the floor again, and with Eddie behind the wheel they sped away. In the darkness, now, the shooting began again, but they got back to the hotel safely.

A little more than a week later, Gilbert and several others decided late one morning to visit some of their pals in another hotel across the square. It was an uncommonly quiet day, sunny and unseasonably warm for December. They went downstairs to look around outside, and then ducked into the subway entrance. When they emerged on the other side of the square, they cautiously surveyed the situation before making a break for the other hotel's entrance. They enjoyed lunch together, most of them talking about the lull in the fighting and wondering why the warring had come to a halt. Heading back to their own hotel, in the peace of the still sun-drenched afternoon, they decided to walk back around the perimeter of the square instead of the subway route. They were not even halfway back when, as Gilbert recalls, "all hell broke loose. The shooting was coming from everywhere but we couldn't see who was doing the shooting. Back and forth at each other, not necessarily at us, but we were there and if we were, we became targets, too. There was artillery going off. We ran from the square into one of the streets. There were a bunch of streets that emptied into the square, like spokes on a wheel, and we ran down one of them. There was stuff going on in those streets, too. We got into a doorway somewhere and waited till things died down."

When they stepped back into the street, they saw an American jeep maybe 100 yards up the street stopped half over the curb. In the jeep a soldier was slumped over the steering wheel. "We've got to go get him," Gilbert said.

"We can't," one of the others said. "We'll get killed going down there."

"Everybody just stood there for a moment," Sergeant Dick later recalled. "Then suddenly Eddie Gilbert bolted away and ran up the street, everybody standing there watching him."

The soldier, it turned out, was an Army Air Corps tech sergeant named Aja, who was badly wounded in the leg, bleeding profusely, but still conscious. "He was moaning and didn't want to move because of the pain probably," Gilbert later explained. "Or maybe he just feared he'd get hit again, I don't know. I told him we had to get out of there or we'd both get killed. I wanted to get him out of the jeep, but he didn't want to go. So, I finally just pushed him over into the other seat and got in and drove the damn thing off. When I did, they started shooting at us, bullets bouncing everywhere."

Gilbert got about three quarters up the block but slowed as the gunfire increased. Just then a man appeared in a doorway opposite them and shouted, waving for them to come inside. Gilbert dragged the sergeant from the jeep, threw him over his shoulder and carried him into the building. "Inside there were a lot of men," Eddie remembers. "There were beds and tables. It was kind of like a makeshift hospital in there. They were all Greeks, but I didn't know what side they were on. All I do know is that they started to take care of the sergeant, cleaning up his wounds and bandaging him as best they could. They had these long tweezers and used them to pull out the bullets or shrapnel or whatever it was."

After the fighting had subsided outside, Gilbert got the sergeant back into the jeep and drove over to the British-controlled sector off Omonia Square. At a hospital operated by the British there, Gilbert left the sergeant.

Eddie had not expected to see the sergeant again, but one afternoon about three weeks later Sergeant Aja, on crutches and carrying a small suitcase, appeared at the hotel where Gilbert was living. Up in Eddie's room, he opened the suitcase, overflowing with drachmas. "I never saw anything like it," Eddie said years later. "There were all these bills, drachmas. Hundreds of them, maybe thousands."

"I'm being sent back to the States," he told Gilbert. "I want you to have this; you saved my life."

"That's crazy, you keep it," Gilbert said.

The sergeant insisted, and then left. "It was a really nice gesture on his part," Eddie later explained. "It was all the money the guy had over there. A whole suitcase full of drachmas. It looked like a million dollars, but the drachma was hardly worth the paper it was printed on at that time. I mean all the drachmas in that suitcase didn't add up to fifty dollars. But it was such a nice thing, his coming over and doing that before he went home."

Eddie's brave action did not go unnoticed in the Air Corps either. Sergeant Dick reported the incident to the colonel in charge of the ATC unit in Athens who in turn recommended Gilbert for the Bronze Star. Though papers were forwarded to Washington for approval, Eddie did not receive the medal during his tour of duty. Back in New York in late 1946 as a civilian, he was surprised one day to receive in the mail the Bronze Star medal and a letter of commendation recounting the incident that sunny, violent afternoon in Athens.

Sergeant Aja was not the only person in Greece who ended up owing Gilbert a debt of gratitude. One night in January 1945, Eddie was once again caught up in gunfire on a street off Omonia Square. In his PX jeep, he was about to speed up to get out of the area when he heard the screams of a young girl. She was in her mid-teens, cowering in a doorway not deep enough to provide much protection and terribly frightened as bullets flew all around her. Gilbert stopped the jeep and ran over to her. Her face, he remembers, was "the most panic-stricken I've ever seen in my life." He put his arm around her and the two of them, hunched over, ran to the jeep. Before they reached it, something exploded nearby and Gilbert felt a sharp pain in the side of his leg. But they made it, and both jumped into the jeep and Eddie drove away. His leg was bleeding, but it did not appear to be anything serious; and there was little he could do about it at the time anyway.

The girl spoke some English and told him her name was Doris Kathezedzis and that she lived about a mile away. Eddie drove her home and returned to his hotel on Omonia Square. A medic there found some shrapnel in the leg, took it out, and patched him up.

The wound did not get better, however, and began to bother him seriously several days later. Over the next two weeks, it became clear the leg was infected. With it festering, his commanding officer decided that Gilbert needed better treatment than he could get in Athens. So Eddie was taken to the Allied air base and put on a plane for Paris. After several days there, he was put on another plane for London where he remained hospitalized for two weeks until the infection was brought under control.

Eddie spent the remainder of the war stationed in Rome. The conflict in Europe would end in fewer than three months from the time he arrived in the Eternal City in February 1945. For Eddie Gilbert, however, the fighting was over. In Rome, he was assigned to the *Stars and Stripes* as a reporter (the editorial command there apparently unaware of Eddie's undistinguished journalistic experience back in Tennessee two years earlier).

One especially memorable moment from his reportorial days in Rome as the war wound down came as a result of a letter from his sister Enid. When she heard he was stationed in Rome, the intellectually-driven Enid wrote to tell Eddie that George Santayana was living there and urged him to try to meet the famous philospher. Although he admitted that he did not even know who Santayana was before his sister wrote to him, Eddie felt maybe an interview might provide an interesting story for *Stars and Stripes*. He investigated and found Santayana living in a convent in the heart of Rome where the philospher-novelist and former Harvard professor had spent most of the war years. Santayana was then 81 years old and in ill health. But he agreed to talk with Gilbert.

"I didn't really interview him," Gilbert explained later. "He was quite ill and weak, and the day I went over there was not a good one for him. We talked for a little while and that was about it." That was too bad, in a way. It might have been a most interesting meeting of dissimilars: the introspective, isolated Santayana and the extroverted, ever-mobile Gilbert. They might well have enjoyed each other in counterbalance on a more propitious occasion.

The war in Europe ended with the capitulation of Germany on May 7, 1945. A few months later, Gilbert returned to Naples, to the same bay near the same pier where the war had begun for him a year-and-a-half before. Once again he boarded a troop ship, this time bound for a much less daunting and much more coveted destination. He was mustered out of the Army Air Corps in October 1945 at Fort Dix, New Jersey.

The historian Stephen Ambrose wrote in his captivating account of the U. S. Army and its battles in Europe from D-Day to the German surrender, *Citizen Soldiers*, "The 'we' generation of World War II (as in 'We are all in this together') was a special breed of men and women who did great things for America and the world. When the GIs sailed for Europe, they were coming to the continent not as conquerors but liberators. In his Order of the Day on June 6, 1944, [General Dwight D.] Eisenhower had told them their mission was: 'The destruction of the German war machine, the elimination of Nazi tyranny over the oppressed peoples of Europe, and security for ourselves in a free world.' They accomplished that mission."

Eddie Gilbert had been part of that liberation force. But what he found as one of its members, perhaps more than anything else, was his own liberation. The discontented college student, youthful and unproven on his own, who had impetuously joined the Army Air Corps, returned a much more worldly young man. He had now the earned self-assurance that he could take matters into his own hands and make things happen.

*Give my regards to Broadway,*
*Remember me to Herald Square.*
*Tell all the gang at Forty-Second Street,*
*That I will soon be there.*

GEORGE M. COHAN, "GIVE MY REGARDS TO BROADWAY," 1904

I n post-war New York, the lumber products company founded by
Eddie Gilbert's grandfather, Hyman Ginsberg, almost a half-century
earlier was doing well. Annual sales at Empire Millwork had reached
about $8 million when Eddie formally joined the firm in the late
1940s, and the company was modestly profitable.

Shortly after his discharge from the army in 1946, Eddie worked at Empire on a temporary basis, mostly unloading railroad cars or in the factory
putting window frames together. But to appease his family, who were determined that he finish college, Eddie returned to Cornell. There, he
found he was far too restless, too anxious to get moving in the business
world to make a go of it. After a couple of unhappy semesters, he dropped
out of Cornell and returned home.

It was then that Eddie decided to launch his career in earnest within
the family firm; but it was not a glamorous beginning. His father had him
serve in the lowly rank of a shipping clerk in the company's headquarters
in Flushing. Harry Gilbert was adamant in wanting his son to learn the
business from the ground up, and Eddie did not disagree. The youthful
Gilbert had bigger things in mind for himself at Empire, even though he
knew he had to learn all aspects of the Empire operation if he were to succeed in the business and to achieve those ambitions. But because Eddie
was a quick study, he picked up just about all there was to know about the

lumber and wood products industry in his first few months on the job.

So during this same period, he began making forays into the world of finance, both involving Empire as well as other companies then flourishing on Wall Street. The stock market fascinated and challenged him; it was just the kind of arena to excite the quiescent gambling instinct (quiescent at least in the 1940s) inside the personality of Eddie Gilbert. He began to invest and trade, initiatiating a career that before the end of the next decade would at first surprise, then dazzle, and eventually leave an indelible mark in the Wall Street financial community.

Within Empire, however, the area of the business that most attracted Eddie was sales. He liked the feel of the competition, he said later, the opportunity inherent in that aspect of the business, and he felt he could have a sizeable impact there within the company. That impact would have to wait for a while, however, at least until his apprenticeship ran its course.

In 1948, when Gilbert was just 25 years old, his father asked him to visit the company's flooring plant in Harriman, Tennessee. There were reports of disturbing problems at that plant, and Harry wanted his son to determine what they were and to remedy them. Eddie took a train from New York and, after several transfers, finally made it to Harriman, a town of about 5,000 inhabitants in east-central Tennessee some 30 miles west of Knoxville. He recognized the problem the first day there. The plant manager had a serious drinking problem. "When I got there, to the plant, I could tell immediately he was drunk, on the job," Eddie remembers. So he called his father and reported the situation: "I told him I was going to fire the guy, but my father said, 'Hold on. We'll send somebody down there.'"

But the youthful and impetuous Eddie Gilbert was not one for waiting around. To him the solution was simple: Get rid of the problem, and fast. "I'm going to fire him as soon as I hang up here," he told his father.

"No! Who's going to run the plant?" Harry Gilbert asked.

"I'll run it," Eddie replied.

"Just wait. I'm going to send someone down there to handle it."

Eddie did not wait. To him, the solution was a clear-cut one. Because the manager was continuously drunk, the place was in a mess. "It was ridiculous," Eddie remembers, "he was just lying around down there, not accomplishing a damn thing. It would make *me* look ridiculous if I didn't act, I felt." The solution was as simple as the problem was clear-cut; so he fired the manager. By the time an Empire vice president, Marcel Weiss, arrived several days later, Eddie was in complete charge of the plant. He outlined the problems he had found to Weiss and what he had begun to do to correct them. Weiss called Harry Gilbert in New York, telling him that everything appeared now to be in good order. He recommended that Eddie stay on to manage the plant, at least until it was running smoothly again. Before the year was out, the plant was back on track; and Eddie returned from Tennessee happily to reenter the far more cosmopolitan atmosphere of New York.

In the late 1940s, Eddie Gilbert also aspired to establish himself as a man about town in the elite and competitive social circles of New York. He was young, aggressive, and self-confident; since returning from the war and from his brief sojourn at Cornell, he rather quickly cemented old friendships and made many new acquaintances within New York's young socialite set. He had discovered the heralded watering holes of El Morocco, the Stork Club, and the Copacabana and such pedigreed restaurants as Le Pavillon and "21"; he was seen in them regularly and usually with a pretty girl on his arm. He was the quintessential Manhattan bachelor.

One of his dates around that time was tennis star Gussie Moran, who was better known in the late 1940s by her nickname "Gorgeous Gussie"; the lace panties she wore on the court were considered downright scandalous at the time. Gussie was a beauty and a quite competent tennis professional as well, participating in all the major tournaments from Forest Hills to Wimbledon. Teamed with Pancho Gonzalez, she won the U. S. indoor mixed doubles in 1949. Teamed with Eddie Gilbert, well, nothing ever developed into a serious romance. At the time Gorgeous Gussie was involved with movie star Burgess Meredith; Eddie had other female interests as well. Nonetheless, Eddie and Gussie captured notice when they arrived together at any one of New York's fashionable nightspots.

Despite the sophisticated lifestyle he had adopted, Eddie had yet to become the cosmopolite he aspired to become, as the following story illustrates. One evening, Eddie arrived at a cocktail party in Manhattan where he noticed a particularly attractive young woman across the room talking with several of his friends. He made his way over to her and introduced himself. She was more than attractive, he decided on closer inspection; she was simply very beautiful. Dressed impeccably and with the allure of a European accent and the carriage of a model, she was something extraordinary, Eddie felt. Once he had maneuvered her away from the others, she confided to him that she was a "baroness" from the Netherlands, furthering her education in America at the exclusive Barnard College. "Royalty, rich, beautiful, smart" Gilbert later reluctantly recalled, "she was something else. I was dazzled." He asked her out, to have a drink ...she said she would love to.

After a few courtly dates ("I was so taken with her, so in awe, I never kissed her, hell, never even held hands with her," Eddie admits), he asked her to come meet his parents and have dinner at their apartment in the Carlyle. She accepted; and he confided to her that his mother was also a "baroness from Hungarian noble stock." The evening went beautifully: Eddie's mother later evaluated the young woman as "educated, refined... a lady." Eddie was thrilled. To him, it seemed like he was embarked on a fairy tale romance.

Until he talked to his friend Huntington Hartford, that is. Hartford, the heir to the A&P grocery fortune and a playboy of international repute, was one of the New York set with whom Gilbert was keeping company in the late 1940s. Eager to impress Hartford, Eddie suggested they go out together on a double date, proudly revealing that he was dating one of *the* most gorgeous girls in town. "Who might that be?" Hartford inquired after listening to the glowing description of Eddie's new girlfriend. When Eddie told him the girl's name, Hartford said, "You're kidding."

"You know her?"

"From the Netherlands, right?"

"Yes," Eddie replied.

"Know her? I screwed her last week. Eddie, she's a hundred-dollar-a-night hooker."

Eddie was sure that Hartford was putting him on and told him he did not think the joke was very funny.

"Half the guys we know in town have been to bed with her," Hartford continued.

Eddie still did not believe him. Hartford reeled off the names of several of their acquaintances. "Call them," he said. And, as an afterthought, "Ask them about the towel, they'll tell you." Eddie did call and each corroborated Hartford's accusation and admitted having paid to have sex with her. The towel: She liked being beaten with one, they told him.

Instead of the double-date with Huntington Hartford, which was to have been a surprise to her—and what a surprise it would have been—

Eddie called her to ask if she would stop by his apartment before going out. She did, and was rather astonished to find the once courtly Gilbert barefoot and in a silk bathrobe with a towel around his neck when he greeted her at the door. Once inside the apartment, he asked her, "How much?" She stared at him blankly. "How much to go to bed with me" He pulled the towel from around his neck and shook it in a clenched fist. "Is it extra for me to hit you with the towel?" Without the slightest change of expression and without a word, she turned and walked out of his apartment.

Many years later, Eddie ran into her in New York, and they acknowledged each other. Still later, Eddie learned that she had married a wealthy foreign businessman, who died and left her a fortune, then married again to a Count who died leaving her an even larger fortune. Proof perhaps that some fairy tales do indeed have happy endings.

Around this time as well, Eddie began to indulge his special interest in opera, continuing to cultivate the taste for it that had been conceived in wartime Italy. Opera would remain among his most ardent passions, and it was not long before he invested in a box at the Met where he could entertain his growing circle of socialites. Later, as a comfortable millionaire, his evenings at the opera with dinner before and partying afterwards were affairs that could only be described as splendid. Even when his fortunes had fallen in later years, Eddie managed to maintain his box at the Met. When it came to surrendering that box, it was to Eddie almost like giving up himself.

At 26 years old in 1948, Gilbert became entranced with another allure of Manhattan life, the Broadway stage. As time passed, he became less and less content with merely sitting in the darkened audiences of the theaters off Times Square. With the spectacle of opening nights, the glitter of the stars who performed, the fanfare of it all, he was fated to become an integral part of it.

The seeds of his desire had been planted much earlier. When Eddie returned to Cornell after his army tour of duty, he met up with another New Yorker, Dick Winston, a nephew of the notable jeweler Harry Winston, whose fashionable emporium Eddie would later frequent. Dick Winston talked a lot about the theater, regularly confiding to Gilbert how much he wanted to be a part of the magic of it (despite the fact, as Eddie later recalled, that Winston really had no recognizable talent for any aspect of the legitimate stage). Eddie, like Winston, had regularly attended Broadway shows since he was a youngster and had enthusiastically dabbled in Cornell's drama club before the war. With typical Gilbert impetuosity and flair (perhaps sounding more like Mickey Rooney and Judy Garland in an old MGM Andy Hardy movie), he one day replied to a Winston theater harangue by saying, "Well, why don't we just produce a show ourselves?" Winston, who knew Gilbert pretty well by that time, was not dismayed by the idea, grandiose as it sounded, and nodded gleefully when Gilbert added, "Look, you go out and find a play that's worth producing, and I'll figure out a way to come up with the money to produce the thing."

That was the end of it... for the time being, anyway. A while later, Eddie dropped out of Cornell and returned to New York to embark on his business career; and Winston left school shortly thereafter as well. So while Eddie worked for his father and began playing the stock market on his own, Winston wandered around other parts of the city searching for a play for them to produce. Although he came up with a script from time to time and brought it to Eddie, "None of them were any good." Eddie remembers. "Not a one had even a chance of making it, and I'd tell him that. But it didn't stop Winston; he'd just go back and try to find another."

Then, in the spring of 1949, Winston got Eddie's attention when he brought him a new script. Whether because Gilbert now had a fair amount of money earned from his market successes, or because he had in recent days become more serious about getting inside the theater world, or merely because he was more intrigued by what he read this time than by anything Winston had previously brought to him, Gilbert expressed a guarded but sincere interest in the manuscript.

The play was *How Long Till Summer*, the creation of a husband and wife playwrighting team, Herbert and Sarett Rudley. The Rudleys were hardly new to the theatrical world, but the manuscript represented their first joint effort at writing a play for the Broadway stage. They had never heard of Eddie Gilbert, and so the production team of Gilbert and Winston, for them, had no credentials for a theatrical production. Winston was able to assure the Rudleys, however, that he and Eddie shared with them a genuine love for the theater; that they both possessed an inbred determination to finish anything they started; and, most importantly, that they could raise enough money to back the show. Winston's assurances seemed to satisfy the Rudleys and they seemed to respond positively, if hesitantly. In point of fact, they had no other offers to produce their play. So Winston next brought the playwrights to meet Eddie who, though cordial, evidenced no more than a cautious interest during that first meeting.

The play without question bore all the marks of Herbert Rudley's first-born child "He was very dramatic, very positive, very enthusiastic about his play, and he wanted to direct it himself," Eddie remembers. "He was also an egomaniac, I learned later."

At this time Rudley was better known for his acting talent than his play-wrighting and directorial skills. In 1949 he was an established character actor on Broadway and especially in motion pictures. His movie credits included such well-known films of the time as *Abe Lincoln in Illinois, The Seventh Cross, Rhapsody in Blue,* and *Joan of Arc.* And in the years after his cherished play *How Long Till Summer* would became nothing more than a withering memory, Rudley landed roles in nearly a score of movies, including *The Silver Chalice, That Certain Feeling, The Young Lions, Beloved Infidel, The Great Imposter,* and his last role in *Falling in Love Again* in 1980.

The theme of *How Long Till Summer* was controversial, especially for 1949: the story of a black youth caught up in and alternately frustrated and terrorized by an unfriendly white world, together with a rather contrived subplot involving the boy's father, a black attorney, running for Congress with the backing of an exploitative white gangster. After talking about the play during their first meeting, Gilbert wanted to think about it some more. Rudley suggested he stage a reading of it: "You've got to *hear* it," Rudley explained. "You can't just read it and get the full impact."

So Eddie suggested they come out to his father's summer home on Long Island Sound the next weekend. Accordingly the Rudleys arrived at the appropriate hour and were ushered into a scene having all the makings of a movie set itself: a beautiful warm day, sun bristling overhead, the waves of the Sound lapping gently at the shore of the Gilberts' private beach. For the reading with Eddie and Dick Winston was a seasoned producer in the legitimate theater, Leon Bronesky, whom Eddie had sought out to invite for the day's audition. Eddie led them all outside across the sprawling, sloping lawn behind the stately country house to a patio table and chairs in the shade of a magnificent elm tree. Only Gatsby and Daisy and some bootleg liquor were missing that soft summer afternoon on the Sound.

Herbert Rudley read the play, acting out each of the roles. "It was pretty good, I thought." Eddie remembers. "Actually he was very good, the way he read it." When Rudley finished, Eddie retired to the house to talk privately with Bronesky and Winston about the reading. The play had promise, Bronesky said, and he agreed to help guide its production if the necessary money could be raised. Winston had little more to contribute than his enthusiasm, but he sat enraptured at the idea of having his dream finally come true. Gilbert and Winston agreed that each would raise 50 percent of the initial financing to get the show going, a total figure projected at $30,000.

Returning to Rudley under the elm tree, Eddie said simply, "I think we ought to do it," And, just as suddenly as the Rudleys' play was Broadway-bound, Eddie Gilbert's theatrical career was launched.

Gilbert came up with $15,000 himself, a relatively sizeable amount for an angel in the 1940s, and assumed an active part in the play's production, with marquee credit as co-producer with Bronesky. Eddie sat in on all decision-making meetings from the start and even introduced his sister Enid to handle the play's costuming.

Bronesky and the Rudleys were able to persuade the well-known folk singer Josh White to play the lead role as the Congress-seeking lawyer. White was much better known as an authentic American troubador than he was as an actor, however. Although he had appeared on the legitimate stage in two earlier plays (the moderately successful *John Henry* on Broadway and in the highly praised off-Broadway production of Maxim Gorky's *Lower Depths*), he was most immediately perceived as one of the nation's premier folk singers. White had entertained at military bases both during and after World War II, as well as in major theaters and concert halls throughout the United States. His renditions of such country ballads as "One Meat Ball," "The House I Lived in," and "The Lass with the Delicate Air" became country standards by the end of the first half of the 20th century. By 1949, Josh White had recorded for five major companies and had sung on all the top radio networks. Less than a decade earlier, he had entertained at the White House for President and Mrs. Franklin D. Roosevelt; and it was the First Lady, Eleanor, who became a special fan of the folk singer and personally saw to it that many of his recordings became additions to the archives of the Library of Congress.

White brought along his nine-year-old son, Josh White, Jr., to play the part of the black youth: just a third-grader, Josh, Jr. was making his first appearance on the legitimate stage (although he had performed on tour with father since the age of four).

For the female lead, the role of Josh White's wife in the play, Rudley wanted to sign the gorgeous singer Lena Horne, even though there were no songs in the show. Horne was an alumna of Harlem's fabled Cotton Club in the 1930s, but was not a stage figure on Broadway at this point in her career. Her motion picture credits, however, were impressive, to say the least. By 1949, she had appeared in more than a dozen films, including *Stormy Weather*, *As Thousands Cheer*, *Ziegfeld Follies*, and *Till The Clouds Roll By*, alongside such stars as Frank Sinatra, Judy Garland, Lucille Ball, Fred Astaire, Gene Kelly, Dinah Shore, and Jimmy Durante. Horne had sung on screen with the bands of Duke Ellington, Harry James, and Xavier Cugat. Herbert Rudley knew Lena Horne from his career in motion pictures and contacted her. She expressed enough interest to come read for the part but in the end decided she was not really interested in the role.

With Lena Horne no longer in the picture, Rudley and Bronesky conducted a "massive search" (according to the *Playbill* blurb), for a woman to co-star with White and settled upon the unknown actress Ida James. "Miss James has had only one legitimate stage appearance previous to her present role...," it was reported in *Playbill*. "This did not deter Director Herbert Rudley when he selected her for the part of Kate because he felt that here was natural talent. Her reading for the part convinced Mr. Rudley that she *was* Kate, and she got the role forthwith after more than 50 actresses tried for it."

The balance of the cast was a seasoned troupe, however. Frank Wilson had an American theater career that dated back to 1907 and had just come off a successful engagement in which he had played alongside John Garfield in the *The Big Knife*; he had also performed in such Broadway standards as *Green Pastures*, *Watch on the Rhine*, *Anna Lucasta*, and *Set My People Free*. The accomplished dancer Fredi Washington had previously had a part in the stage adaptation of Richard Wright's *Black Boy*, featuring Paul Robeson; and she had also appeared in several Hollywood movies. Leigh Whipper had played Crab Man in the Broadway production of *Porgy* and the role of Haile Selassie in the motion picture *Mission to Moscow*.

Eddie Gilbert was immensely enjoying the milieu into which he had been swept. Although he had invested his own money, he had also solicited additional funds from friends and business associates when needed. Dick Winston had been unable to raise any money on his own; so with nothing else to add to the production of the Rudleys' play, he was forced to bow out of active participation in the show. But Gilbert was present and all over the place. He attended rehearsals and the meetings of the producer, director, and other support staff; he went out and bought the antique furniture and props for the set director, Ralph Alswang, one of the most highly regarded set and lighting men on Broadway then; he got Empire Lumber to provide wood for building the sets; he looked over his sister's shoulder to approve the costuming. To Eddie, it was just one helluva lot of fun, this theater thing.

At one point, Eleanor Roosevelt, in New York on other business, came by at the request of her friend Josh White to listen to a cast reading of the play. The former First Lady said later that she was enchanted with it, and her applause for the show was reported in the *New York Times* (something much appreciated by the producers and the cast in the those early days of rehearsal).

But the play had problems. They were apparent in rehearsals, but they were most evident when the show previewed in New Haven. "I went up there with some anxiety," Eddie recalled years later, "trepidation is what I felt, but I thought it could be cleaned up in the out-of-town run. Then the opening...it was the worst thing I'd ever seen in my life. Rudley had taken it upon himself to change the whole script on the train going up there, and when the play opened it was a disaster. Nobody knew their parts, where they were going on the stage, people were missing their lines. The out-of-town reviews were horrible."

Eddie had driven to New Haven with the set and lighting director, Ralph Alswang; Alswang intimated that he had asked a friend, the young author of the acclaimed 1949 hit *Death of a Salesman,* Arthur Miller, to be there for the opening. Eddie was genuinely impressed with Miller's huge success and proud that he was in the audience for the first-night curtain. When it came down at the end of Act II a few hours later, well, that was a different matter.

After the show, Eddie went back to his hotel room not far from the theater and was joined there by Alswang and Arthur Miller. Eddie sat in the only chair in the room, dolefully shaking his head. Miller lounged on the edge of the bed; Alswang leaned against a wall. Finally Eddie said, "Artie, what do you think? Is there anything you could do; I mean, if we came up with the money, do you think you could do something with this show?"

Miller said nothing at first. But when he finally answered, he looked sympathetically at Gilbert: "Well, I'll tell you, Eddie, I can't help you. I really can't. I'd have to write a whole new play."

"Can't you just clean it up?" Eddie implored.

"No. It's impossible, for me anyway. I could write you a whole new show, but that would take me months."

Eddie shook his head gloomily, "Okay, I'll work something else out."

Perhaps Eddie should have taken Miller up on the proposed solution of a new play. (Miller's next playwrighting effort, *The Crucible*, a drama about the Salem witch trials was both highly praised by the critics, enjoyed a successful run on Broadway, and over the ensuing years was adapted as a motion picture and a major television special and reprised countless times in road shows and summer stock.)

The following day, Eddie was on the phone to New York. He managed to get through to two top Broadway directors of the day, Danny Mann and Herman Shumlin, and persuaded both to come up to New Haven and take a look at *How Long Till Summer* with an eye to somehow salvaging it.

After the next night's performance, Eddie met Danny Mann in the lobby. Mann suggested, "I could take it on the road and clean it up, I think. But I'd need $25,000 to do that, and I really can't guarantee it'll be a success."

"Okay," Eddie said. "I'll get back to you tomorrow." He knew, however, that the $25,000 figure was beyond consideration.

So he sought out Herman Shumlin, who had also attended the show that evening. Shumlin was one of the most respected figures in the American theater, having directed Lillian Hellman's classic *The Little Foxes* a decade earlier and her equally well-regarded *Watch on the Rhine* two years later; and he also had a slew of other outstanding productions to his directorial credit. Despite such respect and repute in the theater world, Shumlin was without affectation. Neil Simon, whom Shumlin counseled before *Come Blow Your Horn* opened on Broadway, described him as "... quite dignified, affable, and charming, if not entirely accessible. He wore his experience and success on his person as a notable would unostentatiously wear his little red Legion of Honor badge almost indiscernibly in his lapel." In his autobiography, *Neil Simon Rewrites*, from which the previous quotation was taken, the playwright introduced the director in italics as *"The Herman Shumlin."*

*The Herman Shumlin* was quite cordial that night in New Haven talking with a despairing Eddie Gilbert. Like Danny Mann, he said he could not guarantee the play's success, but he could try to fix it. "I could take it down to Philadelphia and keep it there for a couple of weeks, work with it, then bring it to Broadway."

"How much?" Eddie asked.

Shumlin shrugged. "I would do it for $5,000."

"You think you could turn it around?"

"The only thing I can promise is you won't be embarrassed when it comes to New York. I can't promise anything more than that."

"That's good enough for me."

Eddie did not bother to call Danny Mann the next day.

Without too much trouble, Eddie was able to come up with some of the money. "I needed about $10,000 altogether, $5,000 for Shumlin and $5,000 for the run down in Philadlephia; I was able to get the rest of it from some of my friends. I gave them a little part of the action in exchange."

There was a lot of competition on Broadway when *How Long Till Summer* finally opened at the Playhouse in late December. Among the other shows running concurrently were Henry Fonda starring in *Mister Roberts* at the Alvin Theater on 52nd Street; Judy Holliday playing to full houses in Garson Kanin's hit comedy *Born Yesterday* at the Henry Miller Theater on 43rd Street; Ralph Bellamy in the lead role of *Detective Story* at the Hudson Theater on 44th Street; and Arthur Miller's *Death of a Salesman*, directed by Elia Kazan with Lee. J. Cobb as Willy Loman. (*Salesman* would, later that year, win both the Pulitzer Prize for drama and the Drama Critics Circle Award.) A pair of memorable musicals were on the boards as well: *Gentlemen Prefer Blondes* with Carol Channing and Irving Berlin's *Miss Liberty*. While *How Long Till Summer* was in good company, it was not in the same league. Still it opened on Broadway Tuesday night, December 27, 1949, at the Playhouse Theater.

Eddie made special plans for opening night. First he saw to it that every friend and acquaintance he could round up was in the audience that night: his parents, close friends like Sherman Fairchild and Jerry Stern, some old prep school pals, the social set in which he was currently mingling. It was as if the opening became a big, fancy Gilbert party, with the men in black tie and the women in formal gowns. Along with the 200 or so perennial Broadway "first-nighters" and the friends and colleagues of the cast, the Playhouse Theater was filled that evening, and it was an appreciative audience.

Eddie's friend Norman Denny set up a blind date for Eddie that night, but the fledgling impressario felt he had to be at the theater early on the opening night. In his place he sent an elegant car for her, chauffered by Bill Williams, the Gilbert family butler; Williams, a handsome 35-year-old quite light-skinned Negro, arrived at the date's apartment and told her the car was waiting. She smiled, took his arm and walked to the car; then to his astonishment she opened the front passenger-seat door herself and slipped into the front seat. Sitting next to him there, she did most of the talking on the way to the theater while the docile Williams just listened. When she walked into the theater lobby, again having taken the arm of a still rather embarrassed Bill Williams, she soon came to realize her mistake. Eddie casually walked up to her and said, "Hi, I'm Eddie Gilbert. Sorry I couldn't pick you up myself but I had to be here at the theater."

In New York, unlike New Haven, no one in the cast missed a line or stumbled over one or wandered to the wrong side of the stage. The play's two acts went off flawlessly, with the Gilbert-stacked audience attentive and more than generous when the final curtain came down. Eddie remembers that "the applause went on and on for what seemed like a half-hour. A bunch of curtain calls. Then in the lobby and outside the theater, everybody's coming up to me and saying, 'Eddie, it's wonderful, you're gonna make a million dollars.' I thought we had a smash hit."

After the show, like legions of theater people before and after him, Eddie waited anxiously for the reviews. There was a splashy, raucous party, which Eddie visited briefly; and then shortly after midnight he and Norman Denny with their dates went to the newsstand at 42nd Street and Broadway where the first morning New York newspapers were delivered. In those days, five or six papers reviewed the Broadway openings. Eddie bought a copy of each newspaper and handed Norman Denny several of them. "Here," a gleaming Eddie said. "You read one out loud, and then I'll read one. We'll take turns."

Denny ruffled through the pages until he got to the theater section while the others waited under the street lamp, coat collars turned up, shivering a little in the cold December night. Denny's eyes were focused on the page he sought but said nothing for a few moments. Then, he looked at Eddie and said, "Why don't you read yours first. It's your play."

Eddie shrugged. "Okay," and then found the review page of the *New York World-Telegram*. He read the headline: "How Long Till Summer... Seven Days."

The review by the respected Broadway critic Ward Morehouse explained that the "seven days" had no reference whatsoever to the length of time until summer, but rather to how long he thought the play would last on Broadway.

Most of the other reviews were equally awful. The *New York Times*, however, was less harsh. Brooks Atkinson, then the dean of Broadway drama critics, wrote "Although the theme is vital, the play does not poke beneath the surface. . . . On one side of the stage is a Negro boy who has discovered the color problem the hard way. He has been brutally frightened by the bullying father of his white chum. Unable to understand why he is hated so viciously, the Negro boy is tortured with savage nightmares that represent the terrors of the race. On the other side of the stage, [playwrights] Mr. and Mrs. Rudley tell a hackneyed and diffuse story about a Negro lawyer who is running for Congress. Eager to escape racial barriers, he is secretly accepting the backing of a white gangster who exploits the Negro race. The candidate for Congress is father of the terrified boy on the opposite side of the stage, and the two stories are supposed to complement each other. But the connection is more abstract than dramatic, for it is difficult to see."

Atkinson went on to sling a few barbs at the Rudleys' writing ("studded with cliches" and "stereotyped adults") and especially the direction ("Mr. Rudley has not noticeably befriended his play."). Herman Shumlin's name did not appear in the credits, at his request, because he felt he was only a stage-doctor tending to the play's ailments in Philadelphia; on the other hand, he may well have sensed how right it was *not* to have his name attached to *How Long Till Summer*. Brooks Atkinson had nice words for the adult actors, however, and even nicer ones for the youngsters in the cast: "... this column would rather plump for [Josh] White, Jr., and Charles Taylor, who play the parts of a Negro boy and a white boy, respectively. Both of them are frank, artless, and attractive. Any time a playwright wants to devote a whole drama to them, this column will guarantee every consideration that is ethically possible."

The boys could not save the play, however, and it closed quietly on December 31, 1949 after just seven performances.

Eddie remembers: "To close the show cost me almost as much as to put it on. I had to pay off the theater, the unions. The store that provided the antiques and furniture wouldn't take them back. I was broke for about half a year after that."

In this same period of his life, Eddie Gilbert was also enticed into the commodity market by another New York friend, Tony Reinach. Reinach was a few years older than Gilbert and worked for a Wall Street brokerage firm owned by his father, Udo (who was better known as "The Baron"). Eddie and Tony had done some business together, mostly in stocks which were handled through the Reinach family firm. Tony was an excellent bridge player as well as a moderately good gamesman and gambler, which endeared him even more to Eddie.

In his mid-twenties, Eddie was thriving in stock market investments, but he had little interest, and no experience, in that volatile marketplace where they traded grain, soybeans, pork bellies, and other staples of the American appetite. Reinach spoke to Eddie on a personal level, not a broker's, telling him that they could make a killing in commodities by employing Eddie's mathematical mind and his uncanny ability to assess and evaluate, the same skills that served him so well in his stock market successes. For several months, Eddie paid little attention to Reinach, but like the theatrically driven Dick Winston, Tony persisted with telephone-call pleas as regular as a weekly subscription magazine. One day, Eddie finally succumbed: "All right, send some stuff over and I'll look at it," Eddie told him.

When the material arrived from Tony Reinach, Eddie looked it over and found one commodity that, for some reason or other (Eddie could never explain it, even years later), appealed to him. Eggs.

So he did some research. "I read everything I could find: agricultural journals, the Farmers' Almanac, anything that had to do with eggs. I found out things like chickens lay more eggs when it's cool than when it's hot, so if it was a torridly hot summer they would lay fewer eggs, all that kind of minutiae. I also found that eggs were at the low end of the scale on the commodity market, hadn't been doing well for some time, and I had that certain feeling that this was the time to buy."

The margin was very good on commodities in the late 1940s. One could buy a commodity contract for eggs and put up just 5 percent in cash. So for a $10,000 contract on an egg future, an investor only had to come up with $500 cash. "It was a tremendous leverage," Eddie said later. "So I bought a bunch of contracts. I don't remember how many, but I had maybe $10,000 that I put down, and I ended up committed for quite a few carloads of eggs. Anyway, the price of eggs started to go up, and up, and up. And as it did, I parlayed my investments. By the time I was finished I had about $25,000 of my own money into egg contracts." It was quite a debut in the commodities market. On paper, Eddie Gilbert had a profit of approximately $1 million.

With such good news and a sudden desire to spend some time far from the New York winter, Eddie and his friend Tony Reinach flew south to Cuba. They checked into the old but elegant Hotel Nacional—*the* place to stay in Havana in those days — the well-publicized hang-out of vacationing movie stars, politicians, international jet-setters, and some infamous mobsters from New York and Chicago. The Nacional and its lucrative casino had in fact been controlled by the Mafia since the 1930s when mobster Meyer Lansky, representing the interests of the New York family run by Lucky Luciano, had been sanctioned to operate it by Cuban president Fulgencio Batista. After the war, the Nacional hosted such other crime luminaries as Joe Bonnano, Joe Profaci, Frank Costello, Joe Adonis, Albert Anastasia, and Tommy Lucchese (from New York), and Tony Accardo, Paul Ricca, and brothers Charlie, Joe, and Rocco Fischetti (from Chicago). At one of the meetings held by the mobsters at the Nacional in 1946, Frank Sinatra was flown in as a special "guest entertainer"; and the singer from Hoboken returned to the Nacional many times before the decade ended, both in and out of the company of American mobsters.

While Eddie never met one of the hotel's disreputable guests, nor apparently was ever aware of their affiliation with the Nacional (he never gambled in the casino there, himself), he did patronize other gambling establishments beyond the hotel.

He and Reinach had been in Havana a few days, as Eddie remembers it, "having a wonderful time. There were a lot of beautiful girls around, it was warm and sunny during the day, the night-life was great. This one afternoon we were out at the pool and there were a couple of girls hanging around that I wanted to impress. I was up on the three-meter diving board and I was just about to go... I was going to do a triple somersault for the girls—to show off—because there were very few people who could do a triple in those days."

As Eddie was poised to dive, Tony Reinach came racing out of the hotel, with a newspaper clutched in one hand, shouting, "Eddie, you gotta come down. Eggs have crashed. My god, it's terrible."

For some reason the stunned Gilbert went through with his dive, though the triple turned out to be just a "two-and-a-half" and Eddie landed flat on his back, and had to be helped from the pool. "I was out of it. They carried me up to the roof of the hotel and someone gave me a massage. When I started to come around, I remembered what Tony had yelled up to me. I said, 'What the hell do you mean? What's going on?'"

Reinach told him that the bottom had dropped out of the egg market. "You've been wiped out. We gotta go back to New York right away."

Eddie and Tony returned to New York and went to face The Baron, through whose firm all of Eddie's egg contracts had been handled. Beyond the $25,000 he had invested, Gilbert learned he owed an additional $27,000 — money he could not put his hands on at that inconvenient moment. So when the two walked in, The Baron was furious.

"How could you get this man involved in this thing, you fucking idiot?" he shouted at his son. And without waiting for an answer, then turned to Eddie, "And you, you're going to pay every dime of this back."

"I'll pay you back," Eddie said. "But I don't have the money now. But I'll do it."

"You give me notes. You hear me, you give notes. How much do you make a week? Two hundred? I want a note for fifty. Whatever you make, I want a note for that percentage."

The Baron was not the only outraged party. When Eddie's father heard his son say, "Pop, I lost some money in this egg thing on the commodities market," and then go on to explain that he owed The Baron $27,000 he did not have," Harry Gilbert was equally furious. When asked about a loan to meet the obligation, without blinking an eye, his father said, "No." He stared at Eddie in silence and then added, "You got yourself into this. You never asked me about it, so why should I loan you the money? You've got a job. Go to the bank and borrow it from them."

So Eddie went to the bank, The Manhattan Bank (as it was known before it merged with Chase), one of those where his father did business and happened to be on the bank's board of directors. Eddie explained his predicament to the bank's president, who inquired if the senior Gilbert knew anything about this. "He's the one who told me to come see you," Eddie said.

"Well, I'm going to have to see a financial statement from you, before I can consider a loan." Eddie told him he did not have a statement, in fact he didn't have anything at all, most certainly not any money, which was why he was there. "Well, I'm going to have to call your father." A few minutes after Eddie was summoned back in the president's office. "I can't offer you the money," he said, "Your father won't guarantee it." But in kindness he added just before Eddie was to leave, "Look, call me next week, Let me think about it. I'll see if there's anything I can come up with."

A week later Eddie called the banker who asked him back. "I'm going to do this," he said when Eddie was once again sitting across the desk from him, "I'm going to lend you the $27,000. I don't know why I'm doing this, you know, but I am; but you had better pay it back, every single penny."

The banker knew why, of course. The senior Gilbert had in the meantime agreed to cosign the loan. But it was not until about two years later, after Eddie had paid the $27,000 in full, that the bank president told Eddie that his father had guaranteed the note.

While The Baron was being repaid and Eddie was reconciling himself to his losses, the issue of the eggs, however, did not disappear. Three or four months after eggs tumbled on the commodities market, Eddie received a telephone call. It seems in the frantic trading at the time of the market disaster, one future had not been sold. The voice over the phone informed Eddie that he was the proud owner of a carload of eggs, which was presently sitting on a railroad siding in Jamaica, New York. "I thought: Hey, this is great. At that time a carload of eggs was worth maybe $7,500 or $8,000. I figured I'd sell it and get back a nice chunk of my loss."

Gilbert went to Jamaica, found the boxcar filled with his eggs on a siding there, just as he was told it would be. What he had not been told was that he owed more than $700 for demurrage—charges for freight remaining on a railway car beyond the original unloading date. With finances still rather tight at that particular moment, Eddie knew he could not go to the banker, nor to his father. He could only imagine the look on either of their faces if he asked for another $700 or $800 for eggs. So he talked friend and insurance broker Vic Levin into lending him the money. "We can make a helluva profit," Eddie told Levin. "We can eliminate the wholesaler and sell, what, about $8,000 worth of eggs, direct to A&P [then the nation's largest grocery chain]."

After he had paid the demurrage fee with Levin's loan and gone to A&P, another problem materialized. Gilbert discovered, much to his chagrin, that the eggs had become "outdated" (being a perishable, eggs had to be sold before a certain date). All of a sudden the $8,000 worth of eggs had no value, and now Eddie had to get them off the truck he was renting on a daily basis. He got the idea that maybe the Bronx Zoo would take the eggs and feed them to the animals. So he sent the truck over to the zoo, but the zoo was equally picky about due dates for food stuffs and declined to accept them. Finally Eddie found a dump site that agreed to take the eggs; but when the truck arrived there, the driver was told he could not dump the eggs until a $200 fee was paid. Gilbert was forced to come up with that amount and took it out himself to pay the dump custodian. Where he had hoped for a windfall of $7,500 or $8,000, and even a profit on top of that from the A&P sale, Eddie instead had to add more than $1,000 to his already sizeable loss. But "the goddam fucking eggs," as Eddie referred to them, were finally off his plate. So he thought.

About a year later, the U. S. Department of Agriculture called, summoning him to Washington. They were investigating his purchases of egg futures, which the department considered inordinately high for an individual. So he appeared with an attorney whom he had chosen because of his special expertise in the areas of politics and bureaucracy, thinking all along, "When will this damn thing end?"

A gathering of stern-faced bureaucrats told him that during a two-month period about a year earlier, he, Eddie Gilbert, controlled more eggs than anyone else in America. "What was I up to, they wanted to know," Eddie recalls. "Was I trying to corner the market on eggs? Was I fronting for someone else? Was I going to sell them to Russia? What were my motives? They made it sound like it was some kind of criminal act." With his lawyer's corroboration, Eddie explained how he came to invest in egg futures, how he lost a lot of money, much of which he was still paying back to the Manhattan Bank on the loan they made to him to cover his losses. He concluded by telling them that he would be happy if he never saw another egg for the rest of his life. The agriculture department officials listened, recessed, and finally dismissed him. Thus ended Eddie Gilbert's first and last venture into the commodity market.

Eddie Gilbert returned to the Broadway theater again in 1950, but not because the glamor of the theater world had somehow become richly transfused into his blood; it was simply that he could not stand leaving anything on a losing note. He hated to lose, and especially to be considered a loser. When *How Long Till Summer* came up a loser, Eddie Gilbert's name was right up there in the marquee lights as co-producer. And all his friends and associates he had coaxed to the theater on opening night could not have failed to remember Eddie as the man who had invested big money in a Broadway play that had not lasted even as long as its worst review speculated: seven days. Eddie Gilbert wanted to redeem himself.

So when the set designer Ralph Alswang told Eddie that he had signed on to do a new musical that he was convinced would be a grand success, Eddie asked to be involved. "Talk to Peter Lawrence," Alswang told him. "I know he's looking for investors; it's going to be a big show."

Aspiring to be a producer for the first time, Peter Lawrence was trying to put together a revival of *Peter Pan,* the famous story of the magical boy who did not want to grow up, written by the Scottish novelist and dramatist James Barrie, which had debuted on the London stage in 1904. The first American production came to New York's Empire Theater the next year, with Maude Adams in the title role and Ernest Lawford playing the parts of Mr. Darling and Captain Hook. The play ran for more than a year on Broadway and then toured the United States on and off over the next seven years. The last revival of the show occured in 1928 when Eva Le Gallienne starred in her Civic Repertory Theater production of it in New York, playing to full houses during limited engagements over the next four years.

Peter Lawrence had stage-managed many successful Broadway shows, including *Sing Out Sweet Land* and *Lend an Ear,* but he needed additional financing for *Peter Pan.* He had had a number of problems getting the show on the road, principally because the rights to the play had been willed by Sir James Barrie to The Hospital for Sick Children in London, (known as "Peter Pan's Hospital"). The hospital maintained strict control over those wanting to reprise the play, reserving for themselves the approval of producer and the actors in the lead roles, as well as requiring proof that sufficient reserves had been banked to insure a first-rate production. In America, the safety of the children who would be flying on wires above the stage also came into play, with pressure being brought by a child-labor rights and safety group.

When Eddie Gilbert said he was "broke for a about half-a-year," following the demise of *How Long Till Summer*, it was not a truly accurate statement of his financial condition, an exaggeration perhaps. He talked to Peter Lawrence, who was most happy to welcome him aboard; and Gilbert came up with about $25,000 to be added to the front money for the show. Eddie was under the impression that he was to function as a co-producer, but Lawrence did not share that understanding. So while Eddie maintained contact as the production and rehearsals began, he was not involved at all as he had been with the Rudleys' play.

Lawrence eventually resolved the problems besetting his production, mollifying the Hospital for Sick Children, by signing Jean Arthur for the title role and Boris Karloff as her co-star. Moreover, he had secured a commitment for a new score from the then 30-year-old Leonard Bernstein already acclaimed for the music he had composed for the smash Broadway musical *On the Town* (1944), his ballet *Fancy Free* (1943), and his two symphonic compositions, *Jeremiah* (1944) and *The Age of Anxiety* (1949). Despite his youth, Bernstein, had also conducted symphony orchestras in New York, London, Rome, Prague, Brussels, Warsaw, and Jerusalem. Bernstein was delighted to be asked to score Lawrence's *Peter Pan*. "Until now, all that's ever been asked of me in the way of music had to do with trains and subways," Bernstein told the *New York Times*, referring to *On the Town* (a musical about three sailors on leave in New York who spend much of their time in the New York subway system). As to the safety concern, Lawrence brought in "Kirby's Flying Ballets" from London, known for their experience and success, as they advertised, in "Flying Effects, Somersaulting, Diving and Auditorium Flying." The firm's founder, the father of the Kirby now running the flying ballet company, had been responsible for the flying effects in the 1904 London production.

*Peter Pan* was was a much more extravagant production than *How Long Till Summer*: Peter Lawrence spent 18 months trying to bring the musical comedy to Broadway before Eddie Gilbert became involved. Eddie's initial investment was crucial, however, and his ability to raise additional money, if and when needed, was another major factor. Eddie thought (actually expected) that he was to get billing as a co-producer of the show. But neither of his contributions were deemed sufficiently important enough to earn a formal billing. He had to settle for the role of an uncredited co-producer. Nonetheless, all of Eddie's friends were aware that he had a hand in the production of the show.

When *Peter Pan* opened in the spring of 1950, it came in the middle of what was already a banner year for Broadway. In January George Bernard Shaw's *Caesar and Cleopatra* was revived, starring the 93-year-old Shaw's hand-picked leads Sir Cedric Hardwicke and Lilli Palmer. In February William Inge's contemporary classic, *Come Back Little Sheba,* debuted with Shirley Booth starring. A few weeks later, celebrated poet T. S. Eliot's *The Cocktail Party* opened to enormous critical acclaim. *Peter Pan* also had to compete among the ticket-buying public with Rodgers and Hammerstein's *South Pacific* and Cole Porter's *Kiss Me Kate* (both playing to packed houses) and, later in the year, Irving Berlin's *Call Me Madam* and Frank Loesser's *Guys and Dolls.*

On opening night for *Peter Pan,* Eddie did not send Bill Williams to pick up his date, nor did he have to arrive early at the theater; but he took the occasion to entertain a lot of his friends, carrying his deeply felt, silent hope that opening night would not reprise the theatrical disaster of the previous year.

But he needn't have worried. The show was in capable, professional hands, both on and off the stage. All the reviews were unguardedly positive, and some were raves. Brooks Atkinson of the *Times* praised everything about it: "Although the world may have grown old and cynical, 'Peter Pan' is still a thing of delight... [it] is altogether charming—a fresh and beguiling piece... [presented] with perfect taste."

As to the stars: "Miss Arthur is ideal as Peter. To a pleasant personality she has added the pleasantest kind of acting. When you think how arch and maudlin the part might be in less scrupulous hands, you can appreciate the ease and simplicity of her performance. She is smiling without being coy and friendly without being patronizing. If there seems to be no acting at all in her performance, it is because she is acting it superbly and and has mastered the spirit and technique of the theatre's most winning fairy-story."

Boris Karloff was similarly applauded: "This is Mr. Karloff's day of triumph. As the father of the Darling children and the pirate King, he is at the top of his bent. Although he is best known for the monsters he has played on stage and screen, Mr. Karloff is an actor of tenderness and humor, with an instinct for the exact inflection. His Captain Hook is a horrible cutthroat of the sea; and Mr. Karloff does not shirk the villainies. . . .

There is something of a grand manner in the latitude of his style and the role of his declamation; and there is withal an abundance of warmth and gentleness in his attitude toward the audience."

Atkinson also praised Leonard Bernstein's "melodic, colorful, and dramatic score." The songs would not emerge as contemporary standards, like those of "New York, New York" and "Lonely Town" from *On the Town*, but Bernstein's music was perceived as a major factor in the success of Peter Lawrence's production.

*Peter Pan* played on Broadway for nearly a year, a total of 321 performances, and then it toured successfully throughout the United States. Eddie Gilbert felt redeemed; although at first it seemed a Pyrrhic victory. As Eddie later explained, "I was very happy. I felt we had a great hit and now, at least, I could walk away a winner. But then I got to talking with Peter Lawrence a couple of weeks after the show had opened, and he told me he had misfigured. I forget now the exact figures, but the difference was about a thousand dollars. He had budgeted it to cost us, say, $33,000 a week to keep the show going. Well, we were drawing near full houses and we were only taking in $32,000 a week. So it looked like it was going to have a long run; and the longer it ran, the more money we'd lose. Each week we'd pack the place and lose a thousand dollars. I didn't tell a lot of people about that."

While the shortfall may have lasted a while, eventually *Peter Pan* turned into a money-maker on Broadway; and it earned a lot more on the road afterwards..

Eddie Gilbert, thus vindicated, walked away from the inner workings of the theatrical world. But he never lost his pleasure in the theater and attended Broadway productions on a rather regular basis for years to come. Even his involvement in the enormously successful revival of the Beacon Theater on upper Broadway 40 years later could not lure him back into the role of producer, marquee billing notwithstanding. He had redeemed himself in 1950; that was enough.

## Give him [Eddie Gilbert] a handful of nickels and a pay phone and he could make you a million dollars by lunchtime.

GEORGE BOEHM, FORTUNE MAGAZINE, C.1960

Gilbert had spent nearly a year streamlining Empire's operation in Tennessee before returning to New York. When he returned, there was no particular job waiting for him at company headquarters, so he decided to take some time to look around for the right niche. After a few days, he realized that niche was most likely in the lumber division (which at the time contributed just one-eighth of the sales-dollar volume at Empire Millwork, or about $1 million a year). Most of Empire's sales were generated by the millwork operation. In the lumber division, which Marcel Weiss managed, there seemed to be a big opportunity, at least according to Eddie's way of thinking. Tactfully described as methodical and conservative, Weiss was content with the lumber division's operation and performance as it was — small, steady and somewhat profitable — and did not relish change or the taking of any risks with what he considered a good thing. In short, Weiss's was a business philosophy totally antipodean to what Eddie Gilbert was formulating in his own mind. "He wasn't a bad fellow," Gilbert later observed, "but he was complacent; he didn't want to upset the status quo. I didn't agree with anything he was doing. I figured the best way to show how wrong his approach was, was to get out and show what could be done."

And that is just what Eddie did. In that first year alone, he sold nearly three times what the division had been selling, increasing its sales volume to nearly $4 million total. And by 1950, he had more than doubled that. Marcel Weiss, with whom Eddie had never really meshed, stepped aside.

"In his heart he wanted to build houses," Eddie suggests, "and it was the best thing for him. So he left the company to do that." Harry Gilbert put his son in charge of the burgeoning lumber division; and by 1952 Eddie had raised its sales to $20 million annually, a figure more than *twice* the rest of the entire company's sales.

Eddie's salary, however, seemed hardly commensurate with the job he was doing: "I was making $15,000 a year," he remembers. "Everybody else who was an officer of the company was making $50,000. I said to my father, 'I want to make $50,000 like everybody else.'

"He said, 'That's ridiculous. How can I explain that to the board?'

"I said, 'I don't care how you do it. Just explain it to the board. Explain I'm doing twenty million in sales and making you two million in profit a year. Explain that to them.'"

Harry Gilbert did not take Eddie's proposal to the Empire board of directors. He told his son that he could not recommend such a salary for such a young man (Eddie was just 29 years old at the time). Eddie was furious. He told his father he was quitting, and the family was soon in an uproar. Eddie's mother, ordinarily a soothing influence, said to him, "You can't do that, Eddie. You can't do that to your father. How can you do it to *us*?"

"I can," Eddie told her. "If he won't pay me, I can do it. I have to live, too."

Whether Harry Gilbert was stubborn or saw Eddie's reaction as merely an empty threat is unclear, but he would not back down.

So Eddie quit. Not only did he leave Empire Millwork, but he started his own wholesale flooring business incorporated under the name of Rhodes Flooring Company.

Another major change occurred in Eddie Gilbert's life about the same time. He had met a beautiful young girl named Rhoda Weintraub at a country club dance in Westchester County. She was 18 at the time, an only child, living with her parents in a stylish apartment on Central Park West at 90th Street. Her father was at the time suffering from heart disease, which would shortly take his life. Although Rhoda was seeing another young man when they first met, when Gilbert reappeared in her life some six months after the dance, things changed rather abruptly. They began dating and were married about a year later in a small ceremony at the St. Regis Hotel in midtown Manhattan on October 11, 1951.

Young and strikingly attractive, Rhoda caused heads to turn wherever she went. She became a glittering accessory in Eddie's life. She was quite comfortable in being swept along in the wake of Gilbert's driving ambition and steadily rising stature in New York's elite circles. With his courtship and marriage to Rhoda, Gilbert became a patron of New York's finest jewelers and Rhoda a figure seen frequently at some of the most famous couturiers of the city. Eddie and Rhoda moved smoothly within Manhattan café society, but several years would have to pass before Eddie's net worth would be computed in millions and their names would be mainstays in the gossip columns and social pages of New York's newspapers.

Without Eddie at Empire, the lumber business dried up. By year's end that business was clearly headed back to the stagnant sales level where it had languished before Eddie transformed it into the firm's most lucrative operation. Nearly 80 percent of the $20 million Eddie generated annually in sales for Empire's lumber division disappeared two years after he left. Meanwhile, Eddie got his own company on solid ground, generating sales for Rhodes Flooring of nearly a million dollars in the first year alone. Over the next two years, sales at Rhodes grew steadily. And Eddie Gilbert was drawing a lot more than the annual $15,000 he had been awarded at Empire Millwork.

It did not take a lot of abstruse reasoning for Harry Gilbert to reach the conclusion that both he and Empire Millwork would be much better off with his son back at the firm. So, in early 1955, he went to Eddie and asked him to come back. "I'll pay you the $50,000," said Harry.

"I'll come back," Eddie told his father, but only on the condition that he be permitted to run his own Rhodes Flooring concern on the side. "I did not want to give up something that profitable," Eddie later recalls. "I figured I could handle both. But my father said something to the effect that you can't run six things at once. So he proposed that they buy it and absorb its operation into Empire."

Harry Gilbert took this proposition to the Empire board of directors where there was no opposition because Eddie's company was now an established and profitable operation. Thus Empire Millwork purchased Rhodes Flooring for a little more than $1 million of Empire stock, and Eddie Gilbert, at 32 years old, had made his first million.

Not long after, Eddie and Rhoda moved into a sumptuous ten-room apartment at 817 Fifth Avenue, between 62nd and 63rd Streets overlooking Central Park, and began to fill it with French antiques and important works of art. Life on the grand scale had begun.

Eddie and Rhoda had expressed a desire to have children of their own, but that was not working out. Eddie was led to believe their lack of success was the result of losing a testicle during his Air Corps days in World War II. So they decided to begin their family by adopting. Their first daughter, Robin, arrived in 1955, followed by Alexandra, in 1957.

Upon his return to Empire, Eddie took over running operations in both the lumber and flooring divisions, leaving the profitable millwork division to others in the company. But it was clear to even the most casual observer that Eddie was on his way to taking charge of all operations of the company. Harry Gilbert knew his son's potential, and more, he had tacitly come to accept his son's dynamic business acumen and that Eddie was going to take Empire's business to realms Harry had never even dreamed of on wings of ambition he had never possessed. Eddie had already made the first mark for himself with Rhodes Flooring, which he had sold for more than a million dollars. And at Empire he exuded confidence and assertiveness, especially to his father; but others sometimes described him in such terms as brash or even reckless. One thing was clear, however: There was no controlling him. His father knew that now; he also knew from that point forward he might be the titular head of the company, but he really was just a passenger on the fabulous ride where Eddie was taking Empire Millwork.

While Eddie was in Tennessee looking after Empire's plant there, he first became aware of the E. L. Bruce Company, a hardwood flooring firm headquartered on the other side of the state in Memphis. In the early 1950s, Bruce was the largest manufacturer of hardwood flooring in America — a family-owned, conservative company that was, according to *Business Week* magazine, "strong and moderately successful," whose officers seemed comfortable existing on the financial plateau where the company had come to settle. There was no question about Bruce's dominance in the hardwood flooring market, but its performance had grown stodgy and its stock relatively dormant on Wall Street. Its corporate mentality, as Eddie Gilbert saw it, was Memphis; and that was very far, not only geographically, from the excitement of the New York financial world. But Bruce was far from a regional company; it maintained plants and owned timberland in many areas of the country. The operation had become diversified, adding lumber, wood polishes, and waxes to its various production lines as well as a division that turned out termite-control products.

During those days in Tennessee, Eddie Gilbert was impressed by the company's size and commanding presence in the marketplace. He was later quoted in the *New York Times* when asked what his initial feelings were about the Bruce company in the early 1950s: "It caught my imagination," he said, "and I remember thinking to myself I'd like to be with that company some day." As things progressed for him at Empire, however, Eddie thought less about joining Bruce and more about it as a model, the prototype perhaps, for what he wanted the smaller Empire to become. He set about learning as much as he could about the Bruce company, its operations, the people who ran it, its projections, and its value and trading pattern on the stock market. But as more time passed, Eddie's thoughts of fashioning a company in Bruce's image eventually gave way to acquiring Bruce and fashioning *it* into a company in the image of Eddie Gilbert's ambition. "They weren't running it properly, I could see that," Eddie later clarifies. "I thought I could do wonders with it. That was it. Very simple."

So in early 1955, the 32-year-old Gilbert began talking to his father and a few friends about his ambition of going after the Bruce company. As Eddie later remembered: "They thought it was a joke. To them, it was like an ant eating an elephant. Ridiculous, impossible, those were the words I was hearing. I didn't think so."

In the early to mid-1950s, it was believed the the Bruce family controlled about 60 percent of the common stock in the company, a condition that made its acquisiton even more daunting. By this time Eddie Gilbert was earning a lot of money, both from his position at Empire Millwork and his stock trading on Wall Street. "In 1955, despite what others thought about it, I decided I would try and buy control [of Bruce]," he later told the *Times*. "So I picked up several thousand shares." Bruce common stock was trading then at about $14 a share on the American Stock Exchange. The next year he bought an additional 10,000 shares. "But I got strapped for money on another deal and sold all but about 2,000 shares." This development did not deter Gilbert from his longer-term ambition to buy the company, however; he looked on it as nothing more than a temporary setback, something that only forced him to adjust his timetable. "I decided at the time that, if another recession should hit the building business, and I thought one would, that would be the time to begin [again]."

In the summer of 1957, that recession—or opportunity as Gilbert saw it—made its predicted appearance. The Bruce Company's performance no longer seemed just stodgy; it was slumping. From record-high sales of $35.3 million in 1956, Bruce's sales had dropped to $28.3 million in 1957. And Gilbert again began buying blocks of shares then, small quantities relatively speaking, but enough to keep his dream alive. He also encouraged his friends to do the same. And by this time Eddie had made some pretty powerful friends in New York's financial community, men like Sherman Fairchild, John and Henry Loeb, as well as quite a few rising wheelers and dealers and serious investors, gamblers, and speculators whom Eddie met both in business and Manhattan's café society. Some took his suggestion, others were still skeptical, but the words "ridiculous" and "impossible" were no longer being used when people spoke of Eddie Gilbert's mission.

And indeed he was a man on a mission. In March 1958, his quiet acquisition of Bruce shares had become a full-fledged assault. And then the fireworks in the financial district began. The stock was selling at a low of $16.87 a share at the time. Over the next three months, it would soar to $77 a share before the American Stock Exchange suspended all trading in the stock on June 12.

What occurred during that quarter-year represents a dramatic sequence of events on Wall Street not seen since the devastating crash of 1929. Eddie had succeeded in enlisting the support of his father and the board of directors of Empire Millwork in his aspiration to acquire Bruce. Taking advantage of the new recession affecting the building and flooring industries and the consequent slump in Bruce's sales, Gilbert was suddenly handed another weapon by none other than the enemy itself when Bruce announced that it was suspending its March quarterly dividend. It was the first such omitted dividend in 17 years. "I'd convinced them at Empire that Bruce was a lethargic company, heading in the wrong direction, and very vulnerable. I told them that with Bruce now failing to pay a dividend we had a good opportunity to pick up the stock from disgruntled holders." Eddie furthermore convinced his father and the other board members that Bruce was a company that could be turned in the right direction with aggressive management. "I could make it prosper like it had never propsered before, I told them, and they believed me."

His friends, too, were suddenly buying the stock, having learned now about Gilbert's grandiose intentions and fueled by his guarantee (to some but not all) against a loss on the stock they purchased. Wall Street was suddenly forced to sit up and take notice: Bruce stock, with a trade volume for the month of February of 3,600 shares, saw 158,000 shares trade in April, another 106,000 in May, and a further 15,800 in the early days of June before trade was suspended.

The Bruce brothers, Edwin L., Jr., and C. Arthur, first became aware that Gilbert was seeking control of their company in early April, about the same time Eddie went to Manhattan attorney Benjamin Javits, the brother of New York Republican Senator Jacob Javits, to enlist his representation. Because there were to be some battlefields to traverse before the war was over, Eddie wanted to enlist the best army he could muster. On learning of Gilbert's intention (they were informed in writing, as the law required, by Javits in one of his first actions representing Gilbert), both Edwin and Arthur Bruce made it clear in public and private statements that they were unequivocally opposed to "this unwanted, hostile intrusion by a New York opportunist." Gilbert's ambition was going to be "met and disposed of with every possible means that the company and the [Bruce] family can bring to bear."

When he first approached Javits, Eddie only imprecisely knew what battles lay ahead in the courts and boardroom negotiating sessions, but he knew something would erupt. Javits was intrigued with Gilbert's takeover plan and was impressed with the young man who presented it to him. Anticipating the legal combat looming ahead, with a certain relish, he signed on his firm of Javits and Javits. What neither Javits nor Eddie perceived at that first meeting, nor anyone else at Bruce or Empire or on Wall Street for that matter, was that the planned takeover would turn into the first authentic "corner" in a stock since the market of the early 1920s.

A "corner" is best described as a situation where shares of a given security are so closely held (by one party or several parties) that speculators who "short the stock" (that is, sell borrowed stock in anticipation of later buying the stock and delivering it at a lower price) are unable to buy such stock in order to cover their earlier borrowing. In the spring of 1958, Bruce stock was soaring because Eddie Gilbert and his associates were buying it up, while the Bruce family was tenaciously holding onto their stock, in fact buying up all additional shares they could put their hands on because they finally realized that Gilbert's hostile takeover was under way. Meanwhile, the "short sellers" jumped in with the expectation that they would make a killing when the "vastly overvalued" Bruce stock nosedived. When the stock reached $77 a share in June and the American Stock Exchange suspended trading in it, more than 16,000 shares, or approximately 5 percent of the outstanding Bruce shares, had been sold short. Most of the contracts calling for delivery of shorted shares were held by Eddie Gilbert. But no nosedive took place. To the contrary, after the suspension of trade on the American Exchange, as Gilbert sought to gain control and the Bruces struggled to maintain ownership of the company, Bruce stock continued to rise meteorically in the over-the-counter market, at one point selling for as much as $190 a share.

As Wall Street was experiencing its first corner in decades, the market was also witnessing the first "natural corner" in financial history. According to *Business Week* magazine, "Most of the classic corners, in which big fortunes were made and lost, occurred before World War I [and] were largely manipulated corners, deliberately contrived to trap unsuspecting short sellers." In a "natural corner," however, "cornering of the shorts occurs as a side result of an all-out battle for control. In the case of Bruce, the stock is concentrated in the hands of Edwin L. Bruce, Jr., president, and his brother, C. Arthur Bruce, chairman, on one side, and in another block controlled by Edward M. Gilbert, a director of New York's Empire Millwork Corp., a big family-operated lumber and millwork company."

Most surprising to those on Wall Street was that such a corner could actually happen: Conditions in the American stock market of the late 1950s led otherwise knowledgeable brokers and investors to think it was virtually impossible for a stock to be cornered. Analysts of the situation noted the big increase in the number of most companies' shares listed on the New York Stock or American Exchanges meant there should be an ample supply of stock floating around to satisfy short sellers' purchases. But in the Gilbert-Bruce struggle of 1958, such shares were not floating around. Another surprise was that this was not an orchestrated corner. According to a *Business Week* article, written later, "Gilbert had no intention of helping to create a corner... He disputes the notion that he is a financial speculator or raider." He sought to control Bruce — yes, without a doubt, Eddie conceded in a later interview he gave to the magazine But a corner? "That just happened," he confirmed. "I was as surprised as anyone. I was happy about it, thrilled in fact, but I hadn't tried to bring it about."

All the historic corners or attempted corners had been manipulated affairs, calculated by powerful investors or robber barons of the late 19th or early 20th centuries. The tainted history of this tactic carried all the way back to 1835 when an attempt to corner Morris Canal and Banking Company shares became the first officially noted by the Stock and Exchange Board, which then governed the financial markets.

Perhaps the most intriguing corner attempt occurred shortly after the end of the Civil War when ruthless financiers Jay Gould, the railroad baron, and "Big Jim" Fisk tried to corner the U.S. gold market in 1869. Gould and Fisk, two years earlier, had joined forces to wrest control of the Erie railroad from Cornelius Vanderbilt. (Commodore Vanderbilt, as he was known, engineered several corners himself in the 1860s.) Now, in 1869, they plotted to take control of all the gold circulating in the United States, worth about $15 million at the time. The New York Stock Exchange had just recently established a "Gold Room" solely for commerce in gold, and it had since become a heavily traded and speculative commodity. As Gould and Fisk began to buy gold, its price rose dramatically, as did their confidence. The only thing to dampen their prospects at cornering the commodity was the possibility of the federal government's sale of some part of its $95 million in gold reserves. That would not happen, Gould confided to a few insiders. "His man" was well-placed within the executive branch of the government, his man being A. C. Corbin who just happened to be President Ulysses S. Grant's brother-in-law. Gould said that Corbin would intercede with the president to ensure that U.S. gold would not come into play; but after Gould and Fisk had bought up all the gold then in circulation, Gould's "man," as it turned out, was unable to protect the consortium's interest. He at least was able to tip Gould off in advance of the government's plan to begin selling some of its gold reserves. With such knowledge, Gould publicly kept up the pretense of being a buyer of gold, thus maintaining its price at a lofty level, while secretly selling off large positions of his gold interests at the inflated value. But the scheme collapsed on September 24, 1869 (a day later dubbed "Black Friday") when the U.S. Treasury officially announced it planned to market a significant portion of the gold it held, sending the price plummeting—a loss of 20 percent in value in the first half-hour after the announcement. It shattered the Gould-Fisk corner; but nonetheless Gould profited as a result of his covert sales, netting as much as $11 million by some estimates. Fisk was the big loser, however, never really having an opportunity to recoup his losses because a business partner in the gold-trading scheme shot and killed him in January of 1872.

Between the end of World War I and the corner of Bruce stock in 1958, there were just two notable attempts at manipulators' cornering a stock, and both were quashed when the New York Stock Exchange intervened. The first occured in 1920 when a Wall Street broker masterminded an attempted takeover of the Stutz Motor Car Company (manufacturer of the famous Stutz Bearcat); the other when the CEO of Piggly Wiggly Stores orchestrated a similar attempt to corner the stock in his company in 1923.

So the Gilbert-led takeover of Bruce, and the resultant corner, made big news in the financial pages of the nation's newspapers and periodicals. Gilbert was reduced to spending a lot of time in the summer of 1958 answering questions from the *Wall Street Journal, Business Week, Fortune, Time, Newsweek* and all the New York newspapers. The statements attributed to him were carefully phrased, mellow, and diplomatic — somewhat out of character for the brash young man known around the financial community as consumed by ambition and not known to varnish his positions. He told *Business Week* that "I am a lumberman, and I want to have a voice in the company [Bruce] with the best potential in the industry." And he described the Bruce company to the *Business Week* as "the Tiffany of the flooring industry," implying that his respect for the company only increased his desire to take over its management and expand its business potential.

By August 1958, Gilbert's faction controlled more than 140,000 of the 314,600 outstanding shares of Bruce stock; and the goal, as stated by counsel Benjamin Javits, was "outright control," by owning more than 50 percent, or at least 157,301 shares. But there was a problem.

At the same time trading in Bruce shares was halted by the American Stock Exchange, another ban went into effect, namely the "buy-in" procedure. Short sellers had by law a three-day grace period before having to deliver "shorted shares" on the fourth business day after the trade; and in many instances, brokers to whom the stock had to be delivered granted longer grace periods. If shares were not delivered on the fourth day, brokers had the right under American Stock Exchange rules to enforce its delivery. The buying broker notifies the selling broker that the stock must be delivered by noon of the next business day or the buying broker has the right to go to the floor of the Exchange with an Exchange representative to buy sufficient stock to satisfy the account of the selling broker. But with the temporary ban of the "buy-in" rule, which protected the buying broker, short sellers were relieved of having to deliver their borrowed shares. Gilbert, who had bought almost all of the approximately 16,000 shorted shares at the time of the trade suspension and buy-in ban, could not take delivery of his shares and could not therefore claim control of them.

Then Bruce countered with a tactic of its own. In a joint announcement at company headquarters in Memphis, President E. L. Bruce, Jr., and James R. Welsh, head of Welsh Plywood Corporation (a manufacturer of hardwood plywood for use in home and office construction whose stock was traded on the Midwest Stock Exchange), announced that Bruce was purchasing the Welsh company for 10,000 shares of authorized, but previously unissued, shares of Bruce common stock. By using these new shares to acquire Welsh, a Bruce company spokesman confidently stated to the *New York Times,* "This puts control of the company out of Gilbert's reach."

The response from the Gilbert camp was swift. Javits issued a statement later the same day: "This does not come as a surprise to us," he explained at a news conference. "The first telegram that we sent to the Bruce company [formally announcing to Bruce in April that they were buying stock for the purpose of obtaining control of the company] put them on notice that we would either enjoin them or void any such action as they have now taken." He told the reporters to expect a court action shortly, not stipulating, however, in which court the action would be taken.

Javits kept the Western Union lines busy the next day, shooting off telegrams to the Securities and Exchange Commission, to the Midwest Stock Exchange, and to the Bruce and Welsh companies, among others. The one to the SEC accused the Bruce company management of defrauding its stockholders by putting 10,000 previously unissued shares of Bruce stock into play just to acquire Welsh Plywood. He asked that the SEC "properly scrutinize" any application regarding the Welsh acquisition and to grant a hearing to the Gilbert interests before making any decision on the acquisition. Javits's wire to the Midwest Stock Exchange stated that legal action was forthcoming to set aside Bruce's purchase of Welsh; and in his telegrams to the Bruce brothers and to James R. Welsh, Javits warned that they would be held personally accountable for "an illegal violation of the interest which we [the law firm of Javits and Javits] represent."

Javits and Javits brought suit in the state of Delaware where Bruce was incorporated. Benjamin Javits noted that Delaware law bans the issuance of new stock once company management is notified that its control is being challenged. He then entrusted the case to a young associate in the firm by the name of Tom Field. Field admittedly had little experience in security trading and sec market regulations, but he did have a reputation for being a quick-study and for his tenacity as well as a near-perfect string of winning cases he had thus far handled for Javits and Javits. Field quickly prepared motion papers to present to the Delaware Chancery Court, enlisting the aid of a prominent Delaware law firm in Wilmington, Richards, Leighton and Fingar. The Delaware court chancellor listened and with little delay ruled in favor of the Gilbert faction, disallowing the 10,000 newly issued shares of Bruce stock and barring the company from voting those shares. As Field later recalled, "It was an accomplishment, I believe, because the law is that if a transaction is, from a business point of view, a valuable transaction, has business merits, for the company issuing the stock, it is generally upheld. And in this case, it was easily argued that it was a good acquisition for Bruce. On the other hand, I think the papers we presented so clearly showed that the transaction was done for the purpose of frustrating Gilbert's bid that the chancellor had no choice other than to disenfranchise the stock." And so the Bruce ploy to ward off the Gilbert raid foundered.

While this issue was being resolved to Gilbert's advantage, the short sellers had yet to be heard from. As the American Stock Exchange announced that it had lifted the ban that had deferred closing out of "short" contracts on Bruce stock (meaning short sellers would have to deliver the demanded stock), a number of short sellers sued in court in early September to prevent the American Stock Exchange from requiring them to close out their contracts. Headed by investor Jack E. Blanck, the short sellers wanted to obtain an order in the New York State Supreme Court temporarily preventing the American Stock Exchange from lifting its ban. "The court move was necessary because there was insufficient stock available by which the shorts could cover their position," attorney Lester Migdal argued for his clients. There was little question the shorts were in trouble: Bruce stock was now being traded over the counter for as much as $190 bid, and at the market close on Friday, September 5, the quotation was $140 bid, $160 asked. Many short sellers had bailed out. Of the approximate 16,000 shares sold short when the American Stock Exchange had suspended trade on June 12, just 4,000 remained undelivered when the short sellers went to court. Still a number of short sellers were very hard-pressed and stood to lose substantially if the ban were rescinded.

Eddie Gilbert was in the middle of it all. The 4,000 undelivered shares had been sold to him, and he needed them now in order to acquire control of Bruce. So he went to court to thwart the short sellers. Tom Field had just returned from Delaware that afternoon, and the young associate quickly began the task of preparing a response, working into the night over an affidavit moving to intervene on behalf of Gilbert and opposing the short sellers' motion to enjoin the Exchange from lifting its ban. Sometime after midnight Field made his way up Fifth Avenue to Gilbert's apartment to review the motion and get Eddie's signature on the affidavit.

Although Field was doing what he had to do for his client, he was in a quandary because he was also concerned over the fate of the short sellers. He later explained, "The drama surrounding this action was heightened by the fact that among the short sellers there were people who, clearly, had no business being short sellers. There was a truck driver. There was a widow who had risked her son's college tuition. There was a Rabbi in Brooklyn, who, instead of praying for other things, was praying for the stock to go down. . . . These people would have been enormously hurt financially, perhaps destroyed, if they had to buy in at $190 or $200 a share." On the other hand, he understood his client's position. "Gilbert would have had absolutely no profit from squeezing the shorts, not one penny for it. It mattered not whether they paid $77 or $250 a share, it meant nothing. All that Gilbert was interested in, really — legitimately interested in — was to obtain the stock that he had bought without the faintest idea that he was buying short stock. So, while I was very much in sympathy with the shorts, at the same time I was aware that it was not Gilbert's fault. Not only that, but he needed the stock. He had invested millions and now needed the stock to take control, and he was entitled to the stock."

The case was scheduled to be brought before Justice Henry Epstein in New York Supreme Court on Tuesday morning, September 9. After Field's lengthy consultation with Gilbert that had extended into the early morning hours, he returned to the offices of Javits and Javits to prepare for court. There he learned that Benjamin Javits had decided to argue the motion himself. This met with stiff objection from Field as well as from Harold Held, one of the other senior partners who happened to have been in the office early that morning. This case would be front-page news in New York, and no one sensed that better than Javits, who seldom stepped out of the way of newspaper exposure. Field saw it as "a horrifying prospect because the man had not appeared in court for God knows how many years, and he really was not a practicing lawyer. He was superb in getting clients and with talking to the press, but [in terms of presenting the motion in court] he was not there at all." Furthermore, Javits's only direct contribution to the case up to that time, according to Field, was "that he brought me a Reuben sandwich from a deli that evening while I was preparing [the affidavit]." So Field called on Held. "Harold, who was a dear, old soul, was very upset with the prospect, and he tried to talk Javits out of it. But there was no talking him out of it, He was the senior partner, and he was going to argue it. That was it."

In court, Judge Epstein listened to the case that attorneys Lester Migdal and Powell Pierpont made for the short sellers, that no fair market for the stock existed and that it would be impossible therefore for the short sellers to cover their positions. Not only was the stock too scarce, they said, it was too high-priced for any "fair market" to exist. Javits arose and was succinct; he told the court that his client needed the shares now, before the Bruce board of directors were to meet on October 28. We are entitled to them, he said, ending his demand with the words, "and we'd like to have a quick decision." Field recalls, "He did not say the things that were in the affidavit that I prepared, which made our position equitably appealing." Judge Epstein, a bit taken back by the tenor of Javits argument, fixed a hard eye on Javits and said, "If you want a quick decision, I can give you one—right now."

"It was stated in such an ominous, threatening tone," Field remembers, "that Javits said 'No, No,' three or four times." Judge Epstein nodded, and then announced to the court, "I'll consider the motion and render a decision Thursday."

When court reconvened two days later, after Judge Epstein had read the affidavits submitted by both sides, he concluded that although the situation affecting the short sellers was "unfortunate," their plight "cannot take precedence over the interests of a legitimate investor who had made such investments in good faith." He saw no reason to rule in favor of the plaintiffs. "No charge of fraud or conscious misconduct is made," the judge said. "No sharp practice by the [American Stock] Exchange is observed. No profit by the Exchange is possible or claimed." Barring any obvious fraud or wrongful application by the Exchange in violation of its regulations, he explained, he concluded that he could not interfere with the judgment made by those speaking for the Exchange. Referring to the short traders, he said, "Plaintiffs gambled and lost. It is an unfortunate situation but one not wholly unknown to the marketplace in cases where those who gamble may lose by reason of a battle for the control of a company whose stock has been the object of their speculation."

Over on Wall Street that day, Bruce stock had been trading in the range of $100 asked, $125 offered, but after Judge Epstein's decision was handed down, the stock soared and closed the day at $140 bid, $170 offered.

While it was a major victory for the Gilbert faction, the fight was not over. The plaintiffs went to the Clerk of the Appellate Division and filed an application to stay the denial of the injunction, in a last-ditch effort to protect the short sellers from having to deliver stock. Once the Javits firm had been notified by telephone, Tom Field was immediately dispatched to the Appellate Division, where a judge listened to both sides' hastily prepared arguments. As the case was of "significance and notoriety," the judge stated that he was reluctant to make a decision on his own. So he referred it to a panel of appellate judges who would hear further arguments in special session the following morning. When the panel of judges convened the next day, they in turn ruled against the plaintiffs.

Meanwhile other things were beginning to unfold behind the scenes. With the court's rulings, it was clear to just about everyone now that Gilbert had succeeded in his strategy to take control of the Bruce company. Rumors began to fly that the Bruce family had all but conceded defeat. It was reported that a meeting had taken place between Benjamin Javits and Herbert Brownell, the attorney representing the Bruces. Brownell was one of New York's most prominent attorneys, known for having served as U.S. Attorney General under President Dwight Eisenhower a few years earlier. But he was in an impossible position: He could only protect the Bruces in their capitulation, not in preventing the takeover. Although the meeting was cordial, the only really practical result was the scheduling of a face-to-face meeting between the two factions at a neutral site in New York.

Following the court's decision to lift the ban on the buy-in rule, Gilbert's attorneys announced that his faction now held a majority of shares in the E. L. Bruce Company. Gilbert himself said he was making no demand on the short sellers to deliver their shares immediately. And speaking for Gilbert, Javits explained to reporters that "Mr. Gilbert said yesterday that he hoped to help the short sellers by asking that they agree to deliver the stock within three weeks carrying proxies made out to Mr. Gilbert." The Javits firm also filed an affidavit in the Delaware Court of Chancery claiming that the Gilbert faction controlled 50.28 percent of the Bruce stock, or a total of 158,201 shares. There were two qualifications, however, which were explained in a financial-page article in the *New York Times*. "[Javits] said 17,255 shares were held by friends and relatives of Mr. Gilbert who were not tied up by contract and were therefore not under Mr. Gilbert's control. Wall Street sources have speculated [and Gilbert later corroborated] in recent weeks that some such members of the Gilbert group may have sold their holdings when the stock reached its recent high prices.

"In addition, Mr. Javits said that 2,447 of the 87,710 shares listed as held for Mr. Gilbert by Carl M. Loeb, Rhoades and Co. had not been delivered as of September 12, when the affidavit was signed. The claimed majority of the Bruce stock thus appears to rest in the stock covered by short sales and the shares held by those close to Mr. Gilbert but without contractual agreements."

A date was quickly set for the meeting between Gilbert and the Bruces. It was agreed that on Monday, September 22, the two factions would meet in a suite at the Waldorf-Astoria Hotel. Attending for the Bruce company would be Edwin L. and C. Arthur Bruce and Frank O'Connor, a company vice president and a member of the board of directors, and their counsel Herbert Brownell.

It would prove to be a memorable event.

Eddie Gilbert was accompanied by his father and Robert N. West of the law firm of Shearman and Sterling, now representing Empire Millwork Corporation. Javits and Javits had been hired principally to handle Gilbert's interests for the securities intricacies of the takeover operation and were not the corporation's counsel of record. The two groups assembled in the Waldorf-Astoria suite at the agreed-upon time, but they could not start the meeting, Gilbert informed them, until John Loeb arrived. So they sat there and waited.

A short while later, a limousine pulled up in front of the Waldorf Astoria, followed by an armored car. John Loeb got out of the limo and watched as guards unloaded several boxes from the back of the armored car. They proceeded then to the suite where Loeb, with help from Eddie and his father, began taking stock certificates from the boxes and piling them on a table in the center of the room. By the time they finished, the stack of stock certificates on the table was nearly two feet high, representing, according to Gilbert, a controlling majority of shares in the E. L. Bruce Company.

Gilbert remembers turning to the Bruces and saying, "Look, what's the use of wasting everyone's time? We all came to this meeting for a reason. We have over 50 percent of the stock. There it is. Right on the table. You can count it if you want. But now we're going to lunch. We'll be back in an hour or so. For your acceptance. Here's our terms: We want seven members on the board of directors; you can name the other seven. I want to be president, you [Edwin. L. Bruce] can be chairman of the board. If you don't want to accept that—I don't want to spend all day talking, negotiating this—then we'll take control of the company and you'll get whatever is left, which will probably be nothing. It's up to you."

Eddie, his father, John Loeb, and Robert West then left for lunch, a brief one as it turned out. An hour later they were back at the Waldorf. Neither the Bruces nor their attorneys had counted the stock; it was still in the same haphazard piles on the table that it had been when they left an hour earlier. "Well?" Gilbert asked.

Frank O'Connor, speaking for the Bruces, said they would accept Gilbert's terms.

There was one small touch of irony: "We didn't have 50 percent of the stock," Eddie later tells the story. "I think there was 49.5 or 49.6 there on the table. I knew it. I was gambling they wouldn't count it." He shrugs. "We did have it the next day, though."

The *New York World-Telegram*, also the next day, reported the Bruce capitulation thusly: "Yesterday, 1,000 miles from Memphis, the victory scale swung to the Gilberts. The South had lost another war."

Eddie Gilbert's dream had come true. He had made it happen. He had taken over the nation's largest hardwood flooring company, the very one he had so admired and coveted when he first encountered it down in Tennessee ten years earlier.

On October 28, 1958, the new board of directors of the E. L. Bruce Company convened in Memphis, Tennessee. The composition of the board was a compromise whereby seven members from the previous Bruce board were joined by seven members from the Gilbert-led faction. Besides himself, Eddie brought in his father Harry (still president of Empire Millwork Corporation), longtime friend Jerry Stern (head of Jerome International Corp., New York), Henry Loeb (managing partner of the investment banking firm Carl M. Loeb, Rhoades and Co., New York), George F. Dixon (president of Carlisle Corporation, Carlisle, Pennsylvania), Norman Denny (president of Denny Building Corporation, Philadelphia), and Philip P. Weisburg (director of Franklin National Bank, New York). They joined board members C. Arthur Bruce and E. L. Bruce, Jr.; Bruce vice-presidents Evan L. Fellman, Frank H. O'Connor, and Walter J. Wood; Orville Taylor, senior law partner of Taylor, Miller, Busch and Magner of Chicago; and H. Earle Muzzy, vice-chairman of the Quaker Oats Company, also headquartered in Chicago.

The two significant items of business approved that day were the 25 cent per share dividend (payable to shareholders of record on November 14) and a press release to be issued stating that "the existing policies of the Bruce company will continue and that there will be no changes in personnel."

It marked the beginning of a glorious four-year ride for Eddie Gilbert.

*There was music from my neighbor's house through
the summer nights. In his blue gardens,
men and girls came and went like moths among the
whisperings and the champagne and the stars.*

F. SCOTT FITZGERALD, THE GREAT GATSBY, 1925

The early 1950s saw Eddie Gilbert working long hours at Empire Millwork for an annual salary of $15,000. Now, with the decade drawing to an end, he was positioned at the head of a major national corporation, his net worth in the high seven-figures, and his social status on the rise.

Fueled by front-page coverage of his spectacular takeover of the Bruce company, Gilbert moved beyond his business to establish a Gatsby-like image. Over the next four years, he would acquire a villa on the French Riviera and an opulent town house on Manhattan's east side, to complement the ten-room Fifth Avenue apartment at 62nd Street where he lived with Rhoda and their two little girls, Robin and Alexandra.

Eddie began to acquire significant art objects as well as elegant French and Italian antiques to furnish the Fifth Avenue apartment, which overlooked Central Park. He was determined to make its interior appearance as impressive as its prestigious address. Word quickly spread through the New York art world that the youthful Eddie Gilbert was bent upon becoming a serious collector. He became a regular purchaser of fine paintings at both the Wildenstein and Newhouse Galleries. From the time he made his first million dollars back in 1955 to the day he lost it all in 1962, Gilbert would assemble an art collection that included at one time or another during those seven years paintings by such artists as Rembrandt van

Rijn, Jean-Honore Fragonard, Antonio Canaletto, Claude Monet, François Boucher, Alfred Sisley, Raoul Dufy, Winslow Homer, Eugene Boudin, Hubert Robert, Dirck Hals, Francesco Guardi, and Jean Boldoni.

Eddie's town house on 70th Street, just west of Park Avenue, was a five-story, Tudor mansion; today it is home to the Explorers' Club, which acquired it in 1963 after Gilbert lost it following the Bruce-Celotex debacle. Gilbert had bought the mansion from Stephen C. Clark's widow, who was the heiress to the Singer Sewing Machine fortune. As the house was in a state of some disrepair when he acquired it, Gilbert hired a French architect to restore it to its original grandeur. Carved woodwork on the second floor, as an example, had come from one of Lord Nelson's ships. It was the perfect setting for the high-life parties that Eddie hosted, and he threw a number of them even while the house was undergoing restoration.

When Eddie entertained at all of his residences, the parties were lavish and customarily attracted a dazzling cast of international jet setters and New York's social and celebrity elite. These parties, matched with the Gilberts' New York nightlife appearances were routinely reported in the gossip columns and on the society pages. Eddie even hired the public relations firm owned by *New York Journal-American* gossip columnist Cholly Knickerbocker (the *nom de plume* of Igor Cassini, brother of notable fashion designer Oleg Cassini) as an adviser and advocate in the social shuffle. On one very special social occasion in New York, for example, Knickerbocker writes, "Paris came to New York last night in a double-barreled amalgamation of two of the grandest French events of the year—the visit to Manhattan of General Charles de Gaulle, President of the French Republic, and the advent of the ninth April in Paris Ball to benefit the French Hospital of New York and the American French Foundation Charities." With General de Gaulle at the Grand Ballroom of the Waldorf Astoria were other such notables as former President Harry S Truman, Governor and Mrs. Nelson Rockefeller, U.N. Ambassador and Mrs. Henry Cabot Lodge, Senator and Mrs. Jacob Javits, Fleet Admiral and Mrs. Chester Nimitz, former New York governor and Mrs. Averill Harriman, and the David and Laurance Rockefellers, Knickerbocker reported. Those who were not at *that* dinner were attending the Paris ball at the Astor Hotel where a replica of the famous Paris Opera House facade, 70 feet wide and 50 feet high, was built over the hotel's main Broadway entrance. The group there included Liz Taylor and Eddie Fisher, Elsa Maxwell, Mr. and Mrs. William Paley, Charlton Heston, and chairperson Mrs. Winston Guest. The night was so socially active that Cholly's column covered an entire page of the *Journal-American* the next day. Among those featured was Eddie Gilbert: "A small group composed of Tina Onassis, Mr. and Mrs. Nicholas Goulandris, the Frank Schiffs, and the Edward Gilberts abandoned the Astor for El Morocco...."

It was not just Cholly Knickerbocker reporting, however; the Gilberts were under the watchful eye of other reputation-makers as well. Philip Van Rensselaer, writing for the *Long Island Press* in 1969, remembered those days this way: "Eddie Gilbert... what a vibrant, colorful character he was: a character right out of Scott Fitzgerald's *The Great Gatsby*.... Rhoda and Eddie Gilbert made a smashing debut on the New York social scene ten years ago under the auspices of those two worldly creatures, Elsa Maxwell and Count Lanfranco Rasponi. Elsa was responsible for launching many new characters through the gilded portals of the great world, and Rasponi had a whole stable full of social starlets panting to meet Mrs. Winston Guest and Mrs. William Paley. If you'd just made a couple of million and were hungry for social recognition, Count Rasponi was your man. He had a public relations business and if you paid him $1,000 a month, you'd be invited to his apartment at 535 Park Avenue and could be presented to the reigning social figures on the Manhattan scene such as pretty Peggy Bancroft [now the Duchesse d'Uzes] or pretty Mrs. Francis Farr.

"So suddenly in a blaze of glory Rhoda and Eddie Gilbert flashed meteor-like into the fashionable New York drawing rooms, into the fashionable restaurants, into the fashionable society columns.

"Who on earth were the Eddie Gilberts, everyone was asking? Every day they were in the columns; Mrs. Gilbert was always beautifully dressed and beautifully jeweled. She was seen lunching with Mrs. Frederick Eberstadt or dining with Mrs. Samuel Peabody and photographed at a fashionable charity ball. How rich was Eddie Gilbert, everyone was wondering? Damn rich, came the reply from the Maxwell-Rasponi camp. Were they worth bothering with? Indeed yes.

"Both the Gilberts were attractive and well-dressed and lived in a very grand apartment on Fifth Avenue.... They entertained lavishly, and through Miss Maxwell and Rasponi even got such celebrities as Gian Carlo Menotti to dine on their gilded plates. Gian Carlo had just opened his music festival in Spoleto, Italy, and he was as hungry for money for his festival as the Gilberts were hungry for his company — it was a fair exchange. Besides, in aristocratic circles the high and mighty always patronized artists — and what was $10,000 to a man rumored to have $10 or $20 million?"

Where Gilbert made his biggest social splash, however, was on the French Riviera. He spent the summer months there from the mid 1950s until his financial catastrophe in 1962. From his Army Air Corps days, Eddie had long held a special affection for that part of the world with its natural beauty mixed with the affluence of the international society who lived and played there. At first he rented a small house in Cap d'Antibes located on the grounds of the three-star Hotel du Cap, sharing expenses with Arde Bulova (of the watchmaker family). The next year he leased a villa of his own at Cap Ferrat; followed by the grand villa at Cap Martin, a 20-room mansion perched on a cliff 150 feet above the Mediterranean with a 75-foot swimming pool and a clear view across the bay to Monte Carlo. After renting the villa for several summers, Eddie then bought it. According to Don Forst, writing later in a feature article about Gilbert for the *Saturday Evening Post*, "There, one guest recalls, 'it was open house just about every day with a jazz band for luncheon dancing at the pool and an orchestra at night. . . . It was a motel for the jet set, and Edward had to be introduced to his own guests.'

"Yet he was delighted to run a way station for sycophants and continent hoppers, and was hurt when some people called him a crass climber, a real-life Great Gatsby. 'Names and titles never meant anything to me,' Gilbert [retorted]. 'Rich or poor, it didn't matter as long they were amusing.'"

The Gatsby connection was often made when describing Eddie Gilbert in those days of conspicuous splendor. Besides his lavish parties, Eddie was seen regularly in the summer months in the Casino at Monte Carlo, where he indulged his passion for gambling. Several national magazine stories suggested that Gilbert was known to win or lose as much $200,000 on a given night at the *chemin de fer* table, his game of choice. Eddie claims in fact to have won $600,000 one night at Monte Carlo and admits to having lost as much as $300,000 or $400,000 on other occasions.

John Brooks's chronicle of that era, *The Go-Go Years*, devoted an entire chapter to Gilbert, titled "The Last Gatsby." But much publicity associated with the image was often exaggerated and sometimes simply not true.

Brooks's description of Gilbert, for example, contains these untruths: "Sometimes he lived in a mansion at Palm Beach...." But Eddie never owned or rented any such residence. "He took an immense villa at Cap Martin on the French Riviera, where he mingled when he could with Maria Callas and Aristotle Onassis...." Although Gilbert had met Onassis (and once played a game of backgammon with him), that was the extent of his relationship with the Greek magnate and the opera diva. Another misperception: "Eddie was always the maestro, directing, giving whimsical instructions, trading hospitality for the right to command. 'Let's go bowling!' he might shout to his assembled guests after lunch, so ingenuously that 40 or 50 of the rich and chic or almost-rich and almost-chic of the world would dutifully jump into their cars, or into one of his waiting limousines, and be off to Monaco's elegant four-lane bowling alley to indulge him." But in truth, when Gilbert entertained at his villa, he was always discreetly in the background, never playing the social director that Brooks makes him out to be. Richard Parkes, a British friend of Gilbert's and a regular guest at his villa in the south of France, has said, "Eddie was a wonderful host; he saw to it that only the finest was provided and that everyone had a good time, but he hired people to do that and never got in the way. He was happy just to see people enjoying themselves. Often you didn't even know he was there, and some of the time he wasn't." As for going bowling, Gilbert said, "Never!" To indulge him? "You've got to be kidding. I threw parties, they came, the ones that were invited, that's all. I never went out with any of them afterwards. I don't know where they went after they left, but I doubt if it was to a bowling alley."

In a retrospective *LIFE* magazine feature article about Gilbert's parties on the Riviera, the author claimed that Eddie often "adjourned the party to Le Pirate, the most expensive nightclub along the Côte d'Azur. He liked Le Pirate because it has attracted the likes of Princess Grace, Maria Callas, and Aristotle Onassis. He would churn up to the place in a big powerboat. And when the party was over Eddie — who drank little, often only soda water — personally picked up the check." Eddie states emphatically that he never once set foot in Le Pirate during any of the summers he lived just up the coast from it.

"Where they get these things, I'll never know," Gilbert said later. Curiously though, Eddie was not that uncomfortable with comparisons to Gatsby. He enjoyed his wealth, and he certainly did not try to hide it. He wore it, in fact, almost as a comfortable old coat. There is little question that, as he became more prosperous and prominent, Eddie openly courted the attention and companionship of the rich and famous, those with influence and celebrity.

Although details may often have been in error, stories of Gilbert's entertaining were nonetheless difficult to exaggerate because they *were* on a scale that could only be called grand. There were 12 large bedrooms in the Cap Martin villa along with the master suite. Always on weekends, and often during the week, all 12 were occupied by guests. Each guest bedroom had its own valet and a maid. The kitchen was open at all hours, manned by a first-class chef, so guests could have either an early morning breakfast or a late-night snack upon returning from the Casino or meals at any time in between. There was a staff of 30 who worked at the villa throughout the summer months when Eddie lived and entertained there.

The entire show, so to speak, was directed and produced by a Frenchman named Olivier Coquelin. When Gilbert decided to take the villa and so entertain his friends in a way they would never forget, he set out to find someone who could organize and run the operation for him. Eddie found him through his New York friend, Dick Cowell, then a major player in New York's café society. Cowell jettisoned (or some say capstoned) his playboy image in 1958 when, at 34, he married the 19-year-old beauty, Gail Whitney, daughter of Cornelius Vanderbilt Whitney; Eddie was Cowell's best man. Cowell had just the man to meet Eddie's requirements. Coquelin was in his late twenties at the time and managing a sporting club in Miami Beach to which Cowell belonged. Eddie brought Coquelin to New York for an interview, where he was delighted with the young Frenchman, whom he found to be as cosmopolitan as he was handsome.

Coquelin had also been a World War II veteran, which resulted in even greater regard from Gilbert. As a teenager, Coquelin had served with the honored commando group known as "Stilwell's Raiders," named for its commanding officer, General Joseph W. "Vinegar Joe" Stilwell. Stilwell's Raiders had fought the Japanese in the China-Burma-India theater of operations in the jungles of Southeast Asia from 1942 through 1945. According to Gene Wolkoff, Eddie's friend and attorney, Coquelin's U.S. citizenship was expedited as a result of his service during the war.

Coquelin was hired on the spot and dispatched to the the south of France where his duties included hiring and managing the household staff, arranging the invitations to houseguests, organizing details of the numerous parties, and seeing to the needs of everyone who wandered in and out of the villa — in effect keeping the place whirring at the pace Gilbert wanted. "It was like running a hotel," Coquelin once said, "a very grand hotel where the party never ended." It turned out, to everyone's satisfaction, that Coquelin proved as adept a social director as he was charming to Gilbert's sophisticated guests. So began a friendship, with deep loyalties on both sides, that would last through Gilbert's successes and failures and would not end until Coquelin's death in the early 1990s.

Eddie's sister Enid remembers another party that Eddie hosted which she attended, typifying his extravagance during this period of his life. At the time the 1960 summer Olympics were taking place in Rome, Enid was an aspiring painter living alone in Venice, while her husband remained in New York tending to his urology practice. "Eddie and Rhoda were staying at the Ruspoli palace," she recalls. "Ruspoli, this is one of the great families in Rome, a great, historic family. They have one of the great palaces in Rome. It takes up a whole square block.

"Dado was one of the sons, Prince Dado they called him — I believe he was a drug addict, into things like that — and he and Eddie had become friends somehow. Anyway Dado had them put up in the palace, in one of the apartments there. They had many apartments in the palace; it was huge, it was as big as Bloomingdale's. The apartment Eddie and Rhoda were staying in had its own elevator. The entire elevator was covered in turquoise velvet, I remember.

"Eddie and Dado decided they were going to throw a party. Dado invited his Italian friends, everyone who was anybody in Italy then, nobility, all the richest and the most famous names; Eddie, he invited all his friends, all those who used to come to his house on the Riviera and those who were [in Rome] for the Olympics.

"They took over the main part of the palace for the party — actually it was a ball, not a party. They decorated the place from floor to ceiling, hired Italian interior decorators to come in and do it. It was a magnificent affair. The night of the ball, everyone arrived dressed formally, the women in luxurious gowns. At the entrance there were huge staircases going up each side and on every other step there was a footman in full livery holding a lighted candelabra — there must have been 30 or 40 men on those stairs, and they stood there for the entire evening. I think there were about

400 guests. There was to be a dinner, but I didn't stay for it. There was an orchestra and entertainers. It was all too much for me. Nobody really paid any attention to me either, unless they were desperate for company.

"But here's something interesting. I walked out just before the dinner, and as I went outside and into the street, who do I run into there but Eddie. He said, 'I had to get out of there. It's too much.' I told him that's how I felt. 'Well, I'm going home,' I told him. He just smiled, shrugged, and looked up the sky—it was a beautiful, starry evening—then he said, 'I have to go back.' And I'm sure he did. I went back to my hotel [in Rome] and back to Venice the next day."

One of the most interesting people Gilbert met in the south of France during one of these summer visits was another gambler of international note, the Britisher John Aspinall, who would become a lifelong friend. Aspinall was a tall, rangy man, succintly described almost a half-century later in the *London Times* as "a rakish millionaire who made his fortune in the port-and-cigar world of upper-class gambling tables in London and devoted it to creating country estates for breeding gorillas and tigers."

Like Eddie Gilbert, Aspinall was an outsider of sorts. Born in India, he was sent off to a boarding school in Rugby, from which he was later expelled for being "idle and rebellious." After a three-year stint in the Royal Marines, Aspinall enrolled in Jesus College at Oxford where, it was said "he devoted himself to dandified dress and gambling [and] boasted of never having attended a single lecture." He took a certain pride in telling friends that on the day of his final exams, he feigned illness and instead went to the Gold Cup at Ascot. Like Gilbert at Cornell, Aspinall did not earn his Oxford degree. "But I did bet on the right horse that day," he liked to remind people later.

Aspinall launched his gambling career in London in the mid-1950s, while gambling was still illegal there. The peripatetic game he ran was a version of Damon Runyon's made famous in *Guys and Dolls*, only Aspinall's "floated" among high-class flats and town houses in London rather than in the subterranean haunts of New York. Although eventually shut down, he managed to avoid prosecution. Once gambling was legalized in London several years later, Aspinall opened the Clermont Club, an elegant, private establishment on Berkeley Square that became famous for attracting high-rolling gamblers from all over the world. Annabel's, a club for dinner and dancing in the below-grade level of the Clermont, soon became the most fashionable and exclusive night spot of 1960s London.

Aspinall's obituary in the *New York Times* following death from cancer in the summer of 2000 records, "The success he had in fleecing some of London's more louche aristocrats and rich foreign visitors in his Mayfair gambling clubs and then spending the profits on his own eccentric model of animal protection was sometimes said to have done as much for redistributing the wealth in Britain in the 1960s as the social programs of the liberal intelligentsia who regularly excoriated him for his extreme right-wing views."

Wild animals were as dear to Aspinall's heart as his gambling, so much so that he often said that of his 30 best friends (among whom Eddie Gilbert was counted), half were animals; and on more than one occasion he announced that he preferred the company of gorillas to humans. With the fortune he built from the success of the Clermont Club and Annabel's, Aspinall opened a private zoo in the south of England, called Howletts, just outside of Canterbury, and later, in addition, a grand 400-acre animal park at Port Lympne not far from Dover. At his death, he was recongized as the keeper of the largest private zoo in the world, his two zoological parks containing as many as 1,100 animals of 80 different species, ranging from his adored gorillas to Siberian tigers, rhinos, and elephants.

In the mid-1950s, though, John Aspinall was regularly struggling to make ends meet financially. He was not then well known in Britain or abroad, but, like Gilbert, he had high ambitions.

Their paths first crossed one evening at Cannes on the Cote d'Azur, both were playing *chemin de fer* in the Palm Beach Casino—Gilbert winning, Aspinall losing. Alone that night, Eddie noticed Aspinall and his wife Jane; as Gilbert remembers, she immediately caught his attention. "She was absolutely beautiful," Gilbert said when asked about that first meeting. "As the night wore on, I got to talking with John as we played and found he was as entertaining as she was good-looking."

Aspinall remembered the night in great detail, even many years later. "How could one forget," he mused. "It was such a magnanimous gesture. And it marked the beginning of such a wonderful friendship. I was losing that night, and I didn't really have that much to lose in those days. And somewhere, long before the night should have ended, I had reached my limit. So I turned to Jane and said something like, 'That's it. We'd best be going.' And Eddie looked astonished, that we might be leaving, suggesting we stay around a while longer and then go out afterwards, but I said to him as I rose to leave, 'How do you play this game with no money? I have no more. So I must go.'" Then Eddie pushed a pile of chips in front of Aspinall, about $10,000 worth, and said, "Here, play for me. We'll split whatever you win."

Aspinall resumed his place at the *chemin de fer* table. "I was delighted to continue playing," Aspinall recalled. "And my luck turned. I believe by the end of the evening I'd run it up to about eight thousand pounds [about $40,000 at the exchange rate then]. So I gave Eddie back what I'd started with and we split the rest, which was sizeable, at least at that time in my life. We walked out together quite happy. Eddie then invited Jane and me to a party that he and Rhoda were having at the villa they were living in at the time the next night. 'Be sure to come,' he said, 'and then we'll go out gambling after.' And so we did, and from that time onward, it seems, we were always there for one another."

Whenever the subject of Gilbert's gesture that night in Cannes later came up, which it often did, Aspinall said that Eddie would claim he did it only because Jane was so beautiful; it had nothing to do with John. Aspinall smiles and adds, "That's Eddie, that's what he'd say. But I recollect he just saw a gambler out of luck. Or maybe he just wanted another place to run a bank from. You made your money running banks at the *chemin de fer* table. And Eddie wanted more than anything to win."

Well, that was not altogether true: There were many times in the early days of their friendship that Gilbert wanted to *lose*. Aspinall's biographer Brian Masters writes of those years in The Passion of John Aspinall, when Aspinall was struggling and Gilbert was sailing, "Eddie ... did not embarrass his friend by offering to give large sums as he knew Aspinall ... would lose face if the struggle were to show. Eddie sensed when Aspinall was broke by the way he behaved, and would then suggest some absurd bet which he knew would be taken up, and moreover which Aspinall was bound to win, for Eddie was careful not to propose anything that the other man might lose. These random bets continued on and off for some six years and were often so fanciful that they compared in outrageousness with the 18th-century bets placed at Brooks's when, for instance, one member would bet another that a certain fly crawling up a window-pane would or would not reach the top."

One such bet in Monte Carlo, Masters described, was that Aspinall could not eat a bowl of flowers placed on a table in the lobby of the Hotel de

Paris, which consumption subsequently cost Gilbert $2,000. Another almost ended in tragedy near Eddie's villa at Cap Martin when the two bet that Aspinall could not swim out to retrieve a hat that had blown into the Mediterranean; but in trying, he got caught in a rip tide and could not make it back until Eddie, a strong swimmer all his life, swam out and brought his friend back to shore.

Aspinall was a wonderful storyteller himself, though inclined toward embellishment, and so took special relish in recounting the most outrageous bet the two ever made. "It was in February and Eddie had come over [to the south of France] because he was in the process of buying this villa. He called me in London and suggested we come down and join them. So Jane and I did.

"We were lunching in this French restaurant overlooking the bay, a very fashionable place whose name escapes me, but it was very nice and it was packed that day. Eddie knew I would do anything for money in those days. So he said, 'John, I bet you $3,000 you won't strip down here in the restaurant, throw *all* your clothes off, and then go outside in the road.' It was a very busy road, I might add. 'And you've got to stay out there *three* full minutes.'

"So I immediately jumped on that. That's something I could do . . . it's an easy $3,000. I got up immediately and said, 'Eddie, you've got a bet.'"

Aspinall then arose from their table and began to take off his clothes. People soon began to notice and a hush fell over the dining room. A waiter carrying a tray of drinks stopped in his tracks, staring wide-eyed at the man now standing naked, except for his socks, in the middle of the restaurant. His shoulders thrown back, Aspinall then began walking toward the door. His wife Jane shouted after him, "Aspers, the socks; don't forget the socks." Aspinall stopped, removed the socks and then walked outside.

"It was freezing," Aspinall remembered. "I stood out there on the street stark naked. There were some street workers, I recall, all in blue dungarees, mending the road and one of them stopped and pointed at me with his pick and soon they were all laughing. And the cars were all slowing down. But I stood there. I hadn't a watch so I had to assess the time. I must've stood there for five minutes because I knew Eddie would be counting and I did not want to lose the bet on that point."

A deeply chilled John Aspinall returned to the restaurant. "The maitre'd was staring at me as I walked back in, so I nodded and looking down at him rather snobbishly said, 'A bet!' But he already knew. While I was out-side Eddie had explained to him and apparently to the other patrons of the restaurant as well that it was a bet. And I believe he told them that I was mad. And they all accepted that; they thought all Englishmen were mad." Mad or not, Aspinall was $3,000 richer. After Aspinall opened the Clermont Club in the early 1960s, and the money began to pour in, their *faux* wagers came to an end. Although from time to time in later years when Aspinall found himself suddenly in need of some help, he knew if Eddie Gilbert were riding high he would help out. Unfortunately for both of them, in those following years, Eddie Gilbert was not always to be found at a high point on his personal roller coaster.

As involved as Gilbert was in forwarding his social position, it did not affect how carefully he operated the E. L. Bruce Company. After the takeover, Eddie moved quickly to consolidate the operations of both Bruce and Empire Millwork, and continued to plan for the formal merger of the two companies (for which he had to gain control of two-thirds of the outstanding Bruce stock). At the takeover two years earlier. Gilbert and his allies had amassed just over 50 percent of the Bruce stock and a year later had control of about 55 percent.

During Gilbert's quest to acquire Bruce, Empire Millwork had suf-fered. Most of its liquid assets were tied up in operations. But ever the salesman, Gilbert had convinced the Empire board to buy more Bruce stock, initially some 31,000 shares. As a consequence, the company's bank line of credit line was cut off "on the ground that the company was in no position to engage in a speculative stock maneuver" (or so it was reported in a *Business Week* article). Empire had to repay $4.3 million in bank loans and, in addition, had to find other more costly ways to finance its oper-ating expenses. In consequence, Empire posted a loss of nearly a half mil-lion dollars for 1958 and saw assets drop from $14 million a year earlier to $9.2 million.

Things were quite different for Bruce, however. Under Gilbert's con-trol, the company was growing in prosperity. In the two years prior to the takeover, Bruce's sales had languished in the area of $27 to $28 million. But by the end of fiscal year 1959, the company boasted record sales of $37.5 million with net income of about $800,000. At the end of the first quarter of 1960, sales continued to spiral upward: $20 million compared to $17.5 million for the same period a year earlier.

To bolster Empire's position and to accumulate cash for the purchase of additional Bruce stock, Gilbert began selling off properties. By 1959, he had disposed of Empire's troubled lumber operations, and later that year he sold off the millwork division for $4.5 million in cash. Empire was left with just three remaining divisions: R&M Millwork located in Muscatine, Iowa; the wholesale lumber division that Eddie personally ran; and the building division that produced nearly 500 houses a year. It was a successful approach. *Business Week* concluded when analyzing the sell-offs: "... in lopping off lumber and the millwork division, Empire is stripping itself of its least promising operations. The three remaining operations are all profitable for it. So, despite a big drop in sales, it promises to show bigger profits without tying up large amounts of cash and credit." The magazine noted that Empire had also cut its operating expenses sharply so that it could operate in the black instead of in deficit as it had in 1958.

Although dropping from sales of $26.5 million in 1958 to $20 million in 1959, Empire showed a profit in 1959 (in contrast to the 1958 loss). "More important," according to *Business Week*, "it improved its cash position, paying off the expensive loans it had carried with the factor, and regaining a bank line of credit."

The takeover had been a smooth one, although there had been worries about how the association of the two principals would work out. Eddie Gilbert, in his mid-thirties, was known for his aggressiveness; he could be brash, abrupt, even hyperactive. Edwin L. Bruce, Jr., now in his late sixties and known as "Mr. Ed" to his employees, was quite the opposite: conservative, slow-talking, and deliberate, acting in a carefully calculated if not plodding way. As for their working together, however, the elder Bruce was quoted as saying that he and Eddie Gilbert "have no trouble getting along. I find him a source of ideas," and he fully endorsed the younger man's plans for Bruce's expansion and growth. Optimistic outsiders called it a successful marriage of youthful vigor and the steadying hand of experience.

By late autumn of 1959, Empire Millwork owned 33,386 shares of Bruce stock; and in late November, Harry Gilbert, as president of Empire, announced that the company was exercising its option to buy 124,014 shares of Bruce stock from his son Eddie, thereby giving Empire control of a majority of Bruce stock.

A year later, Harry Gilbert announced that Empire—now officially known as Empire National Corporation—was making a formal offer to buy outstanding Bruce shares for $37.50 a share to reach the crucial two-thirds ownership. Although Empire owned nearly 60 percent of Bruce's 314,600 outstanding shares, in a letter to Bruce shareholders, Harry Gilbert stated that the offer was for a minimum of 65,000 shares and a maximum of 75,000 at this price. Two years earlier, when Eddie Gilbert made his upstart bid to win control of Bruce, the stock's price went from $16.87 to $77 in about three months until the American Stock Exchange suspended its trading (when it then soared to as much as $190 a share in over-the-counter trading).

Two days after Empire made its offer, Edwin L. Bruce, Jr., announced that he was selling all of his Bruce stock to Empire; so that by December 1960, Empire National owned more than 80 percent of Bruce's outstanding shares. In June 1961 the statutory merger of the two companies occured with the surviving corporation's name being E. L. Bruce Company, Incorporated (Empire National Corporation's name would surface, strangely, in another venture of Eddie's in the 1990s).

Two months later, on August 28, 1961, the merger was approved by both boards of directors, the only dissenting voice being that of Bruce board chairman, C. Arthur Bruce (who with his wife owned approximately five percent of Bruce's outstanding shares), brother of Edwin L., Jr. Opposed to the merger from the outset and expressing continuous dissatisfaction with the situation from the time of the takeover bid in 1958, C. Arthur Bruce formally filed for an injunction in Chancery Court in Wilmington, Delaware, to prevent the formal merger. He was unsuccessful, and the merger was finalized in September 1961.

While all this was moving forward, Eddie Gilbert was quietly maneuvering to execute the next move in the creation of *his* empire. Long before the merger of Empire and Bruce was formalized, in fact just shortly after he successfully orchestrated the takeover of Bruce, Gilbert focused his sights on the Chicago-based Celotex Corporation. Like Bruce, Celotex was prominent in the building materials business. Where Bruce manufactured hardwood flooring and related wood and floor care products, Celotex concentrated on insulation board, gypsum wall board, and accoustical materials.

Celotex was half-again as large as Bruce. Even though Bruce had boosted its sales to a respectable record high of more than $42 million in 1961, Celotex posted sales of nearly $62 million for that year. Eddie Gilbert saw it as a perfect marriage: two companies whose joined forces and products would reinforce and enrich each other, enjoying sales well above $100 million a year with him at the helm.

Gilbert had begun personally to buy Celotex stock in the late 1950s. He urged some of his closest friends and business associates to buy it also and to hold it for him. In much the same way he had aggressively pursued Bruce several years earlier, Eddie Gilbert now saw Celotex as the next logical acquisition.

During this time, however, Gilbert made a fateful financial and personal association, one that he coveted at the time, but one he would later bitterly regret. It came about that in early 1960 Gilbert was giving a speech about Bruce to a meeting of the Society of Security Analysts in New York. Afterwards, a young Frenchman approached Eddie and identified himself as Michel David-Weill, whose family were principals in the firm of Lazard Frères, the most influential investment bankers in French financial circles. Michel, it turned out, was in New York to learn the investment banking business under the tutelage of André Meyer in the firm's New York office. After hearing Eddie's speech, he said to Eddie that it might make sense for Lazard Frères and the Bruce company to do some business together. "We would like to pursue this further," Gilbert remembers David-Weill saying. Gilbert was flattered and impressed, well aware of the international reputation of both Lazard Frères and its American impressario André Meyer.

Meyer was an internationally known figure. His reputation as a highly successful financier was known on Wall Street and throughout all other major world markets. David Rockefeller had once described him as "the most creative financial genius of our time in the investment banking field." He was an investment adviser to the Kennedy family and later, after the assassination of John F. Kennedy, would often serve at social functions as Jacqueline Kennedy's escort. In a book about his life, written by Cary Reich in 1983 (*Financier—The Biography of André Meyer*), Meyer is described in these terms: "Lyndon Johnson would often seek his counsel, as would French president Georges Pompidou. He could count among his intimates numerous other statesmen, politicians, and tycoons, including David Rockefeller, RCA chief David Sarnoff, CBS chairman William Paley, and Fiat king Giovanni Agnelli." Especially in the first half of the 1960s, Meyer's stature was sterling. He was admired as one of the world's shrewdest and most successful venture capitalists, brokering huge real estate deals and orchestrating major corporate mergers and consolidations. It would not be until later in his career that his name would become equally synonymous with terms such as greed, ruthlessness, and ethical vacuity.

As far as Eddie Gilbert was concerned, Meyer was an extraordinarily important business acquaintance, a major figure because of his credibility on Wall Street and internationally as a corporate financier. After his initial meeting with Michel David-Weill and his subsequent introduction to André Meyer, and given Gilbert's expressed enthusiasm for a business relationship with Lazard Frères, Eddie knew there would follow months of Lazard's investigation and analysis of the Bruce company. The outcome was that Lazard Frères became Bruce's principal banker, and Gilbert and Meyer struck up what seemed to be a close personal association.

One of the first fruits of this association was Lazard's agreement to purchase $2 million in Bruce's convertible debentures. In effect, this was a $2 million loan to the company at interest that could be called in at a later time at face value or redeemed by conversion into a specific number of Bruce common shares. While at the time, it seemed a wonderful deal, both for Bruce and Lazard Frères, it would come back later to haunt Eddie Gilbert with ferocity.

More than a year after that first financial transaction, Eddie had launched in earnest his plan to acquire Celotex Corporation for Bruce. Once Michel David-Weill learned of his intentions, he called Gilbert the next day. "I spoke with Mr. Meyer and he's enthused about Lazard Frères becoming involved." A short while later Eddie met with Meyer, whom he held in the highest esteem both as a financier and personally as a friend by this time. Although it would later prove to be a major miscalculation on Eddie's part, he laid out in detail his plan to acquire Celotex Corporation and to merge it with Bruce. According to Meyer biographer Cary Reich, "Meyer was enthusiastic about the takeover and eager to help. Meyer offered to have Lazard and some investment-banking partners buy 250,000 shares of Celotex; when the time came for Gilbert to close the deal and merge Celotex into E. L. Bruce, Lazard and partners would trade their Celotex shares for Bruce debentures for at least a 50 percent profit." Gilbert believes Reich to be in error on this point, explaining that the arrangement was informal, one in which Lazard Frères would sell its Celotex shares to Bruce for a profit, the amount of which would be determined at the time when the merger took place; and noting also that Meyer's sights would never have been set so low as "a 50 percent profit."

André Meyer was more than enthusiastic, according to Gilbert; he was ecstatic about the idea of a merger. He had been looking at Celotex himself, he told Eddie, and had in fact hoped to engineer a merger between Georgia Pacific and Celotex, but that deal had foundered. Now Lazard Frères could be *the* major player in this deal, he promised Gilbert, instrumental in helping his young friend pull off what would come to be seen as a *spectacular* financial coup.

Meyer encouraged Gilbert to proceed on his own in acquiring Celotex stock, reassuring him of Lazard Frères' backing and his own personal commitment both to Eddie and to the deal. And Gilbert did just that. He had also enlisted the E. L. Bruce company to participate in the bid to acquire Celotex.

By the spring of 1962, Gilbert's plan had become public knowledge. The *New York Times* reported on April 11, "Edward M. Gilbert, president of the E. L. Bruce Company, has reported to the Securities and Exchange Commission his ownership of more than 10 percent of the stock of the Celotex Corporation, stirring speculation he might start a proxy battle for control." The article went on to say that Gilbert owned 109,000 shares of Celotex personally and the Bruce company an additional 5,000 shares of the 1,018,651 shares of Celotex common stock outstanding at the time.

A week later, the Bruce company had more than doubled its stake in Celotex, having purchased another 6,200 shares, so that the notion of a Bruce-Celotex merger was more like an unfolding news story than simple speculation. The *Times* later quoted Gilbert as suggesting "a consolidation" of the two companies when he spoke at the annual meeting of Bruce shareholders: "In my view [Celotex] has a great profit potential, which is now being realized, [and] both companies could benefit from a single distribution system." Gilbert went on to declare, "It has also been and continues to be my belief that if a substantial amount of Celotex stock were in the hands of persons whose views coincided with my own, it might be possible at some future date to work out a plan for the combination of the two corporations to the mutual advantage of their shareholders."

With his ambitious plan in motion, the backing of his company, and the investment banking support of Lazard Frères and the wily André Meyer, Eddie Gilbert, in the spring of 1962, appeared on the threshold of pulling off a second and even more spectacular financial *coup de grâce*.

There were problems, unseen and unimagined in their magnitude, however, lurking in the shadows of Wall Street.

## Black Tuesday, October 29, 1929,
## Blue Monday, May 28, 1962.

On Monday morning, May 28, 1962, Eddie Gilbert left his motel room in Carson City, Nevada, and went into town to dictate some letters to the stenographer whose services he had been using on a part-time basis during his self-imposed exile there. Just one week remained now to fulfill the six-week residency required in Nevada to clear the way for him to file for a divorce from Rhoda in that state. He could hardly wait.

But when he returned to his motel room later in the morning, that personal part of his life would radically shrink in significance because of events unfolding on Wall Street that day. As he unlocked the door to his room, the telephone was ringing. He hurried to it. On the other end was Francis Farr, his stock broker with McDonnell and Co. in New York.

"I've been trying to get you for the last hour," Farr said. "Where the hell have you been?"

"In town, some business things. What's up?"

"Nothing's up.... Everything's down. And I'm not trying to be funny. You haven't been tracking the market today, I take it?"

Gilbert said he had not, so by the time Francis Farr had finally managed to reach him, Eddie was unaware that Wall Street was in chaos.

The market had been performing poorly all year. The Dow-Jones Industrials average, slipping from a high of just over 726 in January of 1962, tracked a continuing descent over the next five months to the closing bell on Friday, May 25, and had dropped by nearly 16 percent to 612. The steepest decline in this bear market occurred the week of May 21–25, posting a

38.8 point loss in the Dow-Jones, or a drop of nearly 4.2 percent. Robert Sobel's noted book on the history of American stock market disasters, *Panic on Wall Street*, reports that "The value of all listed stocks on the New York Stock Exchange had declined $30 billion, more than the combined gross national products of Australia, Sweden, and Ireland." It was, in fact, the sharpest drop in the American stock market since the Great Stock Market Crash of 1929, which had catapaulted the world into the Great Depression of the 1930s.

At week's end, E. L. Bruce Company shares were trading on the American Stock Exchange at 32⅜, having lost just three-quarters of a point during that bleak week on Wall Street (although its price was down 5¼ points from its year-high of 37⅝). But Celotex, trading on the New York Stock Exchange, had not fared as well during the week. It suffered a 3¼ point loss, sinking to 31 on the New York Exchange at the close on Friday, down more than 25 percent from its 42⅜ high during the year.

Eddie Gilbert was worried, very worried, after reading Friday's closing quotations. Later, he recalled, "I could sense things were going to continue downward, that we hadn't heard the last of it on Friday. And I also had this kind of premonition that something bad would happen the next week, and I would be squeezed." Although he was worried, he felt that his situation would still be manageable. His feelings were tempered, he reminisced years afterwards, by optimism: "Things were going to get worse before they got better, but they *would* get better."

Over the weekend, the nation's newspapers reported a flurry of depressing stories about the stock markets. Although there was surely some dread in the investment world, it was a kind of disappointment rather than shock; strangely enough, the prevailing feeling among investors and market analysts was "let's wait and see."

But there was a lot of speculation nonetheless. Burton Crane, writing in a front page article for the Sunday *New York Times*, wondered: "Is this a mere forecast of a downturn in the business cycle that now seems likely in the third quarter? Is it a mere adjustment of glamour stocks that have lost their appeal, with other stocks hurt merely because they happened to be around? Or is the blow-off a complete correction of the speculative excesses that engulfed the market between 1953 and 1959?" No one, of course, could answer Mr. Crane's rhetorical questions that weekend.

Another article in the *Times*, written by financial journalist John Forrest, made the point: "One encouraging aspect in the market's dismal performance has been the absence of panic selling among investors." And Keith Funston, president of the New York Stock Exchange, corroborated that fact when noting that, "Investors are not panicking... what we are witnessing is a considerable dimunition of their confidence [in the market]." And American Stock Exchange chief, Edwin Posner, similarly suggested that the stark downturn of recent days was nothing more than an adjustment that was taking place in the market as stocks were retreating to what he termed "realistic levels."

Robert Sobel also makes the point that Wall Street's reaction seemed pretty restrained: "For many Americans, the decline of May 20–25 was a new experience.... But one of the most striking elements of the 1962 crash was the almost total lack of panic. To be sure, those who held stock were unhappy at seeing values melt almost overnight, but they remained calm in the face of it.

"The reasons for this calm were not hard to find. Unlike 1929, the banking system was sound; corporations were secure; the government's role as a guarantor of the economy was not in doubt. Stock declines might cause investors to lose money, but margin calls were unlikely, since stocks were usually purchased for cash in 1962 or, at most, on 80 percent margin. Thus, many investors watched the decline with as much fascination as fear, with more interest than panic."

But one thing investors to whom Mr. Sobel was referring failed to take into consideration, something that surely would have diminished their fascination and perhaps fueled their fear, was that after the crash of 1929, the market had not regained its pre-crash high until 1955, 26 years later.

The *Dow-Jones News Service*, in a seeming effort to shore up confidence in the critically ill market, suggested, "Should the industrial average be able to hold around the 610 level, brokers say the dramatic effect alone may prove of near-term help to the market generally."

All told, a surprising, almost reassuring sense of calm prevailed.

Such sentiments — cautious concern and subordination of panic — had so much governed his thinking that Eddie Gilbert had just gone about tending to his business correspondence in Carson City. He was clearly out of touch with what was going on that morning on Wall Street. The calm that everyone felt over the weekend before what would come to be called "Blue Monday," proved indeed to be the proverbial calm before the storm.

Stock prices began to tumble as soon as the market opened. "Yet the atmosphere of panic was still missing," Robert Sobel reported. "Not even when stocks fell from the opening, or when the ticker began to run late after the first half-hour of trading, did the note of fear appear." But by noon, New York time (just as Eddie Gilbert was sitting down to begin dictating his letters at nine Pacific Coast time), the Dow-Jones average on unusually heavy trading had nose-dived below 610, the critical maintenance level that *Dow-Jones* had cited, and it was about to dip below 600. According to Mr. Sobel, "Every group participated in the fall, with the glamours leading the way. The ticker was unable to keep up with the rush and began sending out 'flash prices' of 30 key stocks as early as 10:20 A.M.; at noon, even these had to be dispensed with by the frantic ticker operators. By then, the would-be seller had no idea of current buy-sell prices for his stock, since the ticker was almost an hour late. Floor brokers stuffed orders in their pockets, hoping to fill them whenever possible. In many cases, these orders were simply forgotten.

"The stock-market crash was headline news by noon."

Farr telephoned the grim news to a stunned Eddie Gilbert in specific terms: Bruce stock had plummeted from 32⅜ to 23 in a 15-minute period that morning; and Celotex had similarly dropped from 31 to 25. "It's as big a crash as the one in '29, as I see it," Farr said. "I don't know how far it's going, but it's bad, Eddie. It's very bad."

In his deposition later filed with the United States District Court, Southern District of New York (February 23, 1967), Gilbert described his reaction. "I thought he must be joking, because it didn't sound logical that Bruce could drop nine-and-a-half points or so in a matter of ten or fifteen minutes, which was almost one-third of its value. I started to figure out on a piece of paper, and found that I had lost over $9 million on paper in that short period of time. This put me in an absolute state of shock, and not believing the broker, I called another broker on the phone to verify whether or not he [Francis Farr] was joking with me, because I thought it probably could have been a practical joke."

But it was not a joke, Gilbert's friend and sometime stock-broker Geist Ely confirmed on the telephone only minutes later. The market was in the throes of a real crash.

Eddie called Francis Farr back. "What do you think we should do?" he asked.

"It doesn't look like there's anything that can be done," Farr told him. "Things look very bad right now, and we'll just have to wait and see where it all settles."

Gilbert later explained in court, "I put the phone down and was absolutely shaken. I didn't know what I was going to do. But I knew margin calls would be coming very shortly, as I didn't think the banks or financial operations that had my stock would sit still for this kind of a drop without demanding additional funds. [After the market closed] I sat and thought as to what I might possibly do to shore up my situation. The thought occurred to me that I might buy additional shares to shore up the market and restore my margins by buying sufficient shares, which would bring the market back to the price it was at previously. However, my courage had left me, and I didn't feel like complicating my situation should I buy additional shares and then, after buying them, have the market drop again, if it really was a crash, in effect, and have these ... sums of money to cover in addition to the previous margins that would have been required of me, so I decided to try to just cover the margins ... as best I could."

Eddie calculated that he had somewhere between $200,000 and $300,000 cash in his own bank accounts, but this would be far short of what he would need to cover the inevitable margin calls. The rest of his wealth was tied up in real estate, art and antiques, his stamp collection, and other similarly illiquid assets. Although he did not have hard totals, he figured the margin calls could range from at least a million dollars to several million.

When the frantic market finally closed on Blue Monday, the Dow-Jones Industrial average had lost nearly 35 points, closing at 576.93, a drop of 5.7 percent. The lead sentence of the front page story in the *Times* virtually shouted, "Shares on the New York Stock Exchange lost $20,800,000,000 of values yesterday in the widest one-day drop since 1929." On the New York Stock Exchange, 9,350,000 shares had been traded, making it the fifth most active day in market history, the record having been set on "Black Tuesday," October 29, 1929, when 16,410,030 shares were traded. The American Stock Exchange suffered an even larger loss, 6.3 percent on a volume of 2,980,000 shares traded.

Almost all stocks shared in the horror of the day. Of the record total of 1,375 issues that traded, 1,212 declined, the largest number ever to fall on one day. Several of note: IBM lost 37½ points, closing at 361; A.T. & T. dropped 11 points to 100⅝; and General Motors ended the session at 48⅞, losing 4⅝. Closer to home for Eddie Gilbert, shares in the E. L. Bruce Company closed at 23, down 9⅜, a drop of nearly 29 percent; and Celotex fell 6 points to 25, a loss of a little more than 19 percent.

The *Times* further reported that Western European stock markets were also sharply lower and that financial institutions in those countries, especially Switzerland, were reacting swiftly and forcefully. "Reports of margin calls there echoed here," the *Times* noted, "and banks ... were said to be forcing the sale of stocks.... Brokers were asking cash from under-margined customers.... Throughout the day brokers talked of margin selling. Some of this selling came from Europe, where brokers give more generous credit than is permitted stock exchange members here [the margin being 50 percent in Switzerland, where Eddie had borrowed liberally, as compared with the 70 percent restriction fixed by the Federal Reserve Board]."

After he had finished talking with Francis Farr, Eddie called Irwin Polivy at the Bruce offices in New York. Polivy, the corporate secretary and Gilbert's right-hand man in the company, was aware of the Wall Street bloodbath that day but not entirely aware of how catastrophic its effects were on Gilbert. He quickly learned that, however. Eddie explained the situation: the impending margin calls and the need to protect their position. He then asked Polivy what cash Bruce had on hand in their banks. Polivy checked the books and said, "Somewhere in the vicinity of three million two hundred thousand."

"Irwin, do you think that we could cover these margins from Bruce?" Eddie asked him.

"I don't see why not," Polivy replied.

Gilbert's deposition to the U.S. District Court records, "I told him that we must under any circumstances cover the margins and avoid being sold out and that he should take whatever sums were necessary and pay the margins from the Bruce company." And Polivy agreed.

Irwin Polivy was there to carry out what the company's president told him to do, nothing more. He did not raise the question of its legality; he may not even have been aware of whether that should have been asked. He had no opinions as to alternatives (neither did Eddie Gilbert), but he knew their company was in a crisis and that drastic action had to be taken to avoid disaster.

"When I get back [to New York] I'll straighten it out," Eddie told Polivy. And, clinging to an unfailing optimism, he added, "Let's hope that this is a temporary drop in the market and that the market will go back up again and I will just get my margins back again."

Two factors governed Gilbert's thinking at that moment: The first was that, even given the worst scenario, he felt that he could still scramble, finesse, call in favors, whatever it took, to raise enough money back in New York to replace what would be borrowed from the company's treasury. And secondly, he did not consider what he was doing as *wrong* (as it was from a strictly legal perspective). He knew he would need the board's authorization to loan the money to meet his margin calls. After all, this was not the first time Eddie Gilbert had looked to the Bruce coffers for an advance or a loan for business purposes. On a couple of occasions over the previous three or four years, he had used corporate funds without prior authorization for the sake of expediency, and authorization from his board of directors had always followed without any note of concern from his board. As far as Gilbert was concerned, the present borrowing was not unusual. It was on record, in fact, that during Empire Millwork's takeover of the Bruce company several years earlier, Eddie had called upon company funds without authorization so as to facilitate the merger that was in the best interests of both companies. In that case, the funds were duly restored with subsequent board approval being nothing more than *pro forma,* because the directors trusted Gilbert's actions on behalf of the company.

By four o'clock in the afternoon Nevada time, Gilbert finished talking with Irwin Polivy by phone; and then the telephone calls began coming to him. First was Abdullah Zilkha of the Swiss banking firm Ufitec. S.A. in Zurich. He sounded upset and distinctly unfriendly and got right to the point: He wanted $300,000, and if he did not receive the cash pay-down he would sell Gilbert out.

As Eddie recalls, "I remember saying to him: Let's wait until tomorrow and see if this is a temporary drop... if the margin call is really required." Zilkha said he could not do that. In light of what was happening on Wall Street, the Swiss banks would not hold, and therefore he could not hold. Although Zilkha appeared to be implacable, Eddie pleaded and cajoled and got him to agree to do nothing with Gilbert's stock until noon the following day, New York time. He wanted to buy an extra day's time to see if the market would turn upward the next day, perhaps returning to a respectable enough level to preclude the margin calls. And if it did not, he now knew he could call on funds from Bruce to get Zilkha off his back. Nevertheless, the Swiss financier would call several more times before daybreak in Nevada.

Gilbert received a second call, this one from Armand Boller, another Swiss banker associated with the Societe Anonyme Financiere Ficomer, headquartered in Geneva. For him it was much the same as it had been for Zilkha. Boller required a pay-down of several hundred thousand dollars or he also would be forced to sell Gilbert's stock. Boller's demand was especially distressing to Eddie because the relationship he had with Armand Boller was personal as well as financial and included stays at Gilbert's villa in the south of France as well as other European vacations together over the prior two years. But by the end of his telephone conversation with Boller, Eddie knew that he was dead wrong to count on their personal relationship to help him through this crisis.

Another friend, Jacques Sarlie, called from New York. Sarlie was a wealthy, 47-year-old independent investor who had presumably spent more than $750,000 buying both Bruce and Celotex shares for Gilbert. In his District Court deposition later, Eddie stated: "I would like to put on the record that I considered Sarlie a friend and a man of integrity, and therefore what the two of us said [on the telephone the evening of Blue Monday, May 28, 1962] was said on the basis of dealing with a man who I considered to have honest intentions." The conversation to which Gilbert refers here, went like this:

"Jack, what do you think we should do?" Eddie asked. "This is very serious, and I'm afraid I won't be able to manage all these margin calls. Do you think that we can hold on?"

Sarlie's reply was: "If you have the money, we can hold on."

Eddie said, "How much do you require?" Gilbert then answered the question himself in his deposition, "I believe he told me approximately a half a million dollars would shore up his positions so that he could hold onto the shares which he had."

But as it turned out later, Sarlie did *not* have the shares—at least he had not paid for them. According to his brokerage house, McDonnell and Co. (one that Eddie Gilbert commonly used also), Sarlie had ordered 17,800 shares of Bruce stock and another 11,700 shares of Celotex, but he had not paid for them. After Gilbert later fled the United States for Brazil, Sarlie also left for Paris without resolving his unsettled account for the stock purchases that the McDonnell Company claimed he had not paid. The brokerage firm brought suit against Sarlie later in the year, filing a warrant of attachment against Sarlie which "seeks to collect $754,000 as payment for the Bruce and Celotex stock he had purchased in connection with the fight for control of Bruce." Acting for the plaintiff, the McDonnell Company's attorney contended that Mr. Sarlie had fled to Paris where he remained out of touch from his creditors and other business associates in order "to defraud creditors." Sarlie denied the allegation, claiming that "all during my stay in Europe I was in full communication with my office, the plaintiff, and others." This assertion was news to the McDonnell firm, who claimed that they had "made repeated attempts to contact Sarlie [during that period of time], directly and through his office in New York, all of which went unanswered and unacknowledged." For his defense, Sarlie also stated unequivocally that he had never authorized the purchase of the stock and was quoted in a *New York Times* article claiming that "he had never been associated with Edward M. Gilbert in the fight for control of Celotex." Gilbert would have been shocked by this claim as he talked with Sarlie by phone that night in May 1962, but Sarlie's perspective would not become known to Gilbert until long after Eddie had sent a lot of money to Sarlie's account to maintain his "position."

The New York State Supreme Court concluded, however, that the McDonnell company had not made its case, ruling against the brokerage house and vacating the warrant of attachment against Sarlie. In rejecting the claim, Judge Arthur G. Klein noted in his opinion, "In the light of the factual proof submitted by Mr. Sarlie, the plaintiff's papers are woefully insufficient to indicate that the defendant's departure from the state was with the intent of defrauding creditors or to avoid service of process." He also declared that the plaintiff failed to demonstrate that "Mr. Sarlie had assigned or secreted property with the intent of defrauding creditors."

Several years later, the Bruce company would have to file suit against Sarlie to recover Bruce's funds that Gilbert sent to repay purchases of stock that Sarlie did not own. All Eddie knew that Blue Monday night 1962 when the two talked by long-distance telephone was that he would have to come up with a large sum of money to keep Sarlie from unloading his sizable positions in Bruce and Celotex.

The calls continued to come all night long. "Zilkha called a number of times," Eddie remembers. "Each time it was the same thing: 'What are we going to do now? What are *you* going to do about this?' He kept asking the same questions. I didn't sleep one wink that night, not from worry either; it was from a combination of worry and the telephone calls coming in all night long. I got a telephone call at four in the morning, I remember, another at five in the morning. You see, in Switzerland at ten in the morning it's only four in the morning in New York [or one in the morning in Carson City, Nevada], and I got calls from the time they woke up … until right on through until ten in the morning [Carson City time]." All those callers, coming down hard on Gilbert that gloomy night, agreed nonetheless to wait one more day, or at least until noon the next day.

There was one exception to the telephone gloom and doom. It was, in fact, the last call from Switzerland that Eddie received that night, from Trevor Salathe of the Bank Privée in Zurich. "It was about six in the morning," Eddie remembers. "I sighed in a kind of despair when I answered the phone. I thought he was going to ask me for a lot of money because I had a lot of securities with him." But Salathe did not. "He didn't require anything. He just said: 'Take care of whatever you have to take care of and forget about us.' Salathe was a perfect gentleman that morning. He said to me, 'Eddie, I want to help.'" The paradox of Trevor Salathe's reassurance was that he and the Swiss Bank Privée stood to lose more than any of the firms circling Gilbert that night.

The next morning Eddie also heard from his good friend, Jerry Stern in New York, who had been buying shares in Celotex to help Gilbert. Stern's business, Jerome International, had its position to hold onto, and so he wanted to find out how bad Eddie felt the situation was. Gilbert's later deposition records, "Jerry Stern was a very close personal friend of mine and certainly was not one of the people who wanted to hurt me. He was more or less like Salathe, except that he did tell me he had to have some, any small amount, to help shore up his positions, if I could. But he was not pressuring me as these other people were." It turned out that Stern wanted $55,000; Gilbert directed Irwin Polivy to draw a check for that amount on the account of Empire Hardwood, his solely owned company through which Eddie carried out some of his personal business deals.

To appreciate how enormous was the economic impact of the market's collapse on Monday, May 28, 1962, one had only to look to the White

House. Early on Tuesday morning, President John F. Kennedy called an emergency session of his top economic advisers: Walter Heller, chairman of the President's Council of Economic Advisors; William McChesney Martin, Jr., Federal Reserve chairman; and several cabinet members, including Treasury Secretary C. Douglas Dillon, Commerce Secretary Luther Hodges, and Labor Secretary Arthur Goldberg. Although Kennedy chose not to address the public formally nor even to hold a news conference following the session, it was made clear that the Wall Street collapse was of utmost importance in and around 1600 Pennsylvania Avenue. The only official word from the Executive branch was that no special government action was anticipated at the time. News media sensed that the pervasive feeling coming from the White House was that the sharp market decline, and Monday's nose-dive in particular, was no more than a dramatic reaction to overvalued stock prices, given existing and prospective economic conditions. Kennedy's chief economic adviser Walter Heller called it "a disturbing correction." Treasury Secretary Dillon said, "Business conditions are very sound, and there is no justification for panic selling of stocks"; adding that "at the present time, federal government intercession is unnecessary." Commerce Secretary Hodges told reporters after the White House meeting, however, that he favored "some swift governmental action in order to stimulate economic activity," suggesting an overhaul of existing tax laws so as to cut personal and corporate income tax rates and to liberalize write-off allowances for business taxpayers.

Even though people everywhere were taking sides — in the cabinet, on Capitol Hill, on Wall Street, in corporate boardrooms, and in the minds of investors nationwide — the government's agencies and the Executive Office were nearly unanimous in their optimism about a rebound in the stock market. On his way to Middleburg, Virginia, later that morning for a family celebration of his 45th birthday, President Kennedy expressed his concern about the temporary situation but restated his faith in the strength of the nation's economy. Like so many others, the president also clung to a "wait and see" attitude.

On Wall Street though, analysts and brokers had wide-ranging opinions. The *New York Times* reported, "There were some optimists. One such analyst said, 'This is the climax for which we have been waiting. There will be a tremendous rally Tuesday or Thursday' [Wednesday was Memorial Day when the markets would be closed].

"There were the pessimists, who brushed 30 years of the semantics that have changed 'slump' to 'depression' to 'recession' and revived the old word 'panic.'

"'This is panic selling and we shall probably see more tomorrow,' said one research partner. 'We are in a full-fledged panic now,' said a senior partner. 'The bottom is likely to come Tuesday morning.'"

Well, the optimists were correct, at least as to how trading went on Tuesday, May 29, 1962. The stock market rallied with gusto. A total of 14,750,000 shares were traded—5,400,000 more than during the previous day's descent and the second largest volume since Black Tuesday 1929—and the market reversed its six-day downslide: The Dow-Jones Industrials Average rose 27.03 points, or 4.7 percent; 60 percent of market losses on Blue Monday were recouped in Tuesday's trading. According to Standard and Poor's, Tuesday's market numbers regained $13,500,000,000 of the $20,800,000,000 lost in the previous day's trading. A record 1,399 issues had traded, of which there were 630 gainers, 637 losers, and 132 issues unchanged.

The reason for the rally, according to the *New York Times*, was four-fold: (1) Three of the largest brokerage houses sent out highly optimistic recommendations to buy. (2) Washington news was encouraging. (3) Institutions were reported to be buying. (4) Leading corporations were said to be investing their plentiful cash to repurchase their own shares.

But the Tuesday rally was of no solace to Eddie Gilbert, having little bearing on his own and the Bruce company's market position: Bruce shares gained 5⅜ in the day's trading to close at 28⅜, but the price was still down four points below its previous trading level. And Celotex lost another quarter of a point, dropping to 24¾ on Tuesday.

Gilbert spent the whole morning on the telephone from his Carson City motel room; it was a very depressing situation. "The stocks came back to $28 per share," Gilbert later testified, "which partially mitigated some of the tremendous drop that had taken place previously.... Everybody's confidence was shaken...and even though it [the stock market] went back [up] they all wanted the margin anyway. They were very nervous." Gilbert went over in detail with Irwin Polivy the margin calls coming in. Polivy agreed to cover the margins by withdrawing funds from the Bruce treasury, issuing checks to Rhodes Enterprises, Inc., and Empire Hardwood Flooring Corporation, two companies under Gilbert's sole control; other checks would then be issued to mollify Gilbert's creditors. He again explained by phone to each of his major creditors—Zilkha, Boller, Sarlie, *et al.*—that he would send the required checks, further instructing them to hold their positions with his stock. And the calls kept coming, from all over. "[When] they called me, I said, 'Call Polivy, go over the figures,' because Polivy is an accountant... and he knows the facts, and he knew the figures. He had all of my books in New York." And by the end of that long Tuesday, nearly $2 million had been withdrawn from the Bruce treasury with checks sent on their way to satisfy the flood of margin calls.

On that same day, Gilbert concluded that he had to end his residency in Nevada; the divorce from Rhoda would have to wait. It was essential that he return to New York. He reserved a seat on a flight out of Las Vegas to New York for the following day, which was Memorial Day, conveniently affording him 24 hours of breathing room since the markets were closed for the legal holiday. He reserved a room at The Sands Hotel, an old haunt of his in Las Vegas; and then made hasty arrangements to get from Carson City to Reno for the 375-mile commuter flight to Las Vegas.

Once back in New York, Gilbert checked into a suite at the Waldorf Astoria, spending an uneasy night there. On Thursday he planned to divide his time between raising money on his own and satisfying the relentless parade of creditors marching in on him. The sweet dream of a merged Bruce and Celotex conglomerate, worth in excess of $100 million, had now given way to his struggle to avoid bankruptcy. He also had to concentrate on choreographing his tap dance with Irwin Polivy which might lead either to financial rescue or to a great deal of legal trouble.

So first thing Thursday morning, Gilbert began to search out what he could come up with in cash. Then the most devastating bombshell fell: André Meyer, senior partner in the venerable investment firm of Lazard Frères, was holding more than $2 million of Eddie Gilbert's cash, which he believed he could call upon if things became desperate. But Meyer was in a position to prevent that.

In 1961, Meyer had encouraged Gilbert to continue to acquire Celotex stock on his own, reassuring him of Lazard Frères' backing and his own. Now later, with Gilbert extended in his quest to acquire Celotex and Lazard Frères not having begun to purchase its promised Celotex shares, Meyer surprised Gilbert by saying that he had to redeem half of the $2 million debenture he had purchased before he could feel comfortable in going forward with the Celotex deal. But because the price of Bruce common shares had doubled in value since 1960, the "half" of the debenture Meyer now wanted to redeem had a price tag of $2 million. Because Gilbert did not want anything to impede the Celotex takeover, he saw to it that Meyer's demand was met. He secured a $2 million loan from the Union Planters Bank in Memphis and then turned the proceeds over to Meyer and Lazard Frères so as to redeem the half of the outstanding debentures.

By March 1962, Meyer had acquired 87,000 shares of Celotex, with a promise to buy an additional 163,000. Aware that Gilbert was heavily invested personally and totally committed to having the merger happen, Meyer swooped down again. He told Gilbert that for him to buy those 163,000 shares, the remaining half of the 1960 convertible debenture had to be redeemed. It would cost Gilbert a further $2 million.

Eddie had to comply with this demand since he was getting close to consummating the merger and needed Meyer to resume his promised purchases of Celotex. For the redemption now, Eddie approached Trevor Salathe at the Bank Privée in Switzerland to arrange for the $2 million demanded, half from a personal account he had at the bank and the other half borrowed against his line of credit. The funds were to be held in escrow at a New York bank for Meyer's eventual withdrawal, no earlier than the first week in June 1962.

The day after Memorial Day, on May 31, Eddie Gilbert was in the tightest financial squeeze of his life. He telephoned Michel David-Weill (whom he now considered a friend after several years of socializing together in New York and in the south of France at their respective family residences there). Eddie explained the situation, hoping Michel, through Lazard Frères, could purchase some of his Celotex shares or lend him the money so as to generate funds he so desperately needed to meet the rush of margin calls. David-Weill agreed to discuss the matter with André Meyer.

Gilbert had tried to reach Meyer directly, but the financier had not returned any of the telephone calls. When David-Weill called back, he told Gilbert that there was no way they could presently help him; Meyer had said so himself, according to Michel. Eddie was shaken, but replied, "Well, if you can't help me, please don't hurt me." He asked simply that Meyer and Lazard Frères at least release the $2 million held in escrow so that Eddie could avoid catastrophe. After all, the convertible debenture was still good, and for the second "half" Meyer was still protected. Meyer and Lazard Frères did not require the funds immediately, whereas Eddie did.

"This will kill me, if he calls in that money," Eddie told David-Weill. "Please talk to him for me." David-Weill said he would, and he did. But Meyer was unyielding. And he continued to ignore Gilbert's telephone calls.

Then, the first week in June, Meyer withdrew the $2 million from escrow. It was a disastrous blow to Gilbert's financial position, and it came at the absolutely worst possible time.

Gilbert felt entirely betrayed by Meyer and, according to Meyer's biographer, "brooded upon the unfairness of it all . . . [viewing Meyer as someone who had] helped him hatch the Celotex scheme, who had agreed to bankroll it, and who had then pulled the rug out from under him. Someone who had left him dangling as the margin calls closed in and who had then hidden himself behind an impregnable wall of wealth and power."

As devastating as Meyer's action was, Gilbert did not entirely lack resources. After meeting the payment to Lazard Frères, he had nearly $250,000 in personal bank accounts. And calling upon personal lines of credit at New York banks, he managed to line up an additional $250,000. With that ready cash, Gilbert could deal with creditors who had not already been issued checks by Irwin Polivy from Bruce's funds.

Abdullah Zilkha, dissatisfied with the amount forwarded to him, flew over from Switzerland and was the first to appear at Eddie's hotel room demanding additional money. He got his check and left. It was a very hectic day: ". . . a parade of all of the bankers started to pour into my room on the 31st floor at the Waldorf Astoria," Gilbert later recalled. "From about 11 o'clock in the morning, I handed out checks." When it was finally over, most of the $500,000 or so of Gilbert's personal funds had been exhausted, and $1,958,000 had been withdrawn from the Bruce treasury. Five thousand dollars would later be returned, reducing the later calculation to the $1.953 million figure cited in the Bruce audit and in governmental indictments. The major creditors included Financiere Du Mont-Blanc, Geneva, Switzerland; Societe Anonyme Financiere Ficomer, Geneva, Switzerland; Ufitec, S.A., Zurich, Switzerland; Joseph Danon and Cie., Paris, France; Jerome International Corporation, New York; Dutch American Mercantile Company, New York; and Jacques Sarlie, New York.

Thus Eddie Gilbert began to rescue the position of his company. As he later explained in his deposition, "Had I not covered these margins with these checks, the Bruce company would have suffered insurmountable damage, because they had a large position in Celotex themselves, totaling over $3 million [the Bruce company held 77,300 shares of Celotex], and all of the stockholders of Bruce would also have suffered because the stock would have plummeted had I been sold out of my Celotex and Bruce shares." Besides taking care of his company, he would have to replace funds withdrawn from Bruce to avoid legal problems down the road.

On Monday, June 4, Eddie contacted Paul Millstein, a longtime acquaintance associated with the Ruberoid Company, another building materials firm that specialized in asphalt roofing shingles and floor tiles. Eddie had learned that Ruberoid was also interested in acquiring or investing substantially in Celotex. Paul Millstein's brother, Seymour, was the executive vice president of Ruberoid; so Gilbert telephoned Paul to ask about Ruberoid's possible acquisition of the large Celotex position Gilbert and his friends controlled. It was the most expeditious and only viable alternative he had, Gilbert later admitted. There was very little time. Eddie knew he would soon have to inform his board of directors about the actions he had taken without their authorization.

Shortly thereafter, Eddie finally got a bit of good news. Paul Millstein reported to Eddie on Monday night that his brother Seymour and Ruberoid were seriously interested in acquiring a major position in Celotex stock. On Tuesday, Eddie learned directly from Ruberoid officials that the company was indeed looking to buy a substantial block of stock—as many as 350,000 shares, according to the Millstein brothers in a subsequent conversation. While such an acquistion would not extract Eddie Gilbert from the jaws of personal bankruptcy, it might bail out Bruce and the many friends and business associates who had acquired Celotex stock at Eddie's behest; most importantly, it would permit him to replace the borrowed funds, or at least most of them.

The first person within Bruce to learn of Eddie Gilbert's use of of corporate funds was, not surprisingly, Harry Gilbert. But Eddie had also confided in Bruce's attorneys at Shearman and Sterling two days earlier, informing them of his use of company funds (without going into any specific detail). He believed he now had to make the company aware of what he had done. The last thing in the world he wanted was for his board of directors to learn about it from someone else.

Late on the Thursday afternoon, June 7, 1962, Harry had just returned to New York from a trip to a company plant in Muscatine, Iowa. "[Eddie] came to me, and he said he had withdrawn a large sum of money. And I asked him how much," Harry later explained at a hearing before the Securities and Exchange Commission in New York. When Eddie said it was somewhere in the vicinity of "a million eight or nine," his father was flabbergasted and "angry as hell," but he remained composed. "He wasn't sure because [it] was so damn much—I think it was five or six checks that he had taken to make this total," Harry stated at the SEC hearing. "He said the market had gone against him; and unless he got up this money, they would have sold out Celotex and Bruce and it would have affected him and the corporation and everybody else." When asked his reaction at the time, Harry responded, "What would any human being say to a son who takes a million nine. You give him hell. You raise hell. You are just ready to commit suicide. What the hell can you do? It is the big shock of my life."

According to Harry, he then asked his son, "Can you return it? Put it back?" He remembered Eddie shrugged and then told him, "No. If the market keeps going this way, I'm broke. I haven't got a dime, and I can't put it back."

After talking with his father, they agreed that Eddie should call one of Bruce's attorneys, Robert N. West, a senior partner at Shearman and Sterling, in lower Manhattan. Bob West had also just returned from a business trip to San Francisco, where he had first learned two days earlier about Eddie's unauthorized withdrawal of Bruce funds. "By hearsay," West explained, "I think my partner [George] Dillon first learned of this thing sometime... late on Tuesday [June 5] from Mr. Gilbert because I got to San Francisco... Tuesday evening and... my recollection is that he [Dillon] telephoned me... and told me this."

On the afternoon of Thursday, the 7th of June, the two men finally linked up by telephone, and both agreed that too much was at stake for them to deal with the matter on the telephone. Eddie agreed that he would come to meet with West and his partners in person. Moments after hanging up the phone, Eddie and Harry Gilbert left for the Shearman and Sterling office; once there, Eddie listened to West describe the seriousness of the situation as "a firestorm." While Eddie knew only too well now what his problems were, he explained he had one resource perhaps to pull the whole thing out of the fire. He explained that Ruberoid officials might be interested in purchasing the 350,000-share block of Celotex owned or controlled by Gilbert and the Bruce company. That amount represented approximately one-third of Celotex's outstanding common shares.

Harry Gilbert asked West to call the Ruberoid people; the two Gilberts and Seymour Millstein were also on the conference call. Millstein confirmed Ruberoid's interest. As Harry Gilbert later testified before the SEC, "the price was set at $36 [per share], contingent upon their board and our board approving it."

It was hardly the solution that Eddie Gilbert wanted, as they would lose Celotex and Eddie would lose his dream; but it was the only viable way out at the moment. And Eddie admitted that even if the Ruberoid purchase of Celotex were consummated, he would not be completely off the hook or out of the firestorm. Even after such a sale, Harry Gilbert said, "[Eddie] would have had an equity in that stock of about a million one or two hundred thousand, so he would have still owed some money to the firm."

West asked Eddie what would happen if the Ruberoid deal did *not* go through. Did he have the money to replenish the Bruce treasury, replacing the entire $1.953 million? Gilbert explained how André Meyer and Lazard Frères had refused to help and had taken his escrowed funds for the firm's debenture. The way in which Eddie later described it was less diplomatic, according to Meyer biographer Cary Reich. Eddie is quoted: "'My dear boy,' that's what he used to call me... that son of a bitch. He put his arm around me and squeezed my balls off at the same time."

The Shearman and Sterling lawyers, however, came up with a strategy to cover any discrepancies, whether or not the Ruberoid deal materialized. It would be addressed the following day.

Everyone at the meeting also agreed further that an emergency board of directors' meeting at Bruce should be called to deal with the situation, and the following Tuesday, June 12, 1962, was selected. It would take several days to get all the directors to New York. Chairman Edwin L. Bruce, Jr., was as at the Bruce offices in Memphis, Harry reminded them, and so were Frank O'Connor, Harvey Creech, and Evan Fellman. Others might well be out of town also, so telegrams would have to be sent to each of them the next morning.

On Friday morning, Eddie Gilbert returned alone to West's office. Facing him was a last and desperate act and a most costly one personally. He was there to pledge the majority of his personal holdings. As West later testified, "We secured from Edward Gilbert collateral promissory notes to the order of the Bruce Corporation in the amounts of his respective withdrawals, dated as of the dates of the respective withdrawals together with a general assignment of all Mr. Gilbert's property, specifically including his interest in the Bruce corporation, Celotex Corporation, his real property on the French Riviera, his collections of paintings, his stamp collection and, generally, all his other property and assets." This was to be an important commitment, later.

The real estate specified in the schedule collateralizing the promissory notes included Eddie's house and land known as *Villa del Mare* at Roquebrune, Cap Martin, on the French Riviera; his town house on East 70th Street in New York; and another parcel of land in Bucks County, Pennsylvania. Financial assets included 334,991 shares of common stock in the E. L. Bruce Company; 149,000 shares of common stock in Celotex Corporation; and the $2 million principal amount of convertible debentures of the Bruce company which he had bought back from Lazard Frères. There were also a number of other smaller stock holdings and whatever cash remained in his personal bank accounts. Gilbert had purchased works of art for an aggregate total of $476,750, but they were conservatively evaluated at $2 million. Gilbert's stamp collection, also pledged, was valued at approximately $1 million. And lastly, there were the French and Italian antique furnishings in his various residences.

E. L. Bruce, Jr., arrived from Memphis on Monday afternoon, accompanied by three other directors. Harry Gilbert picked them up at La Guardia Airport and drove the four to the Savoy Plaza Hotel. Riding back to Manhattan, Harry detailed the huge financial dilemma and also disclosed to them for the first time Eddie's negotiations with the Ruberoid Company. Later in the day, Eddie joined them at the Savoy Plaza, holding impromptu meetings first in Frank O'Connor's room and later in Harvey Creech's (even though Eddie added nothing new to what his father had told them earlier). Although he had not heard from Ruberoid, Eddie learned that they had hastily called a board of directors meeting, and so he remained optimistic.

Harry Gilbert reported that Mr. Bruce was "calm about the matter, although I'm sure he was deeply shocked by the situation." The fact of the matter was that E. L., Jr., had grown accustomed to Eddie's often rash and surprising actions since Empire had taken over the Bruce family's company. This was not the first time that E. L., Jr., had witnessed Gilbert's un-orthodoxy, but he liked Eddie Gilbert and where he had taken the company over the last four years. Although he had not always agreed with all of Eddie's methods, he later admitted that "they usually turned for the best in the long run. He had the knack for making things work out." Even on that Monday night E.L. seemed to believe that the present situation would probably be no different from previous occasions and would work itself out. But E.L. was certainly aware of just how serious the situation had become, and how much was at stake.

They talked about the Ruberoid possibility in detail. They also discussed how Eddie would make full restitution of the monies disbursed. And because Eddie had seemed pretty confident that evening that the Ruberoid bailout would happen, there was little talk of what would happen if it *didn't*. All had been informed that Eddie had earlier signed collateralized promissory notes in the offices of Shearman and Sterling.

Shortly after 10:30 Tuesday morning, Chairman of the Board, E. L. Bruce, Jr., called the meeting to order. Present were Harry Gilbert, chairman of the Executive Committee; Henry Loeb, senior partner of the Loeb-Rhoades investment house (who had brought along his own attorney John Cahill); and Frank O'Connor, Philippe Grelsamer, Norman Mason, Philip Weisberg, Evan Fellman, and Harvey Creech. Only Thomas Lenagh was absent. Bruce company officers, although not members of the board of directors, were also present: Secretary Irwin Polivy and Treasurer Vincent E. DeSousa. Attorney Robert N. West was there with his partner George Dillon, representing Eddie Gilbert; and Bethuel M. Webster and Frederick Sheffield attended as counsel for the Bruce company. Because of a feared conflict of interest, West's firm, Shearman and Sterling, who had earlier been chief counsel for Bruce, wished to represent Eddie Gilbert personally, and so asked the firm of Webster, Sheffield, Fleischman, Hitchcock and Chrystie to represent the Bruce company in this situation. As they seated themselves in the Bruce conference room that morning, all directors knew that Eddie had tapped the Bruce company treasury for $1.953 million: Harry Gilbert had contacted each of them personally beforehand to apprise them of that situation.

There were a few inconsequential matters the board first considered and quickly dispatched. But soon the discussion turned to the $1,953,000 borrowed without authorization from the Bruce bank accounts. Harry

Gilbert asked for a vote to ratify authorization of funds Eddie had withdrawn; he made the case that it had been in the best interests of the company because Eddie had done it to protect the company's position in the merger and its investment in Celotex (because the company owned 70,000 shares by that time). Harry later testified before the Securities and Exchange Commission: "It is my opinion, and I think a great many of the Board [that day], that he did this more for the good of the company than he did for himself, because if the market had gone to hell and all of this had strung to a point, Bruce would have taken a hell of a big licking in their holdings in the Celotex Company."

The board was not eager to take a voice vote so early, however. So Eddie Gilbert began to explain how a proposed stock sale had been discussed with Ruberoid officials, indicating their interest in purchasing a block of 350,000 shares at $36 per share. He had learned earlier that morning that Ruberoid's board was meeting on the subject that same morning, and their decision should be forthcoming soon. Should Ruberoid make the formal offer, the Bruce board of directors were universally in favor of it.

Then various directors questioned how Eddie Gilbert planned to restore monies that had been withdrawn from the Bruce treasury and paid to creditors, regardless if the Ruberoid deal did not come to fruition. Robert West arose to inform the directors of the promissory notes Gilbert had signed, pledging virtually all his personal assets against the $1.953 million. But after he passed out copies of the promissory notes, there was surprisingly little discussion about what they represented.

By 11:30, however, the tone of the meeting had begun to change. Accusations and unfriendly comments flew about the room. Some defended Gilbert, others suggested his immediate resignation. Some counseled caution and reserve, others recommended Bruce's immediate disclosure to the SEC and the U. S. Attorney's office. Through it all, Eddie Gilbert was in a daze because the meeting was not, as Bruce board of directors' meetings usually were, in *his* control. "It all kind of swirled around me," he later said. "I was not myself. I didn't react. I wasn't thinking clearly." It had got away from him. He knew that much.

But it was still unclear how any vote might go. Although Eddie's feeling was understandably pessimistic, in retrospect he believes that the outcome of a vote at that point in the morning might have gone either way.

Then came the fateful telephone call from Ruberoid. When it was announced that Ruberoid had decided *against* acquiring the block of Celotex stock, Eddie Gilbert knew it was all over and he was through.

The *coup de grace* came when Henry Loeb's attorney John Cahill took the floor and delivered a stinging denunciation of Gilbert's actions larded with dire warnings about the personal liability that each and every member of the board would have if they condoned his actions.

With outward calm but inner panic, Gilbert suggested that the meeting recess for lunch so as to give everyone a chance to reflect fully on the issues facing them before making any decisions. The motion was agreed to.

But Eddie had already made *his* decision.

He had no intention of having lunch during the break. Instead Eddie returned to his office; he told Grace, his personal secretary, to book him a first class seat on a flight that evening to Rio de Janeiro. He was taking the one alternative sheathed in desperation because he felt he had no other choice. He was going to Brazil, the country best known in 1962 for its rich coffee, rain forests, and the absence of an extradition treaty with the United States—to the city famous for its Carnival, Copocabana Beach, and American fugitives. Minutes later his secretary informed him that she was able to get him the last available seat on the last Varig Airlines flight that evening, which was scheduled to depart at 7:30 from Idlewild Airport (later known as Kennedy International).

Eddie then left the Bruce offices on Madison Avenue for the Waldorf Astoria Hotel on Park Avenue where he had maintained a suite during his estrangement from Rhoda. Days earlier, he had checked out of the hotel but he still had some money and other valuables in a safe deposit box there—in all, about $2,500 in cash and two rare Mauritius stamps from his collection, worth about $14,000. That represented his total liquidity on that moribund Tuesday afternoon—the same Eddie Gilbert whose net worth just a month earlier had been some $25 million.

Back at the office, he took a sheet of company letterhead and wrote in a bold script:

*June 12, 1962*

*I hereby resign as President and director of the
E. L. Bruce Co. and all subsidiary Corp.*

*— Edward M. Gilbert*

Eddie returned to the reconvened board meeting, told the directors that their vote would be unnecessary, and presented them with his hastily written letter of resignation.

Eddie asked only that they wait until eight o'clock that evening before publicly announcing his resignation. He still had one last resort from whom he might obtain the funds to reimburse Bruce its $1,953,000, he told them. But he did not; as far as he was concerned, he had run out of options. He was merely playing for time, fearing that if Bruce's announcement were made immediately, he might be prevented from boarding his flight to Rio. The directors agreed to wait until eight o'clock that evening.

Under the guidance of Bethuel Webster, acting as the Bruce lawyer, a resolution was then drafted and presented as a motion, formally accepting Gilbert's resignation and appointing E. L. Bruce, Jr., to replace him as president and chief executive officer. The resolution also called for the resignation of Irwin Polivy as company secretary and the appointment of Harvey Creech to replace him. The company's accounting firm, Peat, Marwick, Mitchell and Company, were to be notified and directed to make an immediate examination of the company's books and records. And last, it was resolved that "the proper officers of the Corporation be and they hereby are authorized and directed to inform the regional Office of the Securities and Exchange Commission, the American Stock Exchange, the Connecticut Mutual Life Insurance Company, and the Seaboard Security Company of the disclosures made to the meeting today." The resolution passed without dissent.

Eddie returned to his office and dictated a statement to his secretary for release to the press, radio, and television following the company's announcement of his resignation. It was brief and to the point:

The matters which were the subject of a public statement issued today by the E. L. Bruce Company were disclosed voluntarily by me.

I resigned as president and a director to permit the board to have a free hand to take such action with respect to those matters as it deemed advisable.

The actions I have taken were directed to the protection of an acqusition program on behalf of the corporation, and in my judgment were in the best interests of the corporation and its stockholders.

Eddie then gathered his cash, the two Mauritius stamps, and some personal papers in a briefcase and left the Bruce company offices for the last time. As he walked out the door of the familiar building at 660 Madison Avenue late that afternoon, a thin, steady rain persisted, and he without a raincoat or an umbrella. It seemed grimly appropriate, the way Eddie Gilbert's life had gone that fateful day.

After having composed the letter of resignation earlier in the afternoon, he had made arrangements to meet his father and mother and Turid Holtan at his sister Enid's apartment. Enid and her husband Leonard Smiley, a successful urologist with a practice in Manhattan, lived in a handsome apartment on Central Park West at 62nd Street. Eddie later explained, "I didn't want to go to my apartment or to Turid's. I didn't want to go to any place where someone could find me. My sister's seemed like one of the least likely, so I said we'd meet there."

Because the Smileys had a general idea of what was going on, they called their attorney, Richard Vetter, asking him to come to their apartment once they had learned that Eddie was going to stop by there before leaving for the airport. That move was not so much to protect themselves — since they were not involved beyond having bought some Celotex stock at Eddie's urging — as to dissuade Eddie from leaving the country.

Vetter strongly counseled Eddie not to go to Brazil, suggesting instead that he drive to the Catskills in upstate New York, check into some obscure hotel and stay there until things got sorted out. Should he leave the state of New York, Vetter said, he would be labeled a fugitive.

Eddie barely listened to him. Neither did Harry Gilbert, whose biggest concern as Eddie's father was to keep him out of harm's way. He had come to accept the full impact of Eddie's horrible position, and, to the dismay of Enid and her husband (as well as their lawyer), he was in complete agreement with Eddie's decision to flee to Brazil.

Enid remembers, "There was a lot of tension in the apartment that day. He was not normal. He was not the Eddie I knew. So unnerved. I'd never seen him like that before. A state of shock, that's the only way I can describe it. We were in total agreement with our attorney; we tried so hard to talk Eddie out of it, too. But it was no use. He had made up his mind. And our father was urging him to go through with it, to go down there where they couldn't touch him. They paid no attention to us."

When Eddie, his father and mother and Turid left the Smiley's apartment, the rain that had been intermittent all day now cascaded down with a vengeance. That is Eddie's only remembrance of the lonely drive the four of them took to the airport: the rain washing over the car and giving him the feeling as he looked at the flooded windshield that they were driving under water.

At Idlewild, they all went into the airport. At the Varig Airlines counter, Eddie paid for his ticket in cash — $550 for the one-way fare. Then he said his goodbyes. He told Turid that he wanted her to come down to Rio, that he would send for her as soon as he was settled. She took off the beautiful eight-carat diamond engagement ring he had bought for her at Harry Winston's several months before and handed it to him. "If you need money..." she started to say but couldn't finish. Eddie took it and dropped it into his pocket. His father wished him good luck. His mother tried unsuccessfully to keep her composure. Then Eddie was gone.

He went downstairs to get on the plane. "In those days, you walked outside and over to the airplane and then up a staircase they rolled to the plane to get on board. I remember going out onto the apron and looking back up. It was dark where I was. The three of them were in the window, lighted up, looking out at the airplane and then down at me standing on the pavement. It was raining, not as hard as it was during the drive out, but still coming down. I was standing there in the rain, like in one of those melodramatic movies of the 1940s or 50s, looking back up, and I waved and they waved back." Then he turned and headed up the stairway to board the plane.

Back in Manhattan, at eight o'clock that evening, E. L. Bruce, Jr., stood before a gathering of reporters at the Bruce offices on Madison Avenue and announced the resignation of Edward M. Gilbert as president and a member of the board of directors of the E. L. Bruce company, effective immediately. He then passed out copies of the company's official press statement, drafted earlier that afternoon following the board meeting, as well as the Gilbert's brief dictated statement.

"Where's Gilbert now?" one reporter asked.

E. L. Bruce, Jr., shrugged. He had expected Eddie to be at his side. "I don't know," he said, and then ended the press conference.

Within hours, a lot of people would be looking for Eddie Gilbert and not all of them would be news reporters.

*I was a builder... Maybe I would never have*
*stopped building, but somehow the scaffolding collapsed*
*in the middle of a big job.*

EDDIE GILBERT, IN BRAZIL, 1962

B
razil—that land of fabled romance, spectacular natural beauty, exotic women, and famous soccer teams. By far the largest country in South America, it is a sprawling patch of geography comprising jungle and rain forest, threaded with majestic rivers, graced with grand escarpments and a 4,600-mile necklace of shoreline and modern coastal cities in contrast with primitive inland villages. So large is it in fact that Brazil covers nearly half of South America, its borders touching on ten of the other twelve countries on the continent (excepting Chile and Ecuador). Covering more than 3.2 million square miles, Brazil is exceeded in size only by Russia, China, Canada, and the United States.

The country was discovered and claimed for Portugal in 1500 by Pedro Alvares Cabral, captain of a Portuguese armada following sailing directions of the legendary navigator Vasco da Gama. During the 16th century, the new land was settled and governed by the Portuguese until the Brazilians claimed independence in 1822. Portuguese today remains Brazil's first language.

In 1962, Brazil had a population of 71 million (grown to nearly 160 million today) and a viable, although inflation-racked, economy. It was said at the time that its major export to the United States was coffee (comprising more than half of its export production in 1960), while the United States' principal export to Brazil was fugitives. Brazil had the dubious distinction of being the only major country in the world that did not then have a formal extradition treaty with the United States. Eddie Gilbert knew he would find a safe haven there and some breathing room to contemplate the collapse of his personal financial world.

On that rainswept Tuesday evening in June 1962, the first-class section on Varig Airlines' last flight from New York to Rio was fully booked. Eddie Gilbert settled nervously and uncomfortably into the plush seat reserved that afternoon by his now former secretary, but he was in a daze. "I really couldn't think straight," he remembers many years later. "It was all so unreal, like a dream, a nightmarish one, yet I knew it was all too real."

He fastened his seat belt and sat staring straight ahead. But nothing happened for what seemed like an eternity. "We didn't take off. I thought, oh, Christ, they're holding the plane, they found out I'm on it, and they're waiting for the FBI." He imagined law enforcement officers storming onto the plane, with handcuffs and the mortification of being yanked from his seat and whisked off the plane into a waiting police car. "I was truly paranoid. It was the rainstorm outside, of course, that was delaying the flight, but I didn't think that for a second. I kept asking the stewardess when were we going to take off. What the hell was the matter? And she kept saying, 'Don't worry, it's just a little delay.' I was a nervous wreck. Finally I just got up and started pacing back and forth in the aisle, watching the door of the plane up by the pilot's cabin waiting for it to spring open and the FBI to rush in and pluck me out of there.

"The stewardess was really a lovely woman, very attractive. She tried to calm me down. She had a wonderful smile and such a nice way about her. In those days, the stewardess in first class on international flights was more like a hostess. She introduced everybody to each other, tried to make like it was a social event, our all being there together, and she was the social director."

After about an hour, the thunderstorm broke and air traffic began to move at Idlewild. The captain announced their takeoff, and Eddie gave up his pacing. He remembers sitting there, then gazing out the window as the plane taxied onto the runway, and watching the rain still falling—just a slow drizzle now—and noticing the puddles on the tarmac that glistened under the lights of the airport. It was an eery, ominous scene. Then suddenly the plane lurched forward and roared down the runway, and Eddie Gilbert was on his way to Brazil.

## WIZARDS

*Above left: Hyman and Dora Ginsberg, Eddie Gilbert's paternal grandparents.*

*Above right: Hyman Ginsberg, founder of the company that would later come to be known as Empire Millwork.*

*Left: Harry and Yolan ("Toots") Gilbert with Eddie and Enid in 1928.*

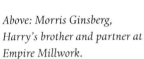

*Above: Morris Ginsberg, Harry's brother and partner at Empire Millwork.*

*Top right: The D. Ginsberg & Sons plant in Corona, Queens, New York. In the 1920s, Harry and Morris Ginsberg would develop this company into the much more prosperous Empire Millwork.*

*Right: Hyman Ginsberg (left) and his three sons in the Empire Millwork plant: Harry, Morris, and Ben.*

Top: The Flushing, New York, residence where Harry Gilbert moved his family in 1925.

Above: Eddie and Enid Gilbert out for a ride in 1925.

Right: Eddie Gilbert at summer camp, circa 1930.

GIS SAILED

*Eddie was a star diver on the Horace Mann High School team (right) placing third in the East Coast Interscholastic Championship Meet in 1940; he dove for the Cornell swim team the following year. Eddie also played serious tennis (far right) both at Cornell and later in 1942 making an appearance in the U.S. Open at Forest Hills.*

*Below right: Harry, Eddie, Yolan, and Enid Gilbert at their summer home in Huntington Beach, Long Island, circa 1940.*

*Opposite: Serving in the Army Air Corps during World War II, Eddie Gilbert is photographed in Rome in 1945 as the war was winding down. For his combat actions in Greece the year before, Gilbert was awarded the Bronze Star and the Purple Heart.*

## REGARDS TO BROADWAY

*Right: King of the Beats Jack Kerouac, with friend, is pictured here in 1965. One of Eddie Gilbert's closest high school friends at Horace Mann, Kerouac used to pen Gilbert's writing assignments, while Eddie did Kerouac's math homework.*

*Below left: Eddie Gilbert was a young Broadway producer in 1949 and 1950. He had both a big flop, "How Long Till Summer," and a big hit, "Peter Pan."*

*Below right: E. L. Bruce, Jr., in his company's Tennessee lumberyard. In 1958, Gilbert took control of the company in what was the first "corner" of a stock on Wall Street since before the crash of 1929. Bruce returned to head the company following Gilbert's resignation in 1962.*

### HANDFUL OF NICKELS

*Above left: Eddie Gilbert,* CEO *of the E.L. Bruce Co., at company headquarters in 1960.*

*Above right: Rhoda Gilbert (right), married to Eddie in 1951, is pictured in New York's Plaza Hotel in 1960 with Princess d'Arenberg and Mrs. Francis Farr. The Gilberts adopted two daughters, and were divorced in 1963.*

*Left: Yolan Gilbert with Eddie and Rhoda's daughters, Robin (left) and Alexandra.*

### BLUE GARDENS

*Top: Eddie and his daughter Alexandra descend the marble staircase at Villa Zamir in Cap Martin on the French Riviera. After renting for five summers, Gilbert bought it in 1960. But before closing, he bought instead the nearby Villa del Mare, thinking its additional vacant real estate more desirable. But he lost the Villa del Mare when the stock market crash of 1962 wiped him out.*

*Below: The grand Villa Zamir as seen from the air in Cap Martin. Perched 150 feet above the Mediterranean Sea, the Villa's vista took in Monte Carlo and its fabled casino, where Gilbert spent much time in those halcyon days. In the style of Jay Gatsby, he entertained lavishly at Zamir, being frequently counseled by hostess Elsa Maxwell; and the Villa's pool provided him a showcase for his diving talents. At Villa del Mare, he had an Olympic-style pool installed after its purchase.*

In the air, Eddie's apprehension about imagined FBI agents in their cars racing toward Idlewild did not abate. The plane, he thought, could still be turned around. The captain could get a radio message; the FBI could order the plane to make a big loop in the night sky and head straight back to Idlewild.

When Eddie first boarded the plane, the stewardess seemed to take a special interest in the most troubled of her passengers that evening and introduced Eddie to the man sitting next to him, André Todor. A soft-spoken and unassuming man, Todor was about five years older than Gilbert. He had emigrated to Brazil from Hungary a number of years earlier, he told Eddie, and was now a Brazilian citizen. A bond of sorts was formed after Gilbert told him that his mother had been born in Hungary, into a family, he added, of some historical aristocracy in that country.

And if Eddie was apprehensive about the FBI, Todor was equally concerned about his seat partner who, when he wasn't pacing the aisle of the airplane ("like a caged animal," Todor remembered), seemed about to spontaneously combust in the seat next to him. But once the plane was airborne, the two began talking and Todor said, "You look awfully upset."

"You'd look upset, too, if you just lost fifteen million dollars," Eddie replied.

Eddie then poured out his story to the man who was quickly captivated by the unfolding tale. "I remember, I wondered if he thought I was full of crap," Eddie said years later, "but I couldn't stop. I guess I just needed to get it all out of my system."

But Todor did not share Eddie's sense of doom and despair. Although he could comprehend Gilbert's state of mind, he recalled later about their conversation, "It occurred to me that what he had done, Brazilians do often enough; and there's no law against it in my country!" When Todor expressed that sentiment to Eddie, the Hungarian-Brazilian cemented a new friendship.

When Gilbert finished his tale of riches to ruin, he asked Todor, "So what do you do with your life?" Todor told him he was in advertising and public relations in Rio de Janeiro and that he owned a company named Due Propaganada Limited and also wrote a social gossip column called "Rio by Day and Night" for the English-language *Brazil Herald*, published in Rio. "Oh, my god," Gilbert said. "You can't write about this. I'm not ready to talk about this, not in public. You've got to understand, I'm going down there to try get my mind straightened out. If I'd known you were a writer, I wouldn't have said all this. You've got to promise me you won't write about what I just told you."

Todor consented. "You have my word," he said. And his word was good; the man never wrote a word about Eddie Gilbert in his column, even though the rest of the Brazilian press flocked to report the story of the surreptitious arrival of the most recent American expatriate (although they could only speculate as to his wherabouts in the country).

Todor was worried about Gilbert. He recalled later that he had never in his life seen someone so distraught. Then, when Gilbert finished his story—at least for the moment—Todor was startled to hear Eddie mumble something like, "So that's it. It's all over now." He watched as Eddie took a pill bottle from his pocket and appeared to pop some of the pills into his mouth. Todor thought the very worst. He went to alert the stewardess. "I think this man may be committing suicide," he told her. Todor explained how agitated Gilbert was, that he had said something about "it" being "over" and then gulped down a handful of pills. Sharing his concern about Gilbert's actions, she entered the cockpit to inform the pilot about the situation.

In his seat by the window, Eddie had just closed his eyes, hoping for sleep to come and help him escape the recollections of the worst day in his life. As he began to nod off, however, he was jarringly brought back to reality. He opened his eyes to see the copilot and the stewardess hovering over him, the copilot shaking him, telling him, "Wake up . . . Come on, on your feet . . . Wake up, Mr. Gilbert." They managed to get him out of his seat and, with each holding him under an arm, half-walked and half-dragged him up and down the aisle, saying, "You have to stay awake. You have to keep moving."

At first, Eddie, being half-asleep, did not understand what was happening; but as they kept jabbering at him and walking him up and down the aisle, he finally realized they thought he had swallowed an overdose of pills. Even when he protested, they paid no attention to him; so he broke free of their grasp and glared at them. "Listen, I just took a sleeping pill," he said. "*One* sleeping pill. All I want is to get a little sleep!" Finally, after a minute or so, he managed to convince them that he was not trying to take his own life, and the dramatic (*comédie noir,* perhaps) scene playing out in the first class cabin of the Rio-bound plane came to an end.

The copilot returned to the cockpit; the stewardess to her duties; and Eddie slumped back into his seat, smiled over at André Todor and said, "Good-night."

When Eddie awoke, the two continued their conversation, and by the time the nearly nine-hour flight was over they had become friends and confidants. Early the next morning, the Varig airliner began its descent into Galeao International Airport, located on Governor's Island in the bay just west of the city. A fiery orange sun edged over the horizon on the Atlantic Ocean, and the sky above Rio was a clear pale-blue; the mood-darkening rains of the day before had been left far behind in the northern hemisphere.

Gilbert had no place to go in Rio de Janeiro, so Todor suggested that he stay with him and his wife, at least until he calmed down a little. He could get a hotel room or an apartment at a less stressful time later, Todor suggested.

Eddie accepted his offer. "They were just the nicest people," Eddie remembers. "The wife, too. Here I show up on her doorstep with just a suitcase, a guy her husband met on the plane who has just run away from a big, big problem in the United States, and she takes me in like it was nothing at all."

It did not take her long to be taken in herself—by Eddie Gilbert and his charm. "He would just get to talking, talking, and then talking some more," she said afterwards. "He had the most amazing mind. Later, I remember, he said we would play a little game. He would ask me for a list of numbers, like 254 and 59 and so on, and told me to write them down on paper. While I added them with a pencil, he'd do the same in his head. And they were long, long lists of numbers. But he always had the answer before I would, and he was always right. He was quite the person."

Eddie confided to Todor that he had brought some money with him to Brazil, not a lot, but enough for him to live on until he could get things back in order. He also told Todor about the diamond engagement ring that Turid had returned to him at the airport in New York and the two valuable Mauritius stamps, none of which he wanted to carry around with him on the streets of Rio. Todor offered to put them in his safe deposit box at the local bank, and Eddie took him up on that, too. Given his state of his mind and the trust he was imparting, Eddie Gilbert was indeed fortunate that he had linked up with an honorable man like André Todor.

Gilbert stayed with the Todors that first day and night. The following morning, with Todor's help, he found a cheap hotel in the Ipanema area bordering on the vast slum section that was central Rio de Janeiro. Its obscurity guaranteed that it would be the last place anyone might look for Eddie Gilbert (and about as far as one could get from Eddie's usual suite at the Waldorf Astoria). While Eddie was trying to acclimate himself to this novel existence, most of the marauding press and media were camped outside the posh Copocabana Palace Hotel or one of the other luxury hotels across from the beach along the Avenida Atlantica where they fully expected to find him.

That same morning, Gilbert and Todor stopped at a newstand to discover blazened in the headline on the front page of a Rio newspaper the name "Gilbert." The two were mystified, however, by the illustration of Eddie accompanying the article: a composite sketch like that of a man on a "Wanted" poster, depicting him with a full head of reddish–blond hair, mustache, goatee, and sun glasses.

Eddie bought the newspaper and the two went to a café where, over a cup of coffee, Todor translated the article for Gilbert. It stated that Edward M. Gilbert, the subject of headlines and feature articles in the *Wall Street Journal* and the *New York Times,* was the most illustrious fugitive to flee to Brazil in some time. The article ended by speculating that the "renegade" Gilbert, according to "informed sources," was using Brazil as a stopping-off point before going into hiding somewhere in Peru or Bolivia. "Where the hell they got that, I'll never know," Eddie said later.

Meanwhile, back in New York, the *Times* described the "developments in the fast-moving situation": E. L. Bruce, Jr., chairman of the board and acting president of the company his family had once owned (and Gilbert had so recently headed), announced he had ordered a complete audit of the Bruce books; he had also accepted the resignation of Irwin S. Polivy, the company's secretary who signed the checks Gilbert had drawn against the Bruce treasury. The *Times* also reported that the Securities and Exchange Commission had suspended all trading in Bruce stock on both the American Stock Exchange and the over-the-counter market. The stock had traded as high as 37⅝ earlier in the year, and closed at 15⅜ on the day Gilbert fled the United States, down 3¼ from the day before (although there were other reports that it had been traded as low as $10 a share in the over-the-counter market just before the SEC suspension of trading). A spokesman for the American Stock Exchange was quoted as saying that it would institute its own investigation "into the Bruce and Gilbert affair."

Gilbert's first days in Brazil were lonely ones. The Todors were the only people with whom he spent any time during that period. Tony Stratton Smith, a British journalist and the author of several sports books whom Eddie met a short while later in Rio, remembered: "He missed his friends badly in those early days. He was constantly fretting over the damage caused them by his collapse." And it was a catastrophic collapse. The journalist Murray Rossant summed up its proportions in the *New York Times* article he wrote shortly after Gilbert was settled in Rio de Janeiro: "In fleeing, Mr. Gilbert left behind a mountain of debts. In some ways, it is like an iceberg, with the nearly $2,000,000 owed to Bruce the only amount above the surface. Beneath the surface are sums owed to various banks and money lenders who are faced with losses on the Bruce and Celotex stock he had pledged to them... Mr. Gilbert also may have made arrangements to guarantee those who bought Bruce and Celotex stock against losses [which Gilbert later confirmed that he had]."

Eddie had taken along just a few clothes when he fled New York. He had not given much thought to his attire that tumultuous Tuesday afternoon. Now, settled in, he dressed simply in a sportshirt, wrinkled slacks and loafers, and perhaps a windbreaker. After all it was the beginning of winter in the southern hemisphere, and although the climate in Rio was temperate, temperatures on occasion could drop to the freezing point. But most often he would be seen walking alone, without loafers, along the sandy Copocabana Beach with its famous backdrop of towering hotels and splendid apartment buildings, or sitting alone at one of the many cafes along the beach promenade. He often telephoned to the United States to talk with his father, with Turid, and his newly hired attorney, Arnold Bauman; but those were the only people he called that first week.

The hotel was especially depressing and dingy, and the neighborhood nearby was as dangerous as it was tawdry. So, he enlisted André Todor's help in finding an apartment closer to the beach. Todor inquired among his friends and located a small, four-room apartment at Number 16 Rua Siqueira Campos, whose tenant was temporarily moving to Portugal. Although the rooms were tiny and the furnishings drab, it was an immense improvement over the transient hotel room; and it was on the fringe of the fashionable Copocabana section of Rio, and also near the beach where Eddie enjoyed spending much of his time.

In seclusion those first few days, he assiduously avoided the press and Rio's paparazzi. He asked Harry Gilbert, Turid, Holtan, and Arnold Bauman not to reveal his exact wherabouts to anyone, at least for the time being. All the newspapers, the wire services, the television networks, and the news photographers were looking for him. They were convinced he was still in Brazil, but they did not know where. His mysterious disappearance had added a dramatic dimension to the business scandal surrounding Eddie Gilbert and the E.L. Bruce Company, and everyone in the business of reporting the news wanted the story directly from the source.

The sleuths of the news world, however, were not the first to locate Eddie Gilbert in Rio. Instead it was those from the darker quarters of that city's society—the fellowship of fugitives. "How they found me, I'll never know," Eddie confided. "No one had a telephone number for me down there. No one in the city, other than Todor, even knew where I was; and I was certain he hadn't told anyone."

During the second day after Gilbert had settled into his new apartment, the ring of the telephone surprised him. "It was about three in the afternoon, and I remember I was especially depressed that day. I wondered who the hell it could be calling me there."

At the time, there were three notorious American fugitives residing in Brazil: BenJack Cage, Earl Belle, and Lawrence Birrell. They and their various escapades prior to fleeing to Brazil had been extensively reported in the United States, from feature articles in *Time*, *Newsweek*, and other national magazines to widespread newspaper coverage. They were living tenuously in Brazil while an extradition treaty signed in January 1961 between Brazil and the United States was awaiting ratification by the Brazilian Parliament. Because the U.S. Senate had ratified the treaty earlier, there was speculation that Brazil's legislature would enact it into law before the year 1962 was over. The question of the treaty's retroactivity was a topic of much discussion in both Brazil and the United States, and it was of special concern to the three expatriates, as it well should have been to Eddie Gilbert. The pending treaty was silent as to the status of fugitives already in Brazil. It was widely understood at the time, however, that because most foreign courts had earlier held that unless a specific clause in the treaty prohibited retroactivity, it would be retroactive. In American legal circles in 1962, it was generally thought that retroactivity would have to be determined on a case-by-case basis.

The notorious three, for reasons that will become obvious, had no desire to return to their homeland. BenJack Cage, 45 years old in 1962, had been there the longest. He arrived in Rio de Janeiro in 1956, shortly after authorities in Texas charged him with embezzling $100,000 from a Texas-based life insurance company, a $15 million company which, according to *Business Week* magazine, Cage had "built and wrecked." After some negotiation and believing a mere slap-on-the-wrist punishment awaited him in Texas, he returned to stand trial. His impression was wrong, though, since he was sentenced to ten years in prison. Released on a $15,000 bond pending appeal of the trial outcome, Cage hightailed it back to the sanctuary of Brazil.

Earl Belle had fled to Brazil in August 1958. He arrived trailing federal indictments in Pittsburgh for stock-watering, price-rigging, and borrowing money from banks under false pretenses. All of the several companies and banks in various parts of the United States with which he had been affiliated had suffered as a result of his wrongful wheeling and dealing. Belle had been accused of masterminding a $1 million swindle before he fled to Brazil.

Lowell Birrell, who arrived in Brazil in August 1959, had been described by the Securities and Exchange Commission as "the most brilliant manipulator of corporations in modern times." Most of his manipulations, however, were well outside the law. The charge of a $14 million stock fraud involving the Swan Finch Oil Company was still hanging over his head in New York.

Gilbert knew about the three fugitives from the New York newspapers; in fact, as he later recalled, the lore surrounding their stories had given him the idea of seeking refuge in Brazil.

When Eddie picked up the phone that afternoon, the clearly American voice at the other end asked sharply, "Is this Gilbert?"

"Who is this?" Gilbert responded.

"Never mind. We know it's you."

"How did you get this number?"

"We have our ways. We want to talk to you."

"I'm not going to talk to you until you tell me who the hell you are."

"Well, I'm not going to tell you. But we *are* going to talk. Let me make that clear. We know what you look like. We've got your address there."

"Are you those guys, I read about... those Americans...?"

"Never mind who we are...."

"Cage and Belle and whoever that other guy is?"

"I'm not going to say." The voice paused. "But you may be on the right track."

"So...."

"Seven o'clock tonight. We'll meet, and we'll talk."

The voice instructed Eddie to be in front of a specific hotel across the street from Copocabana Beach where they would make contact with him. The man then broke the telephone connection.

The call made Eddie very uneasy. He had no idea what they might have in mind, but he feared it would undoubtedly prove to be *not* to his advantage. "The guy didn't scare me," he later explained, "but I was concerned. I wanted to be cautious. I figured I might as well meet them and see what they wanted. They were going to find me if I didn't anyway, so what did it matter. Just get it over with, I thought, what the hell, I decided I'd show up."

In his still unsettled state of mind, though, he decided to go prepared. Just before leaving that evening, he took a long carving knife from the kitchen and slid it inside his trousers, with the blade pointing down. As he put on his jacket before going out, as another precaution, he grabbed a Coke bottle and broke it off at the neck, like some Grade B actor would a whiskey bottle in a movie bar fight. He stuck the jagged neck of the bottle in his coat pocket and went out to meet his mysterious friends. The paranoia that had dogged Eddie since he left New York was apparently still with him.

Eddie reached the specified hotel at seven o'clock. As he awkwardly stood there waiting, looking up and down the street, he realized how bizarre it was to have a broken coke bottle in his pocket and tossed it away. At 7:15, a taxi pulled up in front of the hotel and a face appeared at the back window. According to Eddie's description, "The guy had a little head and big glasses, thick lenses like the bottom of the coke bottle I broke off."

Gilbert looked directly at him, waiting for some word. The man's eyes were scanning the area, Eddie noticed. "Are you..." Eddie started to say.

"Who're you?" the man demanded.

"Eddie Gilbert."

"The hell you are."

"I am." Gilbert shrugged.

"I've seen Gilbert's picture. He's got a beard. You don't look anything like the picture."

"Well the picture was wrong, if you're talking about the sketch in the newspaper the other day."

The man hesitated and then said, "All right, c'mon, get in."

As Eddie lowered himself into the backseat next to the man, the tip of the blade of the carving knife pushed into the inner part of his thigh, and he let out a muffled yelp. He tried to straighten out his leg, grabbing at the cause of his pain, and repositioning the knife.

"What the hell's the matter with you," the man said, startled at Eddie's odd entrance into the taxi.

"Just a cramp... in my leg."

The stranger bought it, and tapped the driver on the shoulder, telling him to start driving.

As they sat in the back of the taxi, Gilbert now recognized the man next to him as one of the three fugitives he had read about, Earl Belle. Sizing him up, Eddie hardly needed the hidden knife (which had left him bleeding and in more than a little discomfort, and which he feared would stab him again if he even moved his leg). Belle was a small, slight man, no more than five-and-a-half feet tall, and with the thick-lensed glasses and splayed ears like Mad Magazine's Alfred E. Newman. Wearing the pouty expression of a teenager, he looked more nerdish than threatening.

Belle was hardly a nerd, however. He had a petulant personality and the self-confidence of a man who had manipulated bankers and toyed with lawyers; he had all the chutzpah of a practiced con man. When he arrived in Rio with practically no financial resources, Belle nevertheless retained his taste for the luxurious lifestyle he had enjoyed while at the top of his game in the United States. His wife had some money, fortunately, enabling him to settle into a fashionable apartment near the beach and to join Rio's exclusive Tios Yacht Club. Once he began to maneuver successfully in Brazilian commerce, however, he shed his American wife and then married a Brazilian woman. By the time Eddie Gilbert had arrived, Belle had two children with his Brazilian wife. Following an ill-fated venture with a small Brazilian machinery manufacturing firm, Belle hit paydirt in the sugar business, turning the profit from a single deal into the ownership of a sugar mill that had been near bankruptcy. His financial success came from a stroke of luck—ironically provided by the nation from which Belle had fled—when the United States stopped purchasing sugar from Fidel Castro's Communist-controlled Cuba in 1959. As a result, Brazil suddenly became a major player in the exportation of sugar to the United States, and Earl Belle happened to be in the right place at the right time.

With Gilbert listening and Belle talking, they drove around the streets of Rio for more than a half-hour. Belle wasted no time letting Gilbert know what he wanted: Gilbert's arrival had suddenly put him and his "colleagues" in a very unstable position in their state of refuge. It had brought them back into the spotlight, Belle explained; and that was not a good thing. However ludicrous it seemed to Gilbert, Belle implied that the extradition treaty presently being considered for ratification in Brazil resulted from Gilbert's recent arrival. Even though they had been paying off Brazilian officials for years to protect them from deportation, Belle said that he had "been informed" that it would now cost him and the other expatriates considerably more to protect their status.

"You're one of us down here now," Belle said. "And you're going to have to come up with the dues."

"Well, if all this is about money, you can forget about it," Gilbert said. "You've got the wrong guy. I don't have any. I lost everything."

"We know about the two million you walked away with. . . . "

Gilbert slowly and painfully explained that the nearly two million dollars he had drawn from the E.L. Bruce treasury had gone to meet his margin calls. He did not have that money nor any of the earlier fortune he once had.

"We know your father has money" Belle persisted. "If you don't have it, [Belle was not convinced that Eddie Gilbert was as penniless as he claimed], you can get it from him."

"No, I can't."

"You may have to," he said threateningly.

Eddie fixed his eyes on Belle. "I want to make this clear. So listen. There's no way my father's going to give me money. I don't even know if *he* has any left. He took a bath in this, just like I did. So you can forget about that, too." Gilbert shrugged, and then looked away.

During the wandering ride about town, Gilbert ascertained that the "we" to whom Belle kept referring included BenJack Cage and Lowell Birrell. And Belle eventually acknowledged who he was. All the while Belle returned to the theme of the danger they all faced because of Gilbert's arrival in what had been, in Belle's words, "our haven, our sanctuary." If something were not done, they would undoubtedly be deported, Belle told him. Although Gilbert did not know it at the time—but Belle surely must have—Brazilian law forbade deportation of the parent of any Brazilian-born child. Belle had two of them at home with his new wife.

"You are going to have to help us . . . financially," Belle again threatened. But Gilbert chose simply to ignore him.

It was approaching eight o'clock when Belle finally realized he was getting nowhere with Gilbert. So he had the driver return them to the hotel where they had met earlier.

"We'll continue this tomorrow night," Belle said as they rolled to a stop. "Be here at the same time, seven o'clock." As Eddie was walking away from the taxi, Belle leaned out the window and called after him, "Give it plenty of thought. We don't play games."

Bullshit, Gilbert thought.

Nonetheless, Eddie showed up again the next night at seven o'clock, although this time he left the carving knife at home. Another taxi pulled up in front of the hotel, this one on time, but the face peering from the back window belonged to an older, balding, and much larger man whom Gilbert recognized immediately as BenJack Cage.

"Mr. Gilbert, how 'bout you joining me?" the man asked with a Texas drawl.

Cage was as large a man as Belle was small. About six-foot-four and 240 pounds, he had played football in college, and he took up most of the taxi's backseat. But unlike Belle's menacing approach the night before, the massive Cage ironically had an openly friendly attitude. With Gilbert settling into the backseat, Cage extended his hand and said, "Hello, son. BenJack Cage. How are you?"

There was to be no driving around town this time. Cage said they were going to an apartment he maintained in Rio.

By 1962, Cage was spending most of his time in Sao Paolo, Brazil's largest city (about 3.1 million residents), nearly three times larger than Rio de Janeiro and 200 miles to the southwest of it. Cage directed his varied business interests from Sao Paolo; and during the six years of his expatriation, Cage became a successful rancher in the Mato Grosso region of west central Brazil. He also had an interest in a prosperous rubber plantation. In still another enterprise, he operated what *Business Week* magazine described as "a profitable sideline... financing other ranchers, whom he supplies with fertilizer and tools for a 50-50 share in the profits while the loan is being repaid. In some cases, this can amount to a 200 percent return within two to four years."

During the cab ride, Cage picked up where Earl Belle had left off, but was much more specific. "We want $25,000 from you," he told Eddie. "We have to pass it on to the [Brazilian] authorities and very soon."

Eddie patiently explained his situation, just as he had to Belle the previous night. But Cage, like Belle, remained unconvinced and seemed to think he was in some kind of negotiation with Gilbert: "If you can come up with a good part of the $25,000, maybe my friends and I can make up the remainder," he told Eddie.

"It was such a scam," Gilbert later said. "Such a transparent scheme to shake me down. I found it personally insulting that they thought I might fall for it."

Cage's apartment was in an upscale building, not far from the beach. When the two arrived, Earle Belle was there along with a young woman whom Gilbert later concluded was BenJack Cage's girlfriend. The apartment was gaudy, Eddie thought: "It was decorated so tastelessly, I thought maybe the girl was a hooker and it was her place," Eddie said years later. As the three men talked about the money they expected from Gilbert, Cage indicated that they were also representing Lowell Birrell, who could not be there that night because of pressing business obligations (Birrell was active in many ventures in Brazil, including mining, business consulting, and money-lending). "They finally came to the conclusion that I wasn't going to contribute to their cause," Gilbert later recalled, "and when they did, Belle, who fancied himself a big-stakes gambler suggested we play chess for $1,000 a game. Now I'm a good chess player, and I'm sure I could have beaten him, but it was a no-win situation. If I won, he wasn't going to pay up, but if I lost they damn well would have wanted the money from me. So I declined."

Gilbert soon left and did not hear from Earl Belle again, although Ben-Jack Cage kept in touch. "He kept calling with one deal or another that he wanted me to come in on with him. They were all shady deals. One was a bank scam, another involved the black market in currencies. I can't remember all of them. But he was creative, always working something."

Cage knew that all kinds of money could be made in Brazil, a country with an inflation rate that had soared to 50 percent during the first six months of 1962 and where money lenders routinely collected 20 percent interest on the money they loaned (and in some cases as much as 48 percent well beyond the 12 percent legal limit). "In fact, I even met with him a couple of times and we had lunch or a drink in the Copocabana Palace Hotel, a lovely place, which is where he liked to hang out when he was in Rio," said Gilbert. "It was a helluva lot better than the sleazy apartment he took me to the first night I met him." Gilbert, however, never entered into any business relationship with Cage, and eventually he stopped calling.

Back in the United States, rumors about Eddie Gilbert abounded. Although no one knew exactly where he was in Brazil, it was fairly common knowledge that he had flown to Rio where he was generally still presumed to be. But not by everyone. One report held there was evidence Gilbert had already moved on to an unidentified South American country where for years he had maintained a "secret hideaway"; another suggested he was in Europe, perhaps holed up with some old friends on the French Riviera. Then just three days after his abrupt departure for Rio, the *New York Times* ran a story on the front page of the business section stating in its lead paragraph: "Edward M. Gilbert is considering taking up permanent residence in Brazil, it was indicated today." The article went on to say that an attorney in Rio de Janeiro named Jorge Chaloupe had informed the *Times* correspondent there that he had heard by telephone from a man identified only as "an intermediary," who had asked for an appointment for Mr. Gilbert, with the lawyer so as to begin the process for Gilbert to apply for permanent residency in Brazil. The *Times* noted that Chaloupe had previously handled residency cases for fugitives Earl Belle and Lawrence Birrell.

In an Associated Press wire service story dated June 15, 1962, it was also reported that "Senhor Chaloupe said Mr. Gilbert planned to fly today to Sao Paolo, the Brazilian business and industrial center about 200 miles from here, to make arrangements with the president of a New York bank 'to handle his interests in New York.' Senhor Chaloupe refused to identify the banker but said he was a close friend of Mr. Gilbert... [Chaloupe also] explained that Mr. Gilbert would need to appear at the U.S. Embassy to obtain certain documents... [but] 'I'm afraid to take him to the U.S

Embassy because it is U.S. territory and they could detain him and take him to a U.S. plane and return him to the United States.'"

Another New York newspaper article implied that Gilbert's legal problems might be of greater consequence than those originally reported in the Gilbert-Bruce Company scandal. New York's assistant district attorney in charge of the fraud division, Jerome Kidder, said that some Bruce officials "seem to suspect that there may be more involved than the $1,953,000." Kidder had spent hours at the Bruce offices poring over records, and had interrogated at some length former company secretary Irwin Polivy. But Kidder's allegation had been adamantly denied by Bruce treasurer John E. Lee, Jr., presently running Bruce's New York office. Lee had already examined the Bruce books and company records related to Gilbert, and said in refutation, "Our audit has just started, but we do not feel it will disclose withdrawals in excess of the $1,953,000 that Mr. Gilbert admitted."

But other dire things *were* taking place. Agents from the U.S. Securities and Exchange Commission had also descended on Bruce's New York offices two days after Gilbert's flight and had seized all of Gilbert's files. "We're trying to reconstruct the situation to see what violations, if any, there were," William Moran, associate regional administrator of the SEC, told the press. He stated that in addition to himself "four or five other SEC officials are continuing the probe." New York District Attorney Frank S. Hogan announced that his office, in addition, was beginning "an immediate and thorough investigation of all phases of the situation involving Mr. Gilbert and the Bruce Company as well as the personal financial activities of Mr. Gilbert."

It was inevitable that the press or the media would eventually find Eddie Gilbert in Brazil, and he knew that. He had just wanted a little time to get his thoughts together in order to formulate an explanation for what even *he* had come to recognize now as pretty bizarre behavior.

Because of all the speculation flying around in New York, the many charges being leveled against him, and what Eddie called the "misinformation" about what he had allegedly done, he decided by week's end that he should make a statement. He arranged to give one to the *Brazil Herald*, the English-language newspaper in Rio to which André Todor was a contributing writer. Not an interview, no questions, just a statement. Todor arranged for it. "Since 'Blue Monday' on Wall Street, I've been all confused," Eddie told the *Herald*. "and now I want to think things over with no outside pressure. That's why I'm here. I have every intention of returning to the United States, but if I returned to New York right now I'd be crucified."

Eddie went on to state that he had never contacted the attorney Jorge Chaloupe, nor had he directed anyone else to approach him. He had no idea where Chaloupe got the idea about a proposed trip to Sao Paolo to see an American banker there. He had been in contact with another lawyer in Brazil named Celso Fontenelle, but that had nothing to do with securing permanent residency in Brazil. Rather, he had enlisted Fontenelle to seek a writ of *habeas corpus* in the Brazilian Supreme Court so as to head off any possibility of arrest in that country or deportation from it. He had also asked Fontenelle to arrange for the extension of his 30-day tourist visa in the event he might extend his stay in Brazil beyond that period. "I am not fleeing American justice," Gilbert went on to say. "I did nothing to hurt anybody intentionally, although a lot of people did get hurt after things got out of control. I withdrew the funds not for myself alone. I did it to protect the position of both the E.L. Bruce Company and myself. This thing would not have happened if I had had the support of the board [the E.L. Bruce Company board of directors]. I felt I was let down by a lot of important people on Wall Street." And then he ended his statement with this personal commitment: "I hope to pay everybody back and make everything whole some day."

The statement was published in full by the *Herald* and picked up by the Associated Press wire service back to the United States.

Then Eddie Gilbert went back into temporary seclusion.

In 1962, *LIFE* magazine, was the second most widely read journal in America after *Readers Digest*, and so it was not surprising that its far-reaching network of correspondents might be able to locate him. It took about a week. But *LIFE*'s Miami bureau chief Richard Billings finally tracked Eddie down and persuaded him to give his first interview since having gone into exile. Along with photographer Cornell Capa, Billings flew to Rio for the interview that he hoped would provide answers to the many questions still floating about in the wake of the Bruce debacle. He sensed a scoop of sorts, and he knew without a doubt that the story was a natural for *LIFE*: a scandal in the loftiest level of the corporate executive suite, one that featured a highly visible and flamboyant member of the international jet set turned fugitive-in-hiding.... So LIFE went after the story with a special zeal.

While Billings and Capa went to South America, a team of researchers at LIFE's offices in New York was also busy investigating and tracking down every bit of background they could uncover about Eddie Gilbert, the boy wonder of Wall Street and bon vivant of New York's storied café society. Chronicling his rise in the business world, poking around the E.L. Bruce Company's offices (and even a company lumber yard), inquiring about his high-flying social life in Manhattan and on the French Riviera, the LIFE staffers were everywhere, treating the Gilbert story as if it were the biggest financial story since the stock market crash of 1929.

In Rio, Billings met Eddie at a sidewalk café overlooking Copocabana Beach. It was chilly that day, the LIFE journalist remembered, "June being the start of winter in that part of the world." Gilbert arrived after Billings did, and as Eddie approached the table, Billings scrutinized him. "His blue eyes were bloodshot," he wrote afterwards. "The fatigue in his face as well as his thinning blond hair made him look older than his 38 years." (Billings' description was something less than accurate: Gilbert's hair was dark brown and his hairline had receded; but the hair he had left was full and far from thinning, as the accompanying photographs taken by Cornell Capa clearly show.)

Following a cursory introduction, Billings noticed that Gilbert seemed uncomfortable when he first sat down. He also remembered Eddie's small talk about the cold weather, something quite uncharacteristic of Eddie Gilbert, as anyone who knew him then or now could corroborate. "At first," Billings wrote, "he seemed reluctant to speak about his troubles with Bruce and the stock market; he needed some coaxing." Eventually Billings got him talking.

"I know they think I brought all that money [the $1.953 million he was accused of taking from the E.L. Bruce Company treasury] in a black satchel or something... [and] the truth is I did bring some money," Gilbert said. At this point, he withdrew a handful of currency from his pocket, no more than a few hundred dollars worth of Brazilian cruzeiros, and held it in front of Billings' face. This constituted about all the cash he had. The nearly $2 million from Bruce had been used to meet margin calls; he did not have it, never did have it "in his pocket," as some speculated. Shaking his head, Eddie said, "I'm living in a room [actually the four-room apartment André Todor had found for him] that cost $7.50 a day. I figure I can live pretty well down here on $20 a day." Then he shrugged.

So Billings got his interviews, first in that café just off Rio's fabled beachfront, and subsequently in Eddie's cramped apartment. Photographer Cornell Capa ran through quite a number of rolls of film, snapping Eddie in the moments when Billings was not questioning him.

The result was a nine-page spread, ample for *LIFE* by any calculation, which appeared the week of June 29, 1962, incorporating 18 photographs as well as a stylized profile that the magazine had commissioned from Gilbert's old school chum, Jack Kerouac, the so-called king of the beatniks and, by 1962, a literary celebrity. Photos showed a barefoot Gilbert strolling the beach alone, another in his sparse apartment in Rio, one of Gilbert in his office at Bruce headquarters in happier days, of employees at work in the Bruce offices (even a staged one of E.L. Bruce, Jr., in one of the company's lumber yards), an earlier one of his estranged wife Rhoda, of Eddie in black tie with attractive but unidentified female companions at the Monaco Casino; there were panoramic shots of his homes in New York and the villa on the French Riviera where he had entertained so lavishly.

Aptly entitled "The Case of Eddie Gilbert vs. Himself," the piece was jointly written by Billings and Herbert Bream, a staff writer from *LIFE's* New York office. The tone was set in the second paragraph: "Edward M. Gilbert, the fugitive financier, went from riches to Rio, a victim of his own overleaping ambition, of bad luck and of the stock-market crash. The undoubted facts are that he filched nearly $2 million from the treasury of the E. L. Bruce Company. . . . "

The word "filched" especially stung Gilbert. He had never "filched" anything in his life, much less the nearly two million dollars to which the *LIFE* article referred. The newspaper business pages had been using a somewhat milder term than filched—"misappropriated"—which was also a verb that especially rankled him. By the time the *LIFE* issue hit the newsstands, Eddie had become, if reluctantly, accustomed to the wording of the accusations; still, in the vocabulary of Eddie Gilbert, he believed what he had done was to "borrow" or "withdraw" the funds.

In the article, Eddie was allowed to explain his position "Sure, I did some wrong things. I'm just an ordinary guy [contrary to *LIFE's* portrait which did not treat him in any way as "ordinary"] . . . . I didn't mean to do anything wrong.... I know I shouldn't have gotten overextended in the first place.... " While admitting to certain human frailties, he was quick to distinguish, "If ambition is wrong, then I'm wrong. I've been ambitious since I was a kid." Then he dug back into his Army Air Corps days for a simile to explain it. "This was a fight for survival. I was like a soldier with a bayonet, waiting on the hill for the enemy to attack. First the guy on my left falls back, then the guy on my right quits. I was left there to fight all by myself."

The article went on to quote a number of individuals from whose "observations today emerges a mosaic portrait that adds considerable insight into Eddie Gilbert's character and personality." The magazine identified just two of them. Harry Gilbert was one, whose offering about his son was nothing more than a nostalgic remembrance of a time past: "As a kid I can never remember him walking. He ran everywhere he went. He was always full of hell and full of life." The other was Igor Cassini, the society gossip columnist who wrote for the *New York Journal-American* under the pseudonym Cholly Knickerbocker: "He was terribly eager to be the richest, the biggest." Cassini, it should be remembered, was Eddie's publicist and someone whom Eddie also considered a friend. But the columnist was still reeling from the $30,000 loss he had suffered in following Eddie's financial counsel to buy Celotex stock; and so he added with characteristic cattiness, "He was always asking if I knew anyone who was bigger or richer at his age."

The others offering mosaic tiles of varying colors—and questionable value—in their quotations were unnamed. *LIFE* framed their observations in this way:

An habitue of Monte Carlo: "I've seen him throw away $100,000 in 15 minutes of baccarat [Gilbert actually played *chemin de fer*] at the Casino in Monte Carlo. He played crazily, without rhyme or reason."

An American poker-playing acquaintance: "He was a lousy gambler—the kind who would draw to an inside straight, bet hard, and be surprised if he didn't fill it."

A former campmate at Camp Winnebago, Maine: "In each of his four years there he was named the camp's best athlete. He was clean-up hitter and shortstop on the baseball team, a crack diver, and fine swimmer. At Cornell he played tennis, boxed, and became a dormitory chess champion...."

An acquaintance: "Eddie had quick, savage strength—really a great athlete. He perfected himself intensely in everything he did. He didn't *play* games; he worked at them.... Once at a club I belong to, Gilbert started talking about how he had once played a great paddle tennis champion. An expert at this club thought Gilbert was boasting, so he challenged him to a game. Gilbert begged off, saying he didn't feel like it. It sounded like he was trying to weasel out. The other guy insisted and Gilbert finally played him one game. Gilbert beat him 21-0.... "

An associate: "He was brusque and actually pretty tough in dealing with subordinates."

A friend: "His wife's (Rhoda) speech wasn't sufficiently distingué for him. He sent her to a school to improve her accent. What he wanted for a wife was a Grace Kelly."

Despite its claim for thoroughness, the comments *LIFE* assembled hardly constituted any kind of substantial portrait of Eddie Gilbert. At most they suggested he was a terrific athlete, a lousy gambler, a man filled with ambition (but worried about his image). No one who knew Eddie Gilbert would challenge his athletic prowess or his ambition; but many knew there was some question as to his gambling ability. (He was known on more than a few occasions to have walked away from the *chemin de fer* table at Monte Carlo with $100,000 more than when he had arrived, but not always). *LIFE's* observations offered little insight into the man himself, and its "mosaic" outlined a bland and superficial picture, not enough to illuminate what indeed had made Eddie Gilbert run.

In a succinct way, *LIFE* did succeed in chronicling Eddie's rise in the business world: starting out with his father at Empire Millwork, branching off on his own, returning to take over Empire, acquiring control of Bruce, and going after Celotex—all the way through to the bitter collapse that left Gilbert broke and in exile.

The one-page profile penned by Jack Kerouac appearing as a sidebar within the article, however, provided the missing insight into the personality and psyche of Eddie Gilbert. The often iconoclastic Kerouac conceded the givens—ambition, athleticism, the chance-taking—but suggested personal traits and character much beyond them.

Kerouac began with his high school remembrance of Eddie Gilbert for *LIFE*. "Among the fantastic wits of the Horace Mann School for Boys in 1939-40," he began his profile, "Eddie Gilbert ranked practically number one—I was just an innocent New England athlete boy suddenly thrown into what amounted to an Academy of incunabular Milton Berles hundreds of them wisecracking and ad libbing on all sides... but when mention of Eddie Gilbert was made there fell a kind of stricken convulsion just at the thought of him—he was insanely witty. . . . "

With stylized prose and stream of consciousness, Kerouac created a mood in capturing his subject. "The sad thing is, though, I could weep tears to think of my boyhood New England summernight trees swishing at my starry window of clear eyed pure hope, I could almost weep as many tears to think of Eddie's room in the old house in Flushing. . . . " The insights into what drove Eddie, what constituted his unique personality—stemming perhaps from Kerouac's own obsessive ambition—were penetrating and on target. He described the competition in which Eddie thrived, the brashness and unorthodoxy of his actions, the inherent ambition not just to succeed but to leave the rest of the pack behind. Unlike *LIFE's* assessment, he alluded to Gilbert's limitless energy and the powerful intellectual resources Eddie had always been able to bring into play.

Kerouac looked upon Eddie Gilbert's meteoric rise in the New York business world with unimpressed eyes, as if it were nothing out of the ordinary—as if in fact it were somehow preordained. "When Wall Street's Walter Gutman told me about two years ago that Eddie had become a 'financial wizard' I wasn't surprised—We'd both decided to become wizards at something or other as we giggled in the halls of Horace Mann among all the other wizards of that class. . . . But Eddie's style in the halls of the school is what I think of: Eddie used to come breezing and bouncing down the hall by himself with a wicked little pale grin and rush by as everybody yelled at him to stop: he was too busy: in other words he was so funny the academy of Wits waited for him in the hall: even the football players (no slouches at being crazy themselves) also watched him with grins: he was always rushing and serious-faced. He rushed down the hall all the way."

Kerouac had encountered his own share of adventures and troubles in his real-life travels, many of which are recounted in the best-selling novel *On the Road*. So he looked upon Eddie's present dilemma almost as if it were just another little problem that hell-raising high school kids might encounter in an otherwise conventional world. "As I read about his recent escapade with the two million dollars I laugh, not because I think it's funny but because *Eddie* is so funny, it seems almost as though he'd pulled this last fantastic joke to tear the funnyguys of Horace Mann apart. . . . "

Gilbert, Kerouac, and many of their Horace Mann pals were just destined for trouble of one sort or another, he concluded. "Eddie threw a big class reunion in 1947 at his estate near Manhasset—About thirty of us drank, swam, played a game of softball, and then at the toasting time at the long table funny Eddie stood up and proposed a toast... and for the last time we were all rolling under the table in stitches—because after that, the young businessmen went their separate ways and now we are all middle-aged and in one pickle or another."

Kerouac left LIFE's readers to ponder this youthful image of the Eddie Gilbert now in exile: "... the neat little boy-bedroom curtains, the swell dresser full of clean socks and shirts the brass handles clicking significantly and softly rich, the closet full of tennis sneakers and rich golden shoe trees making me grip my breast, and the tennis racket on the wall—The smell of bacon and eggs downstairs when we woke up on Saturday mornings—the fresh rain on the front lawn—Eddie bouncing around joking with the maid—the screened porch." Kerouac concludes his portrait enigmatically and thoughtfully: "For all his kidding around a kind of pale green clarity in the sincerity of his gaze—Nobody'll ever know America completely because nobody ever knew Gatsby, I guess."

Funny as Eddie may have been to the Horace Mann crowd, he was not joking a lot as he wandered the beaches and byways of Rio in 1962. He was troubled, dispossessed, his mind in the darkest place it had ever gone in his 38 years. Still, he wanted LIFE's readers to know that he was not disconsolate. "Down here, in a way, it may be worse than going to jail. But at least I'll have a chance to pay back some of my friends. I don't care how long it takes. I have a lot of friends all over the world. They probably hate me now because this thing has wiped them out."

LIFE had allowed Gilbert to say some things in his defense, but the article was ambiguous in its assessment of him. One paragraph led off, "There are those who say now, with hindsight, that Eddie Gilbert was born to be a loser." But four paragraphs later, the authors conceded, "Under his aegis, the company boomed. During Eddie's four years on the board of directors, first as chairman of the executive committee, later as president, E.L. Bruce climbed from $17 million to $28 million in total assets, and annual net sales rose from $26 million to over $42 million." But they could not be unequivocal in their praise, "Although his brazen manner, his total lack of humility, and his unorthodox approach alienated some members of the board, the young president got things done."

Besides business and finance, the magazine also explored Eddie's flamboyant lifestyle, both abroad and in New York. "At his villa at Cap Martin on the French Riviera, Eddie gave afternoon soirees for 200 guests at a time, most of whom he did not know. Often he received them in pajamas and later adjourned the party to Le Pirate, the most expensive nightclub along the Cote d'Azur. He liked Le Pirate because it has attracted the likes of Princess Grace, Maria Callas, and Aristotle Onassis. He would churn up to the place in a big powerboat, and when the party was over Eddie — who drank little, often only soda water—personally picked up the check." To these extravagances, Eddie is in disbelief: He never set foot in Le Pirate, in fact rarely, if ever, went out after one of his parties. "I'd go to bed about eleven or twelve. I never stayed up late. Maybe the others went out afterwards, but I didn't. It wasn't my lifestyle, there, or anywhere else. They were always making those things up. I don't know where they got that information, but they never talked to me about it."

And about Gilbert's life in New York, there was this: "He also acquired a 35-room town house in New York where he liked to give lavish dinner parties which he sometimes interrupted by hiring a fleet of Rolls-Royces to take his guests to expensive seats at hit shows and then bring them back." Some of this Gilbert concedes as true, but he denies ever hiring a "fleet of Rolls-Royces."

Although *LIFE* seemed to portray Gilbert's lifestyle with a certain contempt, the magazine did not overlook Gilbert's charitable instinct: "Although Eddie liked to spend money ostentatiously, not all of his largesse went for wild pleasure. He supported three Korean and three Italian children [actually it was one Korean and one Italian, as well as the three DiNicola sisters who had ministered to him during the war and whom he was also supporting], pledged $100,000 to Harvard, and when Antioch College needed a swimming pool, Eddie Gilbert gave a 75-foot steel model made by one of his firms."

In general, the *LIFE* authors tried to be fairly responsible, but the article contained inflammatory and sensational elements and was judgemental in a "guilty-until-proven-innocent" way. It began with the claim that Gilbert had "filched nearly $2 million from the treasury of the E.L. Bruce Company" and ended on the note that Brazil was for him "simply a reprieve from the jail sentence he is destined to serve." Beyond the innocuous errors about Eddie's "blond, thinning" hair, and baccarat being his preferred game of chance in the casinos, other errors were blatantly misleading. For example, LIFE claimed, "He started out as Edward Ginsberg, son of a well-to-do New York family, but as a teenager he decided to change his name to Gilbert"; in fact Eddie had nothing to do with his family's name change. The suggestion of changing the Ginsberg name had been his sister Enid's, and the choice of Gilbert had been made by his parents while Eddie was still a little boy. When LIFE noted that "The haughty Casino at Monte Carlo permitted him to enter its doors wearing old rope shoes and dirty slacks because he was such a heavy gambler, but it lived to regret the dispensation because he gave the Casino some bad checks and it ultimately had to settle for less than Eddie had lost," the reportage was factually wrong. The facts were that Gilbert had been extended a $250,000 line of credit at the Monte Carlo Casino, something not uncommonly offered to its highest of high rollers. On the occasion of his last visit there he had given the Casino his personal check in the amount of $50,000 as an advance against any future losses. When he left Monte Carlo, before his troubles in the United States began, his losses totalled $32,000; but before he could send a check for that exact amount, the Casino cashed his advance check of $50,000. Once informed by his bank of this, Eddie stopped payment on his earlier check. The Casino, annoyed by this action, then leaked word that Gilbert's check had been returned. Shortly thereafter, an equally annoyed Gilbert issued a check for the exact amount of the $32,000 in losses, and the matter was settled.

True to Jack Kerouac's remembrance of Eddie Gilbert as a jokester, the LIFE article concluded with this: "Aware that his gloom had revealed more of himself than he had intended, Eddie Gilbert made a stab at levity — a mood which still comes and goes in this volatile human being. 'If someone wants to write a book about me,' he said, grinning, 'I suggest he call it, 'How to Lose $15 Million in 30 Days Without Even Trying.'"

The most telling quotation of the entire article, however, was contained in the caption of a photograph of Eddie in his Rio de Janiero apartment: "He was naïve," says a friend. "If Eddie had had a good lawyer, he wouldn't have had to do this."

"Having a good lawyer," or not having one, would turn out to characterize Eddie's brushes with the law, not just in the Bruce matter but later in his life when he would find himself in other legal situations and in courtrooms not even dreamed of in 1962.

*When Eddie talked about millions [of dollars],*
*it was like a carpenter discussing lathes — they were just*
*tools of his trade, not very important in themselves.*

TONY STRATTON SMITH, BRITISH JOURNALIST, 1962

Eddie Gilbert eventually settled into a rhythm of his own in Rio. The first few days remained a blur in his mind: events occuring with effects not fully realized; a detachment from the reality of where he was, as if he were on the outside looking in; a captive of the haunting thoughts of what had so recently transpired and the dilemma of trying to figure out just what to do next. It was a time of agitation and depression, frustration and anxiety. But he came out of it. He had kept to himself for the most part in those first days, distancing himself from everyone, with the exception of the Todors, but even seeing less of them as the days went by. Although they remained his friends throughout his stay in Brazil, they soon resumed their customary life as Eddie came to terms with his new one.

As he began to venture from his self-imposed shell, Gilbert turned to the telephone and began to reach out to his family and those close to him: his parents, his sister Enid (who was living in Venice at the time), Turid, his two daughters Robin and Alexandra who were living with his estranged wife Rhoda in New York, and good friends like Olivier Coquelin, John Aspinall, Sherman Fairchild, Jerry Stern, and a few business associates and lawyers. He used the international telephones lines so much that first month, his telephone bill was nearly $750. Eddie also began writing letters after the *LIFE* crew left, initiating a correspondence that by the end of that same first month saw an average of a dozen or so letters a day arriving at his apartment in Rio.

But what really drew Eddie from the emotional quagmire of those first days in Brazil, was the appearance of New York lawyer Arnold Bauman who arrived at the end of the Eddie's first week there. Bauman, a partner in the firm of Christy, Bauman and Christy with offices at 30 Rockefeller Plaza, had an outstanding reputation as a criminal lawyer, with particular expertise in dealing with federal and state bureaucracies. Eddie's father Harry had secured Bauman's services with a $50,000 retainer (which Harry paid by giving him 5,000 shares of Bruce stock valued at $10 a share). This was quite a substantial sum for a legal retainer in the early 1960s.

Arnold Bauman had entered private practice in 1959 and was approaching his 48th birthday when he took on the Gilbert case. A native New Yorker, he had served as the chief counsel to the U.S. Senate Committee on Investigating Crime and Law Enforcement in the early 1950s and was subsequently chief of the criminal division of the U.S. Attorney's New York office and chief counsel for the New York State Joint Legislative Committee on Government Operations. Bauman was not a congenial man, Gilbert learned minutes after they first met at Eddie's apartment. "He was brusque. He was arrogant. A prima donna," Eddie recalls. "The first thing he said, before even sitting down, was: 'I don't know if I want to handle your case. You've already started doing things down here without my counsel.'" Bauman was not happy about Eddie's having consented to the *LIFE* magazine interview. The $50,000 in Bruce stock safely tucked away in his office safe made it infinitely easier, however, to accept Eddie's case. Still he wanted to set some parameters for their working arrangement. "He was a pain in the ass in many ways, especially in the beginning," Eddie remembers, "but he was trying to protect me, I have to give him that." Bauman knew he had to protect Eddie not only in the inevitable and impending legal skirmishes, from the press and media notoriety sure to surround the case, but most importantly from Eddie himself. He had been forewarned of Gilbert's brashness.

Arnold Bauman arrived in Rio bearing ill-tidings, to say the least, but with a plan. A number of civil court actions against Gilbert had already emerged, with the promise of more to come. Among them: The E. L. Bruce Company had sought a permanent injunction in the New York State Supreme Court preventing Gilbert or his wife Rhoda from disposing of their personal property, which included jewelry, the prominent paintings, and expensive antiques in their Fifth Avenue apartment—those items alone having a value of more than $1.3 million. One of the Bruce attorneys, Manly Fleischman, announced at a press conference that "company lawyers are studying possible further legal action against Edward Gilbert and will make recommendations soon." The Monmouth County National Bank in Red Bank, New Jersey, had filed a lawsuit in Superior Court to recover $75,000 on three of Gilbert's credit notes they believed had been placed in jeopardy by Eddie's flight from the country. In New York, Jacques Sarlie, the Dutch-born financier presumed to be Gilbert's business associate in the effort to amass and control Celotex stock, had been summoned to District Attorney Frank Hogan's office and questioned about any stock dealings with Gilbert. The district attorney was particularly interested in the stock purchased on Sarlie's account, valued at $754,770, in the effort of the Gilbert-led syndicate to take over control of Celotex. Sarlie had just returned from Paris, but had been sought for questioning about Gilbert, Bruce, and Celotex since the first days of the scandal. To Gilbert's dismay and chagrin, Sarlie, it was reported in the *New York Times,* had disclaimed any responsibility for the stock purchases in question and had denied having had any business relationship whatsoever with Gilbert in the failed merger of Bruce and Celotex.

In yet another case before the New York Supreme Court, the Newhouse Galleries on 57th Street in Manhattan had sued for the return of three oil paintings recently purchased by Gilbert but not yet paid for. Rhoda had refused to return them when contacted by the gallery after Eddie's flight to Brazil, claiming the paintings were in storage and retrieving them would be "inconvenient." Newhouse identified the artworks in question as *"Le Chapeau Nouveau"* and *"La Femme en Rouge,"* both by Jean Boldoni, and *"Landscape,"* by Francesco Guardi—the three valued at $19,000.

Bauman explained to Gilbert that grand jury indictments on both federal and local New York levels were imminent and would probably result in charges of misappropriation of corporate funds and perhaps grand larceny. That information came as no surprise to Eddie Gilbert. He knew from the moment he stepped off the Varig jet onto Brazilian soil that he was in for a real fight in New York once he returned.

For the better part of two days, Bauman and Gilbert talked over the cases: Bauman had done his homework about Eddie Gilbert's situation but needed to hear the whole story of the Bruce affair in detail from his client, from the very beginning until he boarded the Varig airliner for Brazil.

Once Eddie had finished telling his story, Bauman assured him that he had nothing to worry about. "There's no crime here," Eddie remembers the attorney saying. Bauman then added he had to return to New York, but promised to return to Rio with one or perhaps several government officials. That had been his plan from the outset, he explained. "I'll bring the right people down here, and we'll get the matter settled right here," Eddie remembers as the way Bauman phrased it. "You just tell them the truth. . . . You tell them the story like you just told me. And we'll make a deal. We'll do it all right here in Brazil, and then you can come back home."

Gilbert told Bauman he was thinking about returning in the relatively near future, but Bauman told him that would not be wise. "Don't come back until I tell you. Settle in down here. It's going to take a little time. But we'll get a deal, and everything will be fine," Gilbert remembers his saying.

Word had leaked out that Bauman had gone to Brazil to meet with Eddie Gilbert. When the attorney returned to New York two days later, reporters were waiting at Idlewild Airport. His arrival at the gate turned into an impromptu news conference. As the questioning began, Bauman cautioned the reporters that no legal action was officially outstanding against Mr. Gilbert. There was no need, nor official request, therefore, for Mr. Gilbert to return to the United States. As to whether Gilbert was planning to return, Bauman could say only, "The decision on that is his and his alone"; and he added that he did not believe that decision had yet been made.

In answer to a question about how Eddie was faring under the circumstances in Brazil, Bauman described him as "a changed man." The once confident, dynamic executive they knew before "is low in spirits, a very sad and very unhappy man, very distressed and very contrite."

"What does he say about taking the money?" one reporter asked.

"He says that whatever he did he did in what he regarded as the interest of the Bruce Company and he stated that that applied particularly to the Celotex acquisition." Then when another reporter suggested that Gilbert made off with the money himself, Bauman shook his head and answered, "Mr. Gilbert has said repeatedly that he did not personally profit one penny from any use of Bruce funds and did not stand to do so. At the time Bruce [the company] and Mr. Gilbert had acquired a controlling interest in Celotex, it would have been a very valuable property to Bruce."

"But what about the reports that Mr. Gilbert arrived in Rio de Janeiro with a very large sum of money?" another reporter interjected.

Bauman shook his head negatively. "Our consultations were held in a microscopic apartment. He is living in circumstances you would find it difficult to believe. I did not see the slightest sign of luxury throughout my two days with him. I did not see any indication that Mr. Gilbert has substantial sums of cash with him."

Bauman then abruptly ended the questioning, saying he had nothing more to say to the reporters about Gilbert's situation as he did not want to see a legal matter tried in the newspapers.

The federal indictment about which Arnold Bauman had warned Eddie was in fact returned within a week of Bauman's return to the United States. Officially entered on June 28, 1962, in the United States District Court, Southern District of New York, U.S. Attorney Robert M. Morgenthau and Llewellyn P. Young, administrator of the New York Regional Office of the Securities and Exchange Commission, jointly announced the 15-count grand jury indictment. Morganthau specified that Gilbert was being charged with violations of the anti-fraud and registration provisions of the Securities Act of 1933; violations of the insider reporting provisions of the Securities Exchange Act of 1934 for his transactions in the stock of the E. L. Bruce Company on the American Stock Exchange; and violations of federal wire and mail fraud statutes "in a scheme to convert to his own use funds of E. L. Bruce Co. [Incorporated] aggregating $1,953,000."

On July 9, 1962, 11 days later, New York state's 12-count indictment for grand larceny in the first degree was also returned. It was filed in the Court of General Sessions, County and City of New York, by District Attorney Frank S. Hogan.

But the most devastating notice, it turned out later, was the letter Gilbert received from the Internal Revenue Service during the last week in June.

Dear Mr. & Mrs. Gilbert:

You are hereby notified that I, the undersigned district Director of Internal Revenue, find that you have designed to conceal your property in order to to hinder and prevent collection of income taxes justly due and to become due for the period January 1, 1962 to June 15, 1962.

In accordance with Section 6851 of the Internal Revenue Code and Regulations thereunder, you therefore are notified that pursuant to authority granted to me I hereby declare the taxable year begun January 1, 1962 and ended June 15, 1962, immediately terminated and the income taxes to become due from you for such taxable period immediately due and payable.

You are further notified that an assessment has been made against you for the income taxes due from you for such taxable period in the following amount:

| Taxable Year | Tax |
| --- | --- |
| January 1, 1962 to June 15, 1962 | $1,723,776.00 |

and that the aforesaid amount of income tax is hereby declared immediately due and payable by you.

You are requested, therefore, upon presentation of this notice to you together with such other or further statement of income taxes as may be presented to immediately pay the full amount to the aforesaid income taxes.

Very truly yours,
District Director

In effect, the IRS demanded that Gilbert immediately pay income tax for the first half of 1962, including income tax it claimed was owing on the $1.953 million that had come from the E. L. Bruce Company treasury.

Shortly after this letter was received, the IRS filed liens against the real and personal property owned by Gilbert and his estranged wife Rhoda in the amount of $3,464,472 for alleged income tax deficiencies (including income taxes the IRS now claimed as owing for years prior to 1962). The IRS's jeopardy assessment, in effect, placed the IRS ahead of all other creditors to collect money that Gilbert owed. More importantly, the IRS thus blocked the E. L. Bruce Company from collecting on the promissory notes that Gilbert had given the company as security for the $1.953 million borrowed from the company treasury. The IRS jumped ahead of Bruce because the company had failed to file its security interest in Gilbert's property included in the promissory notes. Ostensibly, when Bruce went to file, it was informed there was a $10,000 fee required to support any request for a lien against real property (there was none against personal property). Not wanting to pay such a fee, or at least postponing consideration of it for a while, the Bruce company took no further action. The IRS jeopardy assessment then took precedence, as it would not have done had Bruce properly filed. So Gilbert was prevented from using his property to pay Bruce back and was simultaneously being charged income tax on the money he had signed notes to borrow. In a dizzying Catch-22 situation, the IRS actions prevented Gilbert from making restitution; were he not so prevented, he would not have had the IRS tax liability. The actions also left Bruce without the resources it had been given to collect the money it was owed. It was, to say the least, a real mess.

Arnold Bauman had major worries about the press and the media. He had warned Eddie against talking to them before he left Rio de Janeiro, but for the most part Gilbert disregarded his warnings. Although he managed to avoid the beat reporters and local photographers, he was no longer all that reluctant to talk about his predicament after having opened up to the crew from *LIFE*. Evidence of that came just a few days after Bauman left. Murray Rossant, now a top feature writer for the *New York Times* and a journalist Eddie liked (Rossant had written complimentary articles about him for *Business Week* at the time of the Bruce takeover four years earlier), contacted Harry Gilbert in New York. He indicated he would like to go to Brazil and interview Eddie for a major *Times* piece. Harry mentioned this when he and Eddie next talked by phone. Despite Arnold Bauman's counsel to the contrary, Eddie said it would be okay. Rossant caught the first plane out of New York for Rio. The resulting story by Rossant was one of the most insightful and least damning to appear about Eddie Gilbert during this time.

The lengthy feature, along with a UPI photograph of Eddie, received a three-column front-page billing in the Sunday *New York Times* of June 24, 1962, under the headline "Gilbert Story: an Operator's Fall." Rossant characterized Eddie as, "a free-spending millionaire with plans for a $100,000,000 building materials empire... [who] today says he is practically broke and living an almost penny-pinching existence in a modest apartment." Unlike the *LIFE* magazine writers, Rossant avoided loaded terms like "filched," "stole" or "misappropriated"; instead the *Times* writer referred to Eddie Gilbert as the "the man who took nearly $2,000,000 from the E. L. Bruce Company." According to the Rossant article, Gilbert "plans to study Portuguese and stay in Brazil for the time being," and suggested that he might consider "investigating business opportunities in Brazil's lumber industry in the hope of rebuilding his shattered fortune." And he quoted Eddie as saying, "I will pay back everything I owe if it takes me the rest of my life."

It was the only story of the situation that did not infuriate or even offend Eddie's sensitivities in those initial weeks of the scandal.

Less than a week after Rossant's story in the *Times*, the paper carried another feature article, this one about Eddie's father, Harry. Unsurprisingly the elder Gilbert had resigned as chairman of the executive committee of Bruce at a meeting of the company's board of directors at its Madison Avenue offices. At the company's request, however, the 62-year-old Gilbert agreed to retain his seat on the board. E. L. Bruce, Jr., was then elected chairman by the board to replace Harry Gilbert. At a press conference following the board meeting, Bruce took the occasion to announce that the company planned to "transfer a number of the functions and personnel of the New York office to Memphis." The *Times* also reported that "Mr. Bruce had said the company was in a 'very healthy' condition and reiterated previous statements that sales were 'substantially' ahead of those of the corresponding period of last year and that order backlogs were at a record high." Despite the festering scandal, business was obviously going quite well at the Bruce company; and had he been asked at the press conference, Mr. Bruce might have been the first to admit that the healthy sales were directly attributable to the administration of Harry Gilbert's son.

After Murray Rossant returned to New York, Gilbert hooked up with yet another writer, this one living temporarily in Rio. Tony Stratton Smith was a young Englishman, at the time working as a free-lance journalist, reporting on events in South America and the Caribbean Islands and filing his stories with several British newspapers. Smith was 28 years old, tall and reservedly British in manner, and specialized for the most part in stories related to sports, especially soccer. But he was eager to broaden his writing horizons. Gilbert and his newfound friend struck a gentleman's agreement, that Smith would not write any articles about Eddie Gilbert and his present predicament unless they were okayed by Gilbert beforehand. With this understanding, Tony Stratton Smith became Eddie's rather constant companion, keeping a journal of Gilbert's activities in those months of exile. Smith was intoxicated with the Gilbert story and mesmerized by the man telling it. He felt Gilbert's story was much larger than the recent Bruce-Celotex debacle; it appeared to have all the makings of a modern-day, business-world tragedy, Smith later recalled, and worthy of a book. It also seemed to him that such a project might just be the vehicle to whisk him out of the humdrum world of sports reportage.

A vignette Smith recorded from one of the frequent walks the two took along the Copocabana Beach provides a revealing insight into Gilbert's lifestyle in exile and more penetratingly into what motivated Eddie Gilbert the man.

On the beach one day, Eddie was walking along "in baggy, blue shorts, purporting to snatch a little relaxation from his ever-present background of problems," when the two of them encountered, according to Smith, a "barefoot vendor of oranges with a smile as wide as the harbour."

"Hey," said Eddie, "how much for an orange?"

"Ten cruzeiros," said the man.

Eddie looked up at the sky for a moment, then back to the man, "And how much for five?"

"Fifty cruzeiros," said the man, with quickening interest.

Eddie took the man's box of oranges and counted them. There were 21. Then he dropped down and sat cross-legged in the sand with the box of oranges in his lap. "And for the lot?" he asked the man.

The vendor hesitated, then: "Two hundred cruzeiros. It's a bargain, senor."

"I'll give you 120," Eddie said firmly, his clear, blue-green eyes fixed sternly on the man.

"But senor, there is the journey I've had to take to get here, and there's the man I had to buy them from, and my wife and children . . . but maybe I would take 180!"

"150, not a penny more. Take it or leave it."

The vendor took it. Then, with a chuckle, reached down and withdrew an orange from the box and peeled it for himself.

"Get the nerve of that guy," Eddie, with the trace of a smile, said to Tony Stratton Smith. His expression now turned into a full grin, saying to the vendor, "Hey, that's my orange you're eating." The man just continued to smile as he finished eating the orange.

After the man left, Smith asked Eddie why he wanted so many oranges.

"I don't," Eddie said, "but I never could resist a deal."

Gilbert rather liked the idea of a book being written about his life and began sharing with Tony Stratton Smith the details of his meteoric rise in business. At about this same time, Smith learned that the lease on his own tiny apartment in Rio would not be renewed; so Gilbert suggested that he move into the spare bedroom in Gilbert's apartment. That way they could share the expenses and both save some money. And it would facilitate Smith's work on the book about Gilbert. The young British journalist needed no convincing, and quickly moved his few belongings over to 16 Rua Siqueira Campos.

Tony Stratton Smith remembered Eddie Gilbert's earliest days in Rio as beleaguered ones, "filled with sadness and self-accusation, depression, ... for maybe two weeks he was in a state of shock... his doings, he told me, were mostly a mixture of long walks and hot baths at first and later the telephone calls back to the States and the letter-writing." He also observed that "Eddie [in mid-1962, anyway] has an enormous capacity for inventing nightmares. He sits around imagining all the terrible things that could happen to him, then strums out 12 different variations of each one. He comes up with some of the damnedest problems, or rather possibilities sometimes — and insists on kicking them around, whether its breakfast or bedtime."

Smith especially liked the way Eddie characterized himself in one of their earliest conversations. "I was a builder," Gilbert told him. "Maybe I would never have stopped building, but somehow the scaffolding collapsed in the middle of a big job." And, playing on Eddie Gilbert's metaphor, Smith had his own observation, equally incisive, which he added to his journal: "When he talked about millions, it was like a carpenter discussing lathes — they were just tools of his trade, not very important in themselves."

Back in the United States, the Eddie Gilbert story remained a major news item. All the New York newspapers and the *Wall Street Journal* reported on the legal aspects of the story as they took place over those first few weeks. There were small feature articles appearing regularly in issues of *Time, Newsweek*, and *Business Week;* taken together they provide a rather thorough look at the national coverage of the story and its emerging consequences.

Among the first pieces of mail to reach Eddie Gilbert in Rio was a most surprising letter from Albert Ratner. Ratner was about the same age as Eddie and was the head of Forest City Materials, a lumber and building materials company in Cleveland, Ohio. He had been following the national news magazine coverage of Eddie's story. "I'd done a lot of business with them in those days," Gilbert explained. "I sold them a helluva lot of oak flooring, several million dollars worth before the Celotex thing."

The surprise was not that Ratner had written; he felt a close affinity to Eddie Gilbert. Both were young and ambitious men whose companies were on rising tracks much steeper than many other businesses in the early 1960s. The surprise was in the enclosure: Along with a warm and supportive letter was a certified check for $10,000 made out to Edward M. Gilbert. "I hope this will help you get back on your feet," Ratner wrote.

Eddie was thunderstruck. "My mind was still not functioning quite right," he recalls. "I thought, 'I can't accept this.' I wasn't a charity case, but I was very moved by the sentiment." So Gilbert wrote back to Ratner, thanking him for his generosity and thoughtfulness, but returned the check. He explained that he had indeed lost everything and was struggling to put his life back in order, but he still could not accept the money. It just did not seem quite right to accept such a generous gift. But that would not be the end of his correspondence with Albert Ratner.

The issue of *LIFE* containing the article about Eddie reached the nation's newsstands in the third week of Gilbert's exile; shortly thereafter CBS television attempted to reach out to Gilbert for another take on the story. The executives at CBS made it clear to Eddie that they were not going to be outdone by the sprawling feature in *LIFE*. CBS planned a full half-hour on "Eyewitness Reports" to be anchored and reported by their frontline broadcasters, Charles Collingwood, Charles Kuralt, and Roger Mudd. They wanted Eddie's unqualified cooperation.

When CBS executives first spoke with Gilbert, he was naturally reluctant, fearing a hatchet job on national television would further damage his tarnished image in the United States. After giving it some thought, however, he came to the conclusion that a nationally broadcast television show on a major network like CBS might provide him with just the forum he needed to reveal his side of the story (even though it meant ignoring the counsel of Arnold Bauman). "After all, I didn't feel I had done anything wrong," Eddie said later. "I had been caught up in something, and I didn't act rationally. And a lot of people abandoned me, and some actually turned on me, like André Meyer. There were some things I really wanted to straighten out, some things I deeply wanted to say about what had happened." So, for his cooperation, Gilbert insisted that he be able to tell his story upfront, and explain his position. The television executives agreed.

A youthful, slender, and dark-haired Charles Kuralt headed the television crew dispatched to Rio de Janeiro. In 1962, he had the title Chief Latin

American Correspondent and arrived before the technical support crew. Kuralt spent more than a week with Eddie; the two appearing inseparable on the beach and in the boardwalk cafes as Kuralt worked to win Gilbert's confidence.

The show, "Refuge in Rio," aired in late July 1962, about six weeks after Gilbert had taken up residence there. It opened with a panoramic view of the storied Copacabana Beach, filled with land-locked sunbathers and scores of others cavorting in the breaking surf of the south Atlantic, and against the garland of high-rise buildings protecting the playground of the rich and famous from the sprawling slum areas of the city populated by the more than three million *cariocas,* as the locals were known.

The camera slowly zoomed down to focus on two men strolling along the beach as a somber-voiced Charles Collingwood informs the television audience, "On a beachfront promenade in Rio, an American financier named Edward M. Gilbert talks about his future to an American correspondent."

A close-up then on Gilbert's face. He looks youthful despite a prominently receding hairline; and he appears focused and poised. He has his forum, as promised. He speaks slowly, calculatedly, as if he is weighing each word before he lets it escape from his mouth. "I want to prove to everyone, as well as to myself, that what I did was not a criminal act." The self-assurance, so much a part of his character before the disaster that prompted this seaside exile is still there, in his face and in the tone of his voice. "I want to remake my life, my career. Maybe in a different way than before. I want to repay everybody that I owe money to, that lost money in this horrible catastrophe. I intend to do just that."

Back in the New York studio of CBS, Charles Collingwood speaks from his anchor desk and is surprisingly gentle in his choice of words. "Edward M. Gilbert is an American financier, who, after some confusion in his accounts [a new description of his transgression that naturally appealed to Gilbert] recently found asylum in Brazil.... To some, he is a romantic figure there in Rio, a man who gambled for large stakes and, losing, grasped at any straw to give himself another chance. To others, he appears as a fugitive from justice, using a legal quirk to escape the consequences of his acts."

Collingwood goes on to depict Gilbert as an empire-builder, a driven businessman who had taken over the Bruce organization and substantially increased its sales volume and corporate value before going after the acquisition of the even larger Celotex Corporation, only to see the anticipated empire come tumbling down with the the stock market crash a few months earlier.

"Gilbert is gone," Collingwood says, "leaving behind him the abandoned trappings of empire. A ten-room apartment on Fifth Avenue, furnished with a variety of French antiques. He used to pay $1,500 a month rent. He used to collect paintings, especially 18th-century French. The gallery is suing to get three of them back. He used to buy trinkets for his wife at Cartier. But he and his wife are separated, and a bunch of the jewelry recently went back to the store. He had a house on the Riviera, with a 120-foot swimming pool. Gilbert used to move in the kind of circle that treats the Riviera as its backyard."

To explore life in the café society that Gilbert had left behind in New York, CBS went to the *Journal-American's* Cholly Knickerbocker. On the television screen, he speaks without the vindictiveness that had come across in his interview with *LIFE's* correspondent. In fact, the impression he leaves is quite the opposite: "I certainly saw a lot of him in the last few years," Cholly offers. "He sort of appeared on the social scene like a meteor. . . . He used to appear with his wife at El Morocco, and I always remember that I noticed his ruffled shirts. It was anachronistic [sic] for a man who looked like him, a kind of rough and tough type, to be wearing those very fancy shirts. But I think practically everybody felt that he had a Midas touch, that he was a very lucky fellow, that he was very aggressive, that he would be very successful."

Then the CBS program moves back to Gilbert's apartment on the Rua Siqueira Campos. Charles Kuralt continues, asking Eddie the question whose answer on the surface would appear self-evident. "Why did you come to Brazil in the first place?"

Eddie avoids mentioning the absence of an extradition treaty between the United States and Brazil and, with the spin of a seasoned Washington politican, takes the opportunity to dissuade the audience of thinking of him as a fugitive. "Well, Charlie, that's a difficult question to answer... [but] I came here basically to solve some serious personal problems... and I felt that if I stayed in New York, I wouldn't be given the chance... to have the peace and quiet to resolve these problems. I felt that I would be badgered by newspaper reporters, SEC officials [and] company [E.L. Bruce] officials investigating into my affairs, the district attorney investigating. I wouldn't have a minute's peace."

"If you had it to do all over again, would you still come to Brazil?"

"I don't know. I can't answer that question yes or no because there are so many factors weighing on each side in favor of each side. I think I probably would not come, if I had to do it over again. I'm pretty sure I wouldn't."

The show then addresses the question of pending legislation in Brazil's Parliament that would enact an extradition treaty with the United States. A spokeman for Brazil's State Department tells Charles Collingwood that he believes one will be ratified before the year is over but is vague as to its exact provisions and whether it would be retroactive to those American expatriates already in Brazil.

Then Attorney General Robert F. Kennedy appears with CBS correspondent Roger Mudd to answer a series of questions about how the U.S. Department of Justice regards the proposed treaty in general, and how it views the case of Edward M. Gilbert in particular. In regard to the latter, Attorney General Kennedy is cautious, explaining that absolutely nothing at all can be done until a treaty is signed and goes into force. "Even then," the attorney general points out, "there are some problems. He [Eddie Gilbert] was indicted on stock, security fraud here in the United States. The agreement holds, and traditionally these extradition treaties are worded this way, that it has to be a crime in *both* countries. And it would be a question whether this [Gilbert's alleged crimes in the United States] would be covered." Kennedy goes on to explain that because of Brazil's more liberal white-collar crime laws, many acts construed as felonies or misdemeanors in the United States are not such in Brazil. "I would think we'd have a good chance of getting him extradited," Kennedy speculates, and with a facial expression that suggests some doubt, "but there would be that legal problem." The attorney general concludes with this observation: "Now, Mr. Gilbert will have a trial when he comes back to the United States, and he will have the opportunity to answer these charges, and a jury will make a decision."

Although Eddie had had the opportunity to tell his story in his own way, as CBS had promised, he did not take a great deal of solace from the show after it aired because he felt he still came off as a fugitive from American justice, and he did not necessarily view himself as a fugitive. He had made a friend in Charles Kuralt, who became sympathetic to Gilbert's plight. Perhaps it was because Kuralt's credibility was itself then under scrutiny: A Cuban exile had testified before the U.S. Senate's Internal Securities Subcommittee claiming that Kuralt was a communist or at the least an avowed communist sympathizer. This was a charge Kuralt publicly denied and in a letter later sent to Gilbert described as "patently absurd... but oh the dust it stirred up." Kuralt had done his best to see that the prime-time show was fair to Eddie—for a half-hour at least—and showed understanding in its treatment of him. When the show was edited into its final form, he felt he had succeeded in that effort. As he wrote to Gilbert:

*Dear Ed,*

*I have received some reaction to the program, which as you must know by now did turn out to be all about you, with no mention of the "other guys" [Gilbert had expressly told Kuralt he did not want to be listed with the three notorious fugitives, BenJack Cage, Earl Belle, and Lawrence Birrell].... I hope the show didn't pain you; from all accounts I've heard it was an awfully good one, centering around the interview.*

*A man whose opinion I respect, a college teacher of mine, wrote me today that it was "a very sensitive and sympathetic treatment of a man overwhelmed by his troubles—but not done in by them." I guess if it was that, it was what I was trying to accomplish....*

*I send you best wishes.*

> *Very truly yours,*
>
> *Charlie*
> *Hotel Crillon*
> *Lima, Peru*

Olivier Coquelin was the first of Eddie's close friends to visit him in Brazil. The 32-year-old Coquelin had come into Gilbert's life just seven years earlier when he had begun to manage Eddie's villa on the French Riviera and to orchestrate most of the lavish entertaining carried on there. The handsome Frenchman had come to Rio from New York at a time when his own world was on the verge of being shredded into tatters. Coquelin was now manager of Le Club, the New York nightspot in which

Gilbert had earlier been involved and whose board of governors included such luminaries as Rex Harrison, Noel Coward, and Alan Jay Lerner. Le Club had opened to great fanfare the previous New Year's Eve, but was now in deep trouble. Presumably because of Eddie's present financial difficulties and his flight to Brazil, a New York bank had placed a lien on the establishment to secure its $195,000 loan (for the club's start-up financing which Gilbert had arranged before his own troubles erupted). Because of the stock market crash and the bearish mood on Wall Street, most of Le Club's members were reluctant to come up with additional money. There was the very real threat, therefore, that the bank would foreclose and shut down an enterprise that was otherwise doing quite well. And if Le Club closed its doors, Olivier Coquelin would be out of work.

Coquelin, with his European charm and still impeccable sense of tact, never once spoke of his own troubles to Eddie from the time he arrived in Rio until he left five days later. As the Frenchman was quoted in *Time* magazine, his visit was a very simple one: "I have come to see zat Eddee does not go to zee dogs." And, as Gilbert remembers, "He was very supportive. He spent all his time trying to cheer me up." The two spent a great deal of the visit walking the beach together, despite the often cool weather, sitting around cafes, and going to movies. Gilbert recalls that "I was in such a state I'd go to a movie one day and not be able to tell you the name of it the next day." But Coquelin's visit was positive for Eddie. "It was such a help at the time, though. I was so depressed. I didn't know what was going to happen to me. I felt so bad about the people who had been hurt by the Bruce thing, and most of the time I was just trying to figure out how I was going to be able to make it up to them, to get their losses back for them. And then Olivier arrives with nothing but good cheer. 'You'll do it,' he would say. 'Everything is going to be just fine. So let's get on with things!'"

When Coquelin had to return to his own problems in New York, Eddie accompanied him to the Rio airport. After they said their good-byes, Coquelin reached into his coat pocket and brought out his wallet, removing all the bills from it, several hundred dollars worth, and handed them to Eddie. "Here, use this for whatever you need until you've got your things back in order." Then he reached over and plucked a single $20 dollar bill from the roll Eddie was holding. "For the cab from Idlewild," he said, and then hurried off to the departure gate. Eddie was deeply touched.

The next to arrive were Eddie's pals from England, John and Jane Aspinall and Richard Parkes. Aspinall had in fact cabled Gilbert immediately on learning his old gambling and gamboling cohort had fled to Brazil, addressing him c/o the "Copocabana Beach Hotel, Rio de Janeiro":

Only discovered [your] address today. Please call Belgravia 5108 [the Aspinalls' London telephone number]. Anything that I can do to help, just cable. Hope to come to Rio for 10 days to see you. Personal situation intact. Just to us you are still the greatest.

Love — John and Jane

Somehow the telegram caught up with him later and was in fact one of the very first pieces of correspondence Eddie received. Like Olivier Coquelin's gesture, it meant a lot to him.

Both Parkes and Aspinall had taken major hits in the Bruce-Celotex affair. Gilbert had met Richard Parkes through Aspinall on the French Riviera in the 1950s; and in early 1962 Eddie had approached Parkes about buying stock for him on the London stock exchange. Parkes was a tall, handsome young man, who had been heavyweight boxing champion at Oxford. He came from a quite wealthy British family who, at the time, resided in Ireland because of the numbing effects of the British graduated income tax. Parkes' father had been a successful inventor and, among other pursuits, owned three greyhound racing tracks in England. Parkes, Aspinall, and Gilbert had been regular companions at gambling and partying in Europe, especially in London and at Eddie's Cap Martin villa during the preceding half-decade.

"Eddie called me in London one day," Parkes explains. "He asked me on the telephone if I had a stock broker here. Which I had, a good friend of mine he was, too. Eddie wanted me to buy stock in my name, but for him. He told me what a great investment it was and how in the end we would all do very well." The arrangement was a simple verbal one made over the telephone between two friends. Parkes would buy the stock and hold it for Gilbert, and Gilbert would guarantee it against any loss and share with Parkes the anticipated profit. "I, of course, believed Eddie. I had great faith in him and his ability to make money. In addition, he was a wonderful friend. So, I guess, if all be told, I bought maybe £30,000 worth over the next few months. On credit [margin] with my broker. Then that Blue or Black Monday thing in America came along and everything was lost. My broker called and told me of it. Told me I owed the

192                                                    BOY WONDER OF WALL STREET

firm a lot of money. And then I heard that Eddie was in South America."

Aspinall, on the other hand, had invested heavily for himself in the stock of the E. L. Bruce Company, believing in Gilbert's counsel. Made over the previous few years, he valued his investment at £150,000 before the Wall Street debacle of 1962. For John Aspinall, reckoning for his investment in Bruce came at the least propitious time imaginable. His posh London gambling establishment, the Clermont Club, was scheduled to open a month later, so the last thing he needed at that moment was any drain on his liquid assets. Ever since Parliament had legalized gambling in Britain in 1960, Aspinall had been at work to make his lifelong dream come true. He could gratify his deep-seated loves for gambling and the opulent life in one domain, so to speak, over which he would preside and within which he would entertain and be entertained. His own personal resources were quite limited when the market collapse came but not nearly as limited as they had been when he had traveled the exclusive Mediterranean ports of call with Eddie Gilbert a few years earlier. He had signed a 21-year lease for a handsome mansion at 44 Berkley Square in London; it had been built in 1742 for Lady Isabella Finch, known to her friends simply as Lady Bel, one of the daughters of the 7TH Earl of Winchelsea, and later deeded to the first (and last) Earl of Clermont, William Fortescue, in the late 18th century. Fontescue was a renowned sportsman and gambler (known as the "Father of the Turf" for his affinity to horse racing), activities that were so near and dear to Aspinall's heart that he decided to name his new club in the earl's honor. But with an annual rent commitment of £12,500, and a further £90,000 sunk into the restoration of the magnificent residence, Aspinall had stretched himself to his personal limit investing in the Clermont Club.

"It was a disaster," Aspinall observed more than three and a half decades later, "but not one that could not be overcome. I had great admiration and affection for Eddie. He had, after all, been of such great use to me when I could not have been much use to him. He was a rich man, you remember, who constantly bailed me out. He took me to his parties and those of others, looked after me, and I accepted his hospitality. And I never returned it before that time because I didn't have any way to return it. It was a one-way deal in those days [before Brazil]."

On the day after Blue Monday in May of 1962, Aspinall learned that not only had his £150,000 investment been wiped out, but he still owed about half that amount to brokers from whom he had bought on margin. They demanded immediate payment. "I remember, they came in person," Aspinall explained. "A Mr. Irwin and a Mr. Brock. They were a very gloomy pair." He did not have the money, Aspinall told them. All his resources were tied up in the Clermont Club which had yet to open its doors. "They said to me, 'Well, if you don't pay us, we'll get hammered,' which is the word you use in the stock exchange in London. You get hammered—the same as saying 'This man can't meet his commitment.' I said, 'Well, hell, you're going to get hammered then because there's no way I can find £75,000. They weren't very happy with that, I recall." After some searching, though, Aspinall was able to sell his debt to a merchant bank in England. "It took the better part of a year and a half," Aspinall recalls, "paying, I believe it was £5,000 a month to the bank for the debt and the interest they had attached to it, but I finally made good on it, the entire bloody debt."

This episode provides a good illustration of the friendship between Eddie Gilbert and John Aspinall, as reported by Brian Masters, Aspinall's biographer, in *The Passion of John Aspinall:* "He [Aspinall] did not once consider either of the two consequences one would normally expect to flow from such a disaster: He did not cancel plans to open the Clermont Club ... and he did not turn with bitterness or anger upon Eddie Gilbert, the author of his tribulation. The one might be regarded as foolhardy, the other sentimental; but in Aspinall's case both responses were in tune with a personality still rooted in mythical values and boyish enthusiasms.

"When he realized that Gilbert was ruined, Aspinall wept. He could not conceive that a man whose wizardry and will he had so much admired should be brought low, could not bear that the pedestal should be kicked from under one of his heroes—what he could not conceive or bear he would not accept, and he clung to the firm faith he held in Gilbert's resilience and skill."

Or as Aspinall himself put it, upon reflection many years later: "I always knew there was an inherent risk, that we could lose everything. . . . Eddie was a true gambler. He and I are like that. And a real, true gambler will put his reputation at risk. The highest of stakes. He did . . . and I would have to. And though I lost a fortune with him, I never for a minute blamed him for it. If anyone were to blame, it was that horrible fellow André Meyer for what he did at the time, or that other chap John Loeb [Bruce company director] who so let Eddie down at the end. As far as I was concerned, however bad my position was, and it certainly was at the time, the thought to begrudge Eddie never entered my mind, and my position was not nearly as bad as what he was facing. I was not facing jail."

After Gilbert read the cable from the Aspinalls, he called John in London first and subsequently Richard Parkes at his home about 20 miles outside of that city. He assured both that he would make their losses up to them but that it would take time. He explained that he had nothing left, that he would no longer entertain extravagantly on the French Riviera, that there would be no more yachting about the Mediterranean, no more suites at Claridges's or sumptuous dinners at fancy London restaurants. At least for a while, Eddie told both of his British friends. He was scrambling, he said, starting from scratch, but he would turn it around. And they believed him.

As Richard Parkes explains, "I was horrified at first, when I learned how much I'd lost. Quite understandable, one would say. But not with Eddie. I knew Eddie so well. I could not imagine him being down for very long. Then when he called me from South America and said, 'Don't worry. Don't worry, You'll get it all back.' I was certain I would. And incidentally he did pay back every cent that I'd lost, but I really hadn't the slightest doubt he would."

The day after Gilbert called his old pals in England, John Aspinall was on the telephone to Richard Parkes, who remembers the conversation: "Richard, I'm going out with Jane to take Eddie a bit of ready money. Would you like to come along?"

"Well... well, of course."

"Good, settled. Richard, I'll make the arrangements. It's a bloody trip over, no easy way to get there. Oh, and bring along some money for Eddie."

Aspinall was correct: It was not easy to get from London to Rio de Janeiro in 1962. There was a stop in Lisbon, Portugal, and a change of planes in Recife, Brazil; it was a full day's trip.

On the long flight over, they talked about their friend and speculated about what they would encounter when they came face to face with Eddie in his exile. "He sounded fine on the telephone. Well, maybe not fine, but not despondent, anyway. I am a bit worried," John Aspinall said. Richard Parkes said he was not sure what to expect, only that he had great faith in Eddie's ability to bounce back, adding philosphically, "although I'd not known Eddie ever to have had to bounce *back* from anything before." Jane Aspinall said merely, "Eddie is Eddie. Don't worry."

Jane, the head-turningly beautiful former Scottish model, proved the most prescient of the three.

John Aspinall remembered the meeting with Eddie in Rio this way: "He had a smile, so delighted to see us. He was just the same. The same valiant personality. Full of plans. He told us right off he was going to rebuild his fortune, and none of us doubted it. Oh, he was feisty, all right. Cursing André Meyer, cursing a couple of other enemies... and cursing Rhoda. All of us knew she had gone off and bought that $700,000 worth of stuff from Cartier at the worst possible time."

The Aspinalls and Richard Parkes stayed just short of a week. John and Jane had brought some money for Eddie, as they said they would; Gilbert remembers it was approximately £1,000. "It was all they could muster after what had happened. Jane, I believe, sold some of her jewelry to get what added up to a few hundred extra dollars to bring down there"—a fact corroborated in John Aspinall's biography. Richard Parkes remembers bringing another £500 for his friend in need. "It really helped at that time," Eddie mentions. "So, so much, because I was just getting ready to get into some things down there and start making some money again."

One of the things Eddie had in mind was an "arrangement" he hoped to make with a jeweler in Rio whom he had recently met. The man's name was Hans Stern, and he owned a small but apparently successful jewelry store in an exclusive area of Rio de Janeiro. Stern was a Jewish émigré from Germany and had launched his jewelry business in 1945 after having become fascinated with the rich variety of colorful gemstones indigenous to the country where he had settled. Although his business had grown respectably over the next 17 years, it had reached a plateau by the time Eddie met Stern in 1962. After having talked with Stern about his business, Eddie felt the man needed considerable financial guidance. "He told me he had a lot of cash," Gilbert recalls. "And he said he had some ideas about expanding on an international level and also about getting personally involved in investing some of his own money in other areas. I felt I could be of some help to him. I wanted him to hire me to do that."

Eddie explained all this to the Aspinalls, and John then came up with an idea to help his friend. Brian Masters, in his Aspinall biography, writes that: "... [Aspinall engaged] in an elaborate charade to bolster his friend's reputation. Behaving as if he were among the richest men in the world, Aspinall went to the jeweler H. Stern and bought $3,000 worth of precious stones (he actually had only £400 to spend), in order that Stern should be impressed and should then heed his advice to use Gilbert's expertise on the stock market."

Mr. Stern was so pleased with the sale, he invited the Aspinalls, Parkes, and Gilbert to join him and his wife "for a lunch on my yacht." Aspinall remembered it as "a rather uninspired picnic on a little boat," while Parkes recalls that, "The boat was named the *Aqua Marina*. After the stone, I presume, aquamarine. He was a jeweler, after all. It was not much of a boat, however. Certainly not when measured by what Eddie and John and I had been accustomed to in the south of France." Gilbert remembers it as "a long, fruitless afternoon and a lousy lunch." During the luncheon boat-ride, Aspinall made a point of extolling to Stern and his wife Eddie Gilbert's financial acumen and how valuable he could be to a man of Mr. Stern's means. And Richard Parkes added his enthusiastic endorsement. But for whatever reason, Mr. Stern decided not to avail himself of Gilbert's financial wizardry.

As it turned out, Hans Stern did pretty well on his own. According to a recent corporate brochure, by the end of the 20th century, the firm of H. Stern Jewelers, Inc., with its headquarters still in Rio de Janeiro, and additional distribution in 180 stores located in cities throughout the world, had evolved, "from a purveyor of colored stones to the largest family-owned business of its kind [in the world].... " And the H. Stern Gem Museum in Ipanema, housing the private collection of Hans Stern and offering workshop tours, had become one of the most popular tourist attractions in Rio.

When the Aspinalls and Richard Parkes packed up to return to England, Eddie had André Todor retrieve the two rare Mauritius stamps—the 1847 1 p(enny) orange and the 1847 2 p(enny) dark blue—which he had been holding for Gilbert in his safe deposit vault. Eddie turned them over to Aspinall, asking him to sell them at Harmer's in London (where he had bought the two stamps for $14,000 a few years earlier).

"It was a distressed sale," Aspinall remembers with some sadness. "I'd hoped to do well for Eddie, but the story about him was all over London, in all the newspapers. I took them to Harmer's personally as soon as I got back to England, as if I owned them, but they knew where the stamps had come from. After all, the two were quite precious, or rare. They knew at Harmer's they were Eddie's and naturally they slaughtered him. I couldn't do any kind of deal. They offered $8,000 for the two, I believe it was. Awful. Bloody awful. I called Eddie in South America and told him. He was very disappointed. 'But I need the money,' he told me, 'so sell them.' I did, and sent the money on to Eddie." By contemporary standards, the value for them is staggering: According to a recent *Scott Classic Specialized Catalog*, the 1847 1 p orange is valued today at $1,100,000, and the 1847 2 p dark blue at $500,000.

One visitor whom Eddie had not expected, indeed had no desire whatsoever to see, arrived one day during that first month. Eddie called him "an emisarry" of Charles Kandel, the manager of the Sands Hotel in Las Vegas, but he would be better described as a casino bill collector. The Sands, a notorious gambling emporium on the Strip in Las Vegas, was alleged to have been controlled in the 1950s and early 60s by New York mobsters Meyer Lansky and Frank Costello (in league with Chicago's Tony Accardo and Sam Giancana). Entertainers George Raft and Frank Sinatra also held financial interests in the Sands. Gilbert had a $250,000 line of credit at the Sands casino and had left an outstanding debt of $120,000 when he broke off his Nevada residency for divorce earlier in the year and had returned to New York. He had departed so abruptly, in fact, that he had left behind a closet full of clothes in his hotel suite. Having read about Eddie's flight to Rio, Kandel dispatched one of his more versatile debt-resolution specialists to survey and resolve the situation.

Kandel's "emissary" telephoned Eddie once he got to Rio and told him he would like to have a little chat. Realizing he had little choice in the matter, Eddie invited him over to his apartment. The visitor turned out to be pleasant, undoubtedly because Eddie had been a major high-roller at the Sands in the recent past; and he and Kandel had also become friends during the time Eddie lived in Las Vegas.

Eddie explained his financial condition, although that quickly became apparent to his visitor. "He nosed around in each of the four rooms, one at a time, like he was going to rent the place," Eddie remembers, even inspecting the noticeably barren closets. "And then he said: 'This place is really depressing. C'mon I'll buy you lunch somewhere.'"

After the man reported back to his boss in Las Vegas about how Eddie was living in Rio de Janeiro, Kandel shot off this letter on the Sands stationery.

*Dear Eddie —*

*I want you to know how sorry I am about all your troubles and sincerely hope it won't be long until you get everything straightened out ....*

*Now then about your personal effects and clothing which you left here at the hotel — before we could get to the rooms and pack them to send ... a court order reached Las Vegas [confiscating them] and consequently there was nothing any of us could do....*

*If you wish and would want me to I will be pleased to buy you a couple of suits, any other clothing you may need or shoes and pay for them out of my pocket, then some day when you have everything straightened out you can pay me back. If this will help you let me know what you need or want and the sizes and [I] will take care of it immediately.*

*Cordially,*
*Charlie*

Not a mention of the $120,000 Gilbert owed. Writing back, Eddie thanked him for the clothing offer, but declined, telling Kandel that he did not need much in the way of clothing given the turn his life had so recently taken. But he did acknowledge the debt in his note, and his intention to pay it off "just as soon as I get back on my feet." And, in increments, Gilbert did just that over the next few years after he had returned to the United States.

The person Eddie Gilbert most wanted to visit him in Rio, however, was reluctant. After that muddled first week, he had called Turid at her New York apartment every day. Their conversations routinely ended with his asking when she planned to join him and her response of "sometime soon." As Turid remembers of that time, "I didn't know what was going on. I knew Eddie was in trouble, and I wanted to help but I had no idea how I might do that." The truth of the matter was that Turid simply did not understand the situation or where she stood in it, and she was understandably frightened. They had planned to be married as soon as his divorce from Rhoda was final, but now nothing was final, and she had no

TOOLS OF HIS TRADE

199

idea whether her fiance would be on his way to the altar or to the penitentiary.

Eddie's persistence paid off, however; about a month after Eddie settled into his life in Brazil, Turid took some time off from her job as stewardess with Pan American Airways and flew, as a passenger, to Rio. "She looked fabulous," Eddie remembers, "but she seemed very unsettled." Their intimacy was strained, a condition that was compounded when Turid checked into the elegant Excelsior Hotel on the Avenida Atlantica overlooking Copocabana Beach and Sugar Loaf Mountain rather than taking up occupancy in Eddie's tiny apartment, which would have been his preference. Turid acted partly out of her sense of propriety. She liked to refer to herself as an "old-fashioned Scandanavian woman"; and Eddie's precarious personal situation made her especially uncomfortable. "I remember I went down there that first time and I wore a babushka, you know, a head scarf, and sun glasses so no one would recognize me. I was very self-conscious at that time."

Turid's visit was disconcerting for Gilbert in another way as well. Just the day before she arrived, Eddie's attorney Arnold Bauman had returned to Rio with two U.S. government officials who had vested interests in Gilbert: Peter Morrison from the Justice Department and Irving Pollack from the Securities and Exchange Commission. They were there to talk serious business, principally about whether and when Gilbert might be returning to the United States. Turid came to put together in her mind exactly what Eddie's situation was and, just as importantly, how she might fit into it.

Eddie was caught in the middle. He had to juggle a handful of rocky legal problems with a romantic situation that was growing more fragile by the moment.

Gilbert had been under the impression that Bauman's purpose in bringing the government representatives to visit him was to strike a deal as to his return. Bauman had previously telephoned to say he had been working on "an arrangement" with the government. After putting together all the facts of the case, he told Eddie, he would then be able to arrange a proper plea bargain that would enable Eddie to return to the United States. But that is not what happened once they arrived in Rio.

When Bauman brought Morrison and Pollack to Gilbert's apartment the morning they arrived, Eddie said he had every intention of returning to the United States, even though he would not say when, because that depended on what Eddie called "the situation." Although the two government officials were willing to talk about "the situation," they said they had no plea bargain proposal in their briefcases, at least not one that they were willing to lay on the table before him. They wanted Eddie first to turn over his U.S. passport to be held at the U.S. Embassy in Rio de Janeiro. Eddie discussed the matter with Bauman who suggested that relinquishing it would be an act of good faith. So Eddie agreed, especially as he did not intend to travel anywhere outside Brazil anyway. Other than the passport matter, the discussions over the next three days about Eddie's status were rambling and imprecise as to the case against him and the legal issues he faced.

Peter Morrison, representing the U.S. Attorney's office of the Justice Department, was the more important figure as far as Gilbert was concerned, and he appeared to be sympathetic to Gilbert's situation. Although he made no promises, Morrison left Eddie with the impression that nothing dire would come of his return to the United States. There would be *pro forma* court appearances, surely, but his situation could be resolved without much difficulty nor serious consequence for Gilbert. Turid, in fact, has the vivid memory of Eddie's telling her during her visit that the government men had assured him that although he would have to appear before a judge, he would "get a suspended sentence, nothing more, and that would be it." Arnold Bauman took Eddie aside, as the three men were leaving to return to the United States, and assured him of the same thing.

Eddie did not have nearly enough time to spend with Turid during her few days in Rio, but in their few hours together he tried to assure her that he wanted everything to work out between them, that his current expatriot status was just temporary, and that he soon would have everything put back in order so they could resume a normal life in New York. A life much changed, though; they both knew that. Turid listened, but remembers it as a not pleasant situation, and that she felt uncomfortable throughout the visit.

She stayed for just a few days, ultimately telling Eddie that she had to get back to work. She explained rather unconvincingly that she had been on an earned leave of absence that had run out and that she had to return to New York. Altogether it had been an awkward visit, and both Turid and Eddie remember being depressed when it ended.

But before she left, Eddie retrieved from André Todor's safe deposit box the engagement ring that Turid returned to him at Idlewild. He had bought the exquisite eight-carat diamond ring (with a price tag of $40,000) at Harry Winston's in New York. Only Eddie had not paid for it. His credit at the elegant jewelry store had been unquestioned, but then the catastrophe came. In turning over the ring to her again, Eddie asked Turid to return it to Harry Winston when she got back to New York; and a few days later, she did.

As Eddie saw Turid off at the airport that day, despite her reassurances that she would soon return, he had an aching, disconcerting feeling that he might never see Turid Holtan again.

In New York, Turid did not stay on the job at Pan Am for long, however. Less than two weeks later, Eddie learned that she had decided to go to Norway for an indeterminate period of time, staying with her parents in Oslo. All of this unexpected disruption only exacerbated the feeling Eddie had when she had left Rio to return to America. It was uncomfortably reminiscent of that draining feeling of loss and circumstantial helplessness he had experienced so vividly and with such disconsolation when he had first arrived in South America.

*Tall and tan and young and lovely.*
  *The girl from Ipanema goes walking*
*And when she passes, each one she passes*
  *Goes a-a-a-a-h . . .*

*Oh, but I watch her so sadly,*
  *How can I tell her I love her*
*Yes, I would give my heart gladly,*
  *But each day when she walks to the sea*
*She looks straight ahead,*
  *Not at me.*

"THE GIRL FROM IPANEMA"
ANTONIO CARLOS JOBIM AND VINICIUS DE MORAES

As the days of expatriation in Brazil turned into weeks, life for Eddie Gilbert grew routine and unchallenging, as well as financially stagnant. He was not used to being strapped for money nor living at the level he had descended to on the social scale. Six months earlier he had been luxuriating in an art-filled 5th Avenue apartment, or the elegant town house on the upper eastside of Manhattan, or his splendid villa on the French Riviera. In Rio he now lived in a spare apartment with a bedroom the size of an eight-by-ten-foot cell. That half-year before he had nearly $15 million in reserve, now all he had was what was left of the $2,500 he had brought with him and the £1,500 in loans (about $4,000) the Aspinalls and Richard Parkes had provided.

So, shortly after Turid left, Eddie began to think seriously about making some money again. As fate would have it—Eddie Gilbert's kind of fate, that is—he got the stake he needed. It came enclosed in a second letter from Albert Ratner. Eddie's former business colleague once again sent a certified check for $10,000 payable to Edward M. Gilbert, insisting that Eddie accept it. Gilbert acceded to Ratner's wishes this time. And he thought he knew just what to do with the money.

Timber seemed a good place to start; after all, he had been in the lumber business all his working life, and Brazil was rich in forest resources. There were thousands of tree species in the semideciduous and rain forests of Brazil; among them, the most important wood harvested in the 1960s was the Parana pine. Although not a high-grade lumber, it had a variety of commercial applications. There was also an abundance of jacaranda with its expensive rosewood. When Eddie began to look into Brazil's lumber industry in 1962, the country was already producing about 10 percent of the world's roundwood inventory, which is to say timber with its bark removed before being processed into lumber.

Eddie began to study all aspects of the business in order to find his own proper niche. He remembers the time with a shake of his head, "In the United States you've got three or four species [of tree] on a tract. In Brazil you've got maybe 120 different woods growing together. You've got to know which of these species goes where in what industry. That's where I figured I would come in handy."

Tony Stratton Smith chronicled one of Eddie's early forays into Brazilian lumber, describing a trip they took in a "well-worn jeep" which "bounced along the mountain road, sometimes veering dangerously close to the precipitous drop to one side and almost purposely slamming into every pot-hole along the way; it spun like a busy gnat through those high, rain-moody Brazilian mountains."

"Eddie was on the move . . . ." Smith wrote. "This trip was to inspect a sawmill deep in the Sao Paolo State at the invitation of its owner. If he liked what he saw, he was back with a claim in the lumber business, with a percentage in exchange for his know-how.

"The mill foreman was there to meet him, and proudly swept Eddie toward the plant . . . . He led Eddie to the rusting machinery—English-built, circa 19th century—and kicked away a snarling dog. Never one to hide his true feelings, Eddie took one look and said: 'This must be a signed

Louis XV piece.'"

Eddie quickly concluded that this was not the way he wanted to get back into the lumber business, and so he immediately lost interest. But he and Smith decided not to leave until the next morning, because they had even less interest in trying to negotiate the winding, unpaved mountain roads back to Rio in the dark of night.

"He spent the rest of the day practicing homing calls with the pig-man Oscar," Smith writes, "and, in slacks and sweat-shirt, kneeling down to teach Negro housemaids how to build a practical woodfire. 'Being inactive kills me,' he says, 'I'll go out of my way to find something to do.'"

Smith ended the story with the observation, "Eddie feeds on action like a hungry man handling a steak."

Despite his research and several other journeys into the Brazilian woodlands, neither timber nor lumber worked out for Gilbert. He also looked into the charcoal business, which was just getting under way in Brazil, although the prospect of good-quality wood being burned for charcoal "sickened his lumberman's soul," Smith reported. Eddie also considered becoming involved in raising and marketing pigs; he looked at a laundry soap factory just outside Rio and at a plastic bottle-cap company in the city. "He has had overtures about postcards, carnauba wax (an extraction from a Brazilian palm that is commonly used in candles), and real estate. The boot-and-shoe industry interests him," Smith also records.

What proved to be the biggest attraction for Eddie Gilbert, however, was his old friend, the stock market. The Brazilian stock exchange was called BOVESPA, an acronym for *Bosla de Valores de Sao Paolo* or simply the Sao Paolo Stock Exchange; it had been operating in Brazil since 1890.

Eddie Gilbert's entry into it occurred from pure serendipity. In a Turkish bath that had become a regular haunt of his, Eddie was sitting on a wooden bench one July afternoon, wrapped in a towel, sweating it out, when another towel-clad bather approached and sat a few feet away. The tall man, about 60 years old, had an aristocratic air about him, and he nodded pleasantly to Gilbert. So Eddie introduced himself.

After a bit of a double-take, the gentleman said with a strong French accent, "You're *the* Eddie Gilbert, aren't you? The one from America ... the Wall Street wonder?" Eddie said he was. "My name is Gilbert Deschartre," the man replied, "and I've been hoping to meet you."

Gilbert learned that Deschartre had emigrated from France several decades earlier and now owned and operated a small but quite successful manufacturing company in Rio. But the Frenchman also wanted to learn to trade successfully on the Brazilian stock market. He was most interested in Gilbert's ideas and opinions on the subject, he said; and before the two had left the bath, Deschartre said, "I'd like you to come by my office. I should think we could do some business together."

"Perhaps," Gilbert said with a shrug, not wanting to let on just how interested he was.

"Tomorrow, then?"

"Why not?"

When the two sat down in Deschartre's office the next afternoon, the Frenchman indicated that he was very much aware of Eddie's reputation as "the boy wonder of Wall Street"; and he knew all about the present financial misfortunes which had brought Gilbert to South America and "into my life," as he described it. Deschartre really wanted Eddie Gilbert to come to work for him; but when Gilbert demurred, the Frenchman proposed a kind of investment partnership. He had a fair amount of money to invest, he said, but would feel more comfortable investing in the Brazilian stock market if Gilbert were there to advise him The deal would be a simple one, according to Deschartre. Gilbert would study the market for investments to recommend to Deschartre. If he followed Gilbert's counsel and made the proposed investment, Eddie would receive a share of the profits (but would not be responsible for any losses). There would be no salary or draw, no retainer, just a gentleman's agreement. Gilbert thought it was a great idea.

For Eddie, it was an opportunity to get into the market without risking any of the small stake that he had accumulated during the past month in Brazil. He could do it with someone else's money and at someone else's risk. So during the next few weeks he began to look at several stocks. "I only looked at a couple of them, and I got maybe two or three yearly statements about each. One looked pretty good to me, good in the sense that I thought it was underpriced and had a lot of potential to expand. It was a local beer, called Brahma, like the bull, Brahma Beer."

Brahma Beer was the anchor product of Cervejaria Brahma, a company whose brewery was located within Rio's city limits. Gilbert recommended it to Deschartre. The Frenchman asked if Eddie were going to invest in it himself. Eddie said he would invest a little, but he could not afford to put very much into it. Deschartre was convinced and invested heavily.

"It was just luck," Eddie recalls. "It looked good on paper to me, but none of us expected it to do what it did." What Brahma Beer stock did was soar 20 percent in the first two days that Deschartre and Gilbert owned the stock and soon after that had doubled in value. "It was a volatile market down there, and it just skyrocketed," Eddie remembers. "So then we sold it and took a quick profit. I had a check from Deschartre before the week was out for somewhere between $50,000 and $60,000."

Although the trade richly whetted Deschartre's investment appetite, the Brahma Beer deal was the only one that the two men would do together. Eddie went his own way after it, much more healthy financially.

With things moving along so well in exile, Eddie began thinking more and more about the biography that Tony Stratton Smith kept talking about. So he fired off a letter to his old school pal, Jack Kerouac—now a celebrated writer—to get his advice and perhaps some help. Finding the peripatetic author of *On the Road* had never been easy, so Eddie sent his letter to Kerouac's family's address, the way he had managed to keep their correspondence going over the years. Eddie's letters had always caught up to Kerouac and he had always replied. This time was no exception. Kerouac's sister wrote Eddie after the letter addressed to Jack arrived; she told him that Jack was vacationing somewhere in Maine (nobody knew where exactly), so she had forwarded Eddie's letter to Jack's last known address in Orlando, Florida.

Gilbert apparently harbored some doubts as to whether Tony Stratton Smith would be able to pull off writing his life story. As in the old days at Horace Mann, Eddie wondered if Jack might apply his pen on Eddie's behalf. A book, however, was something more than an English term paper; and so Kerouac responded:

*Dear Eddy:*

*. . . I just read your letter 48 hours ago.*

*I know you havent [sic] had time to read my books (I think) but if so, you'll see that I only write about the things I saw with my own eyes—And of course I never ghostwrite—I've had lots of offers to ghostwrite . . . But it's against my plan which is to write only what I see myself and therefore feel and know for sure.*

*Besides, now listen to me: get yourself a good tape recorder... and tell your story into it—Then have a stenographer type it up double space for the publishers—If after he's typed it there are some things you don't like, cross them out, fill in things with your pencil, and have him type it all up again neatly—I happen to know that everybody in the world can tell his story better than anyone else.*

*With the certain bestseller sales for this, plus movie sale, you'll make enough to start paying back the debts, if not all of them... and because of the tremendous worldwide fame you have, and the eagerness of people to hear the fabulous details of your countesses and contessas and villas and all, don't accept peanut-style royalty rates—I'd say for you to insist on a 30% royalty rate on all copies sold....*

*I'm absolutely convinced, Eddy you old bastard, that you can tell your story into that tape recorder better than anyone else can "fix" it for you—Take this as my solemn word if you believe my knowledge about literature—And when I say "Eddy you old bastard" I only mean that's what we used to call each other, remember?*

*Eddy, all the luck in the world... I bet any dough I'll see you again someday and we'll have a good time like we always did.*

*(p.s. when you tell a story into a tape recorder microphone, get a few drinks in you...)*

    *Later*

    *—Jack*

    *Down to the tiniest detail is what makes a story interesting*

Eddie prized the letter, even though he never got that tape recorder. Instead he just went back to telling Tony Stratton Smith about the events of his life; the two remained constant companions throughout the late winter and early spring of 1962 in Brazil. The two not only discussed what might go into the book about Eddie Gilbert's life, but they also went to the opera together, to soccer matches and horse races, played sports, and often made small wagers on everything from the exchange rate between dollars and cruzeiros on a given day to which team would score first in a local soccer match.

Eddie received stacks and stacks of letters during these months, and he replied to each and every one of them; he was forced to hire a part-time secretary with shorthand skills to whom he dictated the letters. He maintained a regular correspondence with his mother and father in New York and with his sister Enid in Venice. He also wrote regularly to Turid in Norway and to his daughters Robin and Alexandra who did their best to answer them with lots of xxx's and ooo's and hand-drawn hearts. Letters were also exchanged with John Aspinall in England, Luciano Ancilotto in Rome, various business contacts in Switzerland, and loyal friends like Jerry Stern, Sherman Fairchild, Olivier Coquelin, and others in New York.

Many of the letters had heartwarming human touches. His former secretary at Bruce, fired from her job, wrote from New York: "On Friday we were told we could buy any of the office equipment we wanted. The office here [E. L. Bruce Company's office on Madison Avenue] will be closed soon. Although I'm not in a position to do so, because I don't know how long it will take me to find a job, I've decided to buy the typewriter for $95. At least when you come back we will have one piece of absolutely essential equipment to start in again."

A former business acquaintance who had lost heavily in the market and had broken his leg around the same time wrote: "I can't even get up to go to the john. If you think you have troubles, try using a bed pan for a solid week and your problems won't seem so aggravating."

Another woman, whom Eddie scarcely knew, wrote: "The people who loved you didn't love you for your $15 millions, they loved you because of your spirit, your intelligence, your wit, your boldness, and your kindness."

Two former maids in the Gilbert household sent him a plaster model of the Infant of Prague. "We had it blessed," they wrote. "Put it somewhere where you can see it. Maybe it will bring you luck." And from Italy, a friend from Eddie's jet-setting days and a self-proclaimed count (who also was another ill-fated investor), suggested, "Is it not possible for you to come here incognito? At least here you would have many friends."

Some of the letters bothered Eddie profoundly, however, such as this one from his Aunt Celia, who had lost $20,000 in the Bruce-Celotex debacle: "If my financial situation were not so harrowing, I would be amused by your request that I look into my vault for stocks and bonds [her reference to a facetious remark Eddie had made in a previous letter]. Eddie dear, everything I had I turned over to you. I was not cagey [sic], and kept nothing to myself. I had no reason to. You see, I never doubted you and in spite of the present situation, I still do not doubt you."

Gilbert's financial life was succeeding so well in Brazil late that summer that he bought a Cadillac convertible, a 1953 model with a lot of miles on the odometer, and hired a chauffeur to drive him around. But most of all he wanted to move from the tiny apartment on Rua Siqueira Campos. Through some of his recent connections in Rio, he found a more commodious apartment on the 11th floor of the building at #45 Rua Inhanga, having a balcony and an ocean view. It belonged to a woman named Simone Delamarr, the alleged mistress of a high-ranking Brazilian governmental minister and, according to a later article in *Newsweek* magazine, "one of King Farouk's flings" earlier. For some reason unknown to Gilbert, she was departing Brazil for Europe and was delighted to sublet her elegant apartment for the sum of $500 per month (princely in 1962 dollars in the Brazilian economy). Eddie hired a full-time maid and then told Tony Stratton Smith to pack his things; they were moving up in the world.

In the United States, things were not quite so rosy. By early August, the Bruce company reported that it had liquidated its holding in Celotex Corporation. They dumped the 69,200 shares they had held since their acquisition while Gilbert was president for $2,076,000 ($30 a share), taking a loss of about $400,000. The stock had been acquired at an average price of $35.76 a share and during 1962 had traded on the New York Stock Exchange for as low as 16.25 a share, and as high as 42⅜ a share. Information about these developments came in a three-page letter from E. L. Bruce, Jr., to the company's shareholders. "The situation of the company is more than ordinarily difficult due to the recent events," he began, "but I and all other officers believe that the basic business of the company is sound." He went on to say that "the sale of the Celotex stock has considerably strengthened the company's cash position." Much more guarded now in his public assessment of the situation than he had been earlier, Bruce added that the auditors' examination of the company's books confirmed that the withdrawal by Edward M. Gilbert amounted to $1,953,000. "It is possible, of course," he wrote, "that our continuing investigation may disclose additional losses or claims against the company as a result of Gilbert's actions." Such a cautionary note was undoubtedly prompted by the company's lawyers, because Bruce had privately said he was quite certain that there were no additional financial complications nor compromising factors as a result of Gilbert's actions. Bruce went on to explain that the ongoing audit continued, but probably would not be finished before the end of August.

He noted that suspended trade in E. L. Bruce Company stock, instituted by the Securities and Exchange Commission after Gilbert's resignation, was still in effect; the suspension would not be lifted until the company's audit had been satisfactorily completed.

E. L. Bruce, Jr., was privately understood to be as optimistic about the condition of the company as he seemed to be in this letter to the shareholders. He was alleged to have said that Gilbert's misdeeds had not extended beyond the checks he had earlier reported to the board of directors. Everything would work out, Mr. Bruce had observed; it would all be settled, it would just take some time. From such reported statements, it was clear that E. L. Bruce, Jr., was still fond of the brash young man who had moved the staid company onto an ascending path that had nearly doubled its value during his four tempestuous years at the head of it.

Gilbert continued to make money in Brazil following the Brahma Beer windfall, regularly exploring a wide variety of business opportunities there. For Eddie, it was still the spirit of the game, the thrill of the chase, whether in Portuguese-speaking Brazil or in the more familiar markets and boardrooms of New York.

One quick way to make cash in the inflation-riddled Brazilian economy, he discovered, was to deal directly in the money market, exchanging American dollars and Brazilian cruzeiros. He had come in contact with Alexander Vamos, the bell captain at the Excelsior Hotel on Copacabana Beach when Turid had stayed there on her earlier visit to Rio. Vamos had made some money on the side by procuring favorable exchange rates for well-heeled guests in the hotel. After talking with him at some length and assessing Vamos's access to the money-exchange trade, Gilbert also assessed the level of volatility in the exchange rate then prevailing in Brazil and concluded that there was a bona fide opportunity to make substantial gains in currency exchanges. So he and Vamos became partners, an arrangement that proved to be wildly successful for them both. How it worked was simple. Vamos needed cruzeiros to provide to wealthy Americans staying at the Excelsior, so Gilbert would buy cruzeiros in the black market with his own dollars at a most favorable rate (American dollars were a prized commodity in the inflation-wracked Brazilian economy). He would then turn the cruzeiros over to Vamos, who would sell them to hotel guests for their dollars at the higher but still favorable "going exchange rate." At the end of the day the two men would meet, and Gilbert would get his dollars from Vamos for the next day's transactions. They would split the day's profits, customarily several hundred dollars apiece; and as other "clients" came into the equation, it was not uncommon for Eddie to pocket as much as $500 or even $1,000 on any given day. It gave him a regular paycheck, so to speak.

During this time, Eddie persisted in his effort not to lose contact with Turid in Norway. He was in love with her and was determined not to let her get away. But it was a difficult time for her. "He wrote almost every day," Turid remembers, "and he called all the time. It was frantic for me. My parents were very upset. We were a very old-fashioned family. They really didn't know what was going on, and I didn't know what was going to happen. My mom had met Eddie, actually it was the day we had gotten engaged." Eddie and Turid had become engaged before Eddie went to Nevada to establish his six-month residency in anticipation of divorcing Rhoda. All of this occured before his recent legal and financial troubles, though. "He'd just given me this big diamond ring from Harry Winston. It was gorgeous. My mother had never seen anything like it. 'God, do you know what you have here?' she said. I did. I said, 'Sure, it's a ring,' and laughed. And I loved it. I wore it everywhere, I remember, even when I was flying. My mother just kept saying, 'Crazy girl… crazy girl.'

"But now things were so different. My father was so very upset. He and Eddie had some very harsh words. On the telephone. My father spoke English well. My mother, she didn't. So it was he who had the communication with Eddie. He was distressed, which was understandable. After all, here I was a 22-year-old, his daughter, with a man who was now a fugitive, and not knowing what was going to happen."

Eddie had the answer to her dilemma, at least in his own mind. Turid should return to Rio to be with him. But Turid chose not to give him an answer about that during those first few weeks when she was with her parents in Oslo.

By September, with his new apartment, a car and driver, and a pocketful of cash, Gilbert was able to resurrect a bit of his flamboyant lifestyle from before Blue Monday. He still entertained with a practiced panache. According to Tony Stratton Smith, "It's at dinnertime that one best sees the range of Eddie's newfound Rio acquaintances. He's kept his gift for surrounding himself with interesting characters. His dinner tables [in his new apartment, but mostly at fashionable Rio restaurants] have included the ex-mistress of King Farouk, a white Voodoo priest who faith-heals by spirit vibrations, a hotel head porter who reads poetry in 12 languages and knew Ezra Pound in the old Paris days, a white hunter who has offered to hole him up in the Mato Grasso jungles anytime Eddie wishes, and the former head of a famous Paris fashion house."

One of Gilbert's favorite dining partners at the time was the American writer John Dos Passos. In early September, the 66-year-old Dos Passos made contact with Gilbert. The writer had taken up temporary residence in Rio while on a tour of South America. Dos Passos was best known for the novel *Manhattan Transfer*, published in 1925, and the trilogy of novels titled *U.S.A.*, comprised of *The 42nd Parallel* (1930), *1919* (1932), and *The Big Money* (1936). Dos Passos knew the story of Gilbert's financial plight and subsequent flight to Brazil and decided he wanted to meet the notorious Eddie Gilbert. Perhaps it was to plumb a possible character for a forthcoming novel, or to discover a human interest element for one of the many travel pieces he was then writing, or maybe it was just out of sheer curiosity. Dos Passos never said, and Eddie Gilbert never inquired.

Gilbert was aware, of course, of Dos Passos's reputation, considered by some in the 1930s and 40s, the contemporary equal of Ernest Hemingway, F. Scott Fitzgerald, and William Faulkner. Eddie had never read any of Dos Passos's writings, but the two still got along splendidly. They had the experiences of war in common. While Eddie had survived the combat of World War II in North Africa and Europe, Dos Passos was a World War I veteran. After graduating from Harvard in 1916, he had gone to Europe to enlist (like Hemingway) for volunteer ambulance service in the French army; and then, when America entered the war, he transferred to the U. S. army medical corps, serving (like Gilbert) as a private until the war ended.

Gilbert introduced Dos Passos to Tony Stratton Smith, who had read several of the author's novels and aspired to move higher on the literary ladder than sports writing. Smith was duly impressed by Dos Passos. "We had several dinners together in Rio de Janeiro, the three of us," he noted in his journal. "Dos Passos shared Eddie's passion for *churrasco*—charcoal-broiled steaks and meats—topped off with a rich dessert of canned guava and cheese. The American writer was also partial to *moqueca*, a seafood stew of sorts served in coconut milk. They talked business and books." In regard to the latter, Smith also remarked that "Eddie admits to having read more in Brazil in a few months than in the U. S. the same number of years... outside of balance sheets, that is." Gilbert does not recall reading any of Dos Passos's books while he was in exile in Brazil, nor discussing them in any of their conversations (although the three men did talk at some length about the book Smith was planning to write about Eddie Gilbert's life).

Over one long weekend, at the suggestion of Dos Passos, the three of them motored down to Angra dos Reis, a village and resort area on the Atlantic coast about 70 miles southwest of Rio, known for its sandy beaches and crystal-clear green waters. There they relaxed, fished, sailed among the offshore islands, ate sumptuously and, according to Smith, "had marvelous conversations on an unending series of topics." Gilbert remembers it as very enjoyable, perhaps his most worry-free time during the four and a half months he spent in South America.

Shortly after their trip to Angra dos Reis, Dos Passos left Rio to continue his travels through South America. He later wrote briefly about his stay in Rio for a travel magazine, but no mention was made of his association in Brazil with Eddie Gilbert and Tony Stratton Smith. He gave Eddie his address at the Dos Passos ancestral farm in Westmoreland (in the tidewater area of Virginia). Eddie wrote him there in mid-October 1962, principally seeking advice about how to get Smith's biography of him published. Apparently Putnam Publishing Company in New York had expressed some interest in the proposed book, which Eddie mentioned in his letter, although Smith had completed only a single, 14-page chapter by that time (which was the sum total of manuscript he would produce).

Gilbert wrote: "Tony and I have been progressing on our book, but we received a letter yesterday, telling us that Putnam were no longer interested as there seems to be a change in the editorial policy in the firm. . . . I do not want to bother you as I know you probably have many of your own projects to think about, but if you have the time I would appreciate your opinion and advice as to what you think we should do from this point. . . . What I am really trying to ask is whether or not you believe we will be best advised to disregard attempting the publishing of our book now and finish it first, or if you think we might be taking too great a risk in spending all of that time and work on this project."

Dos Passos was not much help in the matter, however. The extent of his advice was to suggest they not give up hope. After exchanging several letters during the remainder of that year, their correspondence ended; and their paths never crossed again. Dos Passos died in 1970.

At about the same time, Smith introduced Gilbert to Brazil's most famous soccer player, Edson Arantes do Nascimento, better known as Pele, who had just led Brazil to its second straight World Cup championship. Smith continued to cover sports for various English newspapers while at the same time trying to lay the foundation for a biography of his roommate. He knew there was no larger sports story in all of Latin America than Pele. By then he was well on his way to becoming a legend in the soccer world. Smith had known Pele for several years and had often interviewed him. Smith concluded that the soccer star and his likeness were not being marketed sufficiently in either England or the United States. He approached Pele with the notion of broadening his financial horizons, proposing to represent him in those countries; Pele had showed a modicum of interest. Smith recognized that he needed Eddie Gilbert's business acumen in the equation because of the complicated business arrangements and large sums of money associated with the proposal. Eddie immediately saw the economic advantages for everyone involved, and offered to bankroll the partnership because upfront cash would be needed (and he knew Smith neither had that nor the means to obtain it).

Once he had enlisted Gilbert's support, the exuberant Smith had another idea to expand the project. He had also met and written about Brazil's famed composer and musician, Antonio Carlos Jobim. Jobim had popularized both bossa nova and samba music in the United States, and to a lesser degree in Great Britain. His song, "The Girl from Ipanema," had recently risen to the top of the charts in America, and his score for the award-winning motion picture *Black Orpheus* had extended his reputation as a composer. Although his music had been exported successfully, Jobim the person and the musician had not; Tony Stratton Smith believed his likeness, just like Pele's, was marketable in the United States and England.

Several meetings were held. Gilbert and Smith sat down with Pele and his lawyers at one, and with Jobim and his legal counsel at another. Their plans and promotions were discussed, the percentages of profits and other business details presented. There was a lot to be worked out, but the meetings, as Tony Stratton Smith remembered, "were most positive." Gilbert went so far as to have his Brazilian attorney, Celso Fontenelle, draw up an initial contract for each of the two celebrities.

At the same time, Eddie's heart was really not in it. It was really Tony Stratton Smith's project. It had potential, yes, but there were many more critical things on Eddie's mind in those days, particularly his plans to return to the United States and the unresolved situation with Turid Holtan

In September, Turid made a decision that would ultimately have a profound effect on both her life and that of her fiance. "My father especially was opposed to my going back to Eddie while he was still in South America. He could not understand the situation. He did not want me to make a mistake. But I loved Eddie, and I decided to go back to him."

Gilbert had continued to call and write regularly during the intervening weeks, so the day Turid told him over the telephone that she was returning to Rio, he was ecstatic. "My parents went along with my decision, but I'm not sure it was one they agreed with. My father and some friends took me to the airport in Oslo, I remember, and my father cried."

It was quite different for Turid in Rio this time. Eddie picked her up at the airport in his chauffeur-driven Cadillac and brought her to his new apartment on Rua Inhanga. "It was on a high floor, a penthouse you could call it," Turid remembers. "It was big, with a lovely balcony and a view. There was a maid and decent furnishings. Not grand, but it was nothing like the place Eddie was living in when I first went down there. And he was much better, more settled."

For Eddie Gilbert, the situation was vastly different from what had prevailed during Turid's previous visit as well. He had a respectable amount of money now, his plans to return to America were taking shape, the despair and depression were gone, his anxieties diminished. There was no mention of a hotel for Turid this time. She simply moved into Eddie's apartment and his bedroom (the other still occupied by Tony Stratton Smith). What followed was a movie-fantasy two weeks, romantic and carefree. To Eddie, Turid never looked more beautiful. They walked the beach together and, as the words of Jobim's song danced in Eddie's head, he knew she truly was his girl from Ipanema: "Tall and tan and young and lovely ... and when she passes, each one she passes goes a-a-a-a-h ...." Turid *was* statuesque in her beauty. And the many who watched her did so "sadly," because she looked straight ahead, not at them; and if they smiled when she passed, she didn't see. Turid was interested only in Eddie Gilbert. However, much was still to be resolved for her in their relationship.

BOY WONDER OF WALL STREET

"It was a wonderful time," she recalls. "We did so many things this time. I remember we took the car and drove up into the mountains, other times out into the countryside. We had the beach. We went out to restaurants. We were with interesting people. It was very romantic." Conversations inevitably turned to their future, and then Turid's reservations surfaced. She would ask Eddie when exactly he was coming back to the United States, but he could not give her a definite answer because he did not know himself. She said she could not commit her life to him if he were going to remain a fugitive. He asked her to have faith in him. But nothing was resolved during those days they were together in Rio.

The two-week whirlwind finally came to an end. At the airport, Turid again told Eddie that they could not start a life together until he came home to America, to New York. It was not a sad parting, however, like the previous one had been. Eddie knew he would return to America shortly, and by the day of Turid's departure, he had pretty well convinced her of that fact. Both believed now it was simply a matter of time.

In another way, this departure from Rio was unlike her first. Turid was not traveling alone this time. This time, she was pregnant (although when she boarded the Pan Am plane that day in Rio, she was not yet aware of that fact).

With everything going on in Eddie Gilbert's life as September gave way to October, the most transcendent thought was his return to the United States. He wanted to return and resolve the situation from which he had fled, but he also knew that his future life with Turid depended entirely on his return from exile. He was optimistic. And so he wrote to his sister on September 25:

*Dear Enid:*

*Turid has been with me . . . and we are both very happy. I think we understand each other and I certainly hope that our problems are coming to an end.*

*My situation in the States has greatly improved as Bauman was down here also and just left. It seems that the worst thing that can happen to me in his opinion as of this moment is eight months in jail, but he has great hopes now of getting me off completely free. However, we do not talk about that too much because we do not want to build up our hopes and then be disappointed, but he has come across something which he feels may completely vindicate me and prove that I am in fact innocent.*

*I am smoking a big cigar now while I am dictating this letter and am certain that the worst is over. Things seem to to be picking up each day and I would venture to say that we will all manage to pull through this fiasco and be no worse than we were before.*

*All my love,*

*Eddie*

In early October, as Eddie was preparing to return, putting his things in order in Brazil for the date he now privately projected to be somewhere near the end of the month, he was surprised to read this story in the *New York Times*, which seemed inherently to contradict the many published promises to return that he had routinely made throughout the previous three months.

### BRAZIL DENIES GILBERT PERMANENT RESIDENCE

*Special to the New York Times*

RIO DE JANEIRO, OCT. 2—Edward M. Gilbert, the former American businessman who is wanted in the United States on charges of grand larceny, said today he expects to stay in Brazil for the time being by getting extensions on his tourist visa.

Denied permission to establish permanent residence in Brazil, Gilbert said he had been given a 60-day extension of his visa, which he believed would cover his stay through the first part of November. After that he said he would try for further extensions. Gilbert said, "I like Brazil and its great potentialities." The former president of the E. L. Bruce lumber concern said he had been doing some business in timber options in Brazil.

Bardeau de Carvalho, an official of the Ministry of Justice and Internal Affairs, said Gilbert's request to live and work in Brazil permanently was being denied.

After the surprise piece appeared in the *Times* on October 3, Eddie had some denials of his own to make to people back in the States. Although he was indeed planning to return to the United States, he could not say exactly when. Secondly, his request for permanent residency status had been made months earlier by his Brazilian attorney, Celso Fontenelle; Eddie was not even aware at the time that such an effort on his behalf had been made and only learned about it after Fontenelle's filing. He acknowledged that in the early summer of 1962, shortly after his encounters with fugitives Earl Belle and BenJack Cage, he had become fearful from their intimidations that there might be some truth to the fact that they might be able to railroad him out of the country and back to the United States before he was ready to return. So he instructed Fontenelle to do everything necessary then to prevent his deportation. The Brazilian attorney's stategy was to file for permanent residency, thereby precluding any Brazilian legal actions against Gilbert at least until such a request had been considered. Fontenelle knew that in the slow Brazilian bureaucracy such a request could take months to be acted upon.

Sometime later he had told Eddie about the formal request, explaining that it was just a legal tactic. Once Eddie was convinced he could safely stay in Brazil using temporary visa extensions, he forgot about Fontenelle's earlier request for permanent residency. Several months later, it had obviously made its laborious way through channels and had surfaced for governmental action. After lengthy consideration, it had been denied, but such a decision was irrelevant at this time in October, since Eddie Gilbert had no intention of staying in Brazil beyond his currently valid visa extension.

Just two days after this erroneous report implying that Gilbert sought to remain permanently in Brazil, on October 5, 1962, the E. L. Bruce Company announced from its headquarters in Memphis that the audit of its books by Peat, Martwick, Mitchell and Company had finally been completed. The audit results, according to a Bruce spokesperson, had been turned over to the Securities and Exchange Commission. After its initial study, an official in Washington said the SEC declined to release the results just yet because there were "certain questions" that still "needed clarification." The SEC further announced that trading in Bruce stock on the American Stock Exchange or in the over-the-counter market (where trading had been suspended on June 13) would not be resumed until after the SEC publicly released the Bruce company audit. Asked when that might be, the SEC spokesman replied, "the time schedule is uncertain."

As the early October days dragged on, Gilbert was in continuing contact with his attorney Arnold Bauman. The time was approaching, both agreed, for Gilbert's return to face the grand jury indictments awaiting him in New York. During intercontinental telephone conversations, Bauman regularly assured Gilbert that things were moving along. He was in negotiations with federal authorities and with officials in the New York district attorney's office about the outstanding indictments and was merely awaiting clarification of the final "arrangement." According to

Bauman, the prospects could not be better for Eddie Gilbert, and he believed he would shortly have an ironclad agreement for a "slap-on-the-wrist" punishment if a docile Eddie Gilbert returned voluntarily. Bauman said he would tell Eddie when the time was right to return.

As much as Gilbert wanted to return to the United States, he still had some trepidation. "The fear I live with," he said one day to Tony Stratton Smith, "is how people will treat me when I go back. Even if I pay them back every cent, and show them that I'm just an honest guy who made a mistake, do you think they'll forgive me?" Smith was at a loss for an answer. Gilbert then shrugged, Smith remembered, and added, "You never know with people. You just never know."

Meanwhile, the *Wall Street Journal* reported that Bruce officials had announced at their Memphis headquarters that they had begun to take steps to "tighten the company's operations since Mr. Gilbert's resignation." Bruce's new president, Will H. Gonyea, was quoted as saying, "We want to do whatever is necessary … and this may involve some change in our subsidiaries."

The first change, it was reported, was that Bruce was negotiating to sell its 50 percent interest in American International Housing Corporation, an entity acquired under Gilbert's leadership. Its projected purchaser was All-State Properties, Inc., which already owned the other half of the company. Second, Bruce's swimming pool division (known as Coraloc Industries, Inc., and its subsidiary Sunset Pools, also acquired by Gilbert) was reportedly on the auction block. "The matter is being discussed," Gonyea, said, "but the board of directors has made no conclusion." The *Journal's* reporting went further, noting that one party interested in acquiring Bruce's swimming pool holdings had said negotiations were already under way and hoped that "an agreement will be reached by January 1."

The expansive era at Bruce with Gilbert at the helm was truly over.

By mid-October, Arnold Bauman was expressing confidence about the deals he was seeking to negotiate with federal and New York prosecutors. At least that is what he told Eddie Gilbert by telephone. At the beginning of the fourth week of the month, he called Eddie again to say, "Make your arrangements to come back. Everything's going to work out just fine."

Eddie was relieved when he heard Bauman's words, even excited. "I was ready," he later said. "At that point I just wanted to get on with the rest of my life."

BOY WONDER OF WALL STREET

Bauman was reassuring. "We've got as good a deal on the table as we can hope for. No guarantees, but I'm assured the final resolution will be painless." Eddie needed to show reciprocating "good faith" by his uncoerced return to face the situation.

After talking with Bauman, Gilbert called his father to tell him the news. "I'll be home by the weekend," he said, which then led to a discussion about such contingencies as posting bond, where Eddie would live, and other such details. Eddie next contacted the U.S. Embassy in Rio to relay his plan to return and therefore to request the return of his passport, which they had been holding for nearly five months after he had voluntarily turned it over to them. Arnold Bauman simultaneously informed the federal and state judicial authorities in New York that Edward M. Gilbert was expected to return to the United States voluntarily, and that word swiftly spread among the news media.

Gilbert initially planned to fly back so as to arrive on Saturday, October 27, and booked a first-class ticket on Varig Airlines. But after Bauman said there might be a problem raising bail money over a weekend, Eddie decided he preferred to spend Saturday and Sunday nights in Rio rather than in a New York jail cell. So he rescheduled to a Sunday evening flight that would get him to New York Monday morning.

The U.S. Embassy in Rio de Janeiro informed Gilbert that the passport he had handed over earlier had been voided but that a new one would be issued immediately. It would not be turned over to him, however, until the day he departed for the United States. A State Department official from the embassy, moreover, was to accompany him to the airport to ensure that he boarded an airplane for the United States and not some other destination. This condition proved to be overkill because Gilbert's new passport, dated October 24, 1962, carried this stipulation:

This passport is valid only for direct travel to the United States on or before November 5, 1962. This passport is not to be amended, extended or revalidated without the express authorization of the Department of State.

Michael D. Scarfo
American Vice Consul

The wording clearly left no room for misunderstanding. Gilbert could travel nowhere else in the world but to the United States. Finally admitting that a chaperon to the airport was unnecessary, the State Department acceded to Gilbert's wish to leave Brazil as unceremoniously as possible and allowed Eddie to make his own way to the airport that October Sunday.

Before he could board the plane, however, a startling number of American and international press reporters awaited him, with questions and demands for a statement. Gilbert tried to be accommodating. The front-page story in the *New York Times* quoted him as saying, "I'm returning of my own free will. I'm going under my own name and under my own steam, and nobody's pushing me on the plane." And then he concluded to an Associated Press reporter, "I've got nothing else to say until I get my feet back down on United States soil."

He nonetheless did answer a few other questions, as the *Times* article reported:

Since first admitting that he took money from Bruce's treasury and borrowed from the banks on Bruce's credit lines, Gilbert has portrayed himself as a victim of the market slide last May who fled in panic after being betrayed by his business associates.

He still clings to this version, insisting that the big drop on Monday, May 28, led to his downfall....

But Gilbert refused to disclose what defense he would make against the charges. He said, "I am not a vindictive man. I am only going to try to vindicate myself."

According to Gilbert, he will attempt to make restitution "in every quarter where damage was done." But he refused to estimate the total amounts of his debts [later established at somewhere near $20 million, but impossible to calculate at the time].

Gilbert refused to discuss any of his past transactions. He denied that he made any deal in deciding to return. He said he had gone to Rio because he "was all confused and could not face people." Now he thinks that his return will help "in aiding people close to me who even now find themselves in a difficult position."

He also indicated that his return might make it clear that he was not to be considered in the same category as other American financiers who have sought refuge in Brazil. He denied that he was living in any luxury, although he said that he had managed to make some money during his stay in Rio....

But he expressed hope that he could remake his life in the United States. "I want to live a very quiet, very peaceful life and be left alone," he said.

The *Times* article also pointed out that, if convicted on all counts in just the federal grand jury indictment, Gilbert could face "a prison term of 74

BOY WONDER OF WALL STREET

years and fines of $82,000." The article did not address what consequences might follow the New York grand jury indictment, nor how he might dispose of the more than $3.4 million in IRS tax liens filed against him and his wife Rhoda.

The Eddie Gilbert who walked onto a Varig Airlines jet on Sunday evening, October 28, 1962, was hardly the same Eddie Gilbert who had boarded another Varig airliner on Tuesday evening of June 12, 1962. Dressed in a navy blue suit, a white-on-white shirt and a vertically striped silk tie, he looked fit and prosperous, his stride had authority, and his eyes had that sense of penetration and focus people who knew him associated with his self-confidence and determination. Gone were the paranoia, confusion, the terrible angst that had characterized his desperate flight from New York and the Bruce company back in June. Four and a half months of rest, reflection, and relaxation had allowed Eddie to reassemble his life and to reestablish most of the confidence and determination that had been such integral parts of his nature. As he boarded the plane, he was filled with a hope that things would work out and, just as importantly, that he was ready, even anxious, to confront his accusers and detractors in and out of court. Perhaps the only identical thing about the two flights was that he had a seat in first class.

The Varig flight touched down at Idlewild Airport at 8:15 A.M. Monday morning. Immediately after it came to a stop at the gate, two Justice Department officials, U.S. Marshal Anthony R. Marasco and his deputy Joseph A. Rachon, boarded the plane and approached Gilbert in the first class compartment to inform him that he was being taken into custody. He greeted them with cordiality, a trace of a smile even, then walked with the two marshals off the plane and into the terminal building. They moved quickly through passport control—his freshly minted but restricted passport attached now to the cancelled one in which colorful bouquets of country-entrance stamps on page after page blithely recorded so many trips to London, Rome, Switzerland, the south of France, and other exotic ports of call—and on through customs. Gilbert carried his briefcase and some packages as he cleared customs and stepped into the main terminal at Idlewild. His father and Arnold Bauman awaited him there with a throng of newspaper reporters and photographers behind them.

Greetings and formalities were short, however, and the three men accompanied by the two marshals walked briskly through the airport to two cars that awaited them at the curb just outside the terminal. Reporters fired questions at Gilbert, and flashbulbs blazed from the cameras of the photographers. Gilbert ignored most of the questions but replied to one reporter from the *New York Times* who asked, "Are you glad to be back?" He broke into a broad smile, answering emphatically, "Yes."

The marshals took Eddie in one car while his father and his attorney followed in the other, both cars heading for the Federal Court Building at Manhattan's Foley Square.

Inside that pillared, granite building on Manhattan's lower east side, Gilbert appeared before Federal Judge David N. Edelstein, pleading "not guilty" to the 15-count indictment which accused him of the unauthorized withdrawal of $1,953,000 from the E. L. Bruce Company, wire and mail fraud, selling of unregistered stock, and filing a false "insiders' report" with the Securities and Exchange Commission.

According to the *New York Journal-American*, Arnold Bauman, in Eddie's defense, told Judge Edelstein that "Mr. Gilbert fled to Brazil in a state of shock... but now he has regained control of himself and is able to meet his problems.... Here is a man who in a three-week period was reduced from a very, very rich man indeed to a man overwhelmingly in debt." And, most importantly: "He has returned to the United States voluntarily."

Judge Edelstein then released Gilbert on bail of $15,000, posted by Harry Gilbert.

The entourage then proceeded to a nearby New York police station where Edward M. Gilbert was formally booked, fingerprinted, and photographed for the requisite mug shots.

The next stop was the New York District Attorney's office, where Eddie had to answer to the indictment charging him with 12 counts of grand larceny, each count carrying a maximum penalty of 10 years imprisonment. In the New York State Supreme Court chamber, Judge Saul S. Streit accepted Gilbert's plea of not guilty and released him on a bond of $10,000, also posted by Eddie's father. New York assistant district attorney, Jerome Kidder, told the court that "Our office has discussed the matter with the U.S. Attorney and we both agree that a total of $25,000 bail would be sufficient." The modest bail figure agreed to, Kidder noted, was predicated on Gilbert's "*voluntary* return from Brazil, which has no extradition treaty with the United States."

Assistant U.S. Attorney Peter H. Morrison, who had visited Eddie in

Rio several months earlier with Arnold Bauman, added this recollection, quoted in the *Wall Street Journal*. "At the arraignment, I heard Mr. Gilbert say something like: 'I plead not guilty—for now.' ... Mr. Bauman has also promised that Mr. Gilbert has every intention of cooperating fully with the government in all matters. All this leads me to believe this case may never reach trial." These were most comforting thoughts to Eddie Gilbert, coming from the mouth of a potential prosecutor and one who was believed to be more intimate with the details of Eddie Gilbert's case than anyone else on the government's side. The report reassured Gilbert as to what Arnold Bauman had been telling him over the past few weeks.

To reporters outside the New York State Supreme Court hearing room, Gilbert reiterated the statement made earlier, and reported verbatim by the *Times*. "I originally left," he said, "because I felt too nervous from shock and emotional strain at the time. I came back when I regained my health, both mentally and physically enough to cope with my problems."

One of the most persistent questions being asked was: "Is there some kind of deal?" Eddie Gilbert said there was not: "I came back freely and with no promises or deals." Peter Morrison, speaking for the U.S. Attorney's office, stated emphatically that he knew of no settlement or arrangement that might have been reached or even planned between Gilbert and the government. Even E. L. Bruce, Jr., reached at his New York office, responded flatly, "There has been no deal whatsoever between our company and Mr. Gilbert in regard to his return to the United States." And at Bruce headquarters in Memphis, company president Will H. Gonyea corroborated the chairman's statement. "There has been no discussion about any deal or settlement of any sort," he told reporters. He added that as of the moment, the company planned no special action in the Gilbert situation. Peter Heller, a Bruce attorney, clarified the company's position: "We intend to move along and collect whatever we can." Asked if Bruce would have priority in collecting money owed by Eddie Gilbert, he replied, "Until you get into a case like this, it's hard to say how any one creditor will stand on any one debt." The *Wall Street Journal* also reported that "Mr. Heller said he didn't know when Bruce will begin proceedings against Mr. Gilbert to regain the money it lost. 'Mr. Gilbert has already assigned to us all his property,' the attorney said, 'so we may not have to begin proceedings at all. It all depends on how good the assignment is.'"

Manly Fleischman, another Bruce attorney, speaking from his office in Buffalo, added that the company would have to go to court to get the assets Gilbert had assigned to Bruce to secure his debt. He added that Bruce had already entered a claim against the $750,000 surety bond "which should cover part of the company's losses."

What they all overlooked in the way they were addressing questions about Eddie Gilbert's assets was the more than $3.4 million lien filed against him by the Internal Revenue Service, which had prior standing to all other claims.

When Eddie's day in the several courts had ended, and he was finally able to escape the press and media, he gratefully retired with his father to the family house on Long Island.

Eddie Gilbert's return to the United States had proved to be truly big news in New York. It warranted a front page story in the *Times*, a front page story with a three-column photograph in the *World-Telegram,* a front page story with two-column snapshots in the *Journal American* (and the same in the *Post*), a four-column photo and story in the *Mirror*, and a major feature article without photographs in the *Wall Street Journal*. For whatever reason, all the New York newspapers were oddly preoccupied with Eddie's complexion. The *World-Telegram* story began with this description: "Tanned and apparently refreshed by 4½ leisurely months in Rio de Janeiro, playboy-financier Edward M. Gilbert returned today to fight charges...." The *Journal-American* story began: "Looking like a well-tanned tourist, financier Edward M. Gilbert returned from Brazil today...." Under the headline "TO FACE MUSIC", the caption to the oversized photograph in the *Mirror* stated: "Fugitive financier Edward M. Gilbert looks like the well-tanned tourist as he totes attache case and packages at Idlewild...." Its three-column story opened with: "Razzle-dazzle financier Edward M. Gilbert, 39, came back to face the music yesterday...."

It was some homecoming.

## TEN

*I was a-trembling because I'd got to decide forever*
*betwixt two things, and I knowed it.*
*I studied for a minute, sort of holding my breath,*
*and then I says to myself, "All right, then, I'll go to hell."*

MARK TWAIN, THE ADVENTURES OF HUCKLEBERRY FINN, 1884

T he daring young man on the financial trapeze" was British journalist Tony Stratton Smith's description of Eddie Gilbert in his random journal notes while the two were palling around down in Brazil. Back in New York, Eddie once again climbed up to the platform: As the turmoil caused by his return swirled around him, he stood, poised and anxious, awaiting the trapeze bar to come swinging over so he could grab hold and launch himself back into the acrobatics of the financial world. The fall he had taken before his flight to Rio—with no net beneath—had stunned him, shaken him to the bone, but it had not crippled his desire to try again.

The four and one-half month sojourn in South America had been regenerative to Eddie Gilbert's physical, mental, and emotional well-being. But it had been more than that. He had arrived in Rio with less than $2,500 in cash; when he returned almost five months later Eddie had parlayed that and other cash he had received into a respectable nest egg of approximately $100,000 (owing to his Brahma Beer stock trade with Gilbert Deschartre, a number of Brazilian-American currency exchanges conducted through Alexander Vamos, and a few smaller business "deals" made here and there). And $100,000 in 1962 dollars was hardly an insignificant figure, having the equivalent purchasing power of about $1 million in 21st century dollars. But Eddie was nonetheless obsessed by some nagging questions: the matter of the $1.953 million in 1962 dollars he had removed from the Bruce treasury, the more than $3 million Internal Revenue Service tax lien, and the still-to-be totaled millions he owed others because of his financial collapse.

Gilbert's most pressing concern, however, was legal, namely the two sets of indictments he faced. The first had been handed down by a federal grand jury in June 1962, the other by a grand jury assembled by the State of New York a month later. The 15-count federal indictment specified wire and mail fraud, the selling of unregistered stock, and failing to file the required report with the Securities and Exchange Commission. The 12-count indictment from the State of New York translated Gilbert's appropriation of E. L. Bruce Company funds into a grand larceny felony indictment.

The federal indictment, rendered in the U. S. District Court, Southern District of New York, commenced with this preamble:

1. During the months of May and June, 1962... EDWARD M. GILBERT, the defendant herein, devised and intended to devise a scheme and artifice to defraud and to obtain money and property by means of false and fraudulent pretenses, representations and promises from E. L. Bruce Co. (hereinafter referred to as "Bruce").

2. It was part of said scheme and artifice that the defendant EDWARD M. GILBERT, being president, a director and a controlling shareholder of Bruce, without authorization of Bruce and for his own use, benefit and unjust enrichment, would cause moneys and funds of Bruce aggregating $1,953,000 to be transferred to Rhodes Enterprises, Inc. (hereinafter referred to as "Rhodes") and Empire Hardwood Flooring Corporation (hereinafter referred to as "Empire"), corporations under his sole and complete control.

3. It was a further part of said scheme and artifice that the defendant EDWARD M. GILBERT would cause that the aforesaid moneys and funds of Bruce to be transferred to the accounts of Financiere Du Mont-Blanc, Geneva, Switzerland; Societe Anonyme Financiere Ficomer, Geneva, Switzerland; Ufitec, S.A., Zurich, Switzerland; Joseph Danon & Cie., Paris, France; Jerome International Corporation, New York, N.Y.; Dutch American Mercantile Company, New York, N.Y.; and Jacques Sarlie, in satisfaction of obligations of the defendant EDWARD M. GILBERT....

In detail, the first federal count charged that Gilbert "unlawfully, willfully, and knowingly... transmitted by means of wire and radio communication in interstate and foreign commerce" funds appropriated from Bruce to the Swiss investment bank of Financiere Du-Mont-Blanc. The second count specified his delivering a check by mail which had been written on the account of Rhodes Enterprises and sent to the Joseph Danon Company in Paris. The check so written had been paid by fraudulently acquired money.

Count 3 claimed that "On or about the 31st day of May, 1962... EDWARD M. GILBERT... unlawfully, willfully and knowingly, in the offer and sale of a security, to wit, common stock of said E. L. Bruce Co, by the use of means and instruments of transportation and communication in interstate commerce, and by use of the mails, directly and indirectly, did engage in transactions, practices, and courses of business which operated and would operate as a fraud and deceit upon the purchasers of said security, in that, at the time of said offer and sale of said security, the defendant... failed to disclose to the purchasers of said security that he had stolen, converted, and taken by fraud $795,000 of the moneys and funds of said E. L. Bruce Co." Count 4 specified the same thing, only in regard to a total of $1,411,000 taken on June 1, 1962. The fifth count was addressed to a check drawn on Rhodes Enterprises, allegedly from appropriated funds of Bruce, in the amount of $50,000 and paid to the Joseph Danon company.

The sixth count had to do with a filing error. "On or about the 10th day of March, 1962..." the grand jury charged, "in a report and document required to be filed under Title 15, United States Code, Section 78p(a), and which was filed with the American Stock Exchange at New York, N.Y., and the Securities and Exchange Commission at Washington, D.C., namely a Form 4 Statement of Changes in Beneficial Ownership of Securities, made and caused to be made therein a statement to the effect that he sold or otherwise disposed of 19,142 shares of common stock of E.L. Bruce Co. during the calendar month of February, 1962, which, as the defendant EDWARD M. GILBERT then and there well knew, was false and misleading with respect to a material fact, in that said defendant sold or otherwise disposed of 25,142 shares of said stock during said calendar month." Count 7 charged that Gilbert failed to file the necessary document regarding the changes in beneficial ownership of stock in the Bruce company with the American Stock Exchange and the SEC. The remaining eight counts claimed that Gilbert had used the mails to sell shares of Bruce common stock for which "no registration as to said security (the Bruce common stock) being in effect with the Securities and Exchange Commission."

Facing these indictments upon his return to the United States, intimidating as they all sounded, Gilbert was more determined than ever to fight them and his accusers. He did not deny taking the money—"borrowing" it is the way in which he continually described the act—nor did he dispute that he had done it without the authorization of his board of directors. What he denied was that he took it for his own personal benefit. He had used the money for the benefit of his company's position, he believed, and its investment in the Celotex Corporation, so as to save a merger anticipated to be in the best interests of Bruce. In borrowing the funds for such a purpose, he had not benefitted personally in any way. Nor had it ever been his intention. He tried to ensure that Bruce would be repaid the borrowed funds from the liquidation of his own considerable personal assets. Because of this mindset, he planned to plead "not guilty" to the charges, as he had reiterated to the press, the media, friends and family alike.

The State of New York's grand jury had, in effect, indicted Gilbert for the same crimes as those specified in the federal indictment, claiming that his actions had violated state laws as well as federal statutes. Frank S. Hogan, the District Attorney for New York County, announced the 12-count indictment for grand larceny in the first degree less than two weeks after the federal government presented its case. The wording of charges in the state's case was quite similar to that in the federal indictment. "Said defendant, in the County of New York, on or about, May 28, 1962, with intent to deprive and defraud another of property, and of the use and benefit thereof, and to appropriate the same to his own use, and to the use of someone other than the owner, stole property from E. L. Bruce Co. having an aggregate value of...."

Each of the twelve counts listed a specific check drawn on funds alleged to be those of the E. L. Bruce Company, nine of which were payable to Rhodes Enterprises, Inc., two to Empire Hardwood Flooring Corp., and one to Jerome International Corp., in amounts ranging from $50,000 to $490,000.

The $2.358 million represented by the 12 checks cited in the indictment was, in fact, $405,000 more than the amount Gilbert had earlier been charged with taking from the Bruce company, because the sum ostensibly included some of Gilbert's own personal funds, which he had used to meet the margin calls. There was as well some miscalculation in the sums enumerated in the state's 12 counts.

As Gilbert and Arnold Bauman continued to discuss the financial details

BOY WONDER OF WALL STREET

at length, Bauman simultaneously reassured Gilbert that the "arrangement" he had been working on over the past months was still in the works and that Eddie had no reason to be anguished either by the federal or by the state indictments. Bauman believed that a deal would be worked out with the federal government to avoid a costly and publicity-riddled trial, resulting in a "slap-on-the-wrist" punishment for Gilbert. The State of New York, he felt certain, would go along with whatever ruling the federal court made in the matter. If for some reason New York did not, the defense would have the charges dismissed under the statutory protection against double jeopardy. At best, according to Bauman, Gilbert would receive a suspended sentence or probation in federal court; at the worst, Eddie might have to serve six to eight months in a federal facility, Bauman conjectured.

Bauman's strategy and his own strong belief that Gilbert was innocent of any criminal wrongdoing, left Eddie in a continuing state of dilemma. On the one hand he wanted to plead not guilty, believing, as he had told everyone on his return, that he wanted to be exonerated. He had never backed down from a confrontation, nor given up just to walk away. Gilbert repeatedly told Bauman over the months preceding the trial that he had done nothing wrong. He had made a mistake, he would admit, but he felt that he had done nothing criminal. He had had every intention of paying back the money he had used to benefit both his company and himself, and he had signed promissory notes to cover the borrowing, using his personal and real property as collateral valued at considerably more than the $1,953,000. On the other hand there was another element, a personal one, that nagged at him considerably: He was deeply offended by the press's use of defamatory words like "embezzler" and "swindler" in their descriptions of him and verbs such as "stole" or "filched" to describe the financial transactions he had conducted in order to meet his margin calls. As far as the press and media were concerned, he felt, he had already been tried and found guilty. So the press coverage was something he wanted to correct, and the easiest way to do that was to plead "not guilty" and then go on to win the case.

But Bauman reminded him often that there was the chance that a jury might not agree with him, that he would be found guilty, and could face as many as 74 years in prison on the federal indictment alone. Although neither Gilbert nor Bauman thought such a lengthy sentence was likely (or even conceivable), there remained the prospect of an enormously expensive trial. It should be remembered that Gilbert had not only lost his fortune but also owed millions more. The thought of the inexorably degrading publicity associated with such a public trial was numbing. Bauman said to him more than once: "Why take the chance? You could face five to ten years in prison if they find you guilty. Have faith in the deal I'm making. Take the slap-on-the-wrist and get on with your life." These were Arnold Bauman's routine warnings and assurances. But the dilemma still persisted for Eddie, focused as it was on the conflict warring within him, the tension between Eddie the fighter and Eddie the pragmatist.

A little over a week after Gilbert returned to the United States, the long-awaited audit of the Bruce company books by the Peat-Marwick accounting firm was released. On November 8, the Bruce company announced that it had sustained a net loss of $7,170,545 for the first half of 1962 against net income of $929,363 for calendar year 1961. It was a record loss, caused by what the company referred to as "a number of extraordinary items." Most prominent among those items was Gilbert's withdrawal of $1.953 million, resulting in a net loss to the company of $1,498,103. Other extraordinary items included selected write-offs that the company chose to take, among these a "$1,816,844 provision for losses on the planned disposal of unconsolidated subsidiaries and affiliates—Coraloc Industries, Inc., the Greenmount Building Company, and the American International Housing Corporation." There was a further $1,590,729 loss from terminating its steel swimming pool kit business (part of Coraloc). The accountants also described "abnormal losses on receivables [that] amounted to $768,387 after calculating a tax credit of $224,963." They also made provision for a nearly $500,000 loss owing to a decline in the value of marketable securities (most of which came from the $389,790 loss Bruce realized on the sale of its Celotex stock once the attempted merger fell through).

The audit showed the company to have total current assets of $19,747,116, an increase of nearly $5 million from the $14,868,407 reported on December 31, 1961. Current liabilities, however, stood at $14,842,164 as compared with the $3,588,314 total at the close of 1961. The increased liabilities came from one key item, $9.63 million in short-term notes payable to several banks. Cash on hand was reported at $1,061,481, up from the $780,120 reported at the end of 1961.

Writing as chairman of the board to Bruce shareholders, E. L. Bruce, Jr., said that the company hoped to reduce losses attributable to Gilbert's withdrawals by collecting on a $750,000 surety bond the company had with Seaboard Surety Company of New York. He also mentioned to shareholders that the "serious change in the company's financial position since the end of 1961 . . . created a situation in which the need to conserve cash is of prime importance." The company's need to conserve cash prompted the company to liquidate its interests in American Housing International (the subsidiary engaged in developing a housing project in Argentina), Greenmount Building (the subsidiary engaged in urban renewal in Philadelphia), and Coraloc with its swimming pool business.

The day following the accounting firm's report, the Securities and Exchange Commission announced its permission for resumed trade in Bruce stock on the American Stock Exchange beginning November 19. Bruce's common stock had last sold at its low for the year, 15⅜, when trading was suspended after the market close on June 12 (its high for the year had been 37⅝). But when trading resumed on November 19, the shares plummeted to 8¾, down 6⅝ from the last transaction five months earlier. It had been the most active issue traded on the American Stock Exchange on November 19, a total of 47,000 shares having changed hands.

The effect of this on Eddie Gilbert, who had owned more than 500,000 shares of Bruce stock before the market crash of May 28, 1962, was indirect according to Clyde H. Farnsworth writing in the *New York Times* on November 10. He noted that "for all practical purposes, [Gilbert] no longer has any equity in Bruce." Because Gilbert had pledged most of his stock "for thinly margined loans abroad [and] used the proceeds to acquire stock in the Celotex Corporation of Chicago in order to merge the two companies," there was very little equity left there for Gilbert. Nonetheless, Gilbert's "fortunes are linked to the market performance of Bruce. . . because he is liable for the difference between the funds he was loaned and the proceeds from the sale of the foreclosed stock." In addition to Gilbert's collateral commitments for his international borrowing, Farnsworth also reported that, "Of the more than 500,000 shares Gilbert owned, 207,835 were pledged on two notes from the First National Bank of Chicago. These notes were acquired by a group headed by Will H. Gonyea of Eugene, Oregon, who is now president of the company [E. L. Bruce]. The bank foreclosed on the notes, thereby owning the stock. The Gonyea Group bought the notes by, in effect, paying $10.50 a share for the collateraled Bruce stock."

The *Times* writer could not have known the more interesting tale surrounding those 200,000 shares pledged in Chicago. As the story was later told, an officer at First National Bank of Chicago contacted two of Chicago's wealthiest financiers, Jay Pritzker, founder of the Hyatt hotel chain, and Henry Crown, a principal shareholder in General Dynamics Corporation (and who had, until its sale in 1961, owned the Empire State Building in New York). The officer asked if they might be interested in acquiring the Bruce stock. The bank simply wanted sufficient cash to repay the two notes totaling $2 million for which the stock was held as collateral. Both Pritzker and Crown, multimillionaires by any definition, saw the opportunity as both a worthwhile investment and a certified bargain. So when the two went to the Chicago Loop bank, at the bank's invitation, to discuss the matter, they agreed not to get into a bidding war for the stock and to simply flip a coin to determine the buyer. Jay Pritzker won, buying the block of stock for $10.50 a share, and then aligning himself with Will Gonyea in what the *Times* referred to as the Gonyea Group, before quietly retreating back into the shadows.

Despite his considerable financial problems, life went on for Eddie Gilbert. He settled back into the New York flow as best he could, although life was far different now from the way he had lived there before his flight to Brazil. Gone were the apartment on Fifth Avenue, the town house on east 70th Street, the limousine and chauffeur, the suite at the Waldorf Astoria, the box at the Met, the art and antiques, and all other such trappings of the privileged. Just as he had done 17 years earlier after returning from the war, the 39-year-old Gilbert moved in with his parents and set about looking for a job. By 1962, however, Harry and Yolan Gilbert had moved from the house in Flushing, and settled into a luxurious duplex apartment in the Carlyle Hotel at 78th Street and Madison Avenue.

As for employment, Eddie created his own job: He launched a wholesale hardwood flooring firm, the Northerlin Company, funded mostly by Harry Gilbert and registered in the name of Eddie's mother, Yolan Gilbert. His good friend Tony Reinach, a Wall Street trader at the time, also invested in Northerlin. Eddie also wanted to work Wall Street on his own, but his capital was severely limited.

Another limitation on him was the restriction imposed by his release on bail: He was prohibited from leaving the jurisdiction of the federally defined Southern District of New York, essentially New York City, Long

Island, and Westchester County. But the restriction did not hamper his lifestyle, as his attorneys quickly found ways to get around it. The court routinely granted him permission to leave the federal district for business or personal reasons on 26 different occasions.

Lawsuits to collect money Gilbert owed also proliferated in the weeks and months following his return to the United States. The total would ultimately be tallied somewhere in the range of $20 million. Friends and attorneys counseled Gilbert to declare bankruptcy; but such a course of action was out of the question for Gilbert, given his promises to take personal responsibility for the indebtedness. He was quoted in a 1963 *Saturday Evening Post* article as "planning to pay back every cent he owed, including losses which were only indirectly his responsibility." The magazine further quoted him as saying, "A lot of my friends lost money on Bruce when the price plunged. One day, I want to say, 'Here I am, boys; here it is; we're even.'"

So Eddie went to work. The Northerlin Company's office was located on Madison Avenue at 57th Street, a few blocks from where Bruce was headquartered earlier in the year. But in terms of creature comfort, it was spare and far from the luxury to which Gilbert had formerly been accustomed. Described in a *New York Times* article as "small and cluttered," it contained "a built-in table and an outsize metal cabinet [which] take up most of the space, and what appears to be the concern's entire supply of letterheads, envelopes, invoices and scratch pads is tucked into a set of open shelves above Gilbert's desk." The *Times* article also observed, "There are a few mementos of the days when Gilbert's name was magic on Wall Street—a passport to the higher reaches of gastronomy in the shape of a framed, hand-lettered acceptance in the *Chevaliers du Tastevin* and a brass plaque from the Safari Club in Kenya—but it is all a very long way from the plush executive suite he occupied when he controlled the E. L. Bruce Company." Northerlin had few employees. Besides Eddie—whose principal efforts were in sales—there were a secretary-receptionist and a bookkeeper. Harry Gilbert showed up rather regularly, and Tony Reinach also had a desk in the office.

It was not easy from the outset, because the nation's economy was not strong. This made it especially difficult for a fledgling business. And Gilbert's "situation," the pending indictments, the gargantuan tax lien, the debts, and the lawsuits were further impediments. "I used to order $500,000 worth of lumber on credit, Now I have to pay cash — in advance," Gilbert was quoted in the 1963 *Saturday Evening Post* article. Still, he was optimistic, if frustrated: "I have ideas for making this thing go, but I need 18 Philadelphia lawyers and 75 certified public accountants to check just so I can go to the john."

But Gilbert knew hardwood flooring as well as or better than anyone in the business, and sales had always been one of his special talents. So it was not surprising that Northerlin did well right from the beginning; and it was not long before he was drawing a yearly salary of $50,000. By 1966, after just three years in business, the company had sales of more than $10 million and a net worth of between $1 and $2 million. Gilbert's salary with incentives had grown to about $10,000 a month.

With what he was earning from Northerlin and some success in the stock market, Gilbert began in early 1963 what would become the long and emotionally draining exercise of paying off his astronomical debts. First, 10 percent of his salary was garnished and sent directly to the Bruce company. Behind that stood the banks and investment companies in the United States and abroad, as well as, according to an article in the *Times*, "a scattered army of retailers, craftsmen, doctors, lawyers, florists, and even a pair of dealers who helped Gilbert build a rather valuable stamp collection."

Many outsiders, including many creditors, doubted Gilbert's intentions and ability to make full restitution. One referred to it as "camouflage," several suggested it was simply unrealistic. Gilbert's longtime friend Jerry Stern, who had coincidentally lost a considerable sum in the Bruce-Celotex debacle, was quoted in the press with a different viewpoint, however: "Eddie feels very strongly about restitution," he said, "and it's not just that he's worried about being sentenced. He really thinks he won't be able to hold up his head again until everybody is paid back."

Richard Phalon, writing in the *New York Times* about Gilbert's financial situation in the pretrial days following his return from Brazil, reported that "Friends say that almost all of Gilbert's salary, 'except for the rent and music lessons for the kids,' goes to pay off creditors.... At his current rate of income, it could take Gilbert 70 years or more to make all of his creditors whole, but there is evidence that most of them have been getting something, bit by bit."

Phalon then offered this example. "Max Wasserman, for instance, who now runs Tip-Top shoes at 155 West 72nd Street, used to be one of Gilbert's stamp dealers. Mr. Wasserman was owed $1,600 when Gilbert took off for Brazil.

"Mr. Wasserman says he didn't call Gilbert until 'three or four months after he came back.... I knew he had plenty of bigger things to worry about, but he told me, 'I'll pay you back, but it will take time.'"

"Mr. Wasserman got a check for $1,600 last spring [1966]. 'I was just opening the store then, and I needed every penny I could get,' the dealer says. 'I knew he wouldn't cheat anybody, especially a little man.'"

In the December 1963 *Saturday Evening Post* feature cited earlier, written by Don Forst, the subject of Gilbert's repaying his debts was also addressed. "To the surprise of cynics, Eddie began doing just that," Forst wrote. "Starting with $50 he owed a grocer and $138 due FAO Schwarz, the Tiffany of toy stores. 'I had to start somewhere, so I decided everything under $10,000 comes first,' Gilbert explains. 'A guy in New Jersey I owed $900 allowed me $500 on a watch that had cost me $1,000.' One hundred dollars a month goes to to the house painter who splattereed $2,300 worth of whitewash in that 13-room apartment which Gilbert has since surrendered to Rhoda... 'I wasn't really liable for that paint job,' Gilbert said, 'but I wanted to be a good guy about it.' He was understandably less generous about the $732,000 worth of diamonds, emeralds and pearls Rhoda took home on approval from Cartier's just before his financial disaster...; another $100 monthly goes to a Manhattan stamp dealer [another in addition to Mr. Wasserman]. Eddie, a demon philatelist, figures he used to spend $10,000 or so on stamps each year... He owed $7,000 [to the stamp dealer] when he fled to Brazil. Gilbert points out, 'On account of me, his kids couldn't go to camp this summer.'"

On another front, the hoped-for biography project by Tony Stratton Smith eventually fell apart. Smith had joined Eddie in New York to continue the project, but he was not known in publishing circles there and therefore had no success in interesting a publisher for the project. Meanwhile, Eddie had also been talking with Murray Rossant of the *Times*, one of the few journalists in New York friendly to Gilbert in those days, about the stalemated situation of the book project. Rossant told Eddie he was interested himself and felt certain he could line up a publisher and a royalty advance to complete the project. When Eddie explained this to Smith, he accepted it gracefully; Gilbert and Rossant agreed to buy Smith's research and what he had already written (which was just the single chapter done in Brazil). Gilbert remembers paying Smith something less than $1,000 for the material.

The two other deals Smith proposed, namely to represent Pele and Antonio Carlos Jobim in the United States and England, had similarly failed to progress. With Gilbert and Smith now in New York, the proposals languished on the desks of several Rio attorneys. Faced with his present legal problems and potentially lucrative new business challenges in the United States, Gilbert lost interest. And Smith knew that without Gilbert's involvement, the deals could never be carried off. So, after only a few months in New York, Tony Stratton Smith returned to Brazil and eventually to England, where he had a respected career as a journalist over the next 30 years.

Murray Rossant, on the other hand, had little trouble finding a New York publisher and secured a $7,500 advance, which he split fifty-fifty with Eddie. But a few months after Rossant started to work on the book, he began to have reservations. Because he was still employed as an investigative reporter for the *Times*, Rossant felt a growing conflict of interest. For example, he led off a *Times* article on the state of the stock market in the spring of 1963 with this: "Edward M. Gilbert, the 40-year-old New York financier who fled to Brazil last June and returned under indictment by Federal and state authorities last October, stands out as the most prominent and publicized victim of last spring's big break in Wall Street. But he is not the only victim." And then his story turned into a recapitulation of Gilbert's rise and fall rather than an analysis of the market's recovery. Rossant ultimately concluded that he just could not, in good faith, write the book and still report for the *Times*. Eddie was disappointed, but he could understand Rossant's conflict. They returned the publisher's advance, and the project died. Eddie, of course, had plenty of other things to keep himself occupied.

During those first few months back in New York, Eddie's personal life was in turmoil. He tried ardently to maintain his relationship with Turid, with whom he remained deeply in love. But there were complications. Rather than having a child out of wedlock, Turid had an abortion, despite Gilbert's efforts to dissuade her. Because Eddie was still married, their future continued to be unsettled, in Turid's mind anyway. She had a roommate, a girl from Finland named Muriel who was also a Pan Am stewardess, with whom she shared a small apartment not far from the East River. For the most part then, the arrangements between Eddie and Turid were dictated by Pan Am's international flight schedules. When Eddie was not courting Turid, he was fending off Rhoda, who had become increasingly bitter about her situation in life since Eddie's downfall and her inevitable divorce from him that had been looming since he had first gone to Nevada in the spring of 1962.

Ironically, it was Rhoda who now filed for the divorce in Reno, Nevada; it was uncontested by Eddie and became a reality finally in May 1963. But it was a truly messy affair. The grounds, Rhoda asserted, were "extreme mental cruelty," and reports of the divorce in New York newspapers stated that details of the divorce decree, community property settlement, and custody of the two Gilbert children, Robin and Alexandra, had been ordered sealed by the Nevada court. Custody of the two children had been awarded to Rhoda; Eddie agreed to child support and alimony payments equal to one-third of his annual income. But the "settlement" was far from the end of the matter.

Eddie's financial collapse in May 1962 and his divorce from Rhoda the following year unleashed a fury in her that would rage for years to come and would become a disturbing problem in Gilbert's personal life for some time. Rhoda had already destroyed most of his wardrobe, which Eddie had left behind in their Fifth Avenue apartment when he departed for Brazil; she had also given away or discarded his valuable library of books collected over many years. One of these was his signed first edition of Jack Kerouac's first novel, *The Town and the City*, published by Harcourt, Brace in 1950, which Kerouac had inscribed: "To Ed, in remembrance of our days at HM." The copy was one of a very short first run, published six years before Kerouac's classic *On the Road*, well before he became recognized in American literary circles. Eddie's copy of *The Town and the City* resurfaced in the 1990s and appeared in an auction catalog of a New York rare-book dealer, carrying the notation that it had been discovered at "a tag sale in New York State... then sold to a collector in the Southwest from whom it was purchased by its present owner." Gilbert's accountant in New York, Larry Kaufman, a book collector himself, saw the catalog listing and told Eddie about it. Gilbert bought the book back more than three decades after Rhoda had thrown it out—for $5,000.

Cutting up his clothes and tossing out his books were one thing; more was to follow. Rhoda returned to a New York court about a year after the divorce ruling in Nevada was final, claiming that she was not receiving the one-third of Eddie's income stipulated in the original decree. She filed her lawsuit against Eddie, Eddie's parents, and Turid as well, claiming complicity on their parts in a conspiracy that was meant to deprive her of her full share of Eddie's income. By filing the lawsuit, however, her unorthodox actions preceding its filing became a matter of public record.

According to testimony in the case, after the divorce was final in Nevada, Rhoda had during the period from 1964 to 1966 come to Gilbert's Northerlin office on Madison Avenue on six separate occasions and created such a scene that police had been called to have her removed. On each visit, according to court documents and in front of witnesses, she cursed Gilbert, demanded money, and refused to leave. When she began tearing up business papers and records and throwing them around the office (as she did on all six visits), the police were called. On one occasion, she asked for a glass of water and an aspirin. When they were given to her, she threw the cup of water in Eddie's face. On another visit to the office, she set off a stink bomb: "... she exploded a device in her possession which saturated the office with a noxious odor. At this point the police were called...." On still another, she "approached Mr. Gilbert and with a razor-blade type of paint scraper lunged at Mr. Gilbert. Mr. Gilbert raised his hand to protect himself, pushing plaintiff [Rhoda] away from him, in the process sustaining a severe wound to his arm. The police were called. A policeman appeared at Mr. Gilbert's office, and finding that Mr. Gilbert did not wish to press charges, escorted plaintiff from the premises."

Rhoda also physically attacked Turid. One evening in a French restaurant in midtown Manhattan, while Eddie and Turid were dining, Rhoda arose from another table and strode across the room with a knife in her hand. Eddie glanced up just as she was about to stab Turid and blocked her attempt, sustaining a minor cut himself from her knife. Police were called; this time they took Rhoda to the stationhouse.

Telephone calls and letters also constituted part of Rhoda's arsenal of weapons against Gilbert, his wife, and his parents. Hundreds of harassing telephone calls were made, the contents of which matched that in the letters she wrote. A number of these were introduced as evidence in court as part of the record. The letters revealed her jealousy of Turid for the comfortable life she now had (as compared to the one Rhoda felt was no longer hers); complaints about the "parisites" [sic] she had to contend with throughout her life with Eddie; her depiction of his parents "who didn't care a hoot about my welfare when the chips were down"; how she "suffered boredom in Huntington" as a result of being with them; her unflattering description of Eddie as a "piece of vermin" (among many similar and equally odious epithets); and the profound pleasure she felt following his recent indictments for taking funds from Bruce ("stole" is the verb she used); how she felt that she was being made to "pay for your [Eddie's] crime"; her disgust over Turid's now-enviable financial situation; and her fury over the prospect of "Tootsie" (Eddie's mother's nickname) becoming the guardian of the two girls, Robin and Alexandra. She ends one of her diatribes on the heavily sarcastic note, "Live it up...."

All of the letters are laced with her bitter disappointment at being replaced by Turid, and refer to Eddie's parents with especially vicious racial epithets. Even the envelopes addressed to Turid carry such vulgar and lurid characterizations of her, it is surprising the U.S. Postal Service would deliver them. Harry and Yolan Gilbert, the court records also show, received equally offensive letters and telephone calls from their estranged daughter-in-law.

The suit dragged on for almost five years, during which time a seemingly unending stream of depositions were taken, Rhoda's accusations and claims on one side and Eddie's responses and his accounts of Rhoda's harassment on the other. Finally an agreement was reached in the Supreme Court of the State of New York in late 1971, specifying to two principal measures: a rewriting of the alimony requirement to make it more specific and enforceable and a restraining order prohibiting Rhoda's harassment of Eddie, Turid, and other members of his family. Provision was also made for Rhoda's visitation rights with their two daughters, Robin and Alexandra, then staying with Eddie's mother in her Carlyle apartment. But as the lawsuit was laboriously wending its way through the court system, several problems arose over custody of Robin and Alexandra. In insisting on her need for more money, Rhoda claimed that she could not afford to support the two girls. Eddie simultaneously claimed that Rhoda had made it extraordinarily difficult for him to visit his daughters and so had violated the visitation rights granted him under the original divorce decree. Ultimately, Eddie offered a monetary settlement of $100,000 for custody of their daughters (a sum which he had to borrow), and Rhoda agreed. The girls then officially moved into their grandmother's spacious apartment at the Carlyle.

The uncertain alimony stipulation of "one-third of his income" in the original decree was replaced by specific monthly requirements, $2,000 a month for the first two years, $2,500 for the next two years, and $3,000 from then on until the death of either party or Rhoda's remarriage.

In Article II of the agreement, it was stipulated:

The Wife will communicate only with the Husband and only in the following manner:

(a) By mail addressed to his office address in a plain white envelope containing only the Husband's name and address and the Wife's return address, or

(b) By telephone to the Husband at his office during usual business hours only, or

(c) By mail to the Husband's attorney in a plain white envelope containing only the name and address of said attorney and the Wife's return address, or

(d) By telephone to the Husband's attorney, at his office, during usual business hours only,

Provided, however, that said communications shall not be abusive in nature or quantity and shall be for a legitimate purpose.

Any communication by the Wife to the Husband, members of the Husband's family (other than the children of the parties' marriage...), or the Husband's attorney, other than provided for in the preceding paragraph of this Article, shall constitute a violation of this Article.

The court additionally ruled that Rhoda could communicate freely with the children but only using a separate telephone and number installed for their use at Yolan Gilbert's apartment.

A little over a week after the divorce was finalized, Eddie and Turid were married on May 18, 1963. Sherman Fairchild threw a swank party for them in his 65th Street mansion just off Fifth Avenue, hiring Hoagy Carmichael to entertain at the piano. The wedding was planned to be an intimate affair, with just 40 family members and friends present at the ceremony held in St. Peter's Lutheran Church on East 54th Street. Private guards were also hired to prevent uninvited guests from entering, and to keep the press at bay. Turid remembers it this way: "The day, what a day. I had the most awful dress you've ever seen ... and Eddie's friends and the women with them in their Christian Dior's, all polished and powdered and pampered. My mother helped me through it. Both my parents came over for the wedding. And there I see in the paper in the morning, on the front page, it was the *Daily News* or the *Mirror* or one one of those sensational ones, and the headline is 'Eddie Gilbert, The Crook, Is Getting Married' or something like that. And my parents see that, too.

"And out in front of the church when we pull up are all these other people and photographers; and I did not want to go in, so we drove around the block and then my father insisted and got me out of the car and we pushed our way in, the guards made a way for us."

Eddie remembers it much the same way. "The publicity was terrible. All the papers that were rags treated it like it was some kind of splashy event. They were not kind, and as a result all kinds of people ended up out in front of the church who didn't belong there. It was awful. We had to sneak out the side door of the church after it was over."

A reception followed at Harry and Yolan Gilbert's apartment in the Carlyle, and Eddie and Turid later retired to a suite in the adjacent Hotel where they were badgered with telephone calls from Rhoda until Eddie finally asked the front desk to refuse all incoming calls.

The next day the newlyweds took Robin and Alexandra, then eight and seven years old, to brunch at the Plaza Hotel, and later for a horse-and-buggy ride in Central Park, because, as Turid remembers, "we did not in any way want them to feel excluded, now that we were married." What the two girls did not know that day, as the carriage made its way through the winding, arbored lanes of the park, was that they would soon be joined by a stepsister. Turid, once again, was pregnant: Eddie and Turid's first child, Dominique, would be born on Christmas eve 1963.

From the time of his return from Brazil in October 1962 until the date he went to trial in federal court in September 1964, Gilbert had received 24 continuances, or adjournments of his case. "The reason for so many adjournments," wrote Leslie Gould, financial editor of the *New York Journal-American*, "is that he is 'cooperating' with authorities on a possible securities case involving large Wall Street houses." Other New York newspapers also alluded to the fact that Gilbert was working with the federal government in its investigations of illegal security trading schemes and other assorted financial shenanigans in the stock market. There was a clandestine ring to the reports, but such was not the situation at all. Gilbert had cooperated with federal authorities but only in connection with his own case. The continuances had been sought solely because Gilbert's attorney was attempting to negotiate a plea bargain for his client. It proved to be a protracted process, given the nature of the case and the publicity associated with it. The government was in no hurry, as there was no fear of Gilbert's fleeing again. After all, he had voluntarily returned from the safety of Brazil when he could easily have remained in exile so as to avoid prosecution in the United States. Adjournments, therefore, were no more than formalities, with neither side having any objection to them.

By the early autumn of 1964, however, decisions had to be made. Gilbert continued to maintain that he did not want to plead guilty. Some close to him, like friend Red Chandor and attorney Tom Field agreed, and urged him to make a fight in court. Chandor remembers the situation well: "I guess I was as close to him at the time as anybody. I knew Arnold Bauman, too, just by chance, before Eddie ever heard of him and... all of a sudden he turns up as Eddie's lawyer. I don't know who got [Bauman] for him, but it couldn't have been a friend.... Arnold obviously made a deal. He was *giving* Eddie to them. I mean any damn fool could see that if he [Gilbert] had this written agreement with Bruce [the promissory notes pledging Gilbert's personal assets] that what he did was perfectly legal. Just because the board of directors refused to approve it didn't mean he didn't have the right to do it. He did have the right to do it. And I thought it was ridiculous for him to plead guilty." Tom Field, a young lawyer who had represented Gilbert and the Bruce company in several transactions during Gilbert's tenure at Bruce, expressed the same sentiments. "I heard they are recommending to Gilbert to plead guilty.... I saw Gilbert, and I say, 'Eddie, you're out of your mind to plead guilty. This is not an embezzlement, and if the facts are presented properly, not even a jury of paupers will convict you. And even if they do, it will be reversed. It just wasn't an embezzlement, and you are crazy to plead guilty."

Bauman, on the other hand, was adamant in his stance: Plead guilty; do not take the chance that a jury might find you culpable and send you to prison for a lengthy term. More persuasive, however, was Bauman's contention that he now had a deal with the federal powers involved that would result in a suspended sentence or probation if Gilbert pled guilty. Eddie agonized over the decision; he was in tears about it at one point, Turid remembers.

The court date was September 25, 1964. The night before, Eddie had still not made a decision. Chandor remembers: "I was sitting in his apartment... I'll never forget it. He called Bauman and he said, 'Arnold, I don't want to plead guilty tomorrow.' I agreed with him... and I was going to go down there and be there in court… give him some support… Eddie told him, 'I don't think I did anything wrong, and I want to fight it.' But Bauman said something like, and I don't know the exact words but something like, 'You plead guilty, or I'll resign as your attorney. I gave them my word that you're going to plead guilty. We've got a deal.'" Gilbert got little sleep that night, still agonizing over what he should do the next morning at the courthouse in Foley Square.

As it turned out, Eddie the pragmatist prevailed. Making the biggest mistake since choosing to flee to Brazil more than two years earlier, Gilbert pled guilty to three counts of the 15-count indictment in the federal courtroom of Judge Sidney Sugarman. According to the *New York World-Telegram*, "The slightly built, dapperly dressed Gilbert almost whispered, 'Yes, sir,' when Sugarman asked him if he committed the crimes to which he pleaded guilty." In a front-page article in the *Times*, it was reported that Gilbert "nodded solemnly as his lawyer, Arnold Bauman, said Gilbert intended to make full restitution." The *Times* went on to say, "Mr. Bauman told Judge Sugarman that 'at no time did Mr. Gilbert intend to retain any of the proceeds mentioned in count one, and it is his intention to reimburse Bruce for any money owing. Nothing I have said here is meant to detract from the fact that Mr. Gilbert knew this was an unauthorized withdrawal, but the plea is not tainted by personal gain.'"

The three counts to which Gilbert pled guilty covered the misappropriation of funds from the Bruce company, transportation of said funds in foreign commerce, and the failure to file an "insider's" report with the Securities and Exchange Commission regarding certain Bruce stock transactions he had made. In total, they carried a maximum sentence of 17 years in prison and a fine of $21,000. As part of the deal Bauman had arranged, because Gilbert pled guilty to those three counts, the other 12 were to be dismissed. Judge Sugarman continued Gilbert's release on the $15,000 bail already posted and set sentencing for December 9, 1964. But like so many of the scheduling dates of his trial, this date would be shed along with those in more than 20 subsequent adjournments. The time between his guilty plea in federal court and his sentencing date would prove to be even more protracted than the 30 months it took from the time of his indictment until his appearance at trial.

Bauman had also been negotiating with the New York District Attorney's office, particularly with Jerome Kidder, chief of the frauds bureau, in order to consummate a deal there as well (even though Bauman contended that a deal there might not be necessary).

In October 1964, shortly after Gilbert's guilty plea in federal court, Bauman petitioned the court to dismiss New York's charges on the grounds of double jeopardy. Before the New York state supreme court, Bauman argued in the case of Eddie Gilbert that the division between federal and state proceedings was not one involving "separate and distinct areas of statutory enactments, but rather one involving state and federal prosecutions for the same offense." Bauman also argued that there was no distinction between a prior misdemeanor conviction or an acquittal and a subsequent felony prosecution, citing that the charges against Gilbert were felonies in both the federal and state jurisdictions. The District attorney's office countered: "Because the federal government in a prosecution under the Fraud by Wire statute (Title 18, U.S. code, Section 1343) need not prove a larceny, such proof of larceny in the State Court is an additional element which prevents petitioner from asserting the claim of double jeopardy." Bauman responded by stating, "This theory fails completely to take into account that under the facts in this case the scheme to defraud [federal indictment] and the larceny [New York indictment] were one and the same."

Bauman made his argument for Gilbert's facing double jeopardy in this way: After relating the facts in the case against Gilbert and the particulars of the indictments in both federal and state courts, he argued that the charge contained in Count 1 of the federal indictment to which Gilbert had pled guilty and the charges contained in the state's 12-count indictment were identical. "The federal indictment alleges," he argued, "that the defendant devised a scheme to obtain money and property from E. L. Bruce Co. by means of false and fraudulent pretenses, representations and promises and, further, that without authorization and for his own use, benefit and unjust enrichment caused funds of Bruce aggregating $1,953,000 to be transferred to corporations under his sole and complete control and to use said funds to satisfy his own obligations.

"The present [New York] indictment charges that the defendant, with intent to deprive and defraud E. L. Bruce Co. of property and to appropriate the same to his own use, stole various sums of money from E. L. Bruce Co." Bauman noted that the state indictments entailed a total of $2,358,000 as contrasted with the federal indictment's $1,953,000, the exact amount appropriated from Bruce by Gilbert. Bauman argued that such a discrepancy occured because of errors ("duplicitous allegations," according to Bauman) in several counts of the New York indictment. In the final analysis, allowing for auditing corrections, Bauman asserted that the accurate amount Gilbert was accused of taking was $1,953,000 in both the federal and state indictments. "Therefore, the defendant's position, as supported by the facts, may be stated as follows: Count 1 of the federal indictment, to which the defendant has pleaded guilty, alleges a larceny of $1,953,000 committed by defendant against Bruce; the instant [New York] indictment similarly alleges a larceny committed by the defendant against Bruce in the sum of $1,953,000. The charges against the defendant and the acts committed by the defendant are identical in both indictments. Bauman then quoted from the relevant New York state statute (Code of Criminal Procedure, § 139) to argue against Gilbert's facing double jeopardy:

When an act charged as a crime is within the jurisdiction of another state, territory or country, as well as within the jurisdiction of this state, a conviction or acquittal thereof in the former, is a bar to a prosecution or indictment therefor in this state.

Bauman offered additional documentation from an article of the New York State Penal Law (§ 33):

Whenever it appears upon the trial of an indictment, that the offense was committed in another state or country, or under such circumstances that the courts of this state or the government had jurisdiction thereof, and that the defendant has already been acquitted or convicted on the merits upon a criminal prosecution under the laws of such state, or country, founded upon the act or omission in respect to which he is upon trial, such formal acquittal or conviction is a sufficient defense.

Bauman further cited numerous antecedent cases in which federal court conviction barred subsequent state court prosecutions. And then he concluded, "Therefore, it is respectfully submitted that if the defendant has been convicted in the federal court of the same act with which he is charged in the instant indictment, prosecution of the state indictment is barred by the provisions of Section 139 of the Code of Criminal Procedure and Section 33 of the Penal Law....

"Although the defendant has not been sentenced on his plea of guilty, the plea alone is sufficient to raise the bar against a subsequent prosecution....

"The defendant cannot be placed in double jeopardy for the same crime for which he stands convicted.

"For all the reasons set forth herein, it is respectfully submitted that the motion of the defendant Edward M. Gilbert to dismiss Indictment No. 2688-62 be granted."

Assistant District Attorney Jerome Kidder, representing the state of New York, disagreed with Bauman's basic assumption, that the two indictments, federal and state, were identical. Kidder's contention was that the federal indictment was not for larceny, *per se*, as defined by State of New York law, and, therefore, the state's indictment was not identical to that of the federal jurisdiction. And so he responded in his Memorandum in Opposition to Defendant's Motion to Dismiss the Indictment: "In order to obtain a conviction under the federal indictment in this case it was not necessary to allege or prove a larceny because as pointed out by the United States Court of Appeals (United States vs. Bagdasian, 291 Fed 2nd Series 163), the commission of a larceny or the conversion by the defendant of money or property to his own use is not an essential part of the crime of devising a fraudulent scheme and using interstate wire facilities, for the purpose of executing such scheme...."

"The People of the State of New York are not bound by the language of the federal indictment, and the defendant can not defeat the jurisdiction of this court by pleading to an indictment which incorrectly states the facts and which contains language which is pure surplusage.

"The thefts charged in this indictment were completed common law larcenies, not larcenies accomplished by 'means of false and fraudulent pretenses' as alleged in the federal indictment, and such larcenies could not properly be made the subject of a federal indictment...."

In short, the district attorney declared that the larcenies set forth in the state's indictment were separate and distinct crimes "which are neither alleged nor embraced within the language of the federal indictment."

The New York court sided with the District Attorney, concluding that the two indictments, although there was no dispute that they were for the same act (Gilbert's unauthorized withdrawal from the Bruce company of $1.953 million), were not legally identical.

Gilbert's attorneys appealed this decision but lost in the New York State Court of Appeals. Then, taking their case to the U.S. Supreme Court, they asked for a ruling that the U.S. Constitution's bar against double jeopardy should apply to New York's intended prosecution of Eddie Gilbert. But on October 10, 1966, the U.S. Supreme Court declined to rule on the plea, that action ending Gilbert's hope for a dismissal of the New York state's 12-count indictment.

Bauman again reassured Gilbert that he would negotiate a deal with the district attorney's office as he had with the federal prosecutors. He continued to contend that what awaited Gilbert by way of punishment would be nothing more than a "slap on the wrist."

During these long months of legal wrangling, Harry Gilbert died after a long battle with cancer on April 3, 1966 (the same day, coincidentally, that Eddie and Turid's second daughter, Nina, was born). To the end of his days, Harry remained convinced that his son would be exonerated of any wrongdoing in the Bruce affair. It continually pained Eddie that his father was made to suffer so for the actions and excesses of his only son.

Meanwhile, the case involving the Dutch-born financier Jacques Sarlie finally came to closure in another New York state courtroom. Sarlie had received some of the Bruce funds that Gilbert had appropriated so as to "maintain his [Sarlie's] position," as he claimed at the time, when margins were being called in back in 1962. The total sent to him in four separate Bruce checks, the court ascertained, amounted to $589,150. Sarlie had told Gilbert he had purchased nearly $750,000 worth of stock on his account to support the Gilbert-led syndicate aspiring to acquire Celotex. As it turned out, Sarlie had never bought the stock, although he had accepted funds Gilbert had sent, and so was unable to turn the phantom stock over to Bruce. Bruce brought suit against Sarlie to recover the funds Gilbert had sent to him. In January of 1967, the New York State Supreme Court ordered Sarlie to pay more than $400,000 to the E. L. Bruce Company.

Two months later, in a federal court, where Bruce had also sued, Judge John M. Cannella found against Sarlie, awarding the company more than $825,000 in damages plus interest over four years which, when calculated, would bring the sum to more than $1 million. "By his default," Judge Cannella said as he rendered his decision, "Sarlie had only admitted that between May 28, 1962 and June 7, 1962, he received funds wrongfully withdrawn from Bruce by Gilbert; that Sarlie knew or should have known that the funds were wrongfully withdrawn by Gilbert from Bruce; and that he received them in connection with illegal transactions with Gilbert."

Retrieving the money Bruce was owed was another question. Sarlie was back in Europe, keeping a very low profile.

More than four and a half years would pass between the the day Gilbert was indicted in July 1962 by the state of New York and the actual trial date of February 20, 1967. During those many months, the case appeared more than 20 times on the state supreme court's calendar, but it was postponed on each occasion, with neither party raising objections to the continuances.

Gilbert continued to maintain privately that he was not guilty of any crime, but he again acceded to Bauman's counsel and pleaded guilty to three counts of New York's 12-count indictment in the State Supreme Court that February day in 1967. According to a front-page article the next day in the *Times*, "His plea came as a surprise, and he looked nervous as he whispered, 'Guilty' before Justice Gerald P. Culkin."

The *Times* reported on the specifics of the deal. "The acceptance of the plea to three counts of a 12-count indictment that had charged him with larceny of $1,953,000 was recommended by Jerome Kidder, the chief of the district attorney's fraud bureau. Gilbert's plea to the three counts satisfied the indictment and covered the nine other counts, which in effect are considered dismissed." On each of the three charges to which he had pled guilty, the maximum penalty could be 10 years imprisonment, or a total of 30 years if the terms were to run consecutively. Gilbert's $10,000 bail was continued, and Judge Culkin set sentencing for April 21, 1967.

As winter wore down in 1967, the daring young man on the financial trapeze might better have been characterized as the not-so-daring young man on the legal trapeze. As he dangled out there, the victim of his own guilty pleas, Eddie no longer enjoyed the possibility of making it back to the safety of the platform; he now had to hope that the safety net Arnold Bauman had assured him he had constructed below was as reliable as the attorney said it was.

## ELEVEN

*Good name in man and woman, dear my lord,*

    *Is the immediate jewel of their souls:*

*Who steals my purse, steals trash;*

    *'tis something, nothing;*

*'Twas mine, 'tis his,*

    *and has been slave to thousands;*

*But he that filches from me my good name*

    *robs me of that which not enriches him,*

    *and makes me poor indeed.*

WILLIAM SHAKESPEARE, OTHELLO, ACT III, SCENE 3

T he sentencing of Eddie Gilbert on federal charges was finally set for April 27, 1967, more than two and a half years after he pled guilty to three counts of the 15-count federal grand jury indictment handed down five years earlier (the other 12 counts having been dismissed). Eddie's story made the front page of the *Times*, along with the woes of two other notables: Connecticut Senator Thomas J. Dodd was embroiled in proceedings dealing with his censure by the Senate; and New York Congressman Adam Clayton Powell was appealing his ouster from the U.S. House of Representatives. Neither of those tarnished souls, however, faced the prospect of going to the penitentiary that otherwise pleasant spring day.

Federal District Court Judge Edmund L. Palmieri convened the sentencing hearing in a third-floor courtroom at the United States Court House on Foley Square. Gilbert arrived with his attorney Arnold Bauman.

In discussing Eddie's possible sentencing, Bauman remained convinced that he would get not much more than a slap on the wrist—at the worst, a six-month sentence for all counts; at best a suspended sentence or probation.

Representing U.S. Attorney Robert Morgenthau for the Justice Department that day was prosecuting Assistant U.S. Attorney Michael F. Armstrong. Unlike his predecessor Peter Morrison in the U.S. Attorney's office, Armstrong had little sympathy for Gilbert. Although Morrison felt the case should never have gone to trial, he had left the U.S. Attorney's office not too long after Gilbert had returned from Brazil, so any sway he might have had, had long since disappeared.

When Armstrong stood to address the court, he began with, "Your Honor, this indictment was filed on June 28, 1962. The defendant pleaded guilty on September 28, 1964, to three of the fifteen counts in the indictment...." As he spoke, Gilbert had a visceral sinking feeling about the reassurances Peter Morrison had given when he made his official visit to Gilbert in Brazil (which he had repeated in New York once Eddie had returned to the United States). Gilbert said later that if Morrison had stayed around to see the investigation to its completion, the case would likely never have gone to trial.

The first of the three counts facing Gilbert was wire fraud (for having told Bruce company Secretary Irwin Polivy to transfer funds from the company to Gilbert's private holding companies) which carried a maximum sentence of five years and a fine of $1,000. The second (for having sent stolen funds, $50,000 from the Bruce company, for payment to Gilbert's Parisian creditor) was punishable by a maximum 10 years imprisonment and a $10,000 fine. The last count (for failing to report to the Securities and Exchange Commission his personal transactions in Bruce stock) bore a maximum sentence of two years and a fine of $10,000. The other 12 counts had been dropped. At worst, then, Gilbert could be sentenced to 17 years in prison and fined a total of $21,000. When Armstrong finished his sentencing statement to the court, Bauman stood to make his plea on Eddie's behalf.

He first directed the court's attention to the fact that Gilbert had been "indicted in the state court, the Supreme Court of the State of New York, for the identical acts with which he is charged here." Although it might not be strictly construed as "double jeopardy," Bauman conceded, it was an important mitigating factor in determining the sentence to be handed down. The state court charges and the concomitant plea of guilty by Gilbert "is a different charge in law," Bauman stated, "but no acts of Mr. Gilbert other than those involved in this [federal] indictment are involved in the state court indictment. I should like to point out that Mr. Gilbert faces sentence in the state court indictment, and I should like your honor to [bear] that in mind."

Bauman then brought to the court's attention Gilbert's war record. "After attending Cornell, he served for almost three years in the U.S. Air Force. While he was in service, at the risk of his life, and under heavy machine gun fire, he saved the life of a non-commissioned officer for which act of heroism he was awarded the Bronze Star." Bauman also informed Judge Palmieri that Gilbert's staff sergeant during those wartime days, Gordon Dick, was present in the courtroom and prepared to testify to Gilbert's "acts of heroism and bravery." The judge was not inclined to call upon the sergeant, however, and by this point Gilbert began to think that Judge Palmieri appeared not only uninterested in Bauman's presentation but also at times not even paying attention to Bauman's words.

Bauman next introduced a letter from Technical Sergeant Joseph A. Aja, dated March 28, 1967, and read it to the court:

To whom it may concern:

On December 8, 1944, I was wounded in Athens, Greece. A soldier rushed up to me in a jeep, and risking his life by coming through enemy fire to my rescue. Through his courage and bravery, without regard for his own immediate danger, he got me to a British hospital in a matter of about an hour. I believe I am alive today because of the unselfish act of this soldier whose name was Edward Gilbert.

I did not know him previous to this time nor have I seen or heard from him since, but because of this one act I am able to write today.

Joseph A. Aja
R. F. D. No. 3
Barre, Vermont

Bauman finally concluded his account of Gilbert's wartime bravery with, "I should like further to point out that Mr. Gilbert still wears the scars which he obtained as a result of gunshot wounds during World War

II. As a result of injuries sustained in the war, he was awarded a disability pension which he rather soon declined after he got out of the service."

Bauman next began to trace Gilbert's meteoric rise as a businessman, the financial successes of the Bruce company under his leadership, and the well-conceived but star-crossed attempt to merge Celotex and Bruce. Bauman pointed out that in January 1962, Gilbert had advised the Bruce board of directors that he was personally buying shares in Celotex, eyeing a takeover, and recommended that the company do the same, "and would eventually sell any and all shares of Celotex which he bought to the Bruce Corporation at his cost." Shortly thereafter, Bauman noted, the Bruce company purchased $400,000 worth of Celotex stock; and, on April 17, 1962, the board authorized a further purchase of $3.3 million for the purpose of effecting a merger at some future time. The company had in fact bought 69,000 shares of Celotex worth approximately $2.5 million by May 18, 1962, not for investment purposes, Bauman emphasized, "but rather in pursuance of a corporate program of the acquisition of the Celotex Corporation."

Bauman's argument for sentencing leniency centered on the fact that Gilbert had made the withdrawals of company money to meet margin calls so as to protect Bruce's large investment and to save the merger—an action clearly in the best interests of his company and not calculated for his personal gain.

At one point, though, Judge Palmieri interjected, "Those withdrawals were entirely improper and larcenies, weren't they?" Bauman did not dispute that. "I am trying to explain the reasons for them, not to indicate that they were not violative of the law. And I do want to point out in that connection that while what he did was wrong, while it was the misguided act of a corporate officer, a wrongful act of a corporate officer, in connection with the activities of his corporation, this money was not taken for Mr. Gilbert's personal use; this is not a case where money was taken for wine, women and song; and this is not a case where it was lost at the race track. This is a case that has business origins and where the the wrongful acts took place in connection with a corporation's business, wrongful though these acts might have been."

The reasoning prompting Bauman's arguments was persuasive, other attorneys would later say, but the arguments were out of place in a sentencing hearing. They might effectively have been presented at a trial to determine Gilbert's guilt or innocence in the case; but having had no trial because of his guilty pleas, they were merely after-the-fact explanations.

Bauman offered another convincing argument, but again one that would have better served Eddie Gilbert in a trial, not as a plea for leniency at a sentencing hearing. He stated that Gilbert had executed promissory notes in 1962 and had assigned all his assets over to the Bruce company to secure the notes, the assets representing a substantial enough sum to reimburse the company the entire $1.953 million withdrawn, but the company had mistakenly failed to record its assignment. Because of this oversight, the U.S. Internal Revenue Service was able to file its superior lien against those same assets, in effect preventing proceeds from the sale of them from being used to repay Bruce. Five years later, Bauman explained, "These liens of the Revenue Service still prevent the turn-over of any Gilbert assets to the Bruce Corporation. And I suggest to the Court that the amount still under tax lien [is] very substantial. There is litigation presently pending on the theory that if the proceeds of larceny constitute income, then the return of those proceeds within the same taxable year are a [tax] credit, and the action of the government in asserting its lien has prevented Mr. Gilbert from making restitution and reducing or eliminating his tax obligation." In short, the government deprived Eddie of the ability to use his own remaining financial resources to repay Bruce; it simultaneously imposed a jeopardy assessment for income tax presumably owed on "income"—namely the funds borrowed from the Bruce treasury to cover his margin calls that Blue Monday. It was an impossible situation.

Bauman closed with a plea. "Mr. Gilbert is terribly contrite and sick about what he has done. He wants a chance to work. He wants a chance to care for his family. He wants a chance to remedy the wrong he has done. He wants a chance to repay his obligations. He wants a chance to live a useful and a productive life.

"Your Honor, I respectfully suggest that this is a case that merits the court's sympathy and understanding. This is a case in which I suggest, sir, that justice should be tempered with mercy. This is a case, I suggest, in which a man who has made a mistake, never before involved with criminal law, should be treated with sympathetic understanding and with as much mercy as the court may have."

When Judge Palmieri asked if there was anything Gilbert wanted to say before sentence was imposed, Gilbert responded, "No, sir."

Judge Palmieri was neither moved by Arnold Bauman's tributes to Gilbert's character nor his pleas for clemency. "I don't think anything that was said in court that day had any effect whatsoever," Gilbert later remembered. "I think the judge had made up his mind before he ever sat down on the bench that day as to what he was going to do." What the judge had to say is reproduced here from the U. S. District Court sentencing proceeding of April 27, 1967:

I appreciate all that you have said, Mr. Bauman, and all that you have said, Mr. Armstrong, and I realize that as in all sentences that there are reasons why perhaps the full measure of the law should not be inflicted upon a defendant.

This defendant, as you pointed out, returned voluntarily from Brazil, after apparently having sought haven there. He pleaded guilty and did save the government the trouble of a very expensive trial, because these trials are always much more expensive and more tedious to conduct than other trials.

He has a good war record, and he has cooperated with the government, and he has made at least two bona fide attempts at restitution.

But I cannot overlook the fact that the acts committed were wrongful acts of massive proportions, and he must face the penalties which I am about to impose; in a spirit of accepting them, I hope the true measure of the punishment [is that] which he deserves for the acts that were committed.

Judge Palmieri then sentenced Gilbert to two years imprisonment on each of the three counts, to run concurrently, levied a fine of $21,000, and instructed that following served time he be held to "unsupervised probation for a period of five years [during which time] you may not act as a broker, dealer, or agent with respect to the sales or purchases of any securities and that you shall not act in any representative capacity with respect to any such purchases or sales, except that you may act on your own account or on the account of members of your immediate family." He then released Gilbert on his own recognizance, setting a date one week later, Friday, May 5, for him to report to begin serving his sentence in a federal penitentiary.

The sentence was much harsher than Eddie Gilbert had expected, and Arnold Bauman was also shocked by it, not realizing how it could have happened. Eddie looked at it differently: "I was not a nervous wreck. I was shaken. It was more than I expected, more than I was led to believe I would get. Still I knew I'd only have to serve about eight months [with good behavior he would be eligible for parole after serving one-third of a federal sentence, in those days anyway], and I *could* deal with that."

The *New York Times* reported that Gilbert, after the sentencing, declined to say anything to the press or media already gathered at the courthouse that day to cover his sentencing. "He walked quickly from the courtroom in the United States Court House at Foley Square, his head held high but a glint of tears in his eyes," Edward Ranzal reported the next day on the front page of the *New York Times*.

Gilbert was scheduled to surrender to federal authorities on May 5, a date just three days before he was to appear before the New York Supreme Court for sentencing on the state charges to which he had also pled guilty. On May, 1 Bauman returned to Judge Palmieri's courtroom requesting a postponement, so as to delay Gilbert's reporting date. Bauman's tactical reason was that a sentence imposed in a state court could not be served concurrently with a federal prison term if the federal sentence had begun. In the event he were sentenced to prison time in the New York state proceeding, the federal and state terms would have to run consecutively. If, on the other hand, Gilbert received a state prison term, he could request the director of federal Prisons to grant him permission to serve his federal term while in state custody. Such grants were not uncommon and, if awarded, would have the same outcome as having the sentences run concurrently.

Arnold Bauman did not think this would be necessary, however; he took such a precaution in the unlikely event that the New York court might also impose a prison sentence on his client. All along Bauman had reassured Gilbert that assistant district attorney and prosecutor Jerome Kidman had said that if a substantial sentence were imposed in federal court, the State of New York would be satisfied with a suspended sentence for Gilbert. Bauman had specifically told Gilbert that his sentencing on May 8 in the State Supreme Court building should be no more than a *pro forma* exercise; Judge Gerald P. Culkin had in fact told Gilbert and Bauman at the time of his trial in February that, if he pled guilty, "I'll treat you properly," and with a knowing smile and a nod added, "So, don't worry." Judge Culkin had a reputation moreover for being rather lenient in sentencing.

But Gilbert did not feel quite so comfortable about what might happen at his New York sentencing session. His faith in Arnold Bauman had been shaken because things had not turned out as Bauman said they would, witness the two-year federal term that was to have been a mere "slap on the wrist" in return for his guilty plea.

In the days leading up to the state sentencing hearing, Gilbert asked Bauman to check again with the district attorney's office. Even though Bauman did not think it necessary, Gilbert insisted. But he was not overly surprised, then, when Bauman returned from meeting with Jerome Kidder at the D.A.'s office and told Eddie that he had "a funny feeling" that the "suspended sentence" promise would not be kept. Pressed on the subject by his client, Bauman acknowledged that the New York D.A.'s office had likely changed its minds and might now seek a prison sentence of its own.

Gilbert was terribly upset: "I... became apprehensive and concerned because I had four daughters and a family, and I didn't have very much money at the time, and a jail sentence of two years in the Federal Court, coupled with a sentence on top of that in the State Court, didn't appeal to me very much, and I was worried." Bauman had no idea how to deal with this sudden turn of events either. "He was very concerned, but he didn't know what to do," Gilbert later stated.

So Eddie struck out on his own. "I went to a friend of mine by the name of Mr. Chandor," Gilbert testified in a federal grand jury investigation in 1970, "and I discussed the matter with him and asked if he had any suggestions. How we could make them keep their promise. What we could do. Was there anything... he could suggest? He said he would check and let me know."

Red Chandor was merely an acquaintance of Gilbert's, who traveled in some of the same social circles in New York. Chandor was a dilettante who was more on the fringe of Manhattan's café society than at its center. In fact, in the days before Eddie ran afoul of the law, he often looked after Chandor's well-being. But Chandor had connections around town, and so he was not an unlikley choice for Gilbert to approach given the precarious circumstances. Some of Chandor's connections, unfotunately, were not the most reputable, it would turn out.

"He [Chandor] came back to me the following day," Gilbert testified, "and told me there was a man we should meet by the name of Winterberger." According to Chandor, Robert Winterberger was a politically well-connected public relations specialist (as well as a lobbyist) for U.S. House Minority Leader Gerald Ford, and he might be willing to help, Eddie was told. It should be noted that a spokesman for Minority Leader

Ford later denied that Winterberger had ever been a lobbyist for the Republican congressman, stating that "Mr. Ford had been introduced to Mr. Winterberger by a constituent in 1965 and had seen him three to four times a year from then on [but only] in connection with his [Winterberger's] efforts to have a Dutch doctor legally admitted to the United States."

Nevertheless, Chandor arranged for a luncheon meeting at the Princeton Club near the end of the week before Gilbert's New York sentencing. At that lunch, Eddie told Winterberger with a sense of urgency about the dilemma he faced in the forthcoming state sentencing hearing. When he finished, Winterberger told Eddie and Red Chandor that he could not help personally, but that he "had a lot of political connections, and he had one man in particular who was… Mr. McCormack's [Representative John W. McCormack from Massachusetts, then Speaker of the House] assistant, or worked in Mr. McCormack's office, and this particular man had a lot of influence, and knew a lot of people, and quite possibly if anybody could help me, this fellow could. He didn't know whether the fellow would want to, and he was very busy… but he'd see what he could do."

The individual Winterberger alluded to was Nathan Voloshen, reputed to have far-reaching connections and big-time political power in the federal government. Winterberger then left the luncheon to try to reach Voloshen by telephone, only to discover that Voloshen was out of town, in Washington, he believed, but was expected to return to New York later that day. Winterberger gave Eddie Voloshen's telephone number and suggested he call later that evening, and promised to continue himself trying to reach Voloshen on Gilbert's behalf

Later that evening, Gilbert finally contacted Nathan Voloshen, who by that time had spoken with Winterberger. Voloshen asked Gilbert to come to his office the next morning, Friday, just three days before his anticipated sentencing.

"I went alone," Gilbert recalled in his testimony. "It was in the 40s someplace—43rd Street, or something like that [actually on east 45th Street]. I just don't remember. I came into his office and his secretary said, 'Will you please have a seat?' I sat down and the phone was ringing every minute, and she was saying, 'Yes, Senator'… 'Yes, Congressman'… 'Yes, Your Honor'… 'Yes, Judge'…. I don't know if it was true or not. [But] he was the busiest guy that ever lived, this guy. I'm not sure it wasn't to impress me."

Waiting outside Voloshen's office, listening to his secretary field call after important call, Gilbert could think only that his dilemma was about having to give up several more years of his life. If Jerome Kidder reneged on the promise Gilbert believed he had made to Bauman, he could indeed spend a couple of additional years in prison. He knew his situation was desperate.

"Finally, I was escorted into his office.... He was there with another gentleman, and the other man was a type like Rocky Graziano; a real tough guy, who shook my hand, gave me a very firm grip, and he said to Mr. Voloshen, 'Yeah, that's him; he's all right; I checked him out; he's all right, Nat.' So I thought I was coming into a prize-fighting ring or something. I didn't think I was coming to a lawyer's office. [Gilbert believed that Voloshen was an attorney, but did not learn until later that he was not licensed to practice law in New York.] I couldn't understand it."

Voloshen, 69 years old in 1967, was smooth and polished, as contrasted with his rough associate, Gilbert remembered. The *Times* and the *Wall Street Journal* described him later as "dapper" when Voloshen's own fiefdom came crashing down; he was partial to dark Brooks Brothers' suits and striped ties, exuding an air of affluent sophistication in both looks and manner. Smiling warmly, he asked Gilbert to have a seat. "Now tell me, son, what's your problem?" Gilbert remembers his saying it in a "very fatherly sort of way." Then the phone calls began again. Later describing the situation to the grand jury, Gilbert said, "He'd pick it up and say, 'Okay, Senator, right, I'll be at the dance tonight.... Congressman.... Your Honor.... He talked to every kind of person that I ever heard of in my life.... I was so impressed that I thought this guy would just pick up the phone, I'd go home, and they'd give me the Congressional Medal of Honor.... If he just liked me, I'd win the case. I was so happy. This guy would help me."

Voloshen listened as Gilbert told him the entire story in detail: the misappropriated funds, the flight to Brazil, the guilty plea, the federal sentence of two years, the promise (now quite uncertain) of a suspended sentence by the New York District Attorney's office. And, of course, Eddie's present urgency in that he had to be in court for sentencing the following Monday morning.

Gilbert later gave his testimony as to Voloshen's response: "Oh, not much time, not much time. I don't know what we can do about this; just don't have much time, but let me see what I can do. I'm going to a dance tonight, and I'm meeting a few of the boys [Gilbert understood this to mean judges and politicians] and we'll talk it over, see what we can do."

Gilbert asked Voloshen how much all this might cost, reminding him that he had very little cash on hand at the moment. Voloshen responded with an air of benevolence. "Don't worry about it," he said, "We haven't done anything yet." Gilbert felt relieved, especially after Voloshen added, "Look, I've got a business with some friends of mine in Texas who are going bankrupt, who went bankrupt, and maybe you—you're a good businessman—maybe you can help straighten them out. If we get his thing solved for you, maybe you can help us straighten out our mess." They agreed to meet at a coffee shop across the street from Voloshen's office at 7:30 on Sunday morning.

"I was worried," Eddie later admitted, "concerned, really concerned because if he couldn't do anything to help me then, I had no more time to do anything, because Monday morning, ten o'clock, I was going to be sentenced in State Court." Shortly before 7:30 on Sunday morning, Gilbert arrived at the coffeeshop, and waited, but Voloshen did not show up. "I was there about a half an hour, maybe more than that." Then Eddie went home, very disappointed. He explained to Turid that he had run out of options, that they might as well accept some friends' invitation to spend the day in the country. But for some inexplicable reason, Eddie then decided to try one more time to reach Voloshen. "I don't know what made me do it [but] I telephoned his office and he answered the phone himself [to Gilbert's amazement]. And he said, 'Where've you been? I was waiting for you.' Well, I know I can recognize people, and he was not in that coffee shop, because there were only four or five people in there. But he told me he was sitting there and left about five minutes after eight, which was nonsense. But I didn't want to argue with him."

They agreed to meet at Voloshen's office later that morning. Then Voloshen explained that he had not been able to do anything to resolve Eddie's problem. "I just haven't had the time to get in touch with the right people," Voloshen said. "But don't worry, I'm going to be able to help, I think." Voloshen then urged him to have his attorney seek a continuance, i.e. a postponement of his sentencing. "A week should be enough." Voloshen shrugged, "This is always allowed," he told Eddie. Gilbert later testified that "He assured me that in 99 percent of the cases, if you want to postpone the sentencing, that they practically do it automatically. And I certainly wasn't going to argue with the fellow. He had so many friends, and he said, 'You just tell him [Arnold Bauman] to say new evidence is coming up, new things to interject in the case, and that they will give you some time to think about it."

With the additional week's time, Voloshen assured Eddie that he could work something so as to avoid the New York sentence being tacked onto the federal sentence. Voloshen also planned to be in court the next morning to assist in the process, he told Eddie.

Gilbert left Nathan Voloshen's office no longer dispirited, believing now that things could be worked out. He had a big-league hitter in the batter's box, he felt, as he returned home. It would just take a little time.

Despite his guilty pleas to three counts of grand larceny in the first degree and his loss of faith in the District Attorney's promise of a suspended sentence, Eddie was not worried when he set out for court on Monday. He felt a sense of relief, if not resolution, when he left home that morning. He planned to return to his office after the appearance in court and had told Turid to confirm plans for dinner that evening with friends. He joined Olivier Coquelin and two other friends for breakfast: Eddie was calm and composed, and told Olivier that there was nothing to be concerned about. "Things were in the works," Eddie said. He expected to get a postponement that morning, and the future looked promising. When they finished eating, Coquelin, who appeared more edgy than Gilbert, rode with him to the State Supreme Court House at 100 Centre Street in southern Manhattan but did not enter the courthouse with him.

Bauman had arrived before Gilbert, as had Nathan Voloshen. "I introduced my lawyer to Mr. Voloshen and then told him about his suggestion for a postponement." The three talked for a few minutes, and Bauman agreed it was a good idea. As he had no stratagem of his own to circumvent the state's plan to seek a prison term for his client, Bauman conceded that additional time would likely help; and, like Voloshen, he felt certain the postponement would be granted.

Assistant District Attorney Jerome Kidder, chief of the District Attorney's frauds division and representing District Attorney Frank Hogan, had also arrived early. Well over six feet tall and weighing about 225 pounds, Kidder was an imposing figure with an abrupt and often adversarial manner. Gilbert later remembered that "He had the most emotionless eyes I ever saw." He would remember even more cogently later what Kidder had to say about him in court that day.

Moments after Judge Culkin opened the proceeding, Bauman stood to ask the court for a one-week postponement, explaining that personal and professional commitments had kept him out of the state most of the month of April and was thus unable to serve his client effectively. But more importantly, Bauman added, "It has come to my attention that there are matters of what I regard a very important nature which might well affect this court's sentence.... I should like, if the court would be gracious enough to grant it, a one-week extension, in which to produce to the court certain matters which I sincerely think may materially affect the court's decision."

To the great surprise of Bauman, Gilbert, and especially Nathan Voloshen sitting in the gallery, Kidder immediately rose to object: "Your Honor, first of all I must say the application for an adjournment is based on rather vague and nebulous grounds. We don't know what Mr. Bauman intends to submit to the court which he can't acquaint us with more fully now.

"In addition to that, as I understand it, the defendant is due to surrender in federal court to start a sentence there today, and if he does that we may have difficulties in getting him back here.

"I would think that since February when this man pleaded, anything that should have been brought to the attention of the court could have been brought to the court's attention by this time. And I respectfully oppose any adjournment, and suggest that the sentence be disposed of at this time."

Judge Culkin nodded, then turned to Bauman. "The application is denied, counselor," he said.

Stunned by the unexpected denial of his motion, Bauman introduced the transcript of the federal court sentencing, marking them as an exhibit. He next introduced the matter of double jeopardy which he believed should mitigate his client's sentencing in the state court. "Now, the one point I should like to make utterly clear, your Honor," Bauman began, "is that the basic wrongful act which resulted in both indictments is the same. It has been held by the courts that they do not constitute — that this proceedings [sic] is not double jeopardy — but there is no question on anybody's part that Mr. Gilbert was sentenced in federal court in connection with the theft of $1,953,000 from Bruce Company, and indeed that this $1,953,000 is exactly the same amount upon which he is being prosecuted in this court.

"This is one of those unusual situations where one set of acts results in two different prosecutions. But it is terribly important to me, sir, that I make clear, and I hope your Honor will bear with me, that what Mr. Gilbert has been prosecuted for there and sentenced for there, is exactly the same series of acts, exactly the same misappropriations that your Honor has before you today."

Assistant District Attorney Kidder immediately responded: "Your Honor, I only have to say this: That the federal cases are entirely separate and distinct. The only jurisdiction that could have any jurisdiction of the larceny was this. The first count, which counsel unsuccessfully claimed constituted double jeopardy, really involved the dissipation of the stolen money by sending it to various brokers in Europe. The other counts in the federal indictment I believe were SEC violations of one kind or another.

"I understand that when Judge Palmieri sentenced this man, it was called to his attention that he faced sentence in this court. And nowhere have I heard any representation that Judge Palmieri indicated that he was attempting in his sentence to cover that. In fact, it may well be that by reason of the fact that he was awaiting sentence here, he was as lenient as he was in that court." Gilbert recalls nearly falling out of his chair when he heard this line of reasoning.

As he had in federal court, Bauman again tried to make the case that Gilbert's actions were not for personal gain but for the benefit of the company of which he served as the chief executive officer. With special emphasis, he told the court, "I want to say at this point that Mr. Gilbert never intended to end up owning the Celotex corporation. This was a corporate venture. It is my understanding that the federal court was informed by the Bruce Company that it was a corporate venture, and it is my fond hope, and one of the reasons I wanted to adjourn this sentence ... that this Court has been informed by the Bruce Corporation that the acquisition of Celotex stock was a program undertaken by the Bruce Company...."

Judge Culkin interrupted him here to say, "Well, I don't think anybody quarrels with that," and then addressing Kidder, "You don't quarrel with that statement, do you?"

"No," Kidder replied. "The only thing [is] we must remember that Mr. Gilbert was president of Bruce, and the acquisition was designed to increase his holdings in Bruce, make him a bigger man, make him a wealthier man, and he gambled with a couple of million dollars worth of the company's money in an attempt to accomplish that. And it didn't work."

Bauman replied to this assertion by saying, "Well, I just want to say with respect to what Mr. Kidder says, your Honor, Mr. Gilbert was a corporate president; Mr. Gilbert did what every corporate president does. He looked around for an acquisition for his company. He found one that was good; it was no fly-by-night concern. He thought it was in the company's interest, and for that reason and that reason alone he undertook this program. And I don't think the district attorney adds much by that kind of statement."

"Well, the company didn't actually acquiesce in his using their money to bolster his position in the market," Kidder retorted. "They didn't know about it, and they authorized him, as I recall by the minutes, [only] to make certain specific purchases with their funds...."

Bauman, frustrated and exasperated now, said, "Doesn't your Honor want me to make my statement at this time, and Mr. Kidder to make his later without interrupting?"

Judge Culkin was unsympathetic, adding sharply, "I don't want to hear anything further on the merits of his [Gilbert's] position, because the defendant had pled to three separate counts, which is an admission of guilt...."

"Sir, we do not withdraw from that..."

"Well, that *is* the basic fact..." Judge Culkin interjected. "Whatever happened in the federal court had to do with federal law, acts committed against certain laws of the United States, which he violated in the act of performing the larcenies committed here."

"I understand it. I am...."

Culkin cut him off again: "Technical violations of the law. Here it's a substantive crime. While he has, as indicated, a great war record and everything else, he comes at a point that we are ready on the sentence.

"I have a Probation Department report, a full report. Counsel had an opportunity to contact them, which they did. There are letters in the file from the defendant himself. All those things have been gone into."

"Well, is it in order for me to address the court?" a disconcerted Bauman asked.

"I am familiar with the facts," the judge replied dismissively.

But Bauman was permitted to continue. He spoke of Gilbert's voluntary return from Brazil, the assignment of all his personal assets to the Bruce company, the IRS jeopardy assessment preventing their use for restitution of the money taken, and his client's cooperation with both the federal government and the New York District Attorney's office over their investigations, and his ready availability for all court appearances associated with the cases against him.

But Assistant District Attorney Jerome Kidder had the last word. He summed up the state's position in the Gilbert case with these closing words: "I think that the nature and amount of the crime calls for a jail sentence in *this* court, the amount of which I shall leave to your Honor's discretion."

The court agreed. And in Judge Gerald Culkin's discretion, Gilbert's guilty pleas in the New York court warranted a sentence of not less than two, nor more than four, years on each of the three counts, to run concurrently. He also noted that the New York sentence could not run concurrently with that imposed by the federal government.

And then, most unexpected by Gilbert, he ended the sentencing hearing with the shattering words, "Remand the defendant."

Gilbert was stunned. Bauman said later he, too, was "shocked and shaken." And so, as the *New York Times* reported the next day, "Gilbert, wearing a dark suit and dark tie and carrying a brown attaché case, was led from the courtroom with a bewildered expression on his face." Eddie Gilbert would not be returning to his office that day after all. He would not be returning to his office for quite some time.

This marked the beginning of the most agonizing period in Gilbert's life. He labored under the worry of meeting the daily needs of his family and with the nagging feeling that he had let them down. And he had still to fulfill his earnest intention to repay all the money he owed to friends and creditors alike. But his personal commitment to do so was now severely constrained by the years he was to spend in state and federal prisons. It was a very dark time for Eddie Gilbert.

*I know not whether Laws be right,*
*Or whether Laws be wrong;*
*All that we know who lie in gaol*
*Is that the wall is strong;*
*And that each day is like a year,*
*A year whose days are long.*

OSCAR WILDE. "THE BALLAD OF READING GAOL," 1898

A s the courtroom door closed behind him, Gilbert was in a state of disbelief. This was not what was supposed to happen. He was supposed to be on the way to his office, where he had things to do and people to see. And there was that dinner engagement he and Turid had with another couple that evening. Instead, a uniformed guard was taking him gruffly by the arm, ushering him into a barred holding cell, then slamming the gate behind him with a noise so shattering that he could feel the reverberation course through his entire body.

He remained there for several hours, pacing the floor and occasionally talking with the two other prisoners also being held there, a 70-year-old black man convicted of assault and battery (he had merely been defending himself, he told Eddie), and a young white man with a southern accent who had just been sentenced to six months for what he labeled "a minor mistake." Gilbert chose not to tell them that he had been sentenced for grand larceny in the amount of nearly $2 million.

Once inside the cell, Eddie asked if he could make a few telephone calls. After all, he told the guard, his wife had expected him to return home; he had assured her of that when he left for court that morning. And his business associates expected him at the office. The guard informed him that no phone calls were permitted, and that there were no exceptions to that rule.

He was allowed a visitor, however. After about two hours, Nathan Voloshen appeared at the holding pen; a guard let him in and then locked the barred door. Shaking his head, Voloshen sat down on a bench and told Eddie how appalled he was at what he had seen in the courtroom that day; he was "utterly dismayed" that a postponement had not been granted. Furthermore, he said that he had personally escorted Arnold Bauman to the chambers of another judge, Mitchell D. Schweitzer, a good friend of his, who sat on the New York State Supreme Court. But at the moment nothing could be done, Voloshen stated. At the same time, he wanted to let Eddie know that after Bauman's departure from the judge's chambers, Schweitzer had confided that he believed Eddie had not been competently represented by counsel—"a shocking performance" is the way Voloshen summed it up. Bauman had "mishandled the case and should have let another lawyer handle it; he should have stepped away from it."

Because of the unfairness of it all, Voloshen had now become seriously interested in the case, he assured Gilbert. It was now obvious that Kidder had reneged on his promise not to seek sentencing if Gilbert pleaded guilty in state court and was later sentenced to prison for the federal indictments, Voloshen said. This betrayal, Voloshen believed, could be addressed in court, and he would explore that strategy on Gilbert's behalf. He promised to do everything possible to set things right, and, in that fatherly way of his, putting his hand on Eddie's shoulder, said, "Don't worry about a thing. We'll have you out of here in thirty days." Just before leaving he took $60 from his billfold, handed the money to Eddie and said, "Here, take care of some of the guards. It will make it easier for you."

Nathan Voloshen was indeed a power broker, an "influence peddler" as he would later be characterized in the press. In 1967, Gilbert was unaware of the darker side of Voloshen's background. The seamier details of his life would not be revealed until several years later when a scathing article in *LIFE* magazine would lead to a grand jury investigation of Voloshen and his associate, Martin Sweig, who served as chief aide to Speaker of the House John McCormack (and had been in McCormack's employ for more than 20 years). What Gilbert did know and appreciate at the time, was Voloshen's reputation for getting things done in the sanctums of government, the judiciary, and wherever else the bureaucratic systems in New York or Washington proved to be an obstacle.

Voloshen earned a very good living by making deals. William Lambert, in his 1969 *LIFE* magazine exposé, accused Voloshen not only of making questionable deals but of "fixing" a number of cases. Voloshen and Sweig participated in shady schemes involving building contractors, labor racketeers, arms dealers, and trustees of the Teamsters Union pension fund. They frequently invoked their relationship with Speaker of the House McCormack to wheedle favors and peddle influence; they even impersonated the Speaker over the telephone, the *LIFE* article asserted.

Another article around the same time appeared in *Time* magazine, which accused Voloshen of working a scam with the later-defamed Bobby Baker (a secretary to the Senate Democratic majority leader in 1963) and labor racketeer Jack McCarthy. Their goal was to acquire the Bank of Miami Beach. Baker promised to divert government deposits to the bank, while McCarthy would enhance those with an influx of union funds under his control. According to the *Time* article, "Voloshen was to put together a syndicate to buy the bank. The deal collapsed when Voloshen was unable to meet his part of the bargain." Bobby Baker would later be convicted of theft, conspiracy, and tax evasion; McCarthy would serve jail time for 38 counts of violating federal labor laws.

*Time* also claimed that Voloshen worked *both* sides of an illicit deal. In 1963 he was alleged to have lobbied against the Haitian government of Francois "Papa Doc" Duvalier (delivering votes against ongoing foreign aid to Haiti for a fee of $5,000 per legislator) and yet, on a retainer from the Haitian government the following year, lobbied for a $4.5 million U.S. grant in aid to construct an airport in Port-au-Prince.

Perhaps most disturbing in these exposés were Voloshen's associations with major organized crime figures. The *LIFE* article linked him to the boss of one of New York's most famous Mafia families, Vito Genovese. Voloshen had allegedly been hired to get the Mafia boss released from the federal penitentiary in Atlanta because of his ill health. Although Voloshen had not been successful, Genovese *was* later transferred to the federal prison hospital in Springfield, Missouri, where he died while still in custody. Voloshen later worked with greater success on behalf of Salvatore "Sally Burns" Granello, in order to block the mobster's transfer from the relatively comfortable federal penitentiary in Danbury, Connecticut, to the notoriously harsher federal prison at Lewisburg, Pennsylvania. Granello's attorney had failed through customary channels to block the transfer, but Voloshen called on the services of Sweig in the Speaker of the House's office, and Granello finished out his sentence at Danbury.

Another illustration of Voloshen's influence-peddling in the 1960s involved a hoodlum by the name of Manuel Bello. Bello ran a nightclub in Lowell, Massachusetts, well-known as a Mafioso hangout. He was arrested in 1967 attempting to unload $100,000 worth of stolen securities; he pled guilty, and was sentenced to 15 to 30 months in state prison by New York State Supreme Court Judge Mitchell Schweitzer. Six months later, Schweitzer denied a motion to lighten Bello's sentence because of the prisoner's ill-health.

When Bello became eligible for parole in 1968 — also denied — Voloshen and Sweig swung into action on his behalf. According to the *LIFE* article, "Martin Sweig phoned Russell G. Oswald, New York State Commissioner of Parole. Sweig said that Speaker McCormack wanted it called to Oswald's attention that two Massachusetts congressmen would like to have Bello released from prison because he was seriously ill. Sweig said the congressmen had talked with Judge Schweitzer and that the judge said he would not object.

"Oswald reviewed the Bello file and returned Sweig's call, informing him of Bello's Mafia reputation. Sweig backed off, saying he would convey the message and was sure that McCormack would wish to disassociate himself at once from any effort in Bello's behalf."

But it was not over. Reenter Nathan Voloshen, working behind the scenes and bringing into play his longtime friendship with Judge Schweitzer. *LIFE* reported, "This time the mobster asked to withdraw his original guilty plea on grounds that he had been in ill health and was not properly advised of the gravity of his plea when it was entered in 1967 — though the record clearly showed otherwise. Schweitzer nevertheless ordered a hearing on the motion... [at which] Schweitzer allowed withdrawal of Bello's original plea and permitted the mobster to plead guilty *again* to the *identical charge*. Only this time the judge sentenced Bello to a shorter term, which made him eligible for immediate release. Bello thereupon walked out of the courtroom a free man."

Eddie Gilbert, however, knew nothing of these influence schemes when he sought Voloshen's help in his own situation in 1967.

After Voloshen left Gilbert in his holding cell in the courthouse, and "after what seemed a lifetime [actually about three hours]," Eddie noted in a journal he later transcribed to a yellow legal pad, a guard came, handcuffed him, and took him over to "the Tombs," New York's detention center on White Street in lower Manhattan. An officer there told him that his wife would be phoned and that she could come visit him after 6 P.M.

In his holding cell at the Tombs, Eddie had an unforgettable introduction to prison life. Once in his cell, the guard handcuffed him to a corpulent black man seated on a bench. The man was eating pieces of fried chicken from a grease-soaked box. He glanced at Gilbert but said nothing. Moments later, he got up and, dragging Gilbert along with him, walked over to the toilet bowl at the other side of the cell, sat down and commenced to have what can only delicately be described as an evacuation of major proportion. From the piece of chicken still in his free hand he took another bite, and then offered it to Gilbert who had been pulled into a stooped position next to him by the handcuffs. When Eddie declined, the man shrugged, finished the piece himself, and using the hand linked to Gilbert reached out and tore off a wad of toilet paper and proceeded to wipe himself.

A guard later appeared and uncuffed Gilbert, then collected his wallet, wristwatch and wedding ring and led him down the corridor to a room where he was told to disrobe for a doctor's examination.

The physical was brief. As Eddie later described in his journal: "[The doctor] was a cold, impersonal man who asked me if I had any serious illness. When I replied no, he hardly looked at me, just said in a hard tone. 'Put your clothes on.'" And the physical was over.

"It was about this time that I really became depressed," Eddie recorded in his journal. "They gave me a tray and the first meal I had was some horrible fish cake, spaghetti and cole slaw. I was hungry but could only manage to eat the cole slaw. I was then showed in [sic] a cell about 8 feet long and 5 feet wide with no windows and very dingy with one toilet bowl and a small sink and a piece of aluminum used as a mirror and a double-decker bed."

Turid arrived at the Tombs sometime after six o'clock, and she was horrified. "I went down there and was thrown in with all these other women who were there to see their mates. You had to draw a number and when it was called you could go see him and you have 30 minutes.... And there my husband comes. He had a white shirt on—I remember that—and his hair was combed. But mostly it was his eyes I remember, I saw them and they looked so sad at first and later so angry when he started to talk about the lawyer [Arnold Bauman]. We had to talk on a telephone, there was a big glass between us and we each had a telephone and that's how we talked to each other at that place."

The Tombs was Gilbert's home for the next five days. As depressing as the prison experience was to him, he was typically able to find a redemptive element. "As strange as it may seem, I made many friends in the five days I spent in the Tombs." In his journal Eddie identified four of them and their respective felonies: one for extortion, two for armed robbery, and another for murder and assault and battery. "All four of them were fairly decent fellows," he added.

On the sixth day, at morning roll call, he was called along with about ten others for transport to the state correctional facility at Ossining, infamously known as "Sing Sing," which sprawls across some 55 acres on the east bank of the Hudson River about 30 miles north of New York. Its sweep of notoriety in American lore has been long established, in fiction as well as fact, from a Hollywood creation with slang-spouting Jimmy Cagney ranting in one of its cells ("Angels with Dirty Faces," 1938) to the real-life, electric-chair executions of the Rosenbergs in 1953. In fact, the trip from New York courthouses to Sing Sing—being "sent up the river"—became a common euphemism for being sent to prison. Another nickname for the facility, the "Big House," also became a part of the American vernacular.

The ten prisoners from Gilbert's roll call were joined by ten or so from another cell-block, all then handcuffed to each other. Gilbert's journal records, "Out on the street we were put in a maximum security truck. This was the first daylight I had seen in five days, and it was a strain on one's eyes for a few seconds. There are no windows in the Tombs . . . ."

It took about three hours to reach the gates of Sing Sing. Gilbert often tells the ironic story of his arrival there. As new arrivals were herded into the prison, other inmates in the area began yelling: "Hey, Joe . . . Sam, how you doin' . . . Petey, welcome back . . . ." Gilbert was amazed, "My God, these guys all know each other. What am I doing here?" Less than ten months later, when Gilbert returned to Sing Sing after several weeks back in the Tombs when his case was being reviewed, he heard the voices calling out again; only this time it was, "Hey, Eddie... Look who's back, it's Eddie...." And a profound realization came to him: "My God, *I* am one of them."

Gilbert settled into prison life more easily than might have been expected, given his privileged background and lavish lifestyle. In a way, he looked at it much the same as he had the business world he entered in the late 1940s. Only here the goal was not succeeding, it was surviving. He watched, he paid attention, he picked things up quickly, the do's and the don'ts. Very quickly, in fact. On his first day at Sing Sing, he was walking behind a large man who could have passed for a New York Giants' linebacker. As they walked by a guard who had said something to the linebacker, the man just kept on walking. Eddie tapped the man on the shoulder, "gently and friendly," he remembers. The man wheeled around, eyes ablaze, his face contorted in a sudden rage, saying, "Don't you ever touch me. Do you hear me?" A "don't" Eddie picked up quickly.

Like every Sing Sing prisoner, Eddie was given a job, first teaching math in the prison school, and subsequently being made the school's principal. It was a plum prison job.

Meanwhile, back in New York, mitigation efforts were being made on his behalf. Arnold Bauman was structuring a motion to reduce Gilbert's federal sentence, and Nathan Voloshen was manuevering to have his New York sentence addressed and, he hoped, dismissed.

On May 29, Bauman appeared before Federal District Court Judge Edmund L. Palmieri in the same courtroom where Eddie Gilbert had been sentenced a little more than a month earlier. He filed a motion pursuant to Rule 35 of the Federal Rules of Criminal Procedure to order a reduction in the sentence that imposed on his client; "or, in the alternative, for a modification of said sentence and for other and further relief as to which this court may see just and proper." This language was meant to petition for a decision that the federal sentence imposed by Judge Palmieri be construed as served in the state institution where Gilbert was incarcerated and presently serving his New York sentence.

In his affidavit to the court, Bauman repeated what the New York court had done subsequent to Judge Palmieri's federal court decision, noting especially that the state sentencing was essentially for the same crime, "the withdrawal of the $1,953,000," The only difference between the federal and state indictments, Bauman argued, was "the use of interstate communications media in the federal indictment, a fact necessary for federal jurisdiction." Bauman's point was that Gilbert would unfairly serve two consecutive sentences for the same criminal offense. He also made reference to the additional count to which Gilbert had pled guilty in federal court, namely that he had failed to file with the American Stock Exchange and the Securities and Exchange Commission any statement to reflect changes in his beneficial ownership of his Bruce company stock during June 1962 (arguing that the time for filing the statement had elapsed only because Gilbert had not yet returned from Brazil).

Bauman next reminded the court of Gilbert's actions to restore the funds taken, his assignment of all personal assets, his admirable war record and his cooperation with federal authorities in proceedings against him. Quoting Judge Palmieri at the time of Gilbert's sentencing a month earlier, Bauman stated, "This defendant, as you [Bauman] pointed out, returned voluntarily from Brazil, after apparently having sought haven there. He pleaded guilty and did save the government the trouble of a very expensive trial, because these trials are always much more expensive and more tedious to conduct than other trials....He has a good war record, and he has cooperated with the government, and he has made at least two bona fide attempts at restitution.

"But I cannot overlook the fact that the acts he committed were wrongful acts of massive proportions...."

"From these comments,' Bauman concluded, "it is clear that the court surely had in mind, in imposing sentence, not only the violations of the Securities and Exchange Commission laws but also the misappropriation of $1,953,000, which formed the basis of both the federal and state indictments. It is fair to assume that this court, having considered with great care the full and extensive probation report as well as the remarks of counsel for both sides, concluded that imprisonment for a term of *two* years was appropriate and fair under all the circumstances of this case and that a longer imprisonment was not warranted."

Bauman further argued that Justice of the New York Supreme Court Gerald P. Culkin had imposed concurrently running sentences to each of the three state counts to which Gilbert had pled guilty, appending this statement to his sentencing: "Under the rules the federal court, if it wishes, can make a jail sentence run concurrently with a state sentence, but the state court cannot do the same." To which, Bauman observed, "This is a clear indication that Judge Culkin contemplated that consecutive sentences were not warranted and that this court might well direct that the federal sentence be served at the same time as the state sentence and served in state prison.

"Judge Culkin's remarks about concurrent sentences indicate a belief on his part that consecutive state and federal jail terms might be excessive in this case. While he felt that a term of imprisonment of from two to four years was an adequate sentence, and one which he felt he should impose, his statement suggests that he was powerless to order his sentence to run concurrently with the sentence of this court. If, in fact, Judge Culkin intended that the sentences on the state and federal indictments be consecutive, then it was unnecessary for him to have made mention of the court's power to direct the concurrent service of the sentences.

"Gilbert is now in the custody of the State of New York and has commenced the service of the two- to four-year sentence imposed in the state court. Under the provision of Title 18, USC § 3568, Gilbert's sentence imposed by this court cannot commence to run until he is received at a federal institution. Thus, Gilbert may be subject to imprisonment for as much as *six* years.

"These facts were not before the Court on April 27, 1967, when it concluded that Gilbert should be imprisoned for a period not to exceed *two* years. The state court sentence, which Gilbert is now serving, provides for a minimum of two years' imprisonment and a maximum of four years. Since Gilbert must serve a minimum of two years on his state sentence, the period of imprisonment intended by this Court will, of necessity, be served."

Bauman further explained that under the rules then governing federal imprisonment, Gilbert could be eligible for parole after serving one-third of his sentence, or eight months. But under New York's penal rules, Gilbert must serve two-thirds of the minimum sentence imposed, or 16 months. Bauman then petitioned the court: "Since Gilbert is in state custody, his imprisonment for at least 16 months is inevitable, and he will be released at that time provided his behavior is exemplary. In terms of imprisonment, even assuming that Gilbert is released in 16 months—which is by no means assured—he will have served what would be the minimum time required had a *four-year* jail term been imposed by this court. It is respectfully submitted that such a situation merits the sympathetic consideration of this court."

Bauman asked that the federal sentence, in light of what had occurred in the state, be suspended. "To require Gilbert to serve his state sentence and upon its completion commence the service of the federal sentence would, I submit, be manifestly contrary to the spirit and intent of the sentence imposed by this court," Bauman argued.

Should Judge Palmieri be unwilling to suspend Gilbert's federal sentence, Bauman asked that a request be made of the U.S. Attorney General to agree that the state prison where Gilbert was serving his time be construed as the place of confinement for the federal sentence. In effect, Bauman was requesting concurrency of Gilbert's confinement for his federal and state sentences.

Bauman concluded with this statement, "Unless the sentence of this court is made to run concurrently with the state sentence, Gilbert will be subject to a period of imprisonment of up to *six* years. I do not believe that such was the intention of this Court in imposing a sentence of *two* years... [therefore] your deponent respectfully prays for an order pursuant to Rule 35 of the Federal Rules of Criminal Procedure reducing the sentence of two years previously imposed upon the defendant Edward M. Gilbert to a sentence of two years with the execution of sentence suspended or, in the alternative, for a modification of the sentence previously imposed to include therein a recommendation or direction to the Attorney General to designate the state prison where defendant is confined as the place of confinement on the sentence of this court."

Judge Palmieri agreed to take Bauman's motion under consideration. Just over two weeks later, on June 16, 1967, he announced his ruling:

At the time of the sentence, which was imposed by this Court on April 27, 1967, this Court was aware that there was an outstanding state indictment for misappropriation of funds to which the defendant had pleaded guilty and with respect to which sentence had not yet been imposed. It was not the intention of this Court to preempt in any way the functions of the New York State Supreme Court with respect to the disposition of the plea of guilty then pending before it. The defendant was sentenced in this Court for violations of specific federal statutes—wire fraud... interstate transportation of a stolen check... and failure to file a "Form 4"—and nothing in the proceedings before this Court justifies the conclusion that the functions of the state court were impinged in any way. Each court exercised a separate and distinct function with respect to separate and distinct crimes.

The sentence imposed by this Court followed an intensive study of the case, including the consideration of a pre-sentence report prepared by the Probation Department of this Court. Immediately prior to the imposition of sentence, detailed statements were made to the Court by counsel for both sides. The sentence imposed was a considerate and appropriate sentence based upon a consideration of all the relevant factors and one which cannot in good conscience be disturbed.

The motion is denied in all respects.

Dated: New York, N.Y.    Edmund L. Palmieri
June 16, 1967         U.S.D.J.

The *New York Times* reported the ramifications of Judge Palmieri's decision on its front page the following morning: "Edward M. Gilbert, the former 'boy wonder of Wall Street,' lost a key round yesterday in his effort to avoid serving a maximum prison sentence imposed on him after he pleaded guilty to federal and state charges of grand larceny, fraud and embezzlement.... As a result, Gilbert will have to serve at least four years in prison, less time off for good behavior, instead of a minimum of two years. His attorney, Arnold Bauman, could not be reached for comment, but it was believed Gilbert had few recourses left."

Meanwhile, Nathan Voloshen had visited Gilbert at Sing Sing in early June. His strategy, he told Eddie, was that they would file a petition for a Writ of Error *coram nobis* seeking to vacate the sentence imposed by the New York State Supreme Court on May 8, 1967; and also to vacate Gilbert's guilty pleas to the three state counts made on February 2, 1967. The petition's success would derive from the alleged promise made by Assistant District Attorney Jerome Kidder that, should Gilbert receive at least a two-year sentence on the federal charges, New York would not seek a prison sentence on the counts to which Gilbert had pleaded guilty. "We'll get this thing straightened out and have you home for Christmas," Voloshen predicted.

Voloshen's stategy sounded plausible to Gilbert. As Eddie later testified before a federal grand jury in a related matter, "I was asking for my plea back; the fact that I had pleaded guilty. I didn't think I was guilty, but I had pleaded, on the promise that I would get a suspended sentence; and the original reason I had pleaded guilty was because my lawyer had promised me a suspended sentence. I didn't think I was guilty." Voloshen urged him to talk it over with Bauman and get from him a sworn affidavit about having been promised a suspended sentence.

When Gilbert asked Bauman for such an affidavit, much to Eddie's surprise, Bauman said he could not make such a statement in court. He could not say that Kidder had "promised" a suspended sentence. "But *that's* what you told me," Gilbert said.

"That was my interpretation of what he said... not that there was an outright promise," Bauman replied.

"But that's why you recommended I plead; that's why I pleaded guilty," Gilbert reminded him. As Bauman continued to vacillate, Eddie realized it was clear that he would not say that Kidder had made such a specific promise to him. "So, I proceeded to tell Bauman I had no further use for his services and that Mr. Voloshen was now going to find me a lawyer."

On his next visit, Voloshen suggested that a criminal lawyer named Edelbaum came highly recommended and was known to have worked on a number of important state-related cases. "I was privileged to get this Edelbaum," Voloshen said, according to Gilbert's later testimony. So Eddie said Edelbaum would be fine, "And I asked him what it would cost me."

"Well, we'll discuss that with Edelbaum when he gets up here," Voloshen said.

It was August, however, before Voloshen got Edelbaum to Sing Sing. Gilbert recounted his situation in detail. When he finished, Edelbaum said, "Yes, you've got a good case."

"Do I have a fifty-fifty chance?" Eddie asked.

"Oh, better than fifty-fifty... much better than fifty-fifty," Edelbaum replied.

"Well, what's all this going to cost me?" Edelbaum reflected for a moment or so, then told Gilbert he thought $40,000. Gilbert shook his head. "I don't have [that kind of] money. I lost everything I have." Edelbaum looked at Voloshen, but before either could speak, Eddie added, "Well, I'll tell you what I can do. I might be able to borrow $15,000, or scrape it up, or do something and give you $15,000, and then the other $25,000 when I get out of prison, and if I get back on my feet, and if I have it one day, and if I make any money. I'll pay you that, and you'll just have to take my word for that."

Edelbaum and Voloshen then conferred for a minute or so out of Gilbert's earshot. When they rejoined him, Edelbaum said, "That's okay with me."

And Gilbert said, "This is the way I'm going to pay the $15,000: $5,000 when I have my hearing, $5,000 when I win the hearing, and $5,000 if it goes to an appeal, if the state appeals it and I win it then."

Edelbaum nodded. "That's okay. My man will be up to see you soon, and we'll get into it right away."

As Gilbert later testified, "Within the next week, I got... a message in the prison that a Mr. Feitel had arrived and was there to see me.... He was one of the lawyers in Mr. Edelbaum's office. And Mr. Feitel was a very nice young fellow, very charming, capable fellow.... I told him the whole story... which took about four hours... and he said, 'Excellent case, I'll be back in about four days. I want to check some things.'"

When Feitel returned, he did not seem so positive, however, nor nearly as enthusiastic. With some hesitancy he said to Gilbert, "Well, it's worth taking a shot."

Gilbert, incensed, said, "'Taking a shot?' I don't quite understand what you're talking about. What do you mean? 'Taking a shot?'"

Feitel shrugged, "Everything is 'taking a shot'."

"Wait a minute.... I was under the impression that I had a 90 percent chance of winning this case, and your own boss told me that I had a better than fifty-fifty chance. I don't understand now. I'm 'taking a shot'? I'm not going to pay any $15,000 for 'taking a shot', or $5,000, and jeopardizing my parole.... Now you go back and tell Mr. Edelbaum that unless I have an excellent chance of winning this case, he can forget the whole thing. I'm not 'taking any shots.'"

A few days later Voloshen told Gilbert that Edelbaum was no longer interested in his case.

But a few weeks after that, Voloshen once again contacted Gilbert. He had another lawyer willing to look into the case, Michael P. Direnzo, in private practice with an office on Broadway in lower Manhattan. A close friend of Voloshen's, Direnzo was the attorney of record for mobster Salvatore "Sally Burns" Granello. Voloshen and Direnzo went to Sing Sing to meet with Gilbert. Voloshen had earlier counseled Eddie not to "excite him [Direnzo]..., be very careful..., don't upset him." Voloshen did not want another Edelbaum situation; heeding Voloshen's advice, after a five-hour session, Gilbert agreed that Direnzo would take the case for $15,000, to be paid to the attorney just as Gilbert had arranged to pay Edelbaum.

In reality, Gilbert liked Direnzo. At the grand jury proceeding later, he stated that Direnzo was "... very charming, a very capable lawyer. He tried very hard... [and] did the best he could." Direnzo filed the Writ of Error *coram nobis* in the New York Supreme Court in late 1967, with a hearing scheduled to begin in mid-December 1967 before Justice George Postel. Because Gilbert's presence at the proceeding was necessary, he was brought back to the Tombs where he would be held until his petition was resolved.

The substance of Direnzo's writ was that Assistant District Attorney Jerome Kidder had promised Arnold Bauman (who confided such a promise to Gilbert) that if Gilbert pleaded guilty in state court, New York would not seek a prison term for him if he received a two-year federal court sentence. Given that impression of his fate, Gilbert pleaded guilty in state court. But the District Attorney's office reneged on its promise and recommended imprisonment, in fact a two- to four-year state court sentence. The defendant therefore sought to vacate both his guilty plea and the court's subsequent sentence.

Gilbert acknowledged that no direct "promise" had been made to *him* by Assistant District Attorney Kidder, but testified that this appeal was grounded in what Arnold Bauman had told him, namely what Kidder had promised to Bauman about his sentencing. Gilbert also conceded that neither the judge nor any one associated with the court itself had offered a suspended sentence for the counts to which Gilbert had pleaded guilty.

But as a consequence of his request to vacate his guilty plea, Gilbert had simultaneously been placed in the position of having to admit to lying in his earlier appearance before Judge Culkin in the New York State Supreme Court in February 1967. As to that guilty plea then, this courtroom colloquy during the *coram nobis* proceeding resulted:

KIDDER: [In pleading guilty] Was your answer true to Judge Culkin?

GILBERT: My answer was not true, no.

KIDDER: So you did lie to Judge Culkin?

GILBERT: Then I did, yes.

KIDDER: You were willing to lie then on advice of counsel, weren't you?

GILBERT: My lawyer told me to do that, yes.

KIDDER: I say you were willing to do that, yes?

GILBERT: I was willing to do it: My lawyer told me to.

An additional nail in Gilbert's coffin was revealed in the District Attorney's Memorandum of Law filed after the appeal hearing. "Gilbert also contends that he is innocent of the charges made against him in the

United States District Court. [But] it is interesting to note that he made no attempt to withdraw his plea in the United States District Court even after it became apparent to him that he was going to get a two-year sentence in that court." Direnzo's argument opposing such a simplistic interpretation of the defendant's options was that it had not been "apparent" to Gilbert that he was going to get a two-year sentence in federal court, and so what the District Attorney contended was totally irrelevant to the proceeding in the New York court.

Gilbert testified on his own behalf, particularly about Kidder's alleged promises about sentencing: "He [Bauman] told me that Mr. Kidder had nothing against me personally. I remember him saying this specifically; that he thought that if I were sentenced in the federal court that Mr. Kidder would not insist upon a sentencing in the state court; that he had spoken with Mr. Kidder, specifically, and Mr. Kidder did not seem to . . . have any axe to grind specifically against me, and that he didn't think we presented a serious problem in the state court, because I was indicted first in the federal court, and I would be sentenced first in the federal court. . . . If I was sentenced in the federal court, that the state court probably wouldn't do anything. There was no discussion of a promise at this time, there was no discussion of a deal, excepting that he didn't want to talk to me about deals or anything else. He was going to make his arrangements, and when he felt satisfied that he could accomplish [them], I would get no more than two years [of total confinement for both federal and state sentencings], and that the state court would not do anything if I did get sentenced—I believe he went so far as to say he had spoken with Mr. Kidder. I am not sure if this is right. I know he said [that] at a later date, and Mr. Kidder said to him if I received more than a slap on the wrist in the federal court that he would not ask for anything else for me here. . . . I know he said it as soon as I returned [from Brazil] . . . , that's all he [Bauman] kept mentioning.

"He [Bauman] thought that I should plead guilty to the crimes and that if I did plead guilty he advised me that it was his educated guess that in the federal court . . . if I got one year in prison, he would be pleased; if I got two years, he would think that would be about what it would be; and if I got three years he would be shocked. . . .

"He told me we shouldn't worry about the state court; that he didn't think I would be sentenced there in the first place."

Gilbert testified that he had pressed Bauman for a specific answer before he would agree to plead guilty in the New York state court proceeding. "He told me that Mr. Kidder had promised him that he would stand mute, would not ask for sentence.... Mr. Kidder promised him that if I got more than a slap on the wrist... that he, Mr. Kidder, would not insist upon a sentence."

But Gilbert did testify as to one *caveat* in Kidder's alleged promises. "Mr. Bauman said, 'Mr. Kidder thinks you should serve some time in prison. He has told me so, and that if you do get a suspended sentence in the federal court, Mr. Kidder does believe you should serve some time in prison [which he would seek in the New York case]....'"

The judge then asked Gilbert, "Did he [Bauman] ever tell you what Mr. Kidder's position would be if you received a two-year sentence in the federal court?"

Gilbert was animated and adamant in his answer. "He told me that would constitute more than a slap on the wrist, as far as Mr. Kidder was concerned, it would be satisfactory. He told me that Mr. Kidder promised him he would stand mute at the sentencing... that Mr. Kidder wouldn't ask for me to be sentenced. He told me that Mr. Kidder... would not recommend that I get sentenced but that if I got a suspended sentence in federal court, that I should not get a suspended sentence in state court. He told me that! But Mr. Kidder had promised him he would stand mute. That is what Mr. Bauman had told me."

Gilbert had asked Bauman what had happened. "Did he [Kidder] break his word to you?" According to Gilbert's testimony, Bauman said that Kidder had done so and added, "But so what? What can I do about [it]?"

Jerome Kidder did not remember his conversations that way. His testimony in the court record was that "he had a number of conversations with Mr. Bauman concerning the disposition of the case against Gilbert, but that he never made any promise to Mr. Bauman as to what sentence the defendant would receive in the event that he should plead guilty.

"On the contrary, Mr. Kidder testified that he told Mr. Bauman: 'I want you to understand and I want your client to understand that not only would I not recommend a suspended sentence, and not only will I not remain mute, but I will affirmatively recommend a jail sentence. I want you and Gilbert to know that before he pleads or goes to trial. Whatever you want to do is all right with me.'"

The question before the court in the present hearing for Gilbert was not so much what Kidder had said, but what Bauman had told Gilbert that Kidder had said. And so addressing that question, Direnzo confirmed Gilbert's position by calling three witnesses. The first was attorney Richard H. Wels who was earlier involved in representing Eddie Gilbert in a number of other matters. Wels testified that he had direct conversations with Bauman subsequent to Gilbert's pleading guilty and his sentencings in both courts. During one of those conversations, Wels testified that Bauman had said to him that the state's stiff sentencing of Gilbert was "very rough" and that it breached an understanding he had reached with the District Attorney's office at the time Gilbert was to plead guilty to the New York charges. Wels further testified that Bauman explained to him that if Gilbert received a sentence of imprisonment of two years or more in the United States District Court, his understanding was that the district attorney's office would seek no additional confinement for Gilbert in state court.

Wels elaborated, saying that Bauman had told him New York's imposition of prison time for Gilbert was "very upsetting" to him and that he would prepare and sign an affidavit to that effect for Gilbert's use in whatever action Gilbert might undertake. Wels said that he later learned that, when Gilbert's present attorney Michael Direnzo had requested such an affidavit, Bauman had refused to provide one.

When asked if Bauman had ever spoken of "specific" representations of a suspended sentence for Gilbert in state court, Wels testified that Bauman had always used the word "understanding" in their conversations about the District Attoney's position.

Direnzo next called Gilbert's mother, Yolan, who testified that she and her late husband Harry had spoken with Bauman while Eddie was still in Brazil. "He insisted that he [Bauman] would not let Edward come home until he [Bauman] had made his deal, and that the deal would be, when I asked him... no more than two years in the federal, and that if he got two years or less in the federal, the state would be suspended sentence, and that we didn't have to worry about the state at all."

Mrs. Gilbert confirmed earlier testimony that in the days just prior to Gilbert's decision to plead guilty, Bauman had repeated his assessment of the situation: "Not to worry, that it would be a minor sentence, nothing more than two years, and that the state sentence would be a suspended sentence."

Direnzo's third witness was Eddie's wife Turid. She testified as to a conversation she had had with Bauman on May 18, 1963, about six months after Gilbert had returned from Brazil. She recalled specifically asking Bauman what would happen if her husband pled guilty, and she quoted Bauman as answering, "Don't worry, Turid, if Eddie gets two years or more in federal, then he won't get a state sentence."

New York District Attorney Frank S. Hogan submitted a formal refutation to Judge Postel in a Memorandum of Law dated January 1968, stating, "It is well settled that there should be very cogent reasons for upsetting the *status quo* in a case such as this where the defendant, represented by able counsel, pleaded guilty in open court to charges which had been pending against him for almost five years, and that the petitioner has the burden of proof to show that his constitutional and statutory rights were infringed."

As to Jerome Kidder's alleged promise to Arnold Bauman, District Attorney Hogan wrote, "If we accept the defendant's contention that he had been promised a suspended sentence, it is difficult to explain his conduct on the day of sentence. Any normal human being would instinctively cry out 'What is going on here? I was promised a suspended sentence.' Did this defendant so react? No, it took him seven months to get around to protesting what had happened to him.

"Defendant's claim that he was promised a suspended sentence is based almost entirely on his testimony and he has admitted in these proceedings that he lied to the court on the day that he pleaded guilty to three counts of the indictment then pending against him in this court."

By way of discrediting Gilbert's three witnesses, Hogan asserted there was no record that Bauman told them that Assistant District Attorney Jerome Kidder had ever made any such specific representation to him as a promise. "At best their testimony indicates an alleged promise by an unidentified source." Hogan went on to conclude that "It is reasonable to assume that Mr. Bauman never told either of them that he had made a deal of any kind with Assistant District Attorney Kidder or they certainly would not have hesitated to so testify."

Hogan's Memorandum concluded with a number of telling arguments. First, Kidder testified he never made the promise to Bauman of a suspended sentence. Second, he questioned whether "the People of the State of New York and the defendant would litigate the issue of double jeopardy all the way to the Supreme Court of the United States if there had been a promise of a suspended sentence." And third, what would perhaps prove to be most damaging to Gilbert's petition, "The one person who knows what he told the defendant is his former attorney, Arnold Bauman, Esq. And it is significant that Mr. Bauman, has refused to furnish the petitioner with a supporting affidavit and had not been called as a witness in these proceedings."

In conclusion, Hogan said, "This much is certain. In view of the testimony of Assistant District Attorney Jerome Kidder and the complete absence of any testimony from Mr. Arnold Bauman the petitioner has not even come close to sustaining the burden of proof on the issues raised in this proceeding.... Defendant's petitioner should be denied on the law and the facts."

Direnzo addressed the issues of Hogan's Memorandum in a legal brief submitted to Judge Postel. In it he reemphasized that "the petitioner alleges that a condition precedent to the entry of the guilty plea, to wit: that he would not be the recipient of further penal punishment, induced said plea, that he relied on the promise made to him by his attorney and further, that he felt he was innocent of the charges lodged against him and that he would not have taken the said plea had he known that he would have been sentenced to states [sic] prison."

Direnzo made specific issue of Gilbert's direct testimony: "The court has heard the testimony of the petitioner and likewise heard the answers given to the questions propounded by the District Attorney in a very tenacious cross-examination. The court cannot help but be aware of the petitioner's genuine belief, in his own innocence, which he expressed and continues to express even under such cross-examination. Is there any doubt but that the representations which the petitioner states were made to him by his attorney, were in fact made? Is there any question but that the petitioner relied on those representations and promises? Is there any question but that in reliance thereon he did, in fact, plead guilty to a crime to which he felt he was innocent? Is there any question but that he would not have entered the said plea without such promises or representations?" Direnzo then cited six cases where situations similar to Gilbert's had been addressed in court and were ruled upon in favor of the petitioner.

His written brief concluded, "It is clear that the remedy of *coram nobis* is available where there is a showing of denial of due process requiring corrected judicial process....

"It is submitted that the claim of innocence is an issue which is germane to the issues developed in this proceeding, and that if the defendant is in fact innocent, then a grave injustice has resulted, and the defendant has suffered the deprivation of a fundamental constitutional safeguard.

"The entry of the plea was involuntary in that the petitioner was advised, believed in, and relied upon the representations to him, that he would receive a suspended sentence. He therefore was not aware of the consequence of his guilty plea [the imposition of further incarceration]. The affirmative representation made to him induced the plea, and if the true facts had been known to him, he would not have so pleaded. Such a plea is involuntary.

"It is further submitted that this Court in the exercise of its discretion should permit the accused to substitute a plea of 'not guilty' and have a trial if necessary for the reasons set forth herein on the ground that it is just and fair."

Meanwhile, beyond the courtroom, Nathan Voloshen was busy in ways that Gilbert knew nothing about, but that would not have pleased him. Voloshen had approached Turid Gilbert and Yolan Gilbert in mid-November 1967, insisting that he had to have $10,000 if he were to continue to work for Gilbert's freedom (beyond the $15,000 Gilbert had agreed to pay Direnzo). Yolan Gilbert testified before a grand jury later that she understood such a payment to Voloshen was "for his advice and help." Both women knew that Voloshen was working with Eddie and that Eddie had placed his trust in him. Both drew the implication that the funds Voloshen requested were to help free Gilbert from prison and, in the event that could not be done, to pave the way for his eventual parole. Voloshen told them that, without his help, it was likely that Eddie would have to serve most of his sentence which could mean at least four to six years. Turid remembers, "Mom [Yolan Gilbert] and I had to go downtown to the bank to get the money in cash. She went in to draw out the money, and I stood outside waiting for her. We were both very nervous and scared. It was so much money to have in cash, I remember. But we did, we took a taxicab home, and then Mr. Voloshen came by, and she gave it to him."

Soon thereafter, Voloshen informed Yolan Gilbert that "another $10,000 was due and he said at this time that he knew of another prisoner who had not paid and he never got a parole, so I went and withdrew another $10,000 from the bank and paid him that, in cash again."

　　　　　　　　　　　　　　　　BOY WONDER OF WALL STREET

Some rather unfavorable publicity for Gilbert was also gathering in 1969 about his association with Voloshen, as articles appeared in the New York press and such national magazines as *Time, LIFE, Newsweek*, and *U.S. News & World Report*. Voloshen was reportedly under investigation for fraud and illicit influence peddling, among other offenses. Gilbert apparently did not learn about all of this until after he had been released from prison some time later; in fact, he testified before a grand jury that Voloshen had never told him a single thing about it.

According to the accusatory *LIFE* magazine article written by William Lambert, "Russell G. Oswald, New York State Commissioner of Parole, had a personal call from the Honorable John W. McCormack, Democrat of Massachusetts and Speaker of the U.S. House of Representatives. Oswald had frequently talked on the phone to McCormack during the years Oswald served as corrections commissioner in Massachusetts, and readily recognized the voice. The Speaker said he was a friend of Gilbert's late father and that Eddie himself was a man of 'honesty and respectability.' McCormack recommended that Gilbert be granted an early parole." The *Time* magazine article mitigated the accusation against McCormack by noting that "It is well known in Washington that both Voloshen and Sweig were able to imitate McCormack's voice, a fact of which McCormack was vaguely aware." McCormack vehemently denied that he was "vaguely aware," saying he was "not ever remotely aware" of such a fact; and Sweig later admitted that on occasion he had impersonated McCormack on the telephone.

Speaker of the House McCormack responded to the allegations in a formal statement released to the press. As quoted in the *New York Times*, McCormack adamantly denied ever making a phone call on behalf of Eddie Gilbert. "I never spoke with Mr. Oswald on the Gilbert matter," McCormack said. "In fact, if I ever did speak with Mr. Oswald, it was at least 12 or more years ago when he was Commissioner of Corrections in Massachusetts." McCormack went on to say that prior to the allegation he had had no knowledge of Eddie Gilbert at all nor "any recollection of the Gilbert family or any member of it." He also "denounced the editors of *LIFE* magazine for publishing such 'a malicious article' and subjecting him to 'unwarranted vilification,' a man whose 'public and private life is an open book.'"

Gilbert also felt stung by the way the newswriters were characterizing *him* in articles about the scandal swirling around individuals in McCormack's office. From *LIFE*: "Nathan Voloshen's most notable confidence job was worked on celebrated swindler Eddie Gilbert...." From the *New York Times*: "Edward M. Gilbert, the one-time multimillionaire convicted on federal and state charges of swindling and looting corporate accounts, testified yesterday...." *Time* referred to him as "a convicted corporate swindler," and *Newsweek* as "one-time Wall Street wonder boy turned embezzler." In all fairness, such terms as "swindler" and "embezzler" were sensationalistic in their application to the facts of what had happened. In fact, no one associated with the case—none of the officers of the Bruce company, none of the lined-up creditors, not even the federal or state prosecutors—had suggested that Gilbert had tried to "swindle" or "loot" the company he served as chief executive officer. He had never tried to hide the funds taken. To the contrary, he had forthrightly informed the company's attorneys and its board of directors and had signed promissory notes to the company for the amounts paid out. The act of "borrowing" the money was what he maintained he was doing; even "misappropriating," as the courts eventually decided, was never construed as an act commited for his personal gain but rather as one that would serve the legitimate interests of his company's effort to take over another corporation. John F. Kennedy earlier in the decade may have anticipated the lesson Eddie Gilbert was to learn from all this when he observed that no one ever said life was going to be fair. Such epithets in the nation's press would continue to dog Eddie Gilbert throughout his long business life later.

Inside or outside the courtroom, Nathan Voloshen's efforts on behalf of Gilbert came to nothing. Although Michael Direnzo had built a respectable case, his *coram nobis* petition to vacate Gilbert's guilty plea and consequent sentence in New York court was denied. Judge Postel ruled in favor of the New York prosecutors, it being universally agreed that the most damaging aspect of Gilbert's case was the absence of attorney Arnold Bauman's affirming affidavit.

With his case over, Gilbert returned to Sing Sing in January of 1968 to serve out the balance of his sentence. Shortly after his return, he learned of the $20,000 his mother had had to turn over to Voloshen, and he was outraged. He testified about it before the grand jury investigating Voloshen and Sweig in September 1969; under questioning, Gilbert's responses appear in those court records:

Q. Did you have any conversation with any of the people that you mentioned about any money going to Mr. Voloshen?

A. Yes, my mother.

Q. All right. Tell us the circumstances of that.

A. She told me that she had paid Voloshen $20,000 in cash.

Q. When did she tell you that?

A. I believe right after the first visit I had, when I got back to Sing Sing after my *coram nobis*... and when I was through... my mother, my wife, they and everybody came to visit me.... My mother told me she was quite frightened, when she told me, she was afraid I would be very angry, which I was. I was furious, because I didn't see any reason for him to extort money from my mother.

Q. Did she tell you when she paid the money?

A. She didn't tell me, but my memory was refreshed recently. It was paid November, December, apparently in 1967....

Q. I see. So your mother told you she had paid $20,000, I assume, [informed you of that fact] sometime in '68?

A. She did. She was probably afraid — she could only talk over the phone [at the Tombs] and a few minutes at a time — it would be investigated if she had told me she had paid this guy. That is why she didn't tell me until after I got back to Sing Sing.

There was little that Gilbert could do, however. Voloshen never made it out to Sing Sing again, nor did Direnzo. There were no further communications with either of them. Gilbert certainly had other uses for the $20,000. His creditors would have liked it back in his hands, if only so they could have put their hands on it. Gilbert chose not to try to retrieve the money for other reasons, as he testified:

Q. Mr. Gilbert, the Grand Jury is interested in knowing since the period you have been out of prison, which would be May of 1969, have you made any attempt to contact Mr. Voloshen, presumably in an attempt to retrieve the $20,000?

A. No, I did not.

Q. Did you try in any other way to get the $20,000 back from Mr. Voloshen?

A. Well, when I was in prison, after I heard about this, I was under the impression that he knew every senator, every congressman, worked for the Speaker of the House. I certainly wanted to get out of prison, not stay for the rest of my life, and this fellow frightened me. I thought, maybe, he could keep me in prison, make me do the full time, never get pardoned [*sic*]. I was frightened. However, I was incensed by the whole thing and I mentioned to my lawyer I wanted to do something about this guy. I just didn't want to let it slide. My lawyer [Richard Wels] said, "Look, first, let's get you out." He kept putting me off. Nobody would do anything about it. I changed lawyers. I said the same thing to my second lawyer, and he also advised me as my mother did and everyone else. "Look, this guy can make trouble for you. He is connected, close knit, and God knows what. You can't make trouble for a person like him. You are in prison. Wait till you get out. If you want to do something then, do it then." I was in a very bad position to do something to anybody, being in prison.

Q. You were afraid you would not get paroled?

A. Afraid, much more than [that]—maybe he'd have me sent to prison near the Canadian border, you know, from the things I heard people told. One story he told my mother when he was trying to extort the money from her. . . was that there was some fellow that he was trying to help or something. The fellow didn't pay the money and the guy is still in prison. This was ten years before that and he is still there, never made parole, never made anything, just because he didn't want to listen to him. . . . He was a frightening guy. It's not very pleasant to hear these stories.

Once out of prison, Gilbert had little recourse then either. Just a few months after his release in mid-1969, *LIFE* magazine hit the newsstands with the article about alleged scandals in the office of the Speaker of the House, focusing principally on Martin Sweig and Nathan Voloshen and their shady dealings. The federal grand jury investigation that followed resulted in criminal indictments of both men for fraud, conspiracy, conflict of interest, and 12 counts of perjury. If convicted on all counts, Voloshen faced a maximum penalty of 52 years in prison and $38,000 in fines; but in June 1970, the 72-year-old Voloshen pleaded guilty. Because of his failing health and the fact that he was cooperating with the Justice Department in an ongoing, related corruption investigation, Voloshen was spared a prison sentence, but was fined $10,000 in November 1970. Nine months later, he died of heart failure in New York City. For his part, Sweig (who was never involved in any matters relating to Gilbert) was sentenced to federal prison for a term of two and a half years.

With the failure of the *coram nobis* petition, Gilbert had exhausted all his options to avoid serving out his state-mandated sentence. He could only look forward to a parole hearing to which he was legally entitled, and the best he could hope for then would be a release after serving two-thirds of the minimum sentence, or 16 months. Eddie returned to Sing Sing resigned to make the best he could of a horrible situation.

In one of the most notoriously dangerous prisons in America, he managed to get on fairly well. He knew both the danger of making enemies, and the value of maintaining friends inside the walls. The premium of exchange in Sing Sing was not money, but cigarettes. Packages of cigarettes could get one special meals, favors, and a variety of otherwise inaccesible luxuries. Ever the enterprising entrepreneur, Gilbert picked up on the situation early and soon became a prominent dealer in that commodity in his cell block. He didn't smoke, so he used his ration of cigarettes and the money smuggled to him in prison to corner the cigarette market. It made life inside a lot easier for him.

One of Gilbert's visitors during this period was his old British pal John Aspinall, who remained a true friend throughout Eddie's roller-coaster life, never having forgotten how Eddie had helped him when he so needed it. The two men were quite alike in this respect; fierce loyalty to a friend was an inbred trait common to each of them.

In 1999, Aspinall vividly remembered visiting Eddie in Sing Sing: "I can never forget it," he says wryly. "It was a several-hour drive to Sing Sing. A beautiful drive . . . along the river. Absolutely marvelous. I remember I set off alone that first time, from New York where I was staying.

"When I got to Sing Sing—he had put me down as [an authorized] visitor. And I had to have my fingers printed, of all things. While I'm having these fingerprints—they do each one at a time, you know—I looked up and saw this notice posted to the wall. It said something like: 'Under the Taft Act,' or whatever it was . . . something about 'Under Subsection 4, Paragraph 6, Any visitor found with weapons or giving money to the inmates will be held here in Sing Sing until trial.' Something like that anyway.

"So, I was reading this note and thinking, 'Well, I haven't got a gun for Eddie, nor any money. . . .' So I go in to see him. Or they take me to see him, I should say. It was in a large room with a long table and there was an armed guard at the end of it who stared down at us, a quite menacing man. On my side there were wives and boyfriends, sisters and mothers and what-have-you, all visiting. On the other side of the table were the prisoners. Well, when he first comes in, I can see he is as jaunty as ever. His old unflappable self, Eddie. Well, he sits down and he says, 'Hey, John, would you give me your hand?' I thought he just wanted to shake it. But he didn't let go. 'We have to keep holding it,' he says with that conspiratorial smile of his. 'Really?' I said. I thought he was joking. But he didn't let go, and finally I just said, 'Eddie, what the hell are you doing?'

"'You've got to be my boyfriend,' Eddie whispers, 'that's the reason you're here...my boyfriend,' then nodding toward the guard, 'that's what we want them to think, got it?'

"I said, 'Oh... oh, my,' and then without blinking an eye he said to me, 'So, anyway, John, here's what I want you to do. Tomorrow, I want you to come back and bring a hundred-dollar bill with you. Cup it in your hand and I'll get it when we hold hands like this.'

"Suddenly I was thinking about that sign, and I said, 'Eddie, now...', but he just shook his head. 'Listen to me, John. I'll put you down for a visitor for each Friday.' He knew I was going to be in the States for the next month or so. 'And each Friday you bring me a hundred, and we shake hands, like this.'

"I said, 'Eddie, I can't be doing that....'

"Says Eddie, 'Yes, you can.'

"'Why don't you get Turid to do it, she's your wife....'

"Eddie looked at me like I was mad. 'What kind of heel do you think I am? Ask a woman to do that? My wife! Of all things, John.'"

Aspinall did bring him $100 bills on each subsequent visit and passed them to Eddie without being caught; and unflappable Eddie used the money to help in his scheme to control the cigarette market inside the walls of Sing Sing.

Gilbert was kept busy as a teacher and then principal in the Sing Sing high school. He was surprised that inmates in his class, most of them anyway, were more than casually interested in learning, particularly about mathematics. And for this reason he enjoyed his job. But for him, the worst part of prison life was the loss of his freedom. He writes in his journal, "One never realizes how valuable freedom is until you lose it. When you are [without freedom] it is only then the realization becomes striking and penetrating.... For the first time one realizes how important the small, little every day things are—a comb, a toothbrush, a cigar, a shower, a shave, all of the things that are accepted ordinarily."

Life was decidedly different there, and so were the people around him. "There are various codes in prison," he noted. "The code of stealing (for example) is unusual. Inmates will steal anything they can get their hands on, unless it's from a friend...; in my class they will steal all the pencils but one. That they always leave for me." And the nights, "Then there is the midnight symphony. Any time after lights out you can hear the rhythmic snores, farts, groans, sleep-talking, coughs, throughout the cell block, all like one big symphony throughout the night." The nights were long and especially depressing. "The worst period of the day from my experience," he wrote, "is from about 5 P.M. until about 8:00 A.M. in the morning—because one has time to think, and thinking is very bad in prison."

One inmate whom Gilbert became rather fond of was an elderly black man who had been in Sing Sing since the 1930s. Serving a life sentence for murder, with essentially all of his adult life spent within the prison's walls, he had taught himself several languages as well as how to play chess. By the time Gilbert arrived at Sing Sing, the old man had become so skilled at the game that he had run out of competition. He was delighted to meet Gilbert, the former Horace Mann High chess champion and competitor *extraordinaire*. But they had to play matches in a unique way; "on the run," so to speak. Because of his age, the man was not assigned a prison job and spent his days in, or just outside of, his cell. He set up his chess board outside the cell each morning, and as Gilbert passed en route to the prison school, he would stop, survey the board and make a move. During the day the old man would make his move. On Eddie's way back to his cell after work, he would make his next move. By the following morning, the old man would have made his next move. And so their games went on for weeks and months. When one ended, a new one would commence, until Gilbert had finally served his prison time there.

Like the nights that Gilbert dreaded, the days, too, were long. The routine was nagging and deadly dull. "Probably one of the most painful things in the world is solitude, when there is nothing to look forward to," he observed in a more brooding moment. His term of confinement, although shorter than his army stint, seemed oceanic in its vastness, its end infinitely distant. It could have been Eddie Gilbert in Sing Sing penning Oscar Wilde's words in the gaol at Reading: "...that each day is like a year, a year whose days are long."

It did finally come to an end, however. Eddie was released from Sing Sing on September 24, 1968, the two-to-four year sentence imposed by New York State Judge Culkin satisfied, exactly one year, four months and 16 days from the moment he had been taken into custody. From Sing Sing he was transferred to the federal penitentiary at Danbury, Connecticut, to begin serving the two-year federal sentence he had received in Judge Palmieri's courtroom.

Danbury was like a country club compared to Sing Sing, but it was still prison: Eddie served exactly eight months there, one-third of his sentence, being released on parole on May 23, 1969. In all, he had served two years, two weeks, and three days for the consecutive sentences handed down by the State of New York and the U.S. government.

At the front gate of the Danbury Federal Penitentiary that spring day in 1969, Gilbert walked out as a parolee and stepped into a waiting, chauffeur-driven Cadillac limousine. When Turid had last visited him there, Eddie told her to hire a limo and pick him up at the prison gate. "I want to leave here in style," he told her. "I want to leave like a man."

Suppose everybody cared, everybody shared enough,
wouldn't everybody have enough?
There is enough in the world for everyone's need,
but not enough for everyone's greed.

FRANK BUCHMAN, REMAKING THE WORLD, 1947

During the twenty-four and a half months that Eddie Gilbert had spent behind bars at Sing Sing and the federal penitentiary at Danbury, he had ample time to brood over how this horrendous turn of events in his life had come about. Part of it, of course, had been bad luck. The stock market had selected an inconvenient time to crash, a time when he had been hazardously extended on margin. Another part of it had been a loss of loyalty: The Bruce board of directors withdrew its support of him despite his past successes and his ardent efforts to save the Bruce-Celotex merger; instead they demanded his resignation. But the most salient treachery in the horrible series of events that played out in the spring and early summer of 1962, the one that most dogged Gilbert's mind, was that perpetrated by the man he had thought a trusted colleague, his patron perhaps, and his friend, André Meyer, the legendary financial baron associated with the investment banking firm of Lazard Frères. He had turned on him more viciously than any of those directly associated with Bruce.

In the year or so preceding Gilbert's fall from financial grace, he was in regular contact with Meyer, whom he considered Bruce's "personal banker." Meyer was in his early 60s then: jowly, bespectacled, a bit on the paunchy side, exuding a transcendent air of authority, which could segue without warning into imperiousness. At times, paradoxically, he evidenced a none-too-hidden sense of insecurity, a profound need for regular reassurance. "Without a trace of charm," is one way Gilbert remembers him. A venture capitalist with a portfolio filled with extraordinary successes, Meyer was, according to an article in *Fortune* magazine from this period, "the most important investment banker in the Western world."

But he was also something else, according to his biographer, Cary Reich. "In many ways, André Meyer was not a nice man," Reich wrote. "He was greedy, vindictive, domineering, and often quite sadistic. His constant browbeating and temper tantrums made life unbearable for his business associates and his family. No matter how wealthy he became — and he became *very* wealthy — he could not stop plotting and scheming to build an even bigger fortune. He would allow nothing and no one to get in his way. Once, a Lazard colleague gave some investors the right of first refusal on a deal, after they had given Lazard first-refusal rights on one of *their* transactions. After all, this Lazard partner explained, it was a two-way street. Meyer was furious. 'Where is it written, there is a two-way street?' he demanded."

In 1961 and the first few months of 1962, Meyer was to Gilbert the paragon of power and financial prestige. He would often share the back seat of Gilbert's Rolls-Royce on the morning trip from the Carlyle Hotel, where Meyer maintained a splendid apartment, to Wall Street. They would often have breakfast together and serious conversations well before the market opened. Gilbert soon learned, however, that the road they traveled was not a "two-way street."

In 1970, eight years from the time when the two men had often conferred daily at Lazard Frères' elegant offices and when André Meyer had called Eddie Gilbert "my dear boy," admired publicly his grand plans, and described him to others as a *"wunderkind...* a young man with the greatest of promise," an eternity had passed in their relationship. Gilbert's financial world had collapsed: He had fled the country, returned to plead guilty and serve more than two years in state and federal prisons, been vilified in newspapers and national magazines, and was financially bereft with just a memory of his one-time fortune. Swiftly banished by Meyer when things had begun to sour in 1962, Gilbert, by the end of the decade of the '60s, had ceased to exist in André Meyer's mind.

That was about to change, however. Although Gilbert may have been excised from Meyer's mind, Meyer remained a focal point in Gilbert's.

BLACK AND BLUE

*Above left: Gilbert (left) with Alex Vamos (center) and Tony Stratton Smith in Brazil. Gilbert and Vamos, Bell Captain at the fashionable Excelsior Hotel in Rio, became business partners exchanging American dollars for Brazilian cruzeiros.*

*Above right: Eddie Gilbert becomes front page news, June 14, 1962. The front pages of the* New York Times, *the* Wall Street Journal, *and dozens of other newspapers that day similarly covered Gilbert's story.*

*Left: Displaced Frenchman in Rio, Gilbert Deschartre (left), hired Gilbert in 1962 to advise him on Brazilian stock exchange investments. Gilbert touted him on Brahma Beer shares and walked away with more than $50,000 in commissions.*

COLLAPSING SCAFFOLDS

*Top: The June 29, 1962, edition of* Life *carried a nine-page story on Gilbert's flight to Brazil following his forced resignation from the Bruce Lumber Company; among the article's photos, Gilbert is shown strolling Rio's Copocabana Beach.*

*Above: One of Cornell Capa's candid shots of Eddie in his beach front hotel room in 1962 (reproduced here for the first time, not having been used in the* Life *story).*

*Left: Gilbert's one-time friend—and later bitter enemy—André Meyer of Lazard Frères in 1957. Gilbert's business association and friendship with Meyer collapsed in 1962 when he refused to help Gilbert as the Bruce-Celotex merger began to fall apart.*

*Top: Gilbert and British jour-*
*nalist Tony Stratton Smith in*
*the apartment they shared for*
*several months in Rio in 1962.*
*When the two were not playing*
*chess or attending the opera,*
*Smith kept busy journaling*
*Gilbert's activities, hoping one*
*day to write a biography about*
*the mercurial financier; but the*
*book never came to be.*

*Below:* The New York Daily
News *edition of October 30,*
*1962, pictures Eddie Gilbert with*
*attorney Arnold Bauman re-*
*turning from Brazil to face the*
*federal and state indictments*
*in New York over the $1.9 million*
*he "borrowed" from the Bruce*
*Treasury.*

# In Shock, Plea of Gilbert, Back To Face $1.9 Million Steal Rap

### By NEAL PATTERSON

Edward M. Gilbert was in a "state of shock" and not himself when he fled to Brazil after alleged grand larcenies of $1,953,000 from the E. L. Bruce Co., which he headed, he said yesterday after returning to face federal and state indictments totaling 27 counts.

The former Wall Street hot-shot came back after the Brazilian Ministry of Justice on Oct. 2 turned down his bid to become a permanent resident.

After appearances in two courts, where bail totaling $25,000 was set, the 39-year-old defendant told reporters: "I was in a state of nervous shock and emotional strain when I left. I came back when I regained my health both mentally and physically enough to cope with my problems."

**Pleads Not Guilty**

His attorney, Arnold Bauman, pleaded him not guilty in Federal Court and Manhattan Supreme Court, specifying in the latter: "At this time defendant will not plead guilty."

Basically, the charges in both courts cover the same offenses, Gilbert's unauthorized withdrawals of nearly $2 million from the Bruce concern, America's leading hardwood floor maker, to support his battle for control of the Celotex Corp., a maker of building materials. That bid, along with his financial empire, collapsed in last May's drastic market dip.

"Here is a man who in a three-week period was reduced from a very rich man indeed to a man overwhelmingly in debt," his attorney told Federal Judge David N. Edelstein.

Bauman promised that his client will "cooperate totally" with government authorities. Gilbert, he said, will make every effort toward restitution.

Edward Gilbert (right) is accompanied to Elizabeth St. police station by his attorney, Arnold Bauman.

theoretically could run to 74 years and fines of $82,000.

After posting federal bail, Gilbert was taken to District Attorney Hogan's office and then arraigned in Supreme Court. Bail there was set at $10,000. At the time of the state indictment, Hogan reported that Gilbert went broke for $5 million of his own money and $10 million borrowed from banks and brokerage houses.

Gilbert was taken in custody by U. S. Marshal Anthony R. Marasco and Deputy Joseph A.

Rachon as he landed at International Airport at 8 A. M.

At the height of his prosperity, Gilbert and his svelte, brunette wife, Rhoda, 28, one of the world's best-dressed women, had a 14-room Fifth Ave. apartment and also entertained lavishly abroad in their Villa Zamir, near Cap Martin on the French Riviera.

The couple separated last winter and Gilbert moved out of the apartment.

**(Other picture in centerfold)**

## HEARTS GIVEN GLADLY

*Above: In their Manhattan apartment, Eddie and his second wife Turid are flanked by daughters Robin (left) and Alexandra. At the back of the sofa are Eddie and Turid's young daughters Dominique (left) and Nina.*

*Right: Eddie's daughters with their grandmother "Toots" (second from right) at Alexandra's wedding. From left, Nina, Dominique, Alexandra, and Robin.*

*Top: John Aspinall, Gilbert's loyal and colorful friend, owned the notable London gambling establishment the Clermont Club, as well as the world's largest private zoo in the south of England. For more than 40 years, Aspinall and Gilbert enjoyed the best of times together and saw each other through the worst of times as well.*

*Below: Olivier Coquelin (left) worked for Gilbert as major domo overseeing operations and entertainment at Villa Zamir in the summers before Gilbert's ruinous 1962 debacle. He remained a life-long friend, visiting Eddie in exile in Brazil and in prison. He later became associated with New York's Le Club, several Caribbean ventures, and the failed Beacon Theater Discotheque project.*

SOAP BUBBLE

*Top: Eddie with his third wife,
Linda Watkins. The two renewed
their acquaintance in 1979 and
were married shortly thereafter.
A successful actress, Watkins
played parts in television soap
operas and several Hollywood
movies. They divorced in 1985.*

*Below: In Santa Fe, Eddie Gilbert
enjoys a visit from his good
Ann Arbor friend, Peter Heydon.
In the 1990s, Heydon helped save
the Beacon Theater project for
Eddie as well as a host of other
investors. The two were also
partners in Historic Newspaper
Archives and a number of other
investments following their initial
meeting in 1985.*

## COURT'S ORDERS

*Above left:* BGK, *the real estate company Gilbert conceived in 1987, began over a backgammon game between Gilbert and Fred Kolber. They still play the game, as reflected in this 1998 photo.*

*Above right: The three who lent their names to* BGK, *from left: Eddie Gilbert, Fred Kolber, and Ed Berman (seen here on a Galapagos Islands vacation in 2002).*

*Left: Eddie Gilbert and his fourth wife, Peaches Gore Gilbert, aboard the QE II. The two were married in 1985 and have since adopted their three children from Russia. Peaches persuaded Eddie to move from New York to Santa Fe and, according to Gilbert, was the motivation and driving spirit encouraging him through the launch of his successful career in real estate.*

ON A HANDSHAKE

*Above: Eddie and his three children — Sasha, Beatrice, and Zoe — driving into the 21st century.*

*Right: Eddie and Peaches celebrating his 75th birthday. With more than 100 guests, they took over the Café Carlyle for the December night in 1997, entertained by Bobby Short at the piano with his orchestra.*

Eddie had finally concluded that what Meyer had done (and *not* done) almost eight years before was beyond unconscionable, it was grist for a civil law suit. Meyer biographer Cary Reich quotes Eddie's words: "That son of a bitch. He put his arm around me and squeezed my balls off at the same time." Eddie was now going to do something about it.

Gilbert filed suit against André Meyer and the firm of Lazard Frères on May 14, 1970, in the Supreme Court of New York, County of New York, asking for damages of $25 million, even though the statute of limitations for such an action had presumably already expired. Gilbert's lawyer was Stanley Reiben, a respected attorney who maintained offices at 37 Wall Street and who, like Gilbert, was not overly concerned about the timing of the law suit. Reiben argued that the running of the six-year statute of limitations was tolled by reason of Gilbert's imprisonment for a period of two years and 17 days as well as by Meyer's frequent and lengthy absences from the state of New York during that eight-year period of time. When both of these extenuating circumstances were taken into consideration, Gilbert's law suit was rendered timely within the parameters of existing law. So ran Reiben's contention in the plaintiff's case against Meyer and Lazard Frères.

As developed by Reiben, the action was principally based on Meyer's commitment to Gilbert to purchase stock in the Celotex Corporation of Chicago, Illinois, in pursuit of the goal of taking control of that company and merging it with the E. L. Bruce Company, an arrangement addressed thereafter as their "joint venture." According to the lawsuit's language, "In the fall of 1961, plaintiff [Gilbert] told Meyer and Lazard of his plan to acquire control of Celotex and to merge Bruce and Celotex.

"Meyer and Lazard thereupon told plaintiff that they considered the acquisition of control of Celotex, as well as the proposed subsequent merger of Bruce and Celotex, as excellent business steps. A joint venture was thereupon agreed to and entered upon by plaintiff, acting for himself and for Bruce, and by Meyer and Lazard."

According to one of his depositions, Gilbert at that time explained to Meyer and his colleagues at Lazard Frères that personally, as well as through the Bruce company and various friends and business associates, he would be able to acquire a substantial stake in Celotex. [He felt that with his own resources and those of his associates he could acquire and ultimately control Celotex.]

Meyer, in turn, promised Gilbert that he and Lazard Frères would provide whatever financial backing was necessary to pursue that acquisition, but insisted that no other financial backers be involved in the acquisition effort. This contingency would prove devastating to Gilbert later because, relying on Meyer's promise, which Eddie viewed as a pledge made on behalf of Lazard Frères, Gilbert turned away investment money that could have saved his position once it was apparent that Meyer and Lazard Frères were not going to live up to their side of the agreement. As spelled out in the law suit, "[Meyer] specifically told plaintiff to exclude as unnecessary certain parties with vast financial means who were then willing and able to acquire substantial amounts of Celotex stock for the purpose of carrying out plaintiff's plan and the joint venture to acquire control of Celotex."

The "joint venture" was structured in such a way that Gilbert and his associates would acquire 250,000 shares of Celotex common stock and that Meyer/Lazard Frères, in association with the investment banking firms of Carl M. Loeb-Rhoades and Company and the Wertheim Company, would purchase not fewer than 250,000 shares to achieve the overall goal of financial control of Celotex. According to the lawsuit, "The parties expected, and it was one of the agreed purposes of the joint venture, that upon the merger Bruce would issue to Meyer and Lazard and plaintiff and other holders of Celotex stock in exchange for such stock, a new Bruce security on terms which Meyer and Lazard would recommend to Bruce as its investment bankers, and which terms were expected to be highly attractive to holders of Celotex stock."

As a result of this arrangement with Meyer—their "joint venture"—Gilbert asserted that he had personally purchased shares in Celotex in excess of $10 million and had Bruce purchase approximately $3 million more of Celotex stock. And at Meyer's insistence, he had excluded many other qualified backers who would have purchased substantial positions in Celotex for the sole purpose of helping Gilbert achieve his acquisition. By contrast, Meyer and Lazard Frères had reneged on their promises. They had purchased just 87,000 shares initially of the 250,000 they had agreed to purchase, ultimately buying just 123,000 of the total, but all the while encouraging Gilbert to complete his stock acquisitions because they would eventually meet their obligations under the "joint venture" agreement.

Complicating matters was Lazard Frères' purchase in 1960 of the $2 million Bruce convertible debenture, the first financial transaction between Gilbert-Bruce and Meyer-Lazard Frères. This earlier transaction was unexpectedly brought into the equation after the two parties had mutually agreed that each would buy 250,000 shares of Celotex stock (but before Meyer and Lazard Frères had purchased a single share). Gilbert had already begun in earnest to acquire Celotex shares in 1961 when Meyer called for Gilbert to redeem $1 million of the $2 million debenture for what turned out to be a $2 million expense. (The then-convertible amount of Bruce common stock had approximately doubled in value since the debenture had been issued in 1960.) Gilbert, as expressed in his lawsuit, "acting under duress for the purpose of securing Meyer and Lazard's performance on this joint venture agreement," complied, with the closing date of the transaction being deferred until January 1962 at Meyer's request because of tax considerations. But that did not end the matter. Stanley Reiben outlined Eddie Gilbert's contentions of mistreatment for the court:

After plaintiff had purchased from Meyer and Lazard the $1,000,000 debenture share for $2,000,000 ($1,350,000 of which plaintiff paid in cash), Meyer and Lazard again stated that they would purchase the Celotex shares, which they had previously agreed to purchase, but that rather than buying the shares at the then market price, they would insist on buying first from plaintiff, at plaintiff's cost, Celotex shares theretofore purchased by plaintiff, i.e., at prices lower than the market price prevailing at the time Meyer and Lazard made this statement.

At the time Meyer and Lazard made the demand to purchase plaintiff's Celotex stock, as a precondition of their purchasing of shares in accordance with the joint venture and their original agreement, Meyer and Lazard knew that plaintiff, because of his being an officer and director of Bruce, intended to offer to Bruce at his cost the Celotex shares which he had purchased. In order to obtain this Celotex stock from plaintiff at lower than market price, Meyer and Lazard helped to prepare a statement to be made by plaintiff to the Board of Directors of Bruce to the effect that plaintiff did not consider the time to be ripe for Bruce to purchase any shares of Celotex and that he would, therefore, sell to others the shares of Celotex stock which he had theretofore purchased.

It was Meyer and Lazard's intention and demand to plaintiff that following this announcement by plaintiff to the Board, plaintiff would sell his Celotex shares at his cost to Meyer and Lazard and that thereafter plaintiff would advise Bruce that the time has become ripe for Bruce to make purchases of Celotex stock, with the result that Bruce would be making purchases of Celotex stock at market price, while Meyer and Lazard, rather than Bruce, would have the benefit of buying from plaintiff his lower-priced Celotex stock. Plaintiff consented to and carried out this plan solely by reason of the duress practiced on him by Meyer and Lazard in refusing to perform the joint venture agreement and in the belief that thereafter Meyer and Lazard would carry out their part of the joint venture which would enable Bruce to acquire control of and merger with Celotex; plaintiff concluded that the attainment of that goal (to which the purchases to be made by Meyer and Lazard were an indispendable factor) justified his giving the benefit of the lower-priced stock to Meyer and Lazard, rather than to Bruce or to himself. . . .

Plaintiff thereafter sold to Meyer and Lazard 87,000 shares of Celotex previously purchased (either directly or through friends who had purchased Celotex shares by agreement with plaintiff), the sale being at plaintiff's cost.

Further into 1962, after Meyer's purchase of the 87,000 shares, Gilbert reminded Meyer of his commitment to buy a total of 250,000 shares and that it was an integral part of their joint venture agreement; he wanted that to commence immediately. Meyer replied that he and Lazard Frères would do so but only under one condition: He now demanded that Gilbert redeem the second $1 million of the original $2 million Bruce debenture. This meant that he and Lazard Frères wanted what now turned out to be $2.3 million (based on Bruce's then-common stock value) in order to buy the outstanding $1 million debenture before buying any more Celotex stock. Once again, Gilbert capitulated so as to sustain the acquisition and merger plan, personally raising the money and putting it into escrow in a New York bank. Even then, Meyer and Lazard Frères failed to fulfill their obligation; even though they did buy a further 36,000 shares of Celotex in Switzerland through Dreyfus and Company, bringing their total purchase to 123,00 shares, they still were, significantly, 127,000 short of the agreed-upon 250,000.

Then the stock market crashed on May 28. Margin calls came in, André Meyer stopped taking Gilbert's phone calls, and Eddie Gilbert's financial world collapsed.

But the story was still not over. Following Gilbert's ignominious departure from Bruce, André Meyer's associates and the firm of Lazard Frères arranged a sale of all its Celotex shares as well as those already purchased by the Bruce company to the Jim Walter Corporation, thereby handing over financial control of Celotex to Jim Walter. According to the Gilbert lawsuit, such stock sales created a new but different merger that "plaintiff and Meyer and Lazard had agreed to acquire jointly for Bruce, and for which plaintiff and Bruce had expended vast sums of money and vast effort." As a result of the Jim Walter-Celotex merger on August 31, 1964, the Walter company stock rose to $120 per share from a previous high of $20.50 a share when the Gilbert effort failed in 1962.

Papers dated May 1, 1970, were served jointly on Meyer and Lazard Frères, thereby commencing the lawsuit. Over the next several months, Gilbert was deposed four times by Lazard Frères' in-house attorney Thomas F. X. Mullarkey and one of Meyer's personal attorneys, Edward N. Costikyan. The central issue of these depositions was the assertion that a "joint venture" between Gilbert and Meyer and Lazard Frères existed at all. Former United States District Judge Simon Rifkind, representing both Meyer and Lazard Frères, was one of New York's most influential lawyers—being a senior partner in the prestigious firm of Paul, Weiss, Goldberg, Rifkind, Wharton and Garrison. Rifkind's tack was simple: He brought on a motion for summary judgment, asking the court to rule that as a matter of law, even if all the facts alleged by Gilbert were true, the suit should be dismissed.

The motion outlined, generally denied, but did not directly address specific issues raised in the Gilbert lawsuit; instead Rifkind simply asserted that the six-year statute of limitations precluded any judicial consideration: "The defendants deny the material allegations of the complaint and plead as one of the affirmative defenses that the alleged cause of action set forth in the complaint is barred by the applicable statute of limitations." He didn't miss the opportunity in his brief, however, to dismiss Gilbert's allegations with a few gratuitous couch-side observations: "It is plain that Gilbert's claim against defendants is nothing more than a belated fantasy of psycholgical self-justification common to white-collar miscreants. He is using this lawsuit as a Freudian transfer to shift to defendants the blame for his misappropriation of funds from E. L. Bruce Co... in the Spring of 1962, his fleeing to Brazil to avoid criminal prosecution and his subsequent conviction and imprisonment. Whatever the psychological motivation for the making of these claims, it is clear that they are time-barred as well as untrue."

Rifkind additionally sought to establish for the court that in all of Gilbert's testimony and his counsel's claims there was no concrete evidence of a "joint venture" arrangement between the parties. And in his motion for summary judgment, Rifkind did refer to Gilbert's depositions: "As we have demonstrated," Rifkind claimed, "the allegations of the complaint constitute, at best, a cause of action for breach of contract. From Gilbert's testimony, it is clear that the underlying transactions, as he describes them, similarly give rise to, at best, a cause of action for breach of contract. There is simply no way in which the alleged agreement between plaintiff and defendants can be transformed into a joint venture. Gilbert has shown that he cannot supply the missing elements that would change the agreement into a joint venture, because such elements—according to his own admissions—never existed."

In any event, whether or not the agreement between Eddie Gilbert and André Meyer-Lazard Frères constituted a joint venture was not the issue before the court in the motion for summary judgment. The issue was whether the action could be sustained as a joint venture, which was governed by a ten-year statute of limitations, or a breach of contract to which a six-year statute of limitations applied. The defendants asked the court to throw the case out.

On January 26, 1971, the New York State Supreme Court ruled in favor of the defendants, dismissing the suit. Justice Samuel M. Gold, noted that "the plaintiff had five years in which to sue before he was imprisoned [and] didn't take any steps to commence this action until after the statute of limitations had expired." Moreover, Justice Gold suggested that, to his satisfaction, counsel for the plaintiff had not established a case wherein all the essential elements for a "joint venture" *were* in evidence.

Meyer had been bitterly unhappy from the instant he learned that the suit had been filed. According to his biographer Cary Reich, the one thing the financial mogul most despised was litigation and the publicty concomitant to it, "even if *he* was the aggrieved party." He was reported to have said on learning that Gilbert was suing him, "Loathsome! He is loathsome!" In the days following the filing of Gilbert's suit and its airing of all the allegations about Meyer's conduct during the Celotex debacle, wherein he had been characterized as conniving, duplicitous, and ruthless, the venerable financier alternately stewed in simmering rage or railed at his persecution. When the suit was abruptly dispatched in January 1971, he took little pleasure in his "victory." In fact, it was reported afterwards that he would not entertain any conversation about the case; and when Eddie Gilbert's name was mentioned, he treated it without recognition as if a total stranger had been introduced into the conversation.

Gilbert, on the other hand, took little satisfaction from the discomfort he had caused Meyer. He had not been vindicated, and he was not one to give up easily. After conferring with a new attorney, Peter Fleming (a rising star with the Wall Street-based firm of Curtis, Mallet-Prevost, Colt and Mosle), Eddie decided to appeal the case. Fleming had been recommended to him by Peter Morrison, a member of the government's prosecution team who had visited Eddie in Brazil and had long believed that what Gilbert had done did not constitute a felony; Morrison and Fleming had worked together in the U. S. Attorney's New York office earlier in their careers. Gilbert had asked Morrison in fact to file the appeal, but Morrison sensed a conflict of interest because he had been on the prosecution side of Eddie's case when working for the U.S. Attorney's office in 1962. Fleming was a masterful legal strategist even as a young man in the early 1970s and would in later years defend such notorious miscreants as boxing impressario Don King and Wall Street junk-bond wizard Michael Milken, among others.

In his appeal, as in the original lawsuit, Gilbert was focused on the cause of action, the breach of a joint venture agreement and its consequences; Meyer and Lazard Frères, as defendants by contrast, continued to address the nature of Gilbert's claims as a breach of contract and the timeliness of bringing the matter to court at so late a date. The Statement of the Case to the Court of Appeals of the State of New York indicates that the two sides were clearly arguing different aspects of the case.

Peter Fleming asserts on Eddie Gilbert's behalf:

There was no trial in this case, and there was no evidentiary hearing, Indeed there was virtually no evidence at all. Instead summary judgment was granted after nothing more than a partial pretrial examination of plaintiff by the defendants. Plaintiff had not been asked a single question by *his* counsel and the defendants had not been questioned at all.

Perhaps even more strikingly, summary judgment was granted in these circumstances even though the defendants, the moving parties, never at any time submitted an affidavit by a person having knowledge of the facts. And, strangely, the defendants failed also to submit to the court even the partial deposition of the plaintiff, which had been taken.

For these reasons the statement which follows sets forth the facts as claimed by Gilbert in his complaint, his incomplete examination before trial, and his affidavit submitted in oppposition to the motion for summary judgment.

Simon Rifkind, representing both André Meyer and Lazard Frères, presented much the same argument he had made in his earlier motion for summary judgment:

Appellant's brief to this Court describes a case that never was, a motion never made, and a judgment never rendered.

In fact, summary judgment was granted and affirmed [by an intermediate appellate court] in this case on the single, dispositive ground that the statute of limitations barred plaintiff's cause of action. But appellant's brief is a studied effort to conceal that ground of dismissal. It is first mentioned in passing at page 9 of the brief and thereafter mentioned only rarely and without any discernible attempt to point out that this was the basis for the judgment appealed from. Instead, appellant's brief is a studied attempt to lead the Court into the belief that summary judgment was granted on the merits of the underlying substantive issues, rather than on the merits of the defense of the statute of limitations.

The appeal failed. The seven-judge panel of the New York State Court of Appeals upheld the summary judgment rendered in the State Supreme Court by Justice Gold, while offering no new opinion of its own. It was the end of the legal road. Eddie Gilbert would have to settle for the scant annoyance he had caused André Meyer by bringing the lawsuit to court and the fact that Meyer's deviousness and cupidity had been revealed and reported for public consumption.

And how was André Meyer really affected? Cary Reich stated it this way: "Many years afterward... [Lazard Frères' in-house counsel] Tom Mullarkey was asked about [Meyer's relationship with] Eddie Gilbert and... began laughing uproariously.

"'To his dying day,' said Mullarkey, after he had calmed down, 'André would repeat over and over, "I never knew Eddie Gilbert."'

"'Did he?' Mullarkey was asked.

"'Did he?' chuckled Mullarkey. 'They were like two peas in a pod.'"

Once out of prison, when not developing and pleading his lawsuit against André Meyer, Gilbert eventually went back to the one place where he felt most at home, the stock market. For a short while, he took an executive position with a waterproofing firm in New York, a job for which he was well paid but at which he was generally unhappy. It hardly held the challenge he craved, and he was working directly for someone else, which had not been his style since taking over the Bruce company in 1958. By 1973, he had left that position and began to trade on Wall Street full-time.

And once again it proved to be a lucrative preoccupation, even though the largest share of the successes he had from the stock market went toward paying back the $20 million in debts that had accumulated from the Bruce-Celotex disaster more than a decade earlier. But even before, he had been reducing those debts, bit by bit, since the time he had returned to the United States from his self-imposed exile in Brazil in 1962. It was a grim, draining process that he could have avoided if he had simply followed the advice of more than one attorney and several close friends to declare personal bankruptcy. But early on, while ensconced in Rio de Janeiro, he had announced to all the world on CBS television and elsewhere that he was *not* going to do that, that he was going to make good on what he promised, that he would pay everyone back.

In the early 1970s, Gilbert hired attorney Stanley Reiben to help deal with the myriad lawsuits, large and small, filed against him for money allegedly owed. In 1974, however, that monumental undertaking fell to a young attorney named Gene Wolkoff, recommended to Eddie Gilbert by Reiben. At the time, Wolkoff had a modest legal practice in Manhattan, in the firm of Callahan and Wolkoff (although Parnell J. T. Callahan had died several years earlier). It became one of the most important alliances for Gilbert in his business life because Wolkoff would continue as Gilbert's attorney of record to dispose of nearly 100 lawsuits throughout the next ten years. Beyond that, theirs became a client-attorney relationship and friendship of extraordinary benefit to them both, lasting to the present day and well beyond the eventual settlement of all of Gilbert's $20 million in debts.

While trading in the 1970s, Eddie was usually tight-lipped about how he invested and what issues might have captured his interest at the moment. On occasion, however, he confided to outsiders, as in a piece in the *New York Times* where he was quoted: "'When I really like a stock,' the New York financier said the other day, 'I'll invest every penny I've got, and I'll do it every way I can—leverage, options, everything. Yes. I'm investing aggressively. I just don't do things half way.'" Another writer of the time went into greater detail: "Eddie's precarious trading technique is to obtain the greatest 'leverage' by buying down, 'down and out' or limited price options. Utilizing the lowest margin requirements obtainable, Gilbert attempts to get five times the value from a single investment by using the five-day grace period between placing an order and making payment. Thus, he will invest the same $25,000, for example, on each of the week's five business days, through accounts at different brokerages, gambling that the price of the stock will rise. When it does not, he is obliged to 'finagle' until he sustains the loss or manages to get even by doubling his position. It is an exceedingly nerve-wracking technique—the high wire act of a supremely astute trader."

Although it may seem to be an oversimplification, the bottom line is that Gilbert played Wall Street with the same finesse (and success) in those days of the early 1970s as Jimmy Connors did the court at Wimbledon or Jack Nicklaus the fairways and greens of Augusta. Gilbert made millions during those years, and he repaid millions—as many as $5 or $6 million by 1976—while at the same time forging a comfortable life in Manhattan for him and Turid and the four daughters of his two marriages. He could afford an impressive apartment on Park Avenue at 60th Street, dinners at New York's finer restaurants, seats at the Metropolitan Opera, which remained one of his great passions—even short vacations abroad. A nice existence it was, although far from the lavish and privileged life he had enjoyed during the halcyon days of the late 1950s and early 60s.

It was on a night in 1975 that Gilbert, sitting in a banquette at El Morocco, unknowingly became involved in what would trigger another disastrous plunge in his business life in the months to come. At the request of his daughter Robin, Eddie and Turid had joined Robin and her new boyfriend, a 36-year-old named James Couri, for dinner that night. The 20-year-old Robin had promised to introduce her new amour—known by most as a Wall Street wheeler-dealer wannabee—to her father whom Couri had already known about.

In the years between when he had dropped out of college (following brief stints at Duke and Columbia in the 1950s) to pursue a career in the stock market, Couri had worked on Wall Street as a clerk, an over-the-counter trader, and a registered representative for Ernst and Company. After quitting active participation in the market in 1962, Couri flitted between a variety of business enterprises until he went into business for himself—according to his later testimony, "around '63 or '4 [in the areas of] financial management, consulting, bonds, and selling stock from time to time." Before meeting Eddie Gilbert a little more than a decade later, he had linked up with John Revson, son of the founder of the Revlon cosmetics firm, Charles Revlon. The two young men entered into an investment partnership, operating under the name of John C. Revson and Co. (later changed to Pegasus Company, which was dissolved in 1970 after losing nearly all the money invested in it). Following that, Couri went into business with his father and brother, by starting the company that owned and operated duty-free facilities at Kennedy International Airport. Couri's father, according to *Barron's* weekly, had been head of Customs during the Eisenhower administration and was said to have conceived the notion of duty-free shops at ports of entry. But James Couri had left that enterprise also toward the end of 1974.

By 1975, Couri had no business affiliation. "I was looking for new investments," he testified later, "or, you know, some company to invest in." That year opportunity came knocking, and he jumped to open that door. Robin Gilbert presented an entrée to her father; and Eddie Gilbert was to be, he hoped, his ticket to the long-postponed financial killing on Wall Street he had only dreamt of.

At El Morocco that night, Couri set out to impress the man he knew to be "the boy wonder of Wall Street." Couri acted the host for the evening. There was champagne, a magnificent meal, lively conversation. Couri was charming—"cavalier" was the term Gilbert used to describe his first impression later—and made it clear to Gilbert that he was a man of some affluence himself. He insisted on picking up the check, indeed with such insistence that the senior Gilbert had no choice but to let him. What Gilbert did not know was that James Couri, in contrast to the portrait he painted of himself that evening, then had very little money and was in fact scrambling to meet numerous financial obligations incurred in many of his business dealings.

On the way home that night, Eddie said to Turid, "Gee, what a nice fella. Robin's doing very well." And Turid agreed with him.

A few days later, Couri telephoned to ask if he could come by Eddie's office to talk some business. Investment business.

Gilbert's investment strategy in those days was to concentrate on just a few stocks. Throughout 1974 and 1975, the three he was then buying and selling, were Polaroid, Milgo Electronics, and Conrac Corporation. Investing in Conrac, however, was to lead to Gilbert's second downfall. Conrac was a medium-size, diversified manufacturer of electronic instrumentation; Eddie had first heard about the company while in prison in the late 1960s when it was known as Giannini Controls. Eddie's long-time friend

Sherman Fairchild had brought Giannini to his attention. "He used to write me every week or two while I was in prison," Eddie remembers. "Sherman was a major stockholder in the company, a member of the board of directors, and he wrote to me and told me it was a fabulous buy and that I should get some of it because it was going to do very well." Fairchild was well known and respected in American business and in New York social circles; he was one of the wealthiest men in America, having been a pioneer in photography, aviation, and sound engineering; but perhaps was most famous for having invented the aerial camera during World War I, as well as innovative airplanes developed in the years between the two world wars. He had founded both the Fairchild Camera and Instrument Company and the Fairchild Engine and Airplane Corporation. At his death in 1971, his net worth was estimated to be nearly a billion dollars.

Eddie's friendship with Fairchild dated from the late 1940s. Fairchild's family had an estate on Long Island at Lloyd's Harbor, about a 15-minute drive from the Gilberts' at Huntington Beach. Fairchild entertained friends at his place every summer weekend. He was a great tennis buff, so the weekend activities centered around the game. He had an outdoor court and an indoor court as well, which he had himself designed long before indoor courts became popular. Eddie Gilbert, then an aspiring tennis star who had played in the National Open at Forest Hills in 1942, was invited to the Fairchilds' estate one weekend and played quite well and so made a distinct impression on his host. He soon returned and then became a regular at the weekend gatherings; whereupon the friendship with Fairchild, 25 years Eddie's senior, flourished. In those earliest days of their friendship, Fairchild saw Eddie as "a promising, intelligent young man"; and Eddie looked on Fairchild as a fabulous success story, whose plot-line he wanted very much to emulate; and he especially loved the tennis competition at Fairchild's estate. Fairchild's Long Island retreat was indeed *the* place to be for those weekends, having attracted such tennis stars of the day as Pancho Segura, Bobby Riggs, Gardner Mulloy, and Billy Talbert along with celebrities like Ginger Rodgers, Grace Kelly, George C. Scott, and Howard Hughes. In the years to come, Fairchild and Gilbert became regular companions, frequently talking business over the telephone or over a meal either in some midtown restaurant or at Fairchild's mansion on 65th Street just off Fifth Avenue. Eddie was a frequent social guest at functions hosted by Fairchild in the city or on the Long Island shore; and

Fairchild became a returning guest at Gilbert's villa in the south of France.

When Sherman Fairchild spoke, Eddie listened. While he did not always agree with what Fairchild had to say — the older man being far too conservative for Eddie's instincts — he had great respect for Fairchild's business acumen and his opinions. Later, when Fairchild tipped him to Giannini Controls, Eddie paid attention, even though there was little he could do because he was virtually penniless and in prison. While incarcerated, however, he began following the stock and came to concur with Fairchild's assessment that it would indeed be a good investment. "I think it was selling for about $9 a share when I first started looking at it," Eddie recalls. "I saw it going to $30, maybe even more. I started buying it for around $12 or $13 in the early '70s."

Back to 1975: Another venture Gilbert got involved with took him beyond the stock market. He had agreed to invest $250,000 in Artists Entertainment Complex, a company in Hollywood run by motion picture producer Marty Bregman. Artists had a representational interest in the film star Al Pacino and owned rights to his hit movie *Dog Day Afternoon,* which had premiered earlier in the year. Bregman had produced both *Dog Day Afternoon* and the earlier Pacino hit *Serpico.* Gilbert's investment money was to be paid in five $50,000 monthly payments. In return for his investment, Eddie was to receive stock, stock options, and a percentage share of the profits from the next movie the company backed, which Gilbert was led to believe would feature the marquee-valued Pacino.

In the summer of that year, Gilbert was vacationing in Marbella, Spain, when one of the $50,000 payments came due. Short of ready cash and not wanting to interrupt his vacation, Eddie turned to Couri, because he remained under the mistaken impression that the man was of substantial independent wealth. According to Couri, a business associate of Gilbert's named Lester Kerschner, called him one day to say that Eddie wanted to ask if Couri could advance the $50,000, which Eddie would repay with interest upon returning to the United States in September. Couri did not have that kind of money, but certainly did not want Gilbert to know that fact, so he went to another investor, one with whom he had had some recent dealings, a man by the name of Irwin Robbins. Robbins lent Couri the money, and Couri made the loan to Gilbert, not telling him, of course, that the money had come from someone else. Robbins was also interested in learning what the Wall Street wizard Gilbert was currently investing in.

When Gilbert returned from Spain in September, he repaid the loan to Couri plus $3,000 in interest and, by way of thanks, tipped him about Conrac Corportion. The company's stock had been selling on the New York Stock Exchange in the range of $22 to $23 a share for most of 1974; but in the first seven months of 1975, the price had dropped to about $18. It would recover, Gilbert told Couri, to as much as $30, perhaps $40 a share, and maybe even soon. Gilbert acknowledged that he was heavily into the stock. Couri said that he too was interested in getting into the stock.

By way of a postscript to the Artists Entertainment story, let it be said that it turned out to be a disastrous investment for Gilbert. Following *Dog Day Afternoon*, the company committed itself to the production of a feature film titled *The Next Man*; this, unfortunately, did not include the big box-office draw of Al Pacino. An adventure movie starring Sean Connery as an Arab diplomat who wants to make peace with Israel but spends much of his screen-time running around trying to avoid assassination attempts, the movie was a first-class box-office flop. Artists Entertainment had invested heavily in part because of Gilbert's investment and others like his. Eddie remembers, "I think they had a budget of $3 million, and they spent something like $9 million. Artists went down the tubes. Marty [Bregman] folded up the company. Just shut it down, and vanished. I got nothing for my stock. Later he surfaced, but I never got a penny back."

Conrac was a much better investment, however. By 1975, Gilbert admittedly had already made as much as a half-million dollars trading it, with a goodly portion of the profits dedicated to reducing the huge debts he had incurred more than a dozen years earlier. In October 1975, though, Couri began trading in Conrac stock. A short while later, he would induce John Revson to invest substantially in Conrac as well. Gilbert was delighted. With the increased investor interest in Conrac shown by two well-heeled young speculators, Gilbert felt the stock had a bright future.

At the time, Gilbert had a large position in Conrac stock, bought both in his own name, in those of several corporations he controlled, and in the names of trusts created by his mother and his wife Turid. "Maybe about 50,000 shares," he recalls, "but it was under 5 percent of the outstanding shares [1.3 million in 1975], because you had to report it to the sec if you controlled more than 5 percent." According to Gilbert, Couri said he was interested in acquiring as many as 20,000 shares of Conrac, and asked if Gilbert was expected to accumulate more. Eddie told him he planned to do so, "at least until it gets to $30, or maybe to $40 or $50," which he truly felt it was capable of reaching.

Over the next two and a half months, trading in Conrac stock was volatile. The stock climbed to a high of nearly $31 by December 1, a gain of 13 points or 72 percent in just over two months. Meanwhile word came that the Securities and Exchange Commission had launched an investigation into the very active trading of Conrac stock, their probe reaching back to early 1974. By December 1975, Couri owned some 100,000 shares of Conrac, and Revson had increased his holding to 45,000 shares. All the while, there was considerable buying and selling actively by members of what the SEC would later describe as the "Gilbert group" and the "Couri-Revson subgroup" through a number of separate brokerage houses.

Couri, who had precious few personal resources, was dangerously overextended, having bought much of his Conrac stake on margin and money borrowed to finance his trades. Toward the end of November a bombshell exploded. Gilbert discovered that Couri was not the rich young man he portrayed himself to be; furthermore Eddie learned that he had been misled about the timing and the volume of Couri's Conrac buys and sales. In effect, Gilbert discovered that Couri was trading *against* him. As Gilbert later explained, "Unknown to me, however, Couri was also trading heavily in the stock, both personally and through several of his friends.... He told me that he was personally buying the stock. I did not know that he was selling against my purchases and those of his friends. Apparently, when he learned that I was buying some shares, he would then sell some of his shares; and when he learned I was selling, he would buy. None of these matched trades were known to me and, if they were, I would have cut off all communication with Couri." Couri's position on the subject, as he would later tell the SEC in his plea-bargain testimony, was that he played the dupe in a preconceived "plot of matched-trading" masterminded by Gilbert.

When Gilbert came to realize what Couri's personal finances were and how he had accumulated his Conrac stock, Gilbert knew that a day of reckoning was not only inevitable but imminent; so, quietly, he began to unload his Conrac stock. "I sold mine between $25 and $28," Eddie remembers, "and I made several hundred thousand dollars." The day of reckoning followed soon thereafter: On December 18, 1975, trading in Conrac stock was halted on the New York Stock Exchange, precipitated by Couri's brokers' dumping on the market most, if not all, of the shares he legitimately held (20,000 according to an article in *Barron's*) after he was unable to meet his margin calls. The stock plummeted from about $28 to $23.375 a share when suspension was called. Eddie Gilbert and James Couri were subsequently summoned to appear before the Securities and Exchange Commission in New York.

Trading would not resume in Conrac's shares until January 25, 1976 after the SEC had filed its civil suit alleging a stock manipulation scheme in the trading of Conrac stock, a conspiracy orchestrated by Eddie Gilbert.

The web of trading, Byzantine by any assessment, involved most directly the figures of Gilbert, Couri, Revson, and stock broker Ludwig Cserhat. It would not be publicly unraveled, however, for several years and then only when indictments were handed down by a Grand Jury and the U.S. Attorney's office in New York took the matter and the so-called "conspirators" to court.

A lot more trouble lay ahead for Eddie Gilbert.

In 1977, however, for perhaps the first time since his legal woes took hold in 1962, Eddie Gilbert was able to pick up a newspaper and read something about himself that was actually flattering. The *Wall Street Journal* of April 6 carried a two-column story, with the byline of Jonathan Kwitny under the headline:

EDWARD M. GILBERT ISN'T REALLY A CROOK, APPEALS COURT RULES

NEW YORK—For the past 15 years, common opinion has been that Eddie Gilbert is a crook, and not without reason. After all, he did withdraw $2 million in 1962 from E. L. Bruce Co., the large publicly owned lumber concern he headed, to cover personal stock trading accounts. And he did take off for Brazil that summer, just hours after the Bruce board refused to approve what he had done.

He did stay in Brazil while the Internal Revenue Service, Securities and Exchange Commission, Justice Department, and State of New York filed various charges against him, all of which were fully reported in the press. And to top it all off, he did come home, did plead guilty to grand larceny and securities violations in 1966, and did spend 25 months in jail.

Despite all that, the U.S. Court of Appeals in New York decided this week that Edward M. Gilbert, far from being a thief, is in fact something of a martyr and perhaps even a hero. It pictured him as a man who merely tripped over a legal technicality while risking his own fortune in a sincere effort to save his company's interests during a financial disaster not of his own making.

BOY WONDER OF WALL STREET

It was, in its way, an exoneration. Not that anything could change what had happened to him in the intervening years nor replace those years that he had lost in prison; and nothing would erase all the invective that had been written about him earlier. Still the *Journal* brought the situation into rightful perspective, and Gilbert could take comfort in that. As the article continued:

While various legal issues had been argued in the case, the court ruled strictly on the fact that it didn't think Gilbert stole the money or ever intended to. The court's reconstruction of the incident — which is different from what was widely asserted and published years ago — goes this way:

In late 1961, Gilbert decided that Bruce, of which he was president, principal stockholder and director, could profit from a merger with Celotex Corp., another lumber company. (Bruce has since undergone several changes of ownership and structure). So Gilbert, some associates, and the Bruce treasury began buying Celotex shares. They gained control of over 50% of Celotex and were arranging the merger, which the court specifically found was "highly favorable" to Bruce.

Then came the severe stock market drop of May 28, 1962, which brought heavy margin calls on Gilbert's personal account. He was stuck in Nevada at the time for what the court calls a "personal matter" — actually, his divorce, which required him to stay in the state or lose his residency status. So he telephoned instructions to officers of Bruce to cover the margins with corporate cash because it was the only way to rescue the merger.

"When Gilbert withdrew the corporate funds, he recognized his obligation to repay and intended to do so," the court found. It added, "although Gilbert undoubtedly realized that he lacked the necessary authorization, he thought he was serving the best interests of the corporation and he expected his decision to be ratified shortly thereafter."

Immediately on returning to New York in early June, Gilbert reported his actions to Bruce's officers, directors and outside counsel and executed an assignment to Bruce of "substantially more" than $2 million in assets to cover his debt. This proves, the court said, "that Gilbert at no time intended to retain the corporation's funds."

At a June 12 board meeting, directors suddenly refused to approve Gilbert's action, demanded his resignation and decided to issue a public announcement the next day about the unauthorized withdrawals. Gilbert took off — but, the courts says, left behind enough assets [so] that he couldn't possibly have profited, and therefore can't be billed nor income taxe[d].

While the new decision has no practical bearing on the criminal cases, it does contradict the factual determination that sent Gilbert to jail ....

Despite the court ruling and the exculpatory *Journal* article, the news media would in the years ahead continue to refer to Eddie as a "crook" or an "embezzler" or the executive who "stole" money from Bruce. The belated court exoneration would certainly not return the two years and 17 days he spent in prison nor assuage the decade and a half of personal anguish, but the ruling was corroboration of what Gilbert had claimed from the outset. For those who would listen—and certainly not all did—it was a step toward the restoration of his reputation, which to Eddie Gilbert was a matter of utmost importance.

The income tax case that had clouded Gilbert's skies from its inception back in 1962, accounted for much of what happened to him in subsequent years. If the IRS had not tied up all of Gilbert's assets by slapping its jeopardy assessment on his real and personal property, asset-value derived from those sources would have been more than sufficient to satisfy the $1.953 million in promissory notes that Gilbert had signed over to the E. L. Bruce Company. Had such restitution been made with *his* funds, there would not have been the felony-count charge bringing Gilbert to trial. The matter would have been dropped by the Justice Department, the Securities and Exchange Commission, and the New York District Attorney's office. But with the IRS jeopardy assessment in place, which took priority over any other liens (including the signed promissory notes and assignment of Gilbert's assets to Bruce), Gilbert was prevented from repaying the borrowed money. And the Bruce company, as victim, was denied the opportunity to recoup its loss.

More particularly, the IRS jeopardy assessment filed on June 22, 1962, ten days after Gilbert's departure for Brazil, claimed that Eddie and his wife Rhoda had income tax liabilities for the years 1958, 1959, 1960, and 1962 in the aggregate amount of $3,341,743.95. The bulk of that figure was for income in 1962 (although the year was not yet over), which the government claimed included the $1.953 million taken from the Bruce company, for a total tax liability of $1,723,756.50 The other income tax assessments included $3,836.40 for 1958, $1,119,164.80 for 1959, and $494,986.20 for 1960. Gilbert subsequently paid in full the 1958 deficiency. After audit, the inflated amounts for 1959 and 1960 were reduced by the U.S. Tax Court to $76,598.58 and $18,071.13 respectively. These Gilbert paid in full to the IRS. What remained, carrying forward all the way to 1977, was the figure the government claimed that Gilbert owed from his 1962 appropriation of

Bruce funds. Even this, after further audits, had been reassessed down to the amount of $1,467,536,51.

Gilbert had fought the IRS claim through the corridors of the system, but received no exoneration until the U.S. Court of Appeals ultimately overturned the lower court decisions. For his appeal, Gilbert again enlisted the services of attorney Peter Fleming's law firm, which had earlier handled his appeal in the André Meyer lawsuit. This appeal was handled by Robert D. Whorisky, a tax expert with the firm. Whorisky was not hamstrung this time by any statute of limitations or other legal encumbrance, as Fleming had been in the earlier case. He argued first that Gilbert did not realize taxable income for the year 1962 as a result of his unauthorized withdrawals from the E. L. Bruce Company. "The unauthorized withdrawals by Gilbert," Whorisky maintained, "were not conducted surreptitiously in order to deceive Bruce, but, rather were made in furtherance of a corporate plan of action initiated by Gilbert and endorsed by the [Bruce] Board in which he had made a personal financial commitment of a substantial nature [the promissory notes]. Whether or not the Bruce Board approved of Gilbert's withdrawals, there was a clear recognition by Gilbert and Bruce of Gilbert's obligation to restore the funds." And so, assessment for income tax on those funds was an improper implementation of the law, Whorisky reasoned.

Whorisky next argued to the Appeals Court that the Internal Revenue Service prevented Gilbert from making any repayment in 1962 of the funds withdrawn from the Bruce company. "A deduction is allowed for the repayment of illegal earnings, which were initially included in income," Whorisky argued. "Thus, if such a repayment had occurred in 1962 to the full extent of the amount of the funds wrongfully withdrawn by Gilbert in that year, there would be a reduction for federal tax purposes offsetting the same amount of income... Gilbert, however, did everything in his power to accomplish a full repayment in 1962... [making] an assignment to Bruce of all his assets.... If the assigned assets could have been reduced to cash by Bruce in 1962, Gilbert would have been in a position to have established that an actual payment had been made to Bruce by him in that year.... When the Internal Revenue Service made jeopardy assessments against Gilbert in amounts in excess of the value of the assets assigned by Gilbert to Bruce and filed notices of tax liens, it claimed a prior right to such assets." The conclusion was clear: Gilbert was deprived of the right and the opportunity to make restitution to the Bruce company by the pre-emptory actions of the Internal Revenue Service.

Whorisky's arguments proved persuasive. In a unanimous decision, the three-judge panel reversed the Tax Court ruling and threw out the IRS tax claim. As reported by the *Wall Street Journal*, "Specifically, the appeals panel... ruled that the federal government had no right to collect taxes on the $2 million.... While various legal issues had been argued in the case, the court ruled strictly on the fact that it didn't think Gilbert stole the money or ever intended to." The article went on to say, "While the new decision has no practical bearing on the [prior] criminal cases, it does contradict the factual determination that sent Gilbert to jail." The court's opinion further noted that Gilbert had "pleaded guilty in 1966 because he understood that by doing so, he would avoid a jail sentence, whereas by going to trial, in light of all the bad publicity, he would probably serve time, as well as undergoing the unpleasantness of a court fight."

In response to the long-awaited ruling, Eddie Gilbert also had his say. To a question from the *Journal* reporter about his personal reaction, Gilbert rhetorically asked, "How do I feel now?" Then answered, "I feel like a goddam fool. I've been called an embezzler for 15 years, and it hurts. Bank accounts attached, and being called a thief. All I ever did was try to do the right thing."

To which the *Journal* added the postscript, "Now, at least, a court agrees with him."

# FOURTEEN

*There was never much security with Eddie. It was always up and down from one month to the next. It was like living on a soap bubble. You never knew when it would burst. But somehow he always gets through, he always gets back up again.*

TURID GILBERT, NEW YORK TIMES, 1980

ddie Gilbert might have been able to enjoy what most considered his exoneration in the Bruce-Celotex affair that resulted from the U.S. Court of Appeals ruling of 1977, but his entanglements with the law were far from over. Suspecting that Gilbert was the leader of a premeditated, well-organized effort to manipulate trade in Conrac during 1974 and 1975, the SEC had instituted a quiet but serious investigation into recent trading of Conrac Corporation stock. SEC investigations were customarily carried out under tight security with little information being revealed once a case was initiated. In this case, even the New York Stock Exchange was kept out of the loop: "We turned over what we had to the SEC early on, and we haven't heard anything about it in some time," a spokesman for the Exchange was quoted more than two years after it had turned over the records requested by the SEC. And a Conrac official, speaking on behalf of the company several years after the investigation was under way, told the media, "We're completely in the dark as to what, if anything, is going on."

Eddie Gilbert and James Couri knew what was transpiring behind the closed doors of the SEC, however, because both had been subpoenaed to appear and testify in that *inner sanctum* once the trading in Conrac stock had been suspended on the New York Stock Exchange December 18, 1975. But the stories each told were markedly different.

Gilbert admitted to buying and selling the stock actively, not only by himself but through other sources as well, including small corporations and trusts created by his mother and his wife. Nor did he deny that he had advised or encouraged others to invest in Conrac. Quite the contrary, he made it clear that he had *urged* them to do so because he believed in the company's potential. Active buying of the stock, he asserted, would help increase the stock's value to its real level. Why wouldn't he suggest that others buy a stock he felt certain was headed significantly higher? He maintained that he had done nothing wrong: stock *trading,* sophisticated as it may have been, was well within the law; what he had done was not stock *manipulation,* which *was* contrary to the law. But just as in the Bruce situation in 1962, what Eddie Gilbert perceived as customary and justifiable business practice was not a view shared by government regulators.

Gilbert went on to denounce any idea that there had been a "conspiracy" to manipulate the stock in Conrac. There had been no attempt nor intent artificially to inflate the value of the stock. He adamantly asserted that nothing he had done was in violation of the law or the rules and regulations of trading on the NYSE. But more importantly Gilbert further testified that he had no knowledge at all about most of the trading carried out by Couri in his transactions, especially toward the end when Couri was amassing as many as 100,000 shares of Conrac stock for himself and for John Revson's account. Gilbert explained later in a written statement: "Unknown to me... Couri was also trading heavily in the stock, both personally and through several of his friends. While he told me that he was personally buying the stock, I did not know that he was selling against my purchases and those of his friends. Apparently, when he learned that I was buying some shares he would then sell some of his shares, and when he learned I was selling, he would buy. None of these matched trades were known to me, and if they were I would have cut off all communication with Couri."

Couri, not unexpectedly, directed all the blame at Gilbert. There were certainly several reasons why Couri turned on the man he formerly considered his ticket to success in the market: Most obviously, he needed to protect himself in a situation which looked to have dire consequences ahead. Less obviously, he felt he had been abandoned by Gilbert. Facing margin calls on the 75,000 shares he still held after his brokers had already dumped a reported 20,000 on the market (causing suspended trading in

Conrac stock in December 1975) and without the funds to meet those remaining margin calls, he had gone to Gilbert for financial help. Eddie, who was by then aware of what Couri had been up to, turned him down. Another reason for Couri to turn on Gilbert was that he feared that Eddie, in his testimony, might be selling him out to the SEC, or at best using his knowledge of Couri's trades to strike some kind of plea bargain with the prosecutors.

Whatever his reasons, Couri testified that he had done *nothing* on his own, and that *all* his trades had been dictated by Gilbert, the concert-master of the entire trading scheme. It had been Eddie Gilbert who told him when to buy and when to sell, all aspects of a manipulative plot that Gilbert had hatched to rig the market price of Conrac for his own personal gain. Couri, the victim, had been naively enticed into this scheme and had unknowingly played a part in it as he followed Gilbert's guidance. Over a two-day period, it came later to be known, Couri had given more than 400 pages of testimony to the SEC, all of it especially and directly damning of Gilbert.

As a consequence, the SEC brought civil suit against Gilbert, Couri, and 17 other defendants, including John Revson, broker Ludwig Cserhat, and NYSE specialist Judson Streicher. According to its staff attorney in charge of the investigation, Steven J. Glusband, the SEC contended that Gilbert and the other defendants "embarked upon a scheme to manipulate the price of Conrac stock, creating an illusion of widespread and bona fide buying interest in Conrac"; and that the defendants "dominated and controlled the trading in Conrac causing the price of the stock to reach arbitrarily inflated levels." While the SEC suit was predicated on its investigation, it was substantially dependent on the testimony of James Couri because there was no *direct* evidence of a scheme to manipulate stock outside of what Couri had told the SEC. Nevertheless, the SEC decided to present its charges in court in the form of a civil action.

In an SEC affidavit filed by staff attorney Glusband, the "Gilbert group" consisted of a consortium of individuals and companies, some of whom Gilbert lent money to for the purpose of purchasing stock in Conrac, including "trusts, various corporate entities, some individuals, and the *Banque de l'Union* of Switzerland." The Gilbert group, the SEC contended, accumulated through a network of 25 accounts in two brokerage firms 75,000 shares of Conrac during a period of time in 1974–75 when the price per share rose from $9 to $20. By July 1975, according to SEC calculations, the group had amassed more than 106,000 shares, approximately 8.2 percent of the 1.29 million outstanding shares of common stock in Conrac Corp.

And then James Couri entered the scene in September of that year; and John Revson was involved by Couri shortly thereafter. Couri testified that his first transaction in Conrac stock was at Gilbert's direction to buy 3,000 shares at $19 per share; in return, he would receive a 90-day option to purchase an additional 1,000 shares from Gilbert at the same price as well as a cash payment of $3,000 for executing the buy. This was the $3,000 Gilbert steadfastly maintained represented his interest payment on the $50,000 loan Couri had made to him earlier in the summer so as to meet his Artists Entertainment obligation and had nothing whatsoever to do with any purchase of Conrac stock. As evidence of a "matched trade," wherein two parties arrange to simultaneously buy and sell shares of the same stock (considered illegal only when done for the purpose of artificially inflating the value of a stock, and in which case such intent must be proved), the SEC showed that on the day of Couri's initial purchase of those 3,000 shares, Gilbert's Municipal Street Sign Co. sold off 3,000 shares, and three other members of the Gilbert group disposed of a further 700 shares. Gilbert offered to lend Couri $30,000 if he would buy an additional 3,000 shares of Conrac. Couri testified that, "He [Gilbert] said, 'Look: You were very nice about loaning me $50,000, so I have a proposal for you. If you buy another 3,000 shares I'll loan you $30,000 to pay for it.'" Couri agreed to the arrangement, and on October 3 bought another 3,000 shares, then selling at about $19 a share (the $30,000 being sufficient to cover the trade because Couri's purchase was made on 50 percent margin). But absent an intent to manipulate, none of this constituted any illegal trading in the market.

Couri went on to claim that Gilbert told him he had a net worth of approximately $15 to $20 million and was in a good position to help Couri purchase additional shares of Conrac. Gilbert may have qualified as a millionaire at the time, *but* was nowhere near the net worth Couri suggested, especially since there was still the question of millions of dollars of debt remaining from the Bruce-Celotex affair Gilbert had yet to pay. Eddie emphatically denied ever having made such a claim to Couri. To be sure, there were financial misperceptions on both sides when the two first began talking business. Each thought that the other had a larger net worth than either in fact had. What Couri believed, with certainty, however, was that there was indeed a windfall profit to be made here, and he wanted to be along for the ride. What Gilbert did not perceive at that time was that Couri was planning very shortly to do a lot of the driving himself.

John Revson, 32 years old, was working for his father's Revlon firm in October 1975, holding the position of a division vice president. He had only recently come into a considerable part of his inheritance, including cash and a large position in Revlon stock. He was looking for attractive investments, he later confided. Couri contacted him "on or about October 8,1975," according to court records, and told him of his recent dealings with Gilbert. He then convinced the youthful cosmetics heir of the desirability of not only buying Conrac stock but of giving him power of attorney so as to buy and sell stocks in Revson's name. Shortly thereafter Couri opened a brokerage account for Revson, christening it with the purchase of 5,000 shares of Conrac. There soon followed another buy of 10,000 shares of Conrac; and by October 23, Revson had bought 18,500 shares of Conrac, then worth more than $300,000. Revson now wanted to meet Eddie Gilbert, and so the three—Revson, Couri and Gilbert—met in Eddie's office one day shortly thereafter. Eddie argued the merits to Revson of continuing to invest in Conrac, a stock that he was convinced was on an ascent to at least $30 a share. "I think it's going to be the stock of the year," Gilbert is quoted as saying at that meeting. Revson agreed to add another 12,500 shares to his portfolio. And a few days later, Eddie suggested that Revson increase his position even further; according to Revson's later testimony. Eddie at the same time guaranteed him against any loss. "Based on the fact of [his] guarantee," Revson said, "and the fact that the rising price of Conrac shares appeared to confirm the wisdom of Conrac as a good investment, I decided to purchase an additional 15,000 shares of Conrac to bring my holdings to 45,000 shares, and I asked Couri to place the orders on my behalf."

The SEC investigation uncovered a convoluted maze of stock purchases and sales by Gilbert, Couri, Revson, and others considered in "the group." Much of it had been executed through stock broker Ludwig Cserhat, who was executive vice president of the Wall Street firm of Heine, Fishbein and Co. Cserhat, 40 years old in 1975, was born in Budapest, Hungary; he had become a close personal friend of Gilbert as well as his stock broker.

They were so close, in fact, that of the approximately $200,000 in commissions Cserhat earned in 1975, about 75 percent of it came from investments for Gilbert and accounts related directly to him. Cserhat was also the broker for the Swiss *Banque de l'Union* which likewise had actively traded in Conrac stock during 1975. Consequently, Cserhat became a prime target in the SEC's investigation too.

Judson Streicher was brought into the SEC's case because of an ancillary investigation. At the time, the 52-year-old Streicher was the NYSE specialist in the Western Company of North America., which owned two hotels in Aspen, Colorado. Both Gilbert and Cserhat were investors in Western, and Cserhat had in fact been hired by the firm to generate interest in its stock. How Western fit into the Conrac investigation was later reported in *Barron's*: "It's the SEC's contention, based largely on the information of Couri, who says he got it from Gilbert, that at a dinner meeting in early November the following took place: Streicher and Cserhat told Gilbert that if he took a big position in Western, Streicher would buy some Conrac shares and so, too, would Western's pension fund." The SEC documented that there were some trades involving Streicher and the "Gilbert group," 10,000 Conrac shares on the same day in early November when "Gilbert group" bought 25,000 shares of Western. While much could be speculated about these coincidences, there was nothing illegal about these trades because Gilbert acknowledged he was promoting Conrac shares believing they were undervalued.

When the investigation was concluded, what the SEC had in hand was Couri's uncorroborated assertion that Gilbert masterminded a scheme to manipulate Conrac stock. What the SEC did *not* have, however, was an ironclad case they could make independent of Couri's testimony. No direct, substantial evidence supported the allegation that Conrac stock had been manipulated. So when the SEC announced plans to present its findings to a grand jury months later, Couri refused to testify, claiming he would protect himself under the U.S. Constitution's Fifth Amendment against self-incrimination if called into court. Without Couri's testimony before the grand jury, the SEC was forced to drop its claims and anticipated suit. To help settle the matter, Gilbert and the 18 defendants agreed to sign a consent order, stipulating that they not engage in any illegal activity, such as manipulation, in relation to the trading of stock in Conrac Corp., without admitting or denying any wrongdoing in the past. And so the matter seemed to be over. But it wasn't. The SEC subsequently turned over the results of its investigation, as well as the Couri testimony, to the office of the U.S. Attorney for the Southern District of New York, suggesting that the Justice Department might want to investigate the matter to see if any criminal charges should be brought. Although the case would languish there, it would not die; quietly it percolated behind the scenes before erupting again with unexpected ferocity several years later.

While these machinations were affecting Eddie's business life, his personal life had also been in a state of turmoil. His marriage to Turid had broken down. The two had separated. Eddie had moved out of their Fifth Avenue apartment into a much smaller space on the upper east side, and Turid brought matters to a close by filing for divorce, which was granted on October 26, 1979, bringing their 16 years of marriage to an end. During his separation from Turid, Eddie reconnected with Linda Watkins, the young and beautiful woman who was to become his third wife. When they had met several years earlier in New York, both had been married. Her then-husband, Joseph McInerny, had been seeking one of the U. S. Senate seats from Delaware when the couple came to New York to raise campaign funds. Mutual friends suggested that they approach Eddie Gilbert, although he was not in a financial postion to help them at the time. As she remembers, "It was a comfortable meeting; Eddie was very cordial. We met in his apartment, and he said he was not interested in participating, but he was very good about putting us in touch with some other people who were, as it turned out, helpful to our cause."

As coincidence would have it, they now found themselves on an airplane together, headed from New York to Los Angeles (where Gilbert was on his way to deal with some of the consequences of his ill-fated association with Marty Bregman and Artists Entertainment Complex). Unlike Turid, Linda was not an airline employee; instead she was a fellow first-class passenger traveling on business of her own. At 32, and more than 20 years younger than Gilbert, she was a successful actress with credits in a number of television soap operas, including a major role in "One Life to Live," lesser roles in "All My Children" and "Guiding Light," and appearances in several Hollywood films as well as many television commercials. Unlike Eddie's two former wives, Linda would not be financially dependent on him, because she had an annual income from her profession well into six figures during the latter half of the 1970s.

Once back in New York, they began seeing each other. On their first date, the stylish Eddie picked her up in a limousine bound for Le Club. As their relationship grew more serious, they decided to get married. So they set the date for October 28, 1979, at the *Habitation le Clerc* in Haiti where Eddie's long-time friend Olivier Coquelin held sway. It was a splendid affair with Eddie flying in his mother Yolan as well as his daughters Robin, Alexandra, Nina, and Dominique. Joe Cserhat and John Revson also attended. Returning to New York, Eddie and Linda moved into the apartment she owned on 83rd Street, just east of Fifth Avenue. They would later buy a dairy farm near Goshen, New York, in Orange County, which they would reconfigure into a horse farm to gratify Linda's long-time passion for breeding and training Arabian horses. At its height, the farm stabled 12 purebred Arabians in the newly constructed facilities. Eddie spent most of his time in the city, however, the life of a country gentleman hardly being one to his natural inclination or his financial ambitions.

On July 10, 1978, the Conrac affair came back with a vengeance, riding on the wave of a major feature article in *Barron's*. The italics in the lead paragraph served as the prologue to a long, inflammatory article resurrecting in great detail the entire Conrac affair:

NO SMOKING GUN
JUSTICE DRAGS IN THE 1975 CONRAC STOCK SCANDAL

THURSDAY, DECEMBER 18, 1975. Trading on the New York Stock Exchange in the stock of Conrac Corp., a manufacturer of electronic instrumentation, is suspended. Reason: a cascade of sell orders swamping available bids. Trading halts on the Big Board are scarcely uncommon. But typically they last a few hours, perhaps a day. Conrac, though, fails to show on the tape again that session or the next. Not until January 25, 1976 — more than a month after the suspension — do the shares again change hands. And not before the Securities & Exchange Commission moves in, charging in a civil suit that the stock of Conrac has been the target of a manipulative scheme masterminded by confessed embezzler and ex-convict Edward M. Gilbert.

The piece was based almost exclusively on the testimony that James Couri had provided in the initial sec investigation and subsequent affidavits filed by sec attorney Steven Glusband more than two years earlier. All the key players were in the *Barron's* story — Gilbert, Couri, Revson, Cserhat, Streicher, Kerschner — but only Gilbert was featured as a villain, the others portrayed as mere pawns in his manipulative game. The article laid out an extensive and comprehensive case against Gilbert and then asked why nothing was being done about it, why more than two and a half years after the alleged manipulation the principal manipulator and those who abetted him were still free to do business. In closing, the author states: "And John Revson is still at Revlon. Cserhat is still a member in good standing of a New York Stock Exchange firm, buying and selling securities for customers. As for Edward Gilbert, mum's the word. Through his attorney he authorized the following statement: 'Mr. Gilbert has denied the allegations contained in the SEC's complaint. No further comment is appropriate since the matter is still before the court.'" In the pages that preceded, however, the *Barron's* article presented a devastating indictment of Eddie Gilbert in print, and its effect would be resounding.

Suddenly the government felt a lot of pressure to address what *Barron's* dubbed the "Conrac scandal" and to do something about it. The U.S. Attorney's office accordingly resurrected the case, reviewing all records and transcripts that had been filed away since 1976. With the investigation reopened, old witnesses were called back while new ones were brought in for questioning. The case was assigned to Assistant U.S. Attorney Jeffrey Livingston, a young lawyer who had joined the Justice Department's New York office less than three years earlier. With his assistant Peter J. Romatowski, Livingston's job was to put the case in order and take it to court before the statute of limitations ran out—a rapidly approaching date some six months in the future.

It was an enormous undertaking, according to Livingston: "There was a huge collection of documents, order slips, trading tickets, confirmations, account statements—some of which had been [collated], but many of which had not. And all of these had to be organized and looked into to see if [the U.S. Attorney's office] could match certain trades, to see if you could determine trading patterns....We eventually developed a computer program; we had all the trades computerized, and we could show volume charts—how the volume changed from day to day..., we could trace the pricing on a day-to-day basis. And we were able to match some trades to show certain kinds of... wash sales, sales that would go from one account under his [Eddie Gilbert's] control and one brokerage firm to some other account under his control at another brokerage firm. Of course, a large part of the case was putting together all of those accounts and connecting them to him." Almost as important as showing these trade patterns was the necessity of getting James Couri back in the government's camp and persuading him to testify to everything he had said earlier in his appearance before the SEC.

By late-1979, Couri was in trouble on his own, although it was not common knowledge at the time. He owned a failing art gallery named Plazagal International Corporation; and his dealings in this enterprise had eventually led to a federal investigation for acts of fraud, misrepresentation, and bribery. Facing that investigation, as well as a possible indictment for conspiracy in the alleged Conrac stock manipulation case, Couri concluded that it would be in his best interest to cooperate with the U.S. Attorney's office, especially as they made it clear that they were willing to make a deal in the Plazagal case in exchange for his cooperation and testimony in the Conrac affair. As part of the plea bargain, Couri now agreed to testify against Gilbert, Revson, and Cserhat. On June 18, 1980, Couri was allowed to plead guilty to a single count of manipulation of Conrac stock in return for which he would later receive a one-year suspended sentence, sparing him any prison time.

A July 1980 article in *Fortune* magazine, did not help Gilbert's case either. In a major feature on the subject of top-level businessmen who had served time in prison, Gilbert's profile appeared under the subhead, "The Fugitive Financier." The caption accompanying his picture read, "In 1962, Gilbert, the president of E. L. Bruce Co., fled to Brazil after filching nearly $2 million from the company." (The *Fortune* writer had apparently borrowed the uncomplimentary verb "filch" from the lead line in the *LIFE* magazine story on Gilbert 18 years earlier.) In the body of the *Fortune* article is another insinuation: "[After] Gilbert couldn't meet his margin calls, he started reaching into the company till," and "after some insiders got wind of it, he appeared before the Board to make a confession." The article seriously misstated how it ended at Bruce. The tenor of its profile was that, in *Fortune's* eyes, Gilbert was a thief who had embezzled money from his company, got caught, fled the country and eventually returned, confessed to his crime, and was sent to prison. And even when the article referred to the 1977 Tax Court ruling in Gilbert's favor—a ruling that had put the matter of "theft" aside by stating that "since his equity in the corporation itself is worth well over $1,930,000, it would have been absurd for him to attempt such a theft,"—the vindication was colored unfavorably by *Fortune*: "In his [Gilbert's] view the Court's opinion vindicated him," implying that his "vindication" was solely Eddie Gilbert's interpretation.

Gilbert's attorney, Stanley Reiben, took special umbrage at the article and wrote a letter to the *Fortune* editors protesting these and other discrepancies that combined to paint a most unflattering portrait of his client, Eddie Gilbert. He made special reference to the snide note on which *Fortune's* profile began: "Before he was 39, Eddie Gilbert—born Edward Ginsberg in 1922—had established quite a name for himself." Reiben observed: "I have often noticed that type of lead into a story but never when someone with a Christian name changes his or her name to another Christian sounding name. I believe that sort of quote has no value except that of fanning the flames of anti-Semitism. It certainly is neither material nor relevant to this particular story but when it comes to dealing in money, a little sex is always added to a story if it is clear that a member of the Jewish faith is involved. Whether or not the writer of the story so intended, that is a fact and a bitterly resented one."

There is no question that Gilbert had been sharply stung by the two articles in *Barron's* and *Fortune*; but he could take some solace from a Sunday *New York Times* magazine feature that appeared in October 1980, portraying him and his current problems in a much more sympathetic light. Following this rather prepossessing headline, "Eddie Gilbert: The Highs and Lows of a Wall Street Wonder," the article addressed both his success in the market and the troubles now besieging him in the swirling Conrac controversy. According to the *Times*, "By all accounts, Mr. Gilbert is a man of extremes and passions, and he evokes passionate responses from others. To his detractors, Mr. Gilbert is a wheeler-dealer, a shadowy character, and one of the controversial operators on Wall Street. To his friends and associates, many of whom say they have made considerable sums of money from his stock tips, Mr. Gilbert is a brilliant investor, a charming companion, and an honest man who was unfairly branded by his conviction in the 1960s. They argue that a favorable 1977 tax-case ruling, linked to his earlier troubles, in effect, exonerates him."

The *Times* article also offered insight into Gilbert's personal life. "Mr. Gilbert starts his day early, rising at 6:30 A.M. at his two-bedroom co-op apartment in the East 80s that he shares with his third wife, Linda, a successful actress in commercials and soap operas...

"Without breakfast, Mr. Gilbert is then off to the Sports Training Institute, a fashionable midtown athletic club. After his early morning exertions, Mr. Gilbert walks to his office, always arriving before 9:30 A.M. 'I've got to get to my office and be ready to go before the market opens,' he said.

"There Mr. Gilbert begins plying his craft. He often makes or receives more than 100 phone calls in a day, he eats at his desk (usually chicken salad), and he studies companies. 'I'm always looking at about a hundred companies,' he said, 'but I'm only really studying three or four at a time....'

"What is he after? 'I'm interested in growth and romance in companies,' he replied.

"'Look,' he went on, 'there are hundreds of analysts on the Street— some stink, some are good. But they're focusing on the fundamentals— sales and earnings growth, cash flows, all that. The fundamentals have to be there, but that's not enough. There's a lot of intuition in my decisions. A company has to have pizzazz.'... In gesture and speech, Mr. Gilbert is not given to much sublety. When telling a story, his blue eyes dance and his hands wave to punctuate his narrative....He says the press has treated him shabbily over the years, but he talks and talks. He likes it and he's good at it."

The *Times* further noted that, "There is a disarming openness to the man that is certainly part of his personality" and added an assessment by his second wife Turid, who apparently harbored no ill-feelings about their recent divorce: "Everybody feels better after they've talked to Eddie," Turid said, although she had not forgotten the precariousness of their life together for well over a decade. "There was never much security with Eddie," she offered. "It was always up and down from one month to the next. It was like living on a soap bubble. You never knew when it would burst. But somehow he always gets through, he always gets back up again. He's a fighter, that's for sure."

And a fighter he would need to be. Just a few months before the five-year statute of limitations was to elapse, the lead prosecutor for the U.S. Attorney's office, Jeffrey Livingston, announced criminal indictments of Edward M. Gilbert, John C. Revson, and Ludwig J. Cserhat on three counts, charging that they had "conspired to manipulate trading in the common stock of Conrac Corporation, which was listed on the New York Stock Exchange, in violation of Title 18, United States Code, Section 371." And Gilbert was cited in 33 other alleged violations of securities laws, seven of which charged him with "wash sales" (wherein the buyer and seller of a stock are one and the same person, the sale in essence not re-

BOY WONDER OF WALL STREET

sulting in a beneficial change of ownership); 22 counts charged him with placing "matched orders" (in which two parties respectively agree to buy and sell a given amount of stock at the same time); one count alleged that he effected a series of transactions creating actual or apparently active trading for the purpose of inducing purchases of Conrac stock by others; two counts charged him with failure to file government-required reports of his holdings; and a final count cited him for securities fraud. Each of the counts carried a maximum penalty of five years in prison and a $10,000 fine. Revson was charged with an additional eight counts beyond the initial three, and Cserhat another seven.

A warrant was issued for Gilbert's arrest. When Stanley Reiben, Gilbert's attorney, was so informed, he made arrangements for Gilbert to surrender. At his bail hearing, Eddie appeared before a magistrate, and Jeffrey Livingston argued strongly for a substantial bond because Gilbert had fled the country and the court's jurisdiction 18 years earlier in 1962 when he was certain to face indictments in the Bruce-Celotex affair. Bail was set at $500,000. Gilbert did not have sufficient liquidity to come up with such a large amount, but his friends did. Jerry Stern offered a letter of credit to Eddie for as much as $1 million; as it turned out he only needed to post $200,000 for Eddie, while three other friends came up with $100,000 each: Herb Papock, Al Simon, and Chick Fisdell. So Eddie was not taken into custody and remained free throughout the course of the trial.

Indictments incorporating the name of Eddie Gilbert guaranteed a trial that would be reported on the front pages of New York newspapers as well as nationally in sources like *Time, Newsweek,* and the *Wall Street Journal.* Eddie would need some notable and high-powered representation to defend himself against the government's charges. If convicted of them, he could return to prison for years. He spoke with his long-time attorney Stanley Reiben, who suggested he talk with Herald Price Fahringer, then one of New York's most prominent defense lawyers. In 1980, the 51-year-old Fahringer was a senior partner in the firm of Lipsitz, Green, Fahringer, Roll, Shuller and James, with offices in Buffalo as well as on Madison Avenue in Manhattan. Fahringer's personal client list would come to include such well-known defendants as Jean Harris, convicted murderer of "Scarsdale Diet Doctor" Herman Tarnower; Claus von Bulow, convicted (but later acquitted after a reversal on appeal) of the systematic poisoning of his heiress wife Sunny; Larry Flint, publisher of *Hustler* magazine (whose famous First Amendment case Fahringer argued before the U.S. Supreme Court); Al Goldstein, publisher of *Screw* magazine (in another First Amendment milestone case); the Olin Corporation (accused of dumping 30 tons of mercury into the Niagara River); as well as jazz drummer Buddy Rich and literary critic Leslie Fiedler.

With all his experience and credentials, however, Herald Fahringer lacked a crucial requisite for defending Eddie Gilbert in this case. He did not have a keen understanding of the complex and often curious workings of the stock market, especially as practiced by a sophisticated trader like Eddie Gilbert. And it would prove to be a most complex case indeed. The U.S. Attorney's task was, first, to make the tapestry of stock trading practiced by Gilbert and his associates comprehensible to a jury unschooled in such operations; and, second, to prove their intent to manipulate the stock for personal gain. High-volume trading by an individual or a group of individuals, including "wash" and "matched" trades are not illegal in themselves. They become violations of securities law when it can be proved that there was intent to use the trades artificially to inflate the value of the stock so as to benefit the trader or to mislead other investors as to the value of the traded stock. Eddie Gilbert's defense counsel was faced with the contrary task of refuting the government's charges by convincing a jury, first, that Gilbert's trades were not illegal; and second, that the principal witness for the prosecution, the plea-bargained James Couri, was a dishonest and unreliable witness.

For the U.S. Attorney' Office, Jeffrey Livingston was prepared to present a dog-and-pony show, replete with charts, graphs, and visuals of dazzling variety, to illustrate the intricate web of trading that had occured in Conrac stock. And he had James Couri ready and waiting in the wings to testify as to the collective intent of Gilbert, Revson, and Cserhat to manipulate Conrac stock for their personal interest and profit.

Fahringer told the *Wall Street Journal* that Gilbert was prepared to fight each and every charge: "We assert that Mr. Gilbert at no time ever engaged in any improper conduct or violated any section of the law. The charges involve technical regulatory provisions concerned with the transfer of stock. There is no claim, nor is there any evidence, that anyone lost any money as a result of Mr. Gilbert's conduct."

Both sides expected a lengthy and complicated trial. And that is precisely what they were about to get.

Conrac and James Couri, it turned out, were not Eddie Gilbert's only problems at this time. In 1979, he had been actively trading in the stock of Commodore International, a company manufacturing personal computers, watches, calculators, and other products. Commodore had been incorporated in 1958 as the Commodore Portable Typewriter Co., Ltd., in Toronto, Canada, and had been renamed Commodore Business Machines (Canada) Ltd., in 1962. The company became listed on the American Stock Exchange in May 1974 and had changed its name to Commodore International as it edged its way into the personal computer business two years later.

Eddie Gilbert became interested in Commodore not long after it began trading on the AMEX. It was a highly volatile stock, one which had soared from a low of $7.50 a share to a high of $53.875 in 1978; and then, after adjustments for stock splits, from $22.675 a share in March 1979 to $89.50 by September of that year. The latter escalation, according to the *Wall Street Journal*, prompted the American Stock Exchange to act: "For the first time in about two years, [the AMEX moved] to dampen speculation in a high-flying stock," the *Journal* reported and acknowledged for the first time publicly, "that the Securities and Exchange Commission is investigating erratic price movements in Commodore shares."

Eddie Gilbert had been trading in Commodore shares and had also bought options on Commodore stock through a broker who specialized in such trades, Marc Strausberg of SJS Associates. (His limited partner was none other than William J. Casey, then head of the Central Intelligence Agency, formerly chairman of the Securities and Exchange Commission, and the spin-master who was managing Ronald Reagan's presidential election campaign.) Eddie Gilbert's Commodore problem in 1979 was the result of this significant factor: When Gilbert bought his Commodore options from Strausberg, the broker decided not to protect himself by buying the stock and holding it. Gene Wolkoff, Gilbert's long-time attorney who later helped Eddie successfully fight a suit brought by Strausberg, explains: "Generally what is done with a trader of options [broker Strausberg in this case] is that he will actually buy the underlying stock... to protect himself in the event that the option is called. He would then have the stock physically available and be able to produce it when the option was exercised. If the stock rose significantly, which is the time a trader would exercise the option and take a profit, the option broker would not be hurt.

If he did *not* buy the stock at the time of option or before the stock rose in value, he would have to go out and buy it in order to meet the option call at the then escalated price and would have to absorb the difference. In the case of Ed and Strausberg and the Commodore stock which soared sky-high in 1979, the difference was in the hundreds of thousands of dollars. (Actually, the profit Gilbert would have realized if he had been able to exercise the options was more than $1 million.)

"Strausberg took the money for the option, but he didn't buy the underlying stock. When Ed decided to exercise his option [since the stock had more than tripled in value by that time], Strausberg obviously could not come up with the stock nor with the money to buy the stock and therefore turn it over. He was left holding the bag, and he ended up owing Ed a lot of money."

And Eddie Gilbert now needed the money. He was facing significant attorneys' fees in the Conrac stock manipulation case (for which he had just been indicted) and a stiff bail assessment. But he was not going to get it from Strausberg, who had no intention of meeting his broker's obligation to Gilbert. Even worse, Strausberg decided to enlist the old football maxim: The best defense is a good offense. Armed with the recent announcement of the indictment of Gilbert and the publicity surrounding it, Strausberg hired a lawyer of his own and claimed that he had discovered, to his great surprise, that his client Eddie Gilbert had been manipulating Commodore stock (just as he had the stock in Conrac); and he then made his allegations to the Securites and Exchange Commission. Strausberg charged that Gilbert had "created a fictitious market with the help of a group of associates," which included John Revson and even the chairman of the board of Commodore, Irving Gould. According to Strausberg, Gilbert and "his group" were assisted by inside information provided by Gould. The result, Strausberg claimed, was a series of wash trades and matched trades, conspiracy, and other misdeeds causing the stock to soar in value. Both Gilbert and Commodore chairman Gould adamantly denied the charges. The AMEX then announced that it would place restrictions on the trading of Commodore stock, the principal one being to increase significantly the level of equity an investor must have before making a credit transaction involving the stock. A spokesman for the exchange explained, "We think there is excess speculation in the stock. The exchange has a duty to maintain a fair and orderly market." As a result of the AMEX action and the concomitant announcement of an SEC investigation, Commodore stock's price dropped precipitously.

The SEC eventually dropped its investigation, admitting there was no evidence of manipulation nor collusion between Gilbert and Mr. Gould of Commodore. Still trying to avoid meeting his option obligations, Strausberg brought a civil suit in the U.S. District Court against Gilbert, Revson, Gould, and Commodore; but it was quickly dismissed as meritless. In turn, Gilbert filed suit in New York Supreme Court to collect money owed to him by Strausberg for his Commodore options. Inevitably, Strausberg's strategy of "the best defense being a good offense" collapsed for lack of any structural support; and when the financially strapped broker found himself out of legal alternatives, he declared bankruptcy. Gilbert lost not only the $1 million or so in profit he would have realized by exercising his options but also the cash he had advanced to buy his options in the first place.

Nevertheless the trial against Eddie Gilbert in the Conrac affair commenced on January 12, 1981, in the courtroom of U.S. District Court Judge Charles S. Haight, Jr., and located in the same federal courthouse on Foley Square where Gilbert had pleaded guilty in the Bruce company case in 1967. Although the two cases bore no similarities, the connection between them would have a devastating effect on Gilbert in the Conrac trial. Judge Haight ruled in a pretrial motion by the prosecution that if Gilbert were to testify in the Conrac stock manipulation case, his past conviction could be addressed in cross-examination and played out in detail for the jury; the ruling, in effect, precluded Gilbert from taking the stand. "There is no way we could allow him to appear and open up that line of questioning," Herald Fahringer later explained. "And it was, of course, an awful hindrance to our case."

Another obstacle for Gilbert and his defense team arose during pretrial proceedings. The attorneys for John Revson and Ludwig Cserhat, not surprisingly, requested a separate trial for their clients. Because lawyers for the U.S. Attorney's office had cast Eddie Gilbert as the central figure in "the conspiracy," the other, equally indicted defendants were still perceived as subordinate players to Gilbert. Moreover, for them there was the subject of Eddie's past. The lawyers for Revson and Cserhat thought their clients' best interests would be served if their trial was severed from Gilbert's.

When separation of the trials was broached to Gilbert, he weighed the pros and cons. He could fight the separation, if he so chose; and so the decision was not an easy one to make. By agreeing to the separation, as he saw it, there would be a benefit for his two colleagues, whom he believed were brought into the case only because of "the government's obsession with going after me." On the other hand, separating the trials meant that the two would not testify for Gilbert as to their motives, nor to refute Couri's testimony and to challenge his considerably different interpretation of what had actually happened. At the time, Eddie was under the misapprehension that Revson and Cserhat *could* and *would* testify in his trial. He had talked to them about that particularly and believed he had their assurances that they would be there for him. Whether or not they may have wanted to appear on his behalf, there was no way their attorneys would permit them to do so. Eddie's own attorney Herald Fahringer conceded this when asked about it later, "Eddie very much — and this is to his credit — wanted to help the other two. They had grounds for obtaining a severance, however, whether we opposed it or not. [As to Revson and Cserhat testifying at Gilbert's trial] I don't think anybody worth their salt would ever allow a client to take the stand in a [related] criminal case before their own. If I were representing Revson or Cserhat, I'm not going to let him take the witness stand and give away his whole defense in another trial, under oath, and subject to cross-examination. You can't let the prosecution know your whole case, maybe three or four months before you go to trial. No lawyer would allow that."

So Gilbert's two co-defendants petitioned the court to sever their trials from his. Their argument, as synopsized in the records of the U.S. District Court, was this: "Both Revson and Cserhat contend that they are peripheral defendants who would be prejudiced by a 'spillover' from the Government's proof against Gilbert, the main architect of the alleged scheme and, by reason of a prior securities fraud conviction, other legal proceedings, and a much publicized flight to Brazil.... [They] argue that much of the government's evidence in a projected six-week trial will implicate only Gilbert, thereby giving rise to that 'slow but inexorable accumulation of evidence of fraudulent practices' by major conspirators which was held [in cited cases] to have fatally prejudiced minor participants.... In addition, both defendants claim that they require Gilbert's exculpatory testimony, foreclosed if they are tried together and Gilbert does not take the stand, or purchased at intolerable 'spillover' cost if Gilbert testifies and is cross-examined on his checkered past."

Gilbert had already made his decision, however. He looked upon Cserhat as a friend and Revson as a victim of Couri's manipulation; he did not want to exacerbate their problems. He knew they would be better served with a separate trial. So he offered no opposition, making Judge Haight's decision an easy one.

The case against Gilbert that Jeffrey Livingston prepared for the prosecution was a thorough and well scripted one, and it had to be. He knew he was working relatively new ground, as he later explained. "I don't think anyone had ever been convicted of stock manipulation with regard to a stock trading on the New York Stock Exchange. There may have been some old cases—certainly there were some SEC cases where people used a different method of manipulating which would be just to create rumors… or false information that a stock [has] great value or there is something very positive going on that would cause the stock to go up…. Actually, I believe… it was probably the first time that certain provisions—I think it's under Section 9 of the Securities and Exchange document of 1944—of which there were certain… provisions prohibiting certain kinds of manipulative trades, whether they be wash sales… [or] match transactions. Those provisions, I believe, had not been used. At least there were no cases that we could find in which those had been used."

What the U.S. Attorney's office was seeking at trial, according to court records, was to "establish overwhelmingly that during 1975 Gilbert orchestrated an elaborate scheme to manipulate trading on the New York Stock Exchange in the common stock of Conrac Corporation… [and to show that] Gilbert exercised control over a vast array of accounts spread among numerous brokerage firms for the purpose of manipulating Conrac. These accounts were in his name and in the names of a variety of nominees, including relatives, businesses, friends, and Swiss banks. Dictating the timing, price, and size of countless purchases and sales among these accounts and using classic manipulative devices such as wash sales, matched orders, and coordinated series of trades, Gilbert dominated and controlled the trading in Conrac throughout most of 1975 and succeeded in creating a false impression of widespread investor interest. As a result of Gilbert's manipulation, both the price of Conrac and its trading volume increased dramatically." The "dramatic increase" to which prosecuting attorney Livingston refers was Conrac stock's price rise from $11 a share on January 2, 1975, to a high of $30.25 on November 24 of that year. "Daily volume had averaged approximately 2,000 shares per day in early 1975. In late 1975, the daily volume peaked at 40,000, with Gilbert and his co-conspirators and nominees often accounting for well over 50 percent of the trading." From these activities, the prosecution asserted that Eddie Gilbert and the accounts he allegedly controlled had profited by "approximately $750,000" in 1975.

During the six-week trial, Livingston called 21 witnesses for the prosecution and presented hundreds of charts, graphs, and documents using visual aids to support the government's case. He charged that Gilbert and his co-conspirators traded shares of Conrac through more than 90 accounts at 19 different brokerage houses and that 40 of the accounts were directly controlled by Gilbert. Livingston pointed out that Gilbert used 17 separate accounts with his principal broker and co-conspirator Ludwig Cserhat. Another account that Livingston specially cited was the *Banque de l'Union* headquartered in Geneva, Switzerland: "Armand Boller, a longtime friend of Gilbert's, was introduced by Gilbert to many of his brokers and opened accounts for *Banque de l'Union* [with whom Boller was affilliated] with several of them, including Cserhat. Thereafter, most of the orders for *Banque de l'Union* were placed by Gilbert. And those which he did not place himself he knew about before being told of them by the broker."

Livingston laid the groundwork of the government's case with an intricate paper trail of trades directly involving Eddie Gilbert or accounts that he personally controlled. He then produced James Couri, whose testimony on the stand was much the same as what he had given several years earlier to the SEC. Couri told the jury that Gilbert was the mastermind of the conspiracy to manipulate Conrac stock and that it was a preconceived, carefully plotted scheme. The only other witness whose testimony could be construed as detrimental to Gilbert was Jost Fleck, a business acquaintance, who got caught up in the situation after his own business had collapsed. According to evidence introduced, large blocks of Conrac stock were purchased in Fleck's name. Fleck gave Gilbert a series of blank, presigned checks and endorsed a number of blank checks, according to the prosecution, so that Gilbert could make deposits in, and withdraw funds from, Fleck's accounts. "Fleck, a neophyte in the stock market," Livingston claimed, "thereafter confirmed orders placed by

Gilbert or placed orders himself as ordered by Gilbert. Gilbert was thus able to run Fleck's accounts as if they were his own." Fleck testified to the effect that this had, in fact, happened.

But outside of the courtroom, Gilbert described his relationship with Fleck differently. "He worked for a company I was involved with, and he was very bright. He got in trouble financially, and I tried to help him out. I gave him a job in this lumber company that I'd bought, and I loaned him some money—he was in debt maybe a hundred or two hundred thousand dollars, I remember. I wanted him to run the lumber company; but it was a bad venture, and I eventually had to liquidate it. I told him at the time maybe there was another way I could help him get some money to get himself out of debt. I said I could help him make it in the market, and I agreed to loan him the money to make it. Now that sounds like an imbecilic thing for a guy to do, but I was so confident Conrac was going to do well that both of us would come out on top. I put up the initial money, I loaned him $50,000, I think it was. He put that into an account, and he traded and I traded for him, and there might have been some crosses—I might have been buying when he was selling or selling when he was buying. But all I was trying to do was make some money for him. I loaned the guy money and he was buying and selling shares when I was, but it wasn't to manipulate the stock."

Fleck testified as to the trades but did not accuse Gilbert of trying to manipulate the stock. After a brief cross-examination by Fahringer, Gilbert motioned his attorney back to the defense table and said to him, "Ask him this one question: 'Would he trust Eddie Gilbert?'" Fahringer whispered that he didn't think such a question was a good idea.

"If you don't ask him that question, I'm walking out of here," Gilbert said, seething.

Fahringer could sense Gilbert's determination. "Are you sure you want me to do this?" he asked. "You could lose the whole trial on this one question."

Gilbert reflected for a moment, then said, "Well, I'm losing it anyway. Ask him the question."

Fahringer returned to the witness and and asked the question, just as Eddie had phrased it. Fleck looked over at Gilbert and said, "I would."

Gilbert's defense was both hamstrung and flawed: hamstrung because Gilbert was prevented from testifying to refute the case that Livingston was building; and flawed because defense counsel Fahringer—as effective as he undoubtedly was in other legal areas—proved ill-equipped to challenge Livingston's allegations on cross-examination. As the trial got under way, it became increasingly clear to Gilbert that he was in trouble. It was clear to others as well. One of Gilbert's most trusted attorneys, Gene Wolkoff, although not directly involved in his defense in this case, attended the trial and recalls: "The scene at the trial, I have a vivid picture of it; I was there in the courtroom. They had the jury sitting on one side, and right across from the jury they [the prosecution] had a big easel, and on this easel they'd have a big chart or a graph. They had this SEC expert who would then get up and analyze the trades. They did this dozens and dozens of times. And each time the SEC expert would testify, he would pick up a chart, hold it up, show it graphically to the jury, and recount just what trades [occurred] and how Ed, with the other entities that Ed was allegedly trading for, how they controlled the particular action of the stock on that day or that week. It was a very impressive presentation. But it never proved that anything illegal was done. And practically all of it went unrefuted."

That, of course, is what Eddie Gilbert sat stewing about at the defense table. He was constantly whispering in Herald Fahringer's ear, trying to communicate to his attorney what he would have said had he been able to testify, to show that these trades were legitimate and not as portrayed by Livingston. But his message never got delivered to the jury. "It was very frustrating," Wolkoff explained. "Here you have a man presented with the mantle of years of experience as an investigator in the SEC with these detailed and handsomely done graphs describing in a very erudite fashion what all of it meant. Then you have no cross-examination to establish that they were not *per se* illegal, or an insignificant cross at best the other times. So the jury, while they may not have understood any of it, had to be impressed by the prosecution's presentation and the description by the 'expert'."

It reached a point midway through the trial that Gilbert wanted to fire Fahringer but was dissuaded from doing so by both Stanley Reiben and Wolkoff, who both recognized that it would be disastrous for Eddie's case to change counsel in the middle of a trial.

The testimony Couri gave, despite being uncorroborated, was devastating. Whereas Jeffrey Livingston had portrayed the complicated and interconnected series of trades that Gilbert made, Couri testified as to Gilbert's *intent* to manipulate the stock for his own profit. Showing such intent was essential to proving that Gilbert's trading was illegal. Fahringer was able to show the jury that Couri had plea-bargained his way out of the conspiracy in exchange for testimony against Gilbert; and he was also able to cast some light on Couri's checkered past. But these forays proved to be small consolation because Gilbert was prevented from personally refuting how Couri had characterized the whole business. Further undercutting his defense, of course, was the absence of Revson and Cserhat whose testimony would most likely have contradicted Couri's. Gilbert stood alone, caught again in a Catch 22 situation, not a novel predicament for Eddie in his encounters with the government.

Gilbert could only hope that the jury would not believe Couri. Couri's testimony was *the* overriding factor—although Livingston would later refute that notion, claiming the case was solid on its own merits—and Gilbert thought there was a fifty-fifty chance they might not convict him on the testimony of one witness whose credibility was certainly suspect. "Couri was a liar. That's simple," Gilbert said later. "A liar and an opportunist." As to Jost Fleck, "It was damaging but not in the way Couri's was. I have no hard feelings about Fleck. He did what he had to do, I guess."

The case was turned over to the jury, which returned its verdict on February 25, 1981. It turned out that they believed James Couri. The *New York Times* reported the next day, "Edward M. Gilbert was convicted by a federal jury of 34 counts of violating securities laws by manipulating Conrac Corp. shares in 1975. Mr. Gilbert, 58 years old, was found guilty on the jury's third day of deliberations of all charges in an indictment brought against him last summer by federal authorities.... Each of the 34 counts carries a maximum prison term of five years and a $10,000 fine.... Mr. Gilbert is scheduled to be sentenced April 8 by Judge [Charles S.] Haight, who presided over the six-week trial."

Herald Fahringer was quoted as saying, "We were deeply disappointed in the jury's verdict, but I have never lost confidence in the substantial legal questions we raised in this case and I feel sure we will prevail on appeal."

Gilbert, however, had lost confidence, especially in Fahringer, and was already mulling over who he would hire to handle his appeal. He had no comment to make to the press.

Eddie Gilbert's confidence was buoyed, however, by a letter, dated March 18, 1981, written by Jeffrey Livingston. In it Livingston acknowledged information that the U.S. Attorney for the Southern District of New York had received about James Couri the afternoon after the jury had announced its verdict against Gilbert. The information contained in the letter was dramatic. Livingston wrote that on February 20, 1981, while the Gilbert trial was still in session, Thomas J. Fitzpatrick, chief of the U.S. Attorney's Criminal division (and Livingston's superior) had received a telephone call from former Assistant U.S. Attorney Henry Putzel, now in private practice, requesting to meet the following Monday "in regard to matters which could affect individuals represented by him and Henry H. Korn," another former Assistant U.S. Attorney.

At that meeting on February 23, according to Livingston's letter, Putzel and Korn informed division chief Fitzpatrick that they had information about "a cooperating witness" in one of their cases "who had previously testified as a government witness." The witness was, of course, James Couri, even though when Fitzpatrick asked for the name of the witness, Putzel and Korn stated that they preferred to wait a few days before disclosing it; and Fitzpatrick apparently did not press further for the individual's name. But on the afternoon of February 25, just after the guilty verdict was announced in the government's case against Gilbert, Korn called the U.S. Attorney's office in New York and told Fitzpatrick that the "cooperating witness" was indeed James Couri and that he was facing indictments on a variety of criminal charges relating to his Plazagal company, including defrauding a New York bank. Livingston claimed in his letter of March 18, 1981, that he and his colleague Peter Romatowski had not been informed of that information until the day following the verdict in the Gilbert trial (because he would have been obliged to reveal such information to the defense attorneys had he been aware of it before the trial concluded).

The extent of Couri's alleged criminal actions through Plazagal and the fraudulent dealings with the Manufacturers and Traders Trust Company were a tangled web, but Livingston described them in some detail in his letter. Certain employees at Plazagal provided information that Couri changed some company financial records in order to inflate the sales figures. One employee was asked to inflate the recorded sales figures by treating unsold items as if they had been sold. Other employees were instructed to create false invoices to correspond with the inflated sales figures. These false sales figures were then incorporated into the monthly accounts receivable reports forwarded to the Manufacturers and Traders Trust Company, whose outstanding loan of $1.8 million to Plazagal had been personally guaranteed by Couri. Livingston's letter stated that "the aggregate overstatement of sales was approximately $600,000," a figure later reduced to something between $300,000 and $400,000.

In addition, the U.S. Attorney's office was informed that "figures for inventory of Plaza [the shortened term of Plazagal which Livingston uses throughout his letter], which were from time to time submitted to M and T Bank were greatly in excess of the actual inventory on hand at Plaza." The letter went on to describe a number of Plazagal checks issued on overdrawn accounts, check "kiting" between Plazagal and other Couri-owned companies, use of Plazagal's funds by Couri to purchase speculative securities, Couri's warnings and threats to employees about talking to outsiders about Plazagal's operations or its financial status, etc.

And finally, Livingston concludes in his letter: "There is information that after the M and T Bank began its litigation against Plaza [which the bank was suing so as to collect on the defaulted loan], Couri took a portion of certain payments received by Plaza for certain sales, after directing the employees to enter the receipt of the cash on the books of Plaza and to enter the expenditure of the cash as payments to other companies controlled by Couri. Also since the Bank began its lawsuit several checks were issued by Plaza paying for personal expenses of Mr. Couri, including checks to his attorneys in the aggregate amount of approximately $80,000 to $100,000."

Gilbert and his attorneys immediately saw that the content of the letter provided a rich source of material about Couri that could have been used to discredit the government's star witness during Gilbert's trial; it also seemed suspect that Gilbert had been found guilty just a few hours before the U.S. Attorney's office had learned of Couri's business irregularities and the investigations surrounding them.

For a case that was so tied to the presumed truthfulness of James Couri's testimony, both the information contained in Jeffrey Livingston's letter and the timing of its disclosures were of enormous importance. Hope had returned to the Gilbert camp.

# Trouble follows me.

BILLY MARTIN, NEW YORK YANKEES MANAGER, 1977

Eddie Gilbert hired a new legal team to handle his appeal: It was headed by criminal law specialist Gerald L. Shargel of New York and Alan Dershowitz, who was a faculty member at Harvard Law School and considered one of the nation's preeminent legal theorists. The first step was to file a motion with Judge Haight to grant a new trial because of the recently discovered evidence—information in Jeffrey Livingston's letter of March 18, 1981, about the hitherto unrevealed activities of James Couri. The lawyers' argument was a simple one: Couri's testimony was of overwhelming importance to the U.S. Attorney's case against Gilbert; the significant information contained in the letter, not released until just after the guilty verdict was returned in Gilbert's case, could have been used to further impeach Couri's testimony. Gilbert's lawyers' contention was that, had his defense counsel been in possession of this additional information—which had been floating around the prosecutor's office long before the verdict had been returned— it could have been used to cast an entirely different light on Couri's character and the value of his testimony in Gilbert's case.

In fact Livingston's letter had been addressed to the attorneys representing John Revson and Ludwig Cserhat whose trial was scheduled to begin on March 23, 1981, with copies sent to Gilbert's former defense counsel Herald Fahringer and to the presiding judge, Charles Haight. Received by Gilbert's defense team on Friday, March 20, they requested a suspension of Gilbert's sentencing on March 23 so that the defense could take appropriate legal action in light of the new evidence.

Couri and his attorney were also busy. Because of the charges relating to his dealings with Plazagal and M and T Bank, they were headed into a courtroom of their own. Couri's counsel approached the U.S. Attorney's team prosecuting Cserhat and Revson, headed again by Jeffrey Livingston, on the day the trial began. Counsel informed the prosecution that Couri would not testify at the trial, invoking his Fifth Amendment privilege, unless an agreement was reached limiting his criminal liability in the Plazagal–M and T Bank affair. The U.S. Attorney's office quickly worked out a deal much to Couri's liking. For giving testimony along the lines he had provided in the Gilbert trial, he would plead guilty to two misdemeanor counts of loan fraud. The government would agree not to prosecute him for any other crimes involving Plazagal, and he would be given a sentence of three years' probation. Once again, another Couri plea bargain managed to save him from serving any prison time.

In the case against Revson and Cserhat, however, Couri's testimony, in light of what was now known about him, would not prove to be an important factor. Their trial, which lasted longer than the six-week Gilbert trial, had obvious similarities. The charges were the same, and so was the mass of evidence presented by the prosecution. But there was one glaring dissimilarity: the not-guilty verdict. Gilbert's counsel, Gerald Shargel, described the situation succinctly in his later motion for a new trial. "The Revson-Cserhat trial and the Gilbert trial came as close to constituting a natural experiment as any two trials could possibly be. The indictment was the same. The government's legal theory was essentially the same. As in the Gilbert trial, the government relied on the testimony of Couri. As in the Gilbert trial, the defendants did not take the witness stand. They, like Gilbert, relied on an attempt to attack the credibility of the government's central witness. As in Gilbert, the trial court ruled that if the government's evidence were to be believed by the jury, the defendants' guilt would be established beyond a reasonable doubt.

"This time, however, the defense was armed with massive evidence of 'misrepresentation and fraud' by Couri in his Plazagal dealings. Accordingly, the trial court allowed the defense to cross-examine Couri about these dealings. The defense cross-examination of Couri in regard to Plazagal was devastating. The jury acquitted the defendants, obviously disbelieving Couri's incriminating testimony."

The two trials were for the same conspiracy, but one "conspirator" was found guilty while the other two were acquitted. The two cases against them were almost identical except for the ways in which the juries were able to judge the believability of the government's chief witness, James Couri. The unanswered question remained: How can you have a "conspiracy" if two conspirators are not guilty when their involvement in the trading of the stock was as much in evidence as for the conspirator found guilty?

Prosecuting attorney Jeffrey Livingston, when asked later, said, "Well, the very simple answer to that is the fact that Couri was a conspirator. They [Gilbert and Couri] don't have to be in conspiracy with the two people that were acquitted; [they] were not essential. It only takes two to have a conspiracy. In other words, you've got Gilbert, and you've got Couri; that's two people who, I think, were in a conspiratorial relationship. So, the fact that the other two were acquitted doesn't defeat the possibility of the conspiracy."

Livingston went on to say that he did not believe that Couri's testimony constituted the deciding factor in the guilty verdict against Gilbert. When asked if he thought the information contained in his letter of March 18 might have had an influence on the outcome of the trial, Livingston replied, "I think no, because the documentary evidence in the case was strong. His trading pattern was documented. You could see trading tickets where friends and associates of Gilbert were buyers and sellers in the transactions, and you could see where trades were put in sequentially, increasing the price in a given morning, for example.... And, aside from Couri, there was another [witness] who had these associations with Gilbert... so I think there was a lot of other testimony and a lot of other documentary evidence that I think would have made it very unlikely, in my view, that Eddie would have been acquitted. There was just too much weight in the rest of the evidence."

The Gilbert side disagreed with Livingston's assessment. First, Gilbert believed that the documentary evidence was not sufficient to convict because it did not prove his intent to manipulate the Conrac stock for his own gain; only Couri's testimony directly addressed Gilbert's intent. Although the issue of the fundamental legality of the trades had not been made satisfactorily to the jury in his trial, Gilbert believed that the jury should have had all the facts about the man accusing him, whose character and flawed actions were not fully revealed (even though the jury did know he was not being punished for his part in the conspiracy because he exchanged immunity for testimony against Gilbert in his trial and against Revson and Cserhat in theirs).

On June 9, 1981, Gilbert's attorney filed a motion for a new trial pursuant to Rule 33 of the Federal Rules of Criminal Procedure. Back before Judge Haight, Shargel argued that the content of Livingston's letter which outlined a litany of Couri's misdeeds and felonious acts had been unavailable to the defense in Gilbert's trial; further, that the motive and actions of the U.S. Attorney's office as to its handling of the information contained in the letter about Couri were highly questionable.

Shargel and Dershowitz felt they had a strong case for a new trial or at the very least that the court would grant Gilbert an evidentiary hearing on whether the U.S. Attorney's office had improperly suppressed the new evidence during the trial that might have been exculpatory for Gilbert.

Shargel summarized his arguments before Judge Haight by addressing three crucial areas of governmental conduct. "The first relates to precisely what the government knew or should have known about the Plazagal and M and T Bank situations before and during the Gilbert trial. By the time of the trial, Couri's involvement with M and T Bank was already a tangle of illegalities, misrepresentations and lies...; surely this issue must have come up during the lengthy preparations the government necessarily went through with Couri. The government could not have been certain that all questions regarding these matters would be ruled inadmissible by the trial court. Petitioner is entitled to employ the truth-testing tools of the adversary process to uncover precisely what the government knew, and when it knew it, about the Plazagal-M and T matters."

The second area in question cited by Shargel related directly to government "communications during the Gilbert trial." He noted that on Monday, February 23, while the Gilbert trial was still in process, the chief of the U.S. Attorney's criminal division, Thomas Fitzpatrick, was directly informed that a cooperating witness was involved in various criminal activities. "Upon meeting with lawyers Putzel and Korn, Fitzpatrick's clear obligation was to try to learn which of the government's witnesses was so tainted that two ex-government prosecutors arranged a special meeting to notify the government of the situation. In all probability, Fitzpatrick could have learned the name of the witness in question merely by circulating a memo through the [New York U.S. Attorney's] office; Putzel and Korn had promised, after all, to disclose the name within 'a few days' and thus Fitzpatrick had merely to inquire (if he did not already know) what trial was about to end. Indeed, by promising to disclose the name in a few days, Putzel and Korn for all practical purposes disclosed the name then and there."

Shargel addressed a third issue having to do with the conduct of the U.S. Attorney's office "immediately *following* the verdict in the Gilbert trial." The timing was so obviously gauged to what was transpiring in Judge Haight's courtroom as to be preconceived and carefully planned; regardless, the U.S. Attorney's office should have discovered who the "mystery" witness was by that time. "Within hours after the verdict was announced, Mr. Korn telephoned the United States Attorney's Office to tell the government what it should already have known: Couri was seriously involved in criminal financial dealings. With the verdict in the Gilbert trial safely in, the government proceeded to conduct its own investigation into the matter.

"Yet inexcusably, the government failed even then promptly to inform the court or the defense of the new development. It is difficult to imagine what could have motivated the government at this point—certainly the government prosecutors were aware of their obligation to disclose this vital information to Gilbert. Yet the government waited and waited, allowing the seven-day deadline for Gilbert to pass...."

The U.S. Attorney's reply was simple and brief. Prosecutor Livingston contended, first, that the information about Couri contained in the letter would not have had any material effect on the jury's verdict. Couri's checkered past had been made known to the jury, and despite that they had decided to believe his testimony. The jury, according to Livingston, found Gilbert guilty by virtue of the overwhelming weight of documentary evidence the government presented, to which the testimony of James Couri was merely a supplement. Additional information about Couri's misdeeds and troubles with the law would not have affected the outcome of the case, and so a new trial for Gilbert was not warranted on that account.

Secondly, Livingston vigorously denied any prosecutorial misconduct in handling the information contained in his letter of March 18, 1981, to the attorneys for Revson and Cserhat, nor in the timing of the letter's disclosures or its delivery.

On July 24, 1981, Judge Haight filed his opinion denying the motion for a new trial made by Gilbert's attorneys some six weeks earlier.

In rendering his opinion, Judge Haight cited a prior U.S. Court of Appeals ruling: "To warrant a new trial, it must be shown that the newly discovered evidence is of such nature that it would probably produce an acquittal." And citing another case, he wrote: "...such a motion [to dismiss] 'should be granted only with great caution' and only upon a showing that the evidence could not with due diligence have been discovered before or during trial, that the evidence is material, not cumulative, and that admission of the evidence would probably lead to an acquittal."

Judge Haight then ruled: "Judged by these standards, the present motion must be denied. The post-trial disclosures with respect to Couri's Plazagal-related fraud do not constitute 'direct, exculpatory evidence'; rather, they constitute 'additional evidence tending further to impeach the credibility of a witness whose character had already been shown to be questionable,'... [thus] the evidence at bar is not material but only cumulative; and, in the totality of the circumstances, I cannot possibly conclude that admission of the evidence on a new trial would probably lead to acquittal." In addition, he found insufficient prosecutorial impropriety to warrant a new trial or even an evidentiary hearing.

He concluded: "In sum, the newly discovered evidence underlying Gilbert's motion for a new trial does not rise to the level of materiality required [by Rule 33]. None of the factual issues Gilbert wishes to explore in an evidentiary hearing is germane to resolution of his motion, which in the light of the foregoing authorities, I deny."

At 10:45 on the morning of July 31, 1981, Gilbert and his attorney Gerald Shargel returned to the U.S. Courthouse on Foley Square, in the courtroom of Judge Haight for Gilbert's sentencing. There too were prosecutors Jeffrey Livingston and Peter Romatowski together with their boss, John S. Martin, United States Attorney for the Southern District of New York. After both sides addressed the court in regard to the subject and severity of the sentences at Judge Haight's disposal, the jurist gave a surprisingly long recitation of his thoughts and reasoning in regard to reaching a determination of sentence. He explained that he had studied the presentence report in the case; read the many letters that had been written on Eddie's behalf, testifying to his exemplary character; considered the government's recommendations; even read the results of a lie detector test that Eddie had voluntarily taken in October 1980 which had demonstrated "that Gilbert did not know that what he was doing was wrong."

According to his defense lawyers, the results also demonstrated that there was *no intent* to do anything illegal in his trading.

For that polygraph test, the facts of the case involving Gilbert and Conrac were provided to the polygraphist by Eddie's attorneys Herald Fahringer and Stanley Reiben. Eddie then went to the offices of Scientific Lie Detection, Inc., on West 57th Street and submitted to a test prepared by the firm's polygraph experts. In the affidavit they subsequently submitted, they defined the four pertinent test questions on which their analysis was determined:

1. Were you trading Conrac as you were in order to run up its price?
2. When you were trading Conrac, did you then know that your actions were against the law?
3. When you were trading Conrac, did you then knowingly break the law?
4. Did you trade Conrac as you did in order to commit a fraud?

To each of the questions, Eddie responded "No." The results of the test were then certified in the affidavit from the lie detector firm. "It is the opinion of the polygraphist, based upon The Arthur VI Polygraph Examination of Mr. Gilbert, that he is telling the truth to the above listed questions."

But at the end of the day none of these considerations swayed Judge Haight. He concluded that, "The attempted Conrac manipulation was of a sophisticated nature and constituted, in my judgment, a frontal attack by Mr. Gilbert upon the integrity of the marketplace." He went on to say, "To suggest that an individual as experienced and sophisticated as Mr. Gilbert was unaware of wrongdoing is fanciful....Mr. Gilbert's ability and inclination to manipulate the market constrains me to regard him as a danger to it."

He then sentenced Gilbert to terms of four years' imprisonment on 34 of the 36 counts in the indictment, but to be served concurrently. And he sentenced him to five years' probation commencing after serving his prison term, during which probationary period he would be barred from acting "as a broker, dealer or agent, with respect to the sales or purchases of any securities," although the sentence did permit him to trade on his own account and the accounts of members of his immediate family. This would be an important *caveat* at a period later in Eddie's life.

Shargel announced the defendant's intention to appeal and requested continuation of the $500,000 bail that had been posted by Gilbert. Livingston objected: "I think there is a substantial danger of flight in this case [he cited Gilbert's flight to Brazil in 1962, although not his voluntary return]. I think Mr. Gilbert constitutes a danger to the community in the commission of more crimes." Livingston urged the judge to remand Gilbert to custody immediately. Judge Haight disagreed, however, saying that he did not think it likely that Eddie "would, pending appeal, flee this city, this state, and this country, where his mother is, where his wife is, where his children, in differing degrees of need and dependence upon him, reside." And so he ruled that the terms and conditions of bail remain as they had been previously stipulated, pending the outcome of Gilbert's appeal.

Eddie and his attorneys immediately filed for an appeal. As good as they originally thought their chances looked for winning the motion for a new trial, however, the prospect of winning on appeal now seemed dismal. The case went before the United States Court of Appeals for the Second Circuit, and, by chance, there appeared a ray of hope since J. Edward Lumbard was one of that distinguished panel of three jurists. He had been the appellate judge who authored the opinion that exonerated Gilbert in his tax appeals case back in 1977.

Alan Dershowitz was a recognized appeals process expert and nationally known for his legal brilliance. Although renowned for his persuasive powers, he was fiery in his presentation (so fiery, some thought, that he might have offended the appeals panel) and sharp in his repudiation of how the U.S. Attorney's office behaved in concealing the information about James Couri. But he was not persuasive enough. On December 14, 1981, the Court of Appeals rejected Gilbert's appeal.

Piece by piece, the appellate judges took apart the arguments that had been presented by Dershowitz, "meritless" being the term most frequently used in referring to the separate points of appeal. And with the concluding words in their opinion, "The judgment of conviction is affirmed," it was chillingly clear that Eddie Gilbert was going back to prison.

While the Conrac case was unfolding that year, Gilbert made another acquaintance that would come back to haunt him. In March 1981, a writer by the name of Kenneth Geist approached Eddie, suggesting a project that could be to their mutual advantage. Geist, aware of Eddie's colorful and checkered past, had been following all the current publicity surrounding the Conrac case. He told Eddie that a biography of him would make for interesting reading and provide an unbiased account of Eddie's encounters with the law; it might also prove to be quite profitable. Geist and his agent would seek an advance against royalties from a publisher in the sum of at least $100,000. There would be additional revenue from syndicating magazine articles and perhaps movie and/or television rights. The package had enormous potential.

Geist, who lived in Greenwich Village, had written articles for small publications, mostly about the motion picture and television industries, and had authored a biography of film director Joseph Manckiewicz. Gilbert was intrigued with Geist's idea: He certainly could use the money, especially now faced with costly legal expenses for his defense in the Conrac affair. So, the two struck a deal. They would split the advance and any other income from the book project on a fifty-fifty basis, and Eddie agreed to make himself available for interviews and to provide whatever documentation he had for Geist to prepare a publishable manuscript.

The two began work on the project shortly thereafter. Over the next six months, Gilbert spent much of his time meeting with Geist, narrating his life story (there were hundreds of hours of tapes eventually compiled), and answering Geist's relentless questions. By August 1981, Geist believed they should take the first step: They went to the publisher of *New York* magazine, who expressed serious interest and commissioned Geist to write an article about Gilbert that would, everyone agreed, help to secure a hefty royalty advance from a book publisher.

But in August their relationship took a different turn. During the prior seven months, the two had worked so closely together on the book project that they had come to see each other as friends as well. They socialized on occasion, played tennis together, and sometimes talked about the climate in the business world, the economy, and Wall Street.

Geist had also become increasingly disenchanted with his investment counselor, and so he asked Gilbert for some advice, specifically about the drop in the price of his shares in a firm known as Cray Research. Gilbert looked into that issue and other stocks in Geist's portfolio. About a week later, he suggested that Geist reduce the size of his margin debt by selling approximately 20 percent of his stocks and replacing them with bonds and U.S. Treasury bills.

In early September, as the deadline for the appeal brief of the Conrac trial fast approached, Gilbert was cash-strapped and needed $100,000 to retain his pricey appellate attorneys, Gerry Shargell and Alan Dershowitz. He asked Geist to lend him that amount, but Geist consented to a loan of just $25,000. Eddie obtained the remaining $75,000 from other friends.

At the same time, Geist also decided to replace his investment adviser, seeking counsel for that action from his attorney, his accountant, and Eddie Gilbert. He interviewed several prospective replacements and finally settled on John Westergaard (although he was increasingly seeking advice from Gilbert as well).

Meanwhile, Geist had finished the *New York* magazine article on Gilbert and delivered it in early February 1982. Eddie, Geist, and Geist's literary agent then approached the prestigious New York publishing firm of Random House, submitting an outline of the proposed biography and a sample chapter. Not long after, the magazine rejected Geist's article, and Random House decided to pass on the book proposal.

By this time Eddie had lost his court appeal, and so Geist's access to him was now going to be quite difficult. And with the two rejections, Geist's interest in the book project faded. He talked with Eddie about revising the proposal, about adding another chapter or two to supplement what had been done already, and then resubmitting the proposal, but nothing more was ever done. And as March approached, Eddie Gilbert had much more pressing things on his mind

On March 1, 1982, Gilbert reported to the federal correctional institution at Allenwood, Pennsylvania, to begin serving his sentence. Allenwood was a minimum security facility that housed a number of "white-collar" criminals, although there were plenty of others there with pasts in organized crime and life on the meaner streets of America. Eddie had little difficulty fitting in at Allenwood. After all, he had done time earlier at Sing Sing and Danbury—the former, New York's notorious state prison, a training ground that had prepared him for the very worst that could be expected inside prison walls; the latter, a primer on just what life inside a federal penitentiary could be like.

Survival is the foremost motivation (and skill) at any prison. No one had to tell that to Eddie Gilbert. And Allenwood, minimum security or not, was no exception. It was still a prison with a population comprised of convicted felons. Alliances, not friendships, are made in cell blocks. (But for Gilbert this was not necessarily true, since several of the alliances he made at Allenwood continued as friendships later on the outside.) In fact, one such friendship would challenge his deep-rooted sense of personal loyalty, putting him at odds with the law, and, as we shall see, cause him further grief.

Inside the walls of Allenwood, Gilbert quickly found a most suitable alliance. His name was John, and he was a product of the tougher streets of Brooklyn. On the outside, John had owned a total of 13 saloons, some in Brooklyn, others on Manhattan and one in Queens. He was serving time for what he later described as "conspiracy to possess" (which he claimed was "a bad pinch," although his characterization is disputable). What John was convicted of conspiring to possess were two tractor-trailer loads of hijacked merchandise. John had also been in the coin-operated vending business before his conviction. He was as streetwise as they come, and he had connections. No one in Allenwood messed with John.

"He [Eddie] made a nice impression on me," John later recalled. He was put in my dorm. [Allenwood was a minimum security prison and prisoners were housed in barracks, which some called dorms, rather than cells.] I didn't bother with him for the first couple days — I didn't bother with too many guys there. In fact Eddie was one of the very few, maybe five, six people, I bothered with — in a decent way — the whole time I was there. I just took a liking to him. He seemed like a straight guy . . . a real guy. He didn't whine, didn't walk around talking about what a bum deal he got. Then I started hearing stories about him, who he was on the outside, the big-time money, and I could tell he was very smart. We got to playing cards together. . . and he taught me math. I was getting ready to take my GED test, and he helped me [John passed and got his high school equivalency diploma while he was at Allenwood]. So we became friends."

In a place like Allenwood, one needs friends like John. "We had a couple of wiseguys there," John recalls, "and they knew about Eddie, heard about him being a rich guy, and they were always trying to shake him down. He'd try to avoid them, and they'd try to corner him They were typical wiseguys. I knew them, from the outside. I didn't want to get too involved — you don't do that in there — but I looked out for him. When I thought they were pressuring him too much, I told them to lay off; and they did."

John was not the only one with whom Eddie became allied. One of the wiseguys, an Italian from Queens — not one who had been trying to shake him down — often sat in on card games with Eddie and John. He mentioned to Eddie that he had some cash just sitting around outside, and Eddie told him he should be making money with it. So Eddie gave him a few stock tips. "I was like on cloud nine," the man said later. "I made like a hundred thousand dollars in two months. Hell, I made more there in jail than I ever made on the street."

Eddie had two job assignments at Allenwood. He was an assistant to the man in charge of distributing supplies to the inmates, and he was in charge of the prison's fire department (they even had a fire engine). The jobs were simple and undemanding, a way to pass the time of day. But Eddie was as edgy as ever, and his extra-curricular activites were many and varied. He tutored a number of prisoners besides John and dispensed investment advice to others. The prison had a movie program, but the motion pictures they showed were old and usually grade-B quality. When they were shown, they ordinarily attracted about 25 or 30 inmates. So, when Marty Bregman showed up one visitor's day, Eddie told him he wanted him to get some first-run movies for the prison, and Bregman obliged. Pretty soon as many as 300 to 400 were attending first-run movies on Tuesday night. "He was always organizing something," Hy Gordon, another inmate, remembers. "He was always after something to make things better there, and I think the warden wasn't too fond of that after a while; but he got things done."

Still, it was prison and it was not a nice place. Eddie got by on his wits and his alliances. But he was always on a tightrope. John claims that Gilbert was gullible, that he used to believe everything the other inmates told him, "bragging stuff, sob stories, whatever." But it seemed more that Eddie *wanted* to believe them because the stories were colorful, from streets in the city he would never have ordinarily walked. In a way, it was almost an entertainment to him, a play perhaps being put on just for him. "And they were forever borrowing money from him," John recalls. "There was no way in hell they were going to pay it back. Eddie figured that — he'd done that before at Sing Sing, he told me — but he lent them money anyway or had it sent to their wives or families on the outside. I used to tell him to quit doing it. They're just gonna keep coming to you, but that was Eddie. Maybe he felt he was buying those guys off, maybe he felt he had to to protect himself." What John failed to see was that providing money — which Eddie always seemed to be able to do, inside or outside prison, even when his financial empire was in collapse — offered him a certain opportunity to be in control, and Eddie Gilbert always wanted to be in control. It was an inbred trait, one that his sister Enid had early identified when they were children, and one that anyone who spent much time around Eddie could easily see.

Eddie's habit of lending money or arranging for it on the outside is how John came to learn about Gilbert's prior prison record. "He never mentioned it. Then one day, I have this visitor, a guy [who's] now in the witness protection program. I'm in the visiting room talking to him, and Eddie comes in. He's got a visitor, too, and he sits down. My guy does a little double-take. 'You know that guy over there?' he says. 'Yeah,' I say. 'You know him *good*?' When a guy asks something like that in prison it usually means he's gonna tell you, 'Watch him, he's no fucking good.'

"But he doesn't, he says, 'He's some guy.' Then he tells me he was in Sing Sing with him maybe 15 years earlier. I say, 'You're kidding? Not Eddie.' In Sing Sing? But he tells me he worked in the commissary, and Eddie was a school teacher there. One day the guy's wife and two little girls come to visit him. Eddie sees them and afterwards says, 'You got a nice family, how they doing out there?' And the guy tells him not so good. 'She's trying to work and take care of the kids, money's real tight,' he tells Eddie. 'I got a couple of friends on the street trying to help, but things are pretty tough.'

"So Eddie tells the guy, 'Look, you take this [telephone] number down. Next time you talk to your wife, you tell her to call this broker, and he's gonna buy 5,000 shares of stock for her. I'll tell you which stock.'

"'I ain't got no money to buy no stock,' the guy tells him.'

"'Don't worry about it,' Eddie says.

"So she buys the stock. It's around Christmastime. And three weeks later Eddie tells him to tell her to sell it. She does, for $15,000. The guy tells me it was like $15 million to them. She couldn't pay the rent before, could barely put food on the table. And the guy says, 'He didn't ask me for nothing... never asked me to do nothing for him afterwards.'"

John also recounts another prison story about Eddie that sounds more like it came from the typewriter of Damon Runyon. "Ping pong," John explains, "it was all over a ping pong game. There was this one wiseguy from the Bronx. He was always after Eddie, made bets with him. If Eddie lost, he'd pay up; the wiseguy, when he lost, never did. Anyway, this wiseguy had a kid who was kind of the ping pong champion around there, he was backing the kid. Nobody could beat the kid. Anyway, I'm telling Eddie about it, and he says, 'I can beat him.' 'You never even seen him play,' I say. 'I can spot him and still beat him,' Eddie says. Well, I know Eddie well enough to know he doesn't bullshit. So I say maybe we'll get something going there, meaning we could take the wiseguy. 'But let's be sure,' I tell Eddie. I tell him to go watch the kid; he plays every night down in the gym.

"So we go down the next night. I tell Eddie, don't say anything, don't play him, don't negotiate a game, just watch. After about five minutes, Eddie says, 'This guy don't even have a clue. I can beat this guy.'

"'You're sure?' I say. "Forget about it,' Eddie says, 'I'll kill this guy.'

"Eddie tells me he needs to get into shape, you know, go into training. He hasn't played in like 15 years, he tells me. He's talking like he's going into the ring for the heavyweight championship. I thought it was kind of funny. So I go to the wiseguy and set the thing up. He thinks Eddie'll get slaughtered.

"So, I tell Eddie. 'You gotta go into training,' I tell him. Now I'm having fun with Eddie. Tomorrow morning. We're tying you behind a garbage truck — one of our guys drove the garbage truck — and every morning, six o'clock you're running behind the garbage truck. Well, Eddie says he isn't running behind any garbage truck but he'll do roadwork, he'll get himself in shape. And he does. He's doing push-ups and sit-ups, working out like hell. And he starts playing against some of the guys we know, getting back in practice, and I can see he's as good as he told me he was.

"About three days before the game, one of the guys says he thinks there's a stool pigeon in the dorm, a guy talking to the hacks [prison guards]. So I decide a good way to test him. We start talking about the game. I pass the word that there's $50,000 riding on the game. It's all set up, two guys from New York are coming up and they're meeting in this motel down the road from the prison. There's $50,000 in a satchel, and it'll be transferred in the motel room after the game. Eddie doesn't know anything about this.

"So the game comes up. There's maybe 200 guys there to watch it. Eddie's great, he reels off the first five or six points, then all of a sudden everything goes berserk. The hacks rush in, like it's a raid, from all sides. They grab Eddie and take him off. They know he's a money guy, and they think he's the one behind the $50,000... which of course, there was no $50,000. We were betting commisary money, maybe a couple hundred bucks each. They raided the motel, too, had the state troopers go in, but there wasn't anybody there. Anyway they had Eddie down in the hole and they're grilling him about the $50,000 which he knows nothing about, and the motel, and the guys from New York. And they're threatening to send him to Lewisburg [a maximum security federal prison in Pennsylvania], a place nobody wants to go.

"About two in the morning, I finally got it straightened out. I got to one of the lieutenants and told him the whole thing was a lot of bullshit. It was a scam, a set-up, we just wanted to see if the pigeon would go to the warden. Gilbert didn't have anything to do with it. Finally, the lieutenant or the captain got to the warden; and they all realized there was nothing to it, and so they let Eddie go."

As for the ping pong game, it was never resumed. Gilbert, still thirsting for victory, suggested they finish it the next night; the wiseguy, after watching his kid get shut out until the raid stopped the game, decided he wanted no part of it.

During his two years at Allenwood, Eddie had scores of visitors. His wife Linda came every week, at least for the first year; but an alienation was developing, exacerbated by his confinement and the lifestyle she had developed at their New York horse farm. Her visits grew less frequent; and in his last six months of confinement, they ceased altogether. Their marriage had become irreparably damaged in mid-1983 while Eddie was doing his time at Allenwood, although it would not formally end until mid-1985.

One person who continued to visit on a more regular basis, however, was Kenneth Geist. While the book project had fallen apart, their acquaintanceship had not, nor had Geist's enthusiasm for Eddie's financial advice.

July 1982 saw a bull market on Wall Street, the beginning of a five-year run. Although he was in prison, Eddie followed the market every day and continued to invest what he could and also to offer advice to a select few. He had predicted the unleashing of the Wall Street bull, and there were letters between him and Geist to that effect. So Geist now decided to take part of his portfolio—about $200,000 worth, representing about one-tenth of his investment capital—and put it into an account to be managed by Gilbert's broker Joe Cserhat. The money in this account was to be invested strictly on Gilbert's advice; the rest of the portfolio was to remain with Westergaard. But in October 1982 Geist decided to rely completely on Gilbert for financial counsel and accordingly transferred the major portion of his portfolio from Westergaard to Stuart Sosler, another Gilbert friend and broker, at Bear Stearns.

Gilbert took nothing for providing financial guidance to Geist. In a letter to Geist on August 26, 1982, Eddie wrote: "As you already know, you owe me nothing [for financial advice given]. I am in debt to you to the tune of $25,000." That money, which Geist had lent to Eddie, supposedly to be repaid out of the publisher's advance they were going to get for the book, remained outstanding until it was formally forgiven several months later. Geist admitted that the book project was dead and that there was no way the money could now be repaid according to the terms that they had both agreed upon when he had provided Eddie a quarter of the $100,000 he needed to pay his appellate lawyers the year before.

In exchange for Gilbert's increased role in counseling Geist on his investment transactions, Geist suggested they enter into a business agreement with Gilbert to be compensated at 10 percent of whatever money was earned from his investment advice. It was an arrangement that might be in violation of the terms of Judge Haight's sentence following the Conrac conviction, because that order presumably excluded Eddie's acting as an agent or broker in others' securities transactions. Gilbert wanted to discuss the matter with his attorney, Gene Wolkoff.

In the meantime, Eddie was facing repayment of the final item of indebtedness stemming from the Bruce-Celotex debacle back in 1962. It was a cause of daily anxiety for him that he was not yet done meeting the promise he had made to himself and others that he would retire all those debts. He had repaid or satisfied most of them by 1982, a total of nearly $20 million. A large debt still outstanding was owed to the Swiss banker Abdullah Zilkha. Eddie needed $105,000 to meet it; if he did not, Zilkha would be entitled to much more money later. Eddie told Geist that he was trying to raise the money from other personal sources, but if he were unsuccessful he would like Geist to lend him the money, the loan to be evidenced by a note repayable in full by March 1984.

Geist wrote to Gilbert in April 1983, again bringing up the subject of a possible financial arrangement between them, but decided to send the letter to Gene Wolkoff at the offices of Callahan &Wolkoff at 67 Wall Street.

*April 15, 1983*

*Dear Ed:*

*There are many things I could not say comfortably in our telephone conversation on Wednesday. You have made me wary of what I write to you and I am equally cautious of what we say to each other by phone.*

*That is why I am sending this letter to Gene Wolkoff. At his discretion, he can either forward it to you or excerpt it over the phone. . . .*

*I requested. . . of you that we make a percentage deal based on profit and loss and establish an equitable management fee based on the size of the portfolio. (I appreciate that, under the present circumstances, this may be difficult to legally formalize with you.)*

*But I think it is what you and I must do now, on at least a verbal basis. . . . I also believe that this loan [$105,000] must be predicated on an agreement between us concerning a management and/or percentage agreement for your future advice and supervision of my portfolio. . . .*

*Ken Geist*

Wolkoff discussed the letter with Gilbert. In regard to the question of whether Eddie could legally accept compensation, Wolkoff could not give an immediate answer, saying he would have to research it. But he did tell Gilbert that a bona fide loan would not be construed as compensation. He therefore advised Gilbert to take the needed $105,000 strictly as a loan, with appropriate collateral and without predication of any sort on a compensation agreement between himself and Geist. Gilbert relayed this to Geist who, a few days later, agreed to make the loan on this basis.

With Gilbert now serving as chief investment adviser, Geist's financial situation experienced a dramatic change. According to later court documents, "The value of his portfolios increased by more than $800,000 from April 29 to June 24. (At Bear Stearns his 'total equity' increased from $2,354,680 to $2,938, 852. At Baird Patrick his 'liquidating value' increased from $674,018 to $932,175.)" In August, Geist then told Gilbert that he now needed additional tax deductions and asked him to modify their agreement about the outstanding $105,000 loan. Instead of waiting for the maturity date of March 31, 1984, Geist preferred to convert some or all of the loan into an investment advisory fee, which he could then write off as a deduction from his 1983 tax return. Gilbert again conferred with Wolkoff who, by this time, had researched the legal issues, and advised Gilbert that he could, in fact, accept the compensation in question. He later gave Gilbert a written opinion to that effect.

Eddie Gilbert was released from the correctional facility at Allenwood on December 20, 1983, and moved into a halfway house in Manhattan. According to the terms of this confinement, he was free to go about his business during the week but had to spend nights and weekends at the halfway house for the next two months.

Shortly after his release but before the end of the year, Gilbert and Geist negotiated their compensation agreement, that Geist agreed to pay a fee equal to 10 percent of the profits realized from the investments for which Gilbert was advising him. Gilbert subsequently received two payments from Geist totalling $110,000. He, in turn, paid off the $105,000 loan to Geist and also purchased for $5,000 an investment that Geist wanted to rid himself of.

But it all went downhill after that. The agreement was for 1983 only, and as no written agreement was reached for 1984, the two were continually arguing points about interim advisory compensation and specifics about how and when their agreement could be terminated. While Geist did make one payment of $8,000 to Gilbert in March 1984, Geist's investments headed down the slope, taking with them the closeness of his relationship with Gilbert.

By August, the relationship had come to a vituperous end. Geist claimed he had, in 1984, lost enormously in his stock market holdings as a result of Gilbert's advice, "more than half of my portfolio." Dated August 27, a three-page letter from Geist to Eddie was delivered to Gene Wolkoff at his law office on Wall Street. It began, "As every phone call from you inflicts new wounds—such as today's assertion that you were unaware of the size of my debit at Bear Stearns—I think our phone calls as well as our relationship should now be terminated." He went on to state, "I cannot forgive myself for trusting your 'superior' judgement to the tune of over $2 million. That loss has hurt me every day this past year ... and I can never withstand the financial risks necessary to recoup it. That money not only represents years of worry and torment, but the chance of a getaway house, world travel, and venture capital to participate in theater and film production." And within the litany of his discontent, a veiled threat also emerged. Referring to Eddie's first wife Rhoda, whose wrath at their divorce in 1963 had still not subsided even by the mid-1980s, Geist wrote, "She wants you to experience her daily pain, and now, so do I. This letter is only an indictment before two of your closest friends [it was carboned to Wolkoff and Ludwig Cserhat], but we can easily widen that audience." He signed his letter, "Farewell."

What Geist wanted back was the $118,000 he had paid to Gilbert. What Gilbert had to say to Geist was that, yes, he had lost money — so had Gilbert—in the recent market downturn. But overall Geist had not lost anything when taking into account earlier profits he had earned with Gilbert's advice. Indeed, there was a net gain. There had never been any kind of contingency or responsibility for Geist's losses in their agreement. Eddie therefore contended that he owed Geist nothing and told him — in terms much less delicate — to go away. Geist did not go away, however. Over the next several years, he wrote letters to, and frequently phoned, Gene Wolkoff demanding repayment. When those efforts failed, he brought an equally unsuccessful arbitration proceeding against Ludwig Cserhat (and his firm of Baird Patrick), Stuart Sosler (and his firm of Bear Stearns), and John Ligums (and his Massachusetts brokerage house of J. Edmund & Co.), all of whom Geist used for trades in connection with his advisory relationship with Gilbert.

The civil lawsuit, however, was the least of the problems that Kenneth Geist was going to cause his onetime biographical subject, friend, and financial adviser.

*I don't think Mr. Gilbert makes a particularly good
probationer, either because he won't or he can't, or a combination of the two, because he has within him an inherent
refusal or ability to pay sufficient attention to the court's orders
[hence] I'm not interested in extending his probation.*

JUDGE CHARLES HAIGHT
U. S. DISTRICT COURT, SOUTHERN DISTRICT OF NEW YORK, 1989

When Eddie Gilbert walked out of Allenwood just before Christmas in 1983, he was once again financially
strapped. But unlike when he left the Danbury federal
prison in 1969, he was not saddled with millions of dol-
lars of debt. He still had to start all over and again from the bottom. He
had little capital and a lot of ongoing liabilities: two alimonies, child support, the responsibility for his 83-year-old mother, legal bills...

Financial dealings with Kenneth Geist, now that the biography was a
dead issue, were troubling but constituted only a minor part of Eddie's
business life. He planned to return to the stock market, which had served
him so well before, trying as before to head the roller coaster back up the
track. After two months in the halfway house and estranged from his wife
Linda, he was officially released; and he moved into the elegant duplex
apartment in the Carlisle Hotel that his mother still owned and occupied.
Shortly thereafter, he leased a small office on Madison Avenue to carry on
his business dealings.

One of the most important events to happen during this time of his
life, however, had nothing to do with his business world. Yet it would
prove to be an asset of inestimable value to him in the years to come.

Good friends at the time, Alan and Sally Lubell, suggested to Eddie, now that his latest marriage to Linda was *de facto* over, that he should meet a young, unattached woman whom they knew. Her name was Gail Gore, although everybody called her Peaches. She was vibrant, very attractive— a former model—and exceptionally bright, they told him. Thirty-two years old and divorced, according to the Lubells, she owned the popular boutique called *Mabel's* on Madison Avenue at 79th Street. "My first, thought," Eddie later recalled, "was what interest could she possibly find in me; I was 61 years old, just out of prison, broke...." He politely declined the Lubells' suggestion.

The Lubells did not give up, however. They told Peaches about Eddie, and the speculation game went back and forth for a while until Eddie's curiosity got the best of him. They met through the window pane of *Mabel's*: Eddie had gone there clandestinely to get a look at the woman whom the Lubells described so glowingly and was peering through the window when she first saw him. Having had him described in detail by the Lubells, she thought the man outside—dressed in a lime-colored leisure suit—who left shortly after making eye contact was probably Eddie Gilbert. Strange, she thought.

And then he called her for a date, still thinking the likelihood of anything coming of it was remote. She accepted, and he took her to dinner at Le Club, the private establishment he had helped to launch some 20 years earlier but which had now drifted into the winter of its existence, a moribund relic of better, more prosperous times in his life. But they hit it off, to no one's greater surprise than the two of them. Peaches observed later, "It's amazing to me that Eddie and I could sustain a relationship because we're both so headstrong and so determined to have our own way. But for some peculiar reason, I guess we both just give in at the right time or something. I don't know what it is, just amazing, because we really are two difficult personalities." No one who knew them both would ever doubt that.

They were markedly different, not just in age. Financially Eddie was in the cellar, and Peaches had a suite on the ground floor. *Mabel's*, named for her cat which roamed the store with the same freedom and familiarity as the only slightly more famous cat that wandered the Algonquin Hotel lobby several miles across town, was an offbeat and thoroughly unique shop that specialized in animal-inspired clothing, designer furniture, jewelry, and other items that were, according to Peaches, "a menagerie really of things inspired by nature and whimsy." It was a financially successful enterprise and considered very special by its devoted clientele, which included chic New Yorkers, movie stars, European aristocrats, the rich, and the celebrated. Eddie, on the other hand, had been out of social touch, so to speak, with anyone other than his fellow inmates at the Allenwood federal prison over the last two years. But Eddie was used to having his own way, too, with women especially, who, with the exception of his previous wife Linda, were totally dependent on him. Peaches was dependent on no one, and the thought of such subordination was appalling to her. She had previously been married for five years to Jamie Gore, cousin of Al Gore, later U.S. Vice President and presidential candidate. Peaches lived comfortably in a town house she owned on 69th Street between Park and Madison; while Eddie was back home living with his mother.

For some reason, about as easily explainable as the quantum theory, they meshed. They continued to see each other, and soon their flagrant differences didn't seem so different, at least to them. Eddie's divorce from Linda was finalized in June 1985. A month later, he and Peaches were married in a small ceremony in a faux 18th-century Italian garden behind a restaurant in the New York theater district and then boarded the QE II for their European honeymoon.

What was most interesting about this turn of events in Eddie Gilbert's life was the fact that for the first time he would be with a woman who would have an impact on his life, who would be an influence and a motivation instead of an accessory, who would criticize him as much as she would champion him; and she would change his life forever.

As time passed and the numerous telephone calls and letters from Kenneth Geist to Gilbert and Gene Wolkoff received no satisfactory response — or no response at all — Geist embarked on another course. He threatened a civil law suit. And even more threatening to Gilbert's precarious freedom, Geist went to Eddie's parole officer, Michael Higgins, in November 1985 and reported that he had been "ripped off" by Gilbert to the tune of $1.4 million and that Gilbert's actions were in direct violation of his probation terms forbidding the brokering of stocks set by the court; hence his parole should be revoked and he should have to return to prison.

Gilbert had already informed Higgins of his now bitter relationship with Geist, however. Six months earlier, on April 2, 1985, Gilbert told the parole officer that Geist was making some charges, especially the one that

Eddie had violated the federal order of his five-year probation by *placing* stock orders for Geist with the brokerage firm of Bear Stearns. Gilbert told Higgins that such a charge was patently untrue. Because he had never placed orders, he therefore had never acted as Geist's agent. Gilbert had been compensated for financial advice given, he further told the parole officer; but, according to the written opinion rendered by attorney Gene Wolkoff, that did not violate the terms of his probation.

Geist lodged his complaint to Higgins and another parole officer, Joel Weber, at the Probation Department, who noted it but concluded that the allegations did not constitute grounds for a probation violation. That ended the matter, at least for the time being. Gilbert later went on record with Higgins in February 1986, when he was being released from his parole status, to tell the officer that Geist was continuing to make public allegations that Gilbert was violating the terms of his probation.

Nothing of any significance came of it until 1988 when Geist contacted Jeffrey Livingston, the Assistant U.S. Attorney who had prosecuted Gilbert in the Conrac trial. Although Livingston had left the U.S. Attorney's office in New York for private practice, Geist described in detail to him all the treacheries he attributed to Gilbert. And Livingston listened. Livingston then referred Geist to another attorney, Henry Korn, James Couri's earlier attorney and one of the two former assistant U.S. Attorneys mentioned in Livingston's March 18, 1981 letter, who, together with Henry Putzel, had contacted the U.S. Attorney's office about Couri's allegedly illegal Plazagal dealings. Korn agreed to represent Geist in his quest to recoup alleged losses attributable to Gilbert's advice.

After drawing up their case against Ludwig Cserhat, Stuart Sosler, John Ligums, and their respective brokerage firms, Geist's attorneys brought it to the National Association of Securities Dealers Arbitration Division in July 1988, by filing for a "demand for arbitration and statement of claims." According to Geist's petition, Gilbert "orchestrated with respondents Sosler, Cserhat, and Ligums the elaborate scheme... to defraud petitioner [Geist] and engaged in the racketeering activity...to deprive petitioner of a substantial inheritance and petitioner's equity."

One count of Geist's petition demanded an award from the respondents of "an amount equal to three times petitioner's compensatory damages of actual losses, commissions and margin interest paid, which is not less than $1,425,000, or $4,275,000 when trebled" plus $1 million in punitive damages; and for the other counts of the petition, "an amount in excess of $1,100,000 ... representing petitioner's losses; an amount in excess of $325,000, representing excessive commissions and margin interest..., an amount in excess of $1,000,000 as punitive damages because respondents' conduct in handling petitioner's discretionary accounts was willful, egregious, and so contrary to public policy."

The brokers responded to the petition with a detailed, formal computation of the results of Gilbert's investment advice to Geist. The computation laid out all the trades that Geist had made through the three brokerage houses, as well as the profits and the losses from them. It also detailed funds that Geist had withdrawn from the accounts during 1983 and 1984. The bottom line of these calculations was that Geist had not lost any money at all and, in fact, had realized a $270,000 profit.

The difference of opinion between Geist and the brokers was in how one views the calculation of loss. If, for example, an investor starts out with a portfolio worth $1 million, watches its value increase to $2 million, but later sees it decrease to $1,200,000, has that person lost $800,000 or made $200,000? Geist's accounts indeed had lost a substantital amount of money, but the loss he claimed was from the highs he had achieved through Gilbert's tutelage. According to the brokers, Geist had in fact made a profit above the amount initially invested; according to Geist, he had simply lost a large amount from Gilbert's poor advice and the connivances of the three brokers.

The NASD arbitrators listened to both sides and without lengthy deliberation ruled in the brokers' favor, dismissing Geist's petition.

Unfortunately for Gilbert, that was not the end of it. With Korn still representing him, Geist took his case to the U.S. Attorney's office in New York, claiming that Gilbert had violated the terms of his probation by taking money for his investment consultation and advice. Assistant U.S. Attorney Bruce Baird listened. Gilbert and parole officer Higgins were summoned for questioning. Baird concluded that he disagreed with Higgins's judgment three years earlier that there had been insufficient evidence of a probation violation. Baird also concluded that the U.S. Attorney's office would investigate the Geist allegations and consider initiating probation-violation proceedings against Gilbert.

This was an extremely serious matter. If Gilbert were to be found in willful violation of the probation terms set by Judge Haight in the 1981 sentencing, he could go back to prison for *five* years, two and a half times his original sentence, and by 1988 Gilbert was 65 years old.

No one knew the seriousness of the matter more than Gilbert himself. So he approached Jed Rakoff, a prominent New York attorney especially known for litigating federal matters. Rakoff attended the first hearing with Gilbert but, due to other commitments, said he would not have the time to represent him satisfactorily. Rakoff recommended Douglas Eaton, another highly respected lawyer with extensive federal litigation experience, a former U.S. Attorney who would later be appointed a U.S. Magistrate for the Southern District of New York. Rakoff himself, incidentally, would later become a U.S. District Court judge in the same Southern District of New York.

At about the same time, another factor was introduced into the situation. The U.S. Attorney's office was informed that Gilbert had hired a former fellow prisoner in violation of the court's order, which prohibited associating with other convicted felons while on probation. Hy Gordon had served time at Allenwood with Eddie. A part owner of the notorious New York night club, Plato's Retreat, Gordon had been convicted of federal income tax evasion and was on parole from Allenwood in 1986. He had been unsuccessful in attempts to find employment, so he had gone to Gilbert. He needed to earn a living, especially because he had to pay his deaf son's law school tuition.

Gilbert had been introduced by his friend of long standing, Herb Papock, to a business owned by two young French friends of Papock's, known as Historic Newspaper Archives, based in Rahway, New Jersey. Papock, along with another investor, Peter Heydon of Ann Arbor, Michigan, who was also a good friend of Eddie's, had some interest in acquiring the firm if the deal was right.

Heydon and Gilbert had met one July evening in 1985 while dining with their wives at the Connaught Hotel in London where Eddie and his new wife were honeymooning. Peaches recognized Heydon's wife Rita as one of her customers at Mabel's and so went over to speak with her. They introduced their husbands, and this marked the beginning of an extremely close friendship and business association between Gilbert and Heydon that would carry into the 21st century, Peter coming to be known as Eddie's "Jiminy Cricket," always there on Eddie's shoulder to help protect Eddie from himself.

The Historic Newspaper Archives became one of the first solid acquisitons Eddie Gilbert made after getting out of Allenwood. It was a company that had collected more than 4 million old newspapers and then resold them in attractive packaging. The sales promotion was this: Give someone for his or her birthday (anniversary, etc.) an original newspaper published by the *New York Times* or the *Chicago Tribune* or any of the more than 100 other newspapers from throughout the United States that had been inventoried (there were even a few foreign newspapers like the *London Times* and the *Montreal Daily Star*) from the very day commemorated.

Papock, a real estate developer, had thought about acquiring the company for himself and accordingly asked Eddie to look at the business and give him his valued opinion. Historic Newspapers sales had begun to flatten out — its annual sales were about $700,000 in 1984 — but Gilbert, after studying it, thought there might be some real potential there, given better management and merchandising. Papock's interest, for some reason or other faded, but Eddie's interest was now piqued; and so he discussed it with Peter Heydon. Heydon was, among other things, a member of the board of directors of the prestigious publishing firm of Farrar, Strauss and Giroux in New York and an English professor at the University of Michigan, and therefore had a reverence for the written word. He came to share Gilbert's enthusiasm, and the two decided to buy the company themselves.

Heydon agreed to serve as president of Historic Newspaper Archives in 1986, but like Gilbert was looking for someone to manage the firm's operations in New Jersey. Eddie recommended Hy Gordon, and after an impressive interview, Heydon hired him. But Gilbert's parole officer, Michael Higgins, got wind of the situation in 1988 when Gordon's parole officer offhandedly mentioned to Higgins that his parolee, Gordon, had finally landed a job with a company named Historic Newspaper Archives. Gordon's parole officer had been unaware that Gilbert was one of Historic's owners; but Higgins of course had only a short while before learned that Eddie was trying to acquire the company. He cautioned Gilbert, telling him that he could not permit Eddie to hire Hy. Gilbert ignored him because Heydon, as the company's president, had really done the hiring. And besides, "The man needed a job desperately," Eddie later explained. "We weren't into anything remotely illegal. It was a great opportunity for him. Why should I deny him that? It was a dumb rule to begin with." Hy

Gordon continued to manage Historic Newspaper Archives while the U.S. Attorney's office descended on Eddie Gilbert.

After his release from Allenwood, Eddie Gilbert entered into what is best described as a "deal-making" phase of his life. Although playing the stock market remained his most lucrative occupation, he began putting together a number of "deals" of varying sizes and values. One was for the purchase and remortgage of a building in mid-Manhattan, the income from which helped him get by day to day. Another was his involvement with an old associate, Chick Fisdell, in Fisdell's father's hardware business. Not all ventures were successful; some were in fact dismal failures. One example: He invested heavily in a New Jersey high-tech firm called "Fifth Dimension," which, after years of nurturing by Gilbert and many of his friends who were also investors, floated into bankruptcy on a wave of cancelled government contracts. Eddie was left holding the largest number of valueless shares outstanding as well as the real estate and headquarters building where the company operated in Trenton. Eddie had taken the real estate as collateral to secure a loan necessitated by an earlier company cash shortfall.

Eddie was clawing his way back up the roller-coaster tracks, and it was a steep climb. Along the way, he had to do business with many people he did not like — whose business practices were often at odds with his own and whose business knowledge was far less sophisticated than his — and some of whom would come not to like him either. He was a deal-maker, and that was how he planned to get himself back to the top. His biggest ally during this time of resurgence was his new wife Peaches. Peter Heydon remembers this extraordinarily difficult time in Eddie's life, "She kept him in focus. Always there to motivate, to get Eddie to see the bad parts or the bad people in a deal. She had an uncanny sense of people. She could see through the phonies immediately; she could see those who were trying to take advantage of Eddie. She got involved [something totally alien in Gilbert's relationships with his three former wives]. You see, she had great faith in Eddie, that he *could* come back. They were really a partnership through all of this, and that is just what Eddie needed."

Another opportunity presented itself shortly after the Historic Newspaper deal, but it also presented a somewhat larger risk; perhaps thinking back to the days in the late 1940s when he had insinuated himself into the world of Broadway as a co-producer of *How Long Till Summer* and *Peter*

*Pan*, Eddie was intrigued. The historic Beacon Theater on the upper west side of Manhattan stood empty in 1986, a relic of the movie palace era that had thrived in the middle years of the 20th century. Once one of the grandest movie theaters in New York (with 3,000 seats, it was the next-largest theatrical venue in New York after Radio City Music Hall), it had deteriorated to a second-run movie house in the late 1960s; by the mid 1970s it had been converted to a concert hall; and in 1983, after the close of New York's Palladium, to a venue specializing over the next two years in rock concerts and prize-fight simulcasts. But now its doors were closed.

How the deal developed is illustrative of how the man Eddie Gilbert thought. His long-time friend Olivier Coquelin, the one-time Stillwell's Raider who later had been the major-domo at Eddie's villas on the Riviera in the late 1950s and early 60s (and still later ran Le Club for him in New York), was in trouble in 1985. He owned a fashionable hotel in Haiti, the *Habitation le Clerc* (in which Gilbert, incidentally, had a stake), but it was a property he was about to lose because his drinking had become a major problem. Olivier called Eddie in New York and related his situation. Eddie was forever grateful and loyal to Olivier—never forgetting the French-man's visits to him in Brazil and later in prison and his offer of financial help during those difficult times—so he told him to get on a plane for New York. The two met with Gilbert'a attorney Gene Wolkoff at a restaurant in the South Street Seaport on Manhattan's lower east side. Eddie remembers that, "He was in bad shape, had the shakes...; he was broke, I don't think he had any idea what he could do next, where he was going." After talking for a while, Gilbert said, "All right, Olivier, tell me: What do you think you do best?" Coquelin thought briefly and said he would like to run a club again or maybe a discotheque. Discotheques had been popular for some time, a number of them having thrived in New York. Olivier, in fact, had previously run and was part-owner of Hippopotamus, a quite popular New York discotheque. So Eddie told him to look around the city, see what he could locate. "Maybe I'll get some people, and we'll put together a deal. We'll open one, and you can run it." It was like the Eddie of old, telling his college chum Dick Winston to find a decent play, and he would produce it.

Coquelin spent the next few weeks looking around Manhattan. What he found was the boarded-up Beacon Theater on Broadway at 74th Street, and then he brought Gilbert to look at it. Eddie had misgivings, "but I wanted to do something for Olivier, I wanted to help him get back on his feet. He was such a loyal friend to me. He came down on his own to Brazil when I had my troubles back in 1962, brought money with him for me." And Eddie Gilbert never forgot a loyal friend. Looking at it for its business potential, as he always did, Eddie also thought it might not be such a bad idea. Studio 54, which Coquelin said he hoped to use for his model, had become a New York institution by 1985 and a veritable cash machine. Eddie talked to a few people. Given the general popularity of discos, he thought they might just make a go of it. He enticed several investors to buy into the deal with him, including his longtime friend Jerry Stern, his recent friend Peter Heydon, and his lawyer Gene Wolkoff. Other investment money came from Chick Fisdell and Rudy Slucker, who was an officer of Fisdell's hardware business that Eddie became involved with after leaving the halfway house (Eddie shared office space with Fisdell on Madison Avenue at the time), and Bob Peltz whose family owned a large food-supply and warehousing business. The investment partnership signed a ten-year lease and moved toward converting the Beacon into a 1980s discotheque.

But the conversion to a discotheque never happened. Andy Feltz, who had been Beacon's ticket manager before it closed and was later hired by Eddie to be manager of the Beacon (a job he has retained since 1987), remembers: "There were a lot of problems. You see the Beacon had landmark status in New York [and its interior is listed in the Department of the Interior National Register of Historic Places in Washington, D.C.]. The community was not happy with the idea of a disco; there were a lot of obstacles thrown up... there were environmental impact studies, various stalling tactics." It was an expensive proposition to hire preservation architects and to renovate the theater given the limitations posed by the theater's landmark status; but what the investment group underestimated was the resolve of the residents and the merchants in the neighborhood of Broadway and 74th Street. They organized, raised money on their own from the neighborhood, and instituted a lawsuit to prevent the Beacon's reopening as a disco. As the months went by, Eddie and his partners saw their invested funds steadily draining away.

By November 1986, the money had run out. The group had put about $1.5 million into the project by that time—lease payments, architectural services, permit fees, attorney costs, etc. Eddie's enthusiasm was waning and no one else wanted to put any more money into the project. For protection, the syndicate filed for Chapter 11 bankruptcy — by this time they owed a lot of money to architect Charles Platt for his work to design "non-irreversible" changes to the interior of the theater, to the lessor, and various utilities and other service providers. Eddie and his investors were not yet ready to bail out of the project, but they needed the court's protection from their creditors if they were to have any chance of seeing the Beacon Theater project through.

With Eddie's concurrence (because he had talked with promoter Ron Delsener about the prospects), Feltz went to Olivier Coquelin and suggested that they reopen the Beacon for a few rock concerts, at least until building permits for the disco operation were issued. Because of the neighborhood lawsuit, these permits were not imminent. Olivier reluctantly — his focus was still completely on his planned discotheque — took the idea to Eddie and the three sat down to discuss it. Feltz was convincing. So Eddie told him to go ahead and see what he could do. The Beacon reopened in February 1987, featuring a concert by the British rock band "The Kinks." Feltz signed up a few more dates, even though the concerts were still considered an interim action. Efforts to secure building permits for the disco, however, were going nowhere. The lawsuit had yet to be heard, and time was running out as far as the investors were concerned.

In the spring of 1987, the investors gathered in Eddie's New York office for a crucial meeting. Gilbert was fed up now; he was thinking about taking the step to a Chapter 7 bankruptcy filing and getting out of the Beacon altogether. Most of the others seemed to be leaning that way as well. But Peter Heydon did not agree. He argued that some money was coming in from concert dates, and perhaps more could be done that way. He thought they had not given it enough of a chance. Heydon felt pretty sure they were on the verge of turning it around as a theater venue. He suggested that they give it three more months. There was not a lot of enthusiasm for the idea. Operating expenses were running at about $40,000 a month; so Heydon said, "Look, I'll back the first month myself. I'll write a check for $40,000, if the rest of you will pick up the other two months." After a pause, Jerry Stern said, "I'll take part of a month." Then some others said they would participate. Eddie, overcoming some reservation, said he might later on. They would give it another three months.

By the end of those three months, the Beacon Theater was doing much better. Growth was steady, income was coming in, and six months after their crucial New York meeting, the Beacon Theater came out of bankruptcy. With the discotheque no longer a consideration, Olivier Coquelin told Eddie he wanted out, and Gilbert bought out the share he had given him at the outset. Coquelin, with no other prospects, left New York and returned home to France where he died in Paris a few years later.

For the Beacon, perhaps the most dramatic turning point occurred in January 1988. Because of its historic interior, the theater was taken over for the party after the Broadway premiere of Andrew Lloyd Webber's *Phantom of the Opera*. More than 2,000 guests were in attendance at the Beacon that night along with scores of journalists and other members of the media. The Beacon was written about in every newspaper the next day—the front page of the *New York Post*—and talked about on every television news and entertainment show.

During the 1990s, because of its seating capacity of nearly 3,000, the Beacon became recognized as a highly regarded venue in New York for promoters' presentations, like Rockefeller Center's Radio City Music Hall, but much smaller. During the decade, it hosted smaller performances by many notable rock stars of the age: Bruce Springsteen, James Taylor, the Allman Brothers, among others. Comedian George Carlin's live specials for HBO are performed at the Beacon; UNICEF took it over for a benefit; magazines such as *Sports Illustrated* and *Gentleman's Quarterly* occasionally leased it for their Sportsman and Man of the Year galas. By the early part of the new century, the Beacon enjoyed considerable public appreciation for a former movie palace, and was an integral part of its neighborhood again. It had, without question, also become a notable part, albeit small, of the larger New York entertainment scene.

As it ironically turned out, it was provident that the community around the Beacon Theater rose up to prevent its conversion to a discotheque— a nightlife phenomenon that soon went out of vogue. In turn, the revival of the Beacon as a concert hall proved to be the first successful deal of Eddie Gilbert's new life after he left Allenwood prison and before he entered the real estate business.

For Eddie Gilbert, however, life had not just become one of ovations and encores. There was still the serious matter of his alleged probation violations. And so he returned to court, in a critical battle to keep him a free man.

With two counts in hand and an evidentiary hearing scheduled just days before his parole was to have ended, the U.S. Attorney's office initiated proceedings against Gilbert for violating two conditions of his court-ordered probation. In the summer of 1989, his case was brought before Judge Charles Haight, the same judge who had presided at Gilbert's Conrac trial. Arguing the case for the government was Assistant U.S. Attorney Reid Figel. The charges against Gilbert were—

The probationer violated the special condition barring him from acting as a broker or paid representative in securities trading.

The probationer failed to follow a specific instruction of the Probation Officer relating to employment of a convicted felon.

The government's case in the first count was predicated on the charges brought by Geist. Attorney Douglas Eaton's refutation centered on several facts. Principal among them was that Gilbert never acted as a broker, agent, or representative of Geist's, but had served only as an adviser and had been compensated only for that role in Geist's investments. Additionally, Eaton argued that Gilbert had not acted in bad faith by receiving compensation, having relied on the written opinion of his attorney (an officer of the court); nor had he acted in bad faith to his probation officer because he had concealed nothing from Higgins about the Geist situation. In regard to the second count, relating to Historic's hiring of Hy Gordon, defense counsel Eaton asked that it be considered *after* resolution of the first count and then recommending that it be sent back to Parole Officer Higgins for reconsideration thereafter.

Before Judge Haight this time, Gilbert had counsel with whom he felt comfortable; but he was still justifiably worried. The thought of going back to prison at this time in his life—newly married, his business life and financial status beginning to improve again—was devastating and frightening.

Judge Haight rendered his decision on December 21, 1989. With regard to the first count, that Gilbert had violated his probation by his investment association with Geist, the judge said that in reaching his ruling he was most concerned with Gilbert's not having revealed to his parole officer the arrangement with Geist when officer Higgins had asked him about his employment plans while Gilbert was still at the halfway house following release from Allenwood, when he was already well into his role as Geist's financial adviser. Nor had he shared with his parole officer the fact that he had sought and received his attorney's written opinion as to the legality of his advising Geist. Judge Haight wrote in his Memorandum Opinion, "[Gilbert] is intelligent, shrewd, and powerfully motivated by self-preservation. His minimal and misleading disclosures to Higgins about Geist speak volumes on the key issue of his mental state [reference to Gilbert's acting in good faith]. Gilbert knew that the Geist relationship, past and anticipated, and the financial benefits to Gilbert that relationship generated, violated the special probation. At the the very least, Gilbert did not wish to be told they did by his probation officer.... This is not the profile of a probationer seeking in good faith to comply with the terms of his probation.... Had Gilbert been motivated by that good faith, his primary concern would have been to obtain his probation officer's approval of any conduct that might conceivably run afoul of the special condition."

In essence, Judge Haight based his ruling as to the first count not so much on the matter of Eddie's being compensated for financial advice (the charge that he had acted as Geist's agent and placed his orders for him had been dismissed by this time), but on his failure to disclose the complete situation to his probation officer so that Higgins could make a formal ruling. "I conclude," the judge wrote, "that the government has sustained its burden of proof on the issue of Gilbert's mental state by a preponderance of the credible evidence."

Gilbert did not fare well on the other count either, although he had, in fact, admitted his guilt in that matter. Judge Haight chose not to remand the count back to the probation officer, as Douglas Eaton had requested. Judge Haight explained, "Counsel's premise fails, since I convict Gilbert on the first charge, but I would not have adopted the suggestion in any event. Gilbert acknowledges his guilt on the second charge. Higgins told Gilbert not to employ Gordon. Gilbert deliberately disregarded that order. It is for the court, not the Probation Department, to weigh the gravity of that offense. I will perform that function at the time of sentencing...."

In summation: "The court convicts the defendant on both specifications of probation violation. A new pre-sentence report must be prepared. Sentence will be passed on March 8, 1990."

The sentencing was postponed once and reset for April 4. Eddie Gilbert was a nervous wreck for three and a half months. As damning as

Judge Haight sounded in ruling on the case, he seemed almost compassionate when he spoke from the bench at the sentencing hearing. Before that, however, he heard from both defense counsel Eaton and prosecutor Reid Figel.

Eaton reminded the court that Gilbert had not committed a crime since 1975, when he was convicted in the Conrac case (probation violations not being crimes in themselves). "For sentencing purposes," said Eaton, "it is relevant to note that Geist profited from Gilbert's advice. At one point, his profits were enormous. But even after he lost back most of those profits, Mr. Geist had a net profit of $270,000, after paying all the commissions and all the margin interest to the brokerage firms and after paying the fees to Mr. Gilbert." In regard to the second count, Eaton had this to say: "In 1986 Hy Gordon was on parole, and he could not find a job. He was struggling to pay the law school tuition of his handicapped son. Mr. Gilbert and Mr. Peter Heydon were in the process of acquiring Historic Newspaper Archives.... Mr. Gilbert recommended [the hiring of] Hy Gordon. Mr. Gilbert's act was contrary to the directions of officer Higgins. And Mr. Gilbert apologized on the witness stand. But here again there are mitigating facts. The job was an excellent rehabilitation program for Hy Gordon. And it enabled him to put his son through law school. Hy Gordon's parole officers discovered the facts in the summer of 1988. And yet they allowed Hy Gordon to keep the job, they brought no charges against Hy Gordon, and on January 23 of this year, they released Hy Gordon from parole."

In view of all these mitigating factors, Eaton asked the court to limit sentencing to a new term of probation, "a period of two years and eight months [which] would keep Mr. Gilbert under supervision until December 1992 when he will be 70 years old."

Assistant U.S. Attorney Figel did not agree. "There are two reasons," he told the court, "why the government feels that a term of incarceration is appropriate. The first is, quite simply, it's hard to imagine a more flagrant violation of the court's order, a defendant who's been given wide berth to the securities accounts of others to essentially act as an investment adviser for pay from a federal prison. These activities began before Mr. Gilbert ever surrendered; they commenced, according to the evidence, a month after he was sentenced. Mr. Gilbert was given ample warning... [that] further activities in the securities market or in the accounts of others would be dealt with harshly. And on two separate occasions he has disregarded those admonitions." And that was all Mr. Figel had to say at the sentencing hearing.

In his pre-sentencing remarks, Judge Haight had addressed the subject of restitution, sought for Geist by attorney Henry Korn (in the amount of $2,467,261) and introduced by the prosecution during the probation violation proceedings, Judge Haight said he would offer no ruling on the matter of restitution to Geist. "It would be entirely wrong for me to make an order of restitution in any amount in Mr. Geist's favor. And I decline to undertake that particular task. And so there will be no order of restitution." Judge Haight suggested that Geist seek remedy in civil court if he still thought it was worth pursuing, but from the way the judge reasoned in his remarks, Geist's prospects for winning such a case seemed quite remote indeed. Perhaps that is the reason why Geist sought restitution from the brokers only, and not from Gilbert.

Then, his sentencing remarks: "There is an element of mitigation in the Gordon situation, I would be wrong to deny that. And as far as the investment advice is concerned, it is the only incident of giving investment advice to others in this period of time with which I'm concerned, that I am aware of, or that has been suggested in the government's evidence. And I think it is worthwhile reflecting on the fact that Mr. Gilbert did not seek out Mr. Geist; Mr. Geist sought out Mr. Gilbert.... If forces had not combined to place Mr. Geist in Mr. Gilbert's path, I think it unlikely that these proceedings would have taken place. That is not to excuse Mr. Gilbert's giving of investment advice and receiving compensation from Mr. Geist. But it is to say that, somewhat in contrast to the crimes that brought Mr. Gilbert here before, we are dealing with an isolated incident. And there is, as I have said, no indication that Mr. Gilbert, in violation of the terms and conditions, was attempting to give investment advice to anyone else.

"Were I presented in this case with a violation of the special terms and conditions, involving a retail business of Mr. Gilbert's, giving investment advice, seeking to profit from it, to a number of people, I would take a more serious view of the case than I do."

But contrary to defense attorney Eaton's preference, Judge Haight disagreed with the suggestion of extended probation: "I don't think Mr. Gilbert makes a particularly good probationer, either because he won't or he can't, or a combination of the two, because he has within him an inherent refusal, or inability to pay sufficient attention to the court's orders [hence] I'm not interested in extending his probation."

In announcing sentence, after all this, he drew a collective sigh of relief from those solemnly and nervously assembled at the defense table. "I am going to require him to serve six months of consecutive weekends in a halfway house or a community treatment center. The weekends beginning on Friday at six and terminating Sunday at six."

Douglas Eaton, Gene Wolkoff, and most of all, Eddie Gilbert, viewed this as a strong but single slap on the wrist, accompanied by a smart sting perhaps, but nothing so punitive as the prison time Eddie could have received: 26 weekends in a Brooklyn halfway house with no extension of his probationary period, compared to five years (four if his behavior were good) in a federal penitentiary. Eddie and his friends had good cause to celebrate.

## SEVENTEEN

*Look, I've known Ed umpteen years... he's one*
*of the handful of people in the world that I would do*
*business with on a handshake.*

FRED KOLBER, PARTNER, BGK REALTY, 1998

T he biggest deal that Eddie Gilbert would ever put together in his
life was just beginning to take shape as he was fighting to stay
out of jail. By 1987, Eddie was already involved in several successful ventures: Historic Newspaper Archives was beginning
to experience increased sales under Hy Gordon's management; the Beacon
Theater was becoming recognized as a good venue for productions and promotions, thereby permitting the theater to come out of bankruptcy; and
Eddie was making money, as usual, on the stock market. Still, he was looking for something grander. And he found it at a backgammon game.

Eddie had already had some successes in real estate investments before
that afternoon in late 1987 when he sat down at a table at the Park 65
backgammon club (the name derived from its location in a hotel at 65th
and Park Avenue) with Fred Kolber, a casual acquaintance and a frequent
backgammon competitor. Kolber, in his late 40s, had been an options
trader on Wall Street and later formed the partnership bearing his name,
which he established to manage money in the equity and derivative markets. By the late 1980s, through his company, Kolber had developed a
hedge fund managing more than $300 million in wealthy clients' invest-
ments. But by the late 1980s he had grown tired of trading on the options
market, in particular because it had become computerized. Because of his
own successful investments on Wall Street and elsewhere, he had contemplated getting out of his business altogether. Just about that time, he
sat down with Gilbert for a game of backgammon at Park 65.

The two had known each other for about ten years, but had had no business association nor any social contact besides their mutual interest in a little gambling at the backgammon table. They had one thing in common, however. Both had attended Cornell earlier in their lives, and neither had graduated. Seventeen years younger than Gilbert, Kolber was born in Brooklyn and raised on Long Island. He went to Cornell to study physics but dropped out after three years. His first job on Wall Street in 1961 was with the firm Goodbody and Company (which was later acquired by Merrill Lynch). He remained a broker, moving from company to company, but became ambitious to trade for himself. So in 1968, Kolber and a few other brokers began their own brokerage house, trading on the American Stock Exchange and then later on the New York Stock Exchange. By the early 1970s, the company was thriving and was then acquired by a large California investment house, National General Corporation. But Fred Kolber was not happy working with the people from California, so when his employment contract expired, he left and bought a seat for himself on the American Stock Exchange. "After a few years of trading on my own there," he remembers, "the options thing started. It was a whole new business, started in Chicago and also started on the American Stock Exchange. With my background in trading, it was a natural. And in those early days of options trading, it was extremely rare to find people who knew what they were doing in it, it was so new to everybody, but a few of us kind of figured it out." Figured it out so well, in fact, that Kolber's enormous success in the burgeoning options market soon made him a wealthy man.

Kolber likes to tell a story about his evolving relationship with Eddie Gilbert. About two years after they had begun investing in real estate together, both had got into predicaments of their own. "It was 1989," Kolber recalls. "I was having some health problems, and I was going in for a liver transplant. Eddie, he was having some legal problems [the hearing for probation violations] and was going on trial again. We were talking about it one day, and I said, 'Here we are, two nice guys. Me, I may be dead. You, you may be in prison. What happened to us?'

"Eddie goes, 'Yeah, what's happened to us?'"

The gloom of that conversation did not last, however. After several setbacks, Kolber recovered from his transplant, and Gilbert did not have to go back to prison. "The other thing about that, I remember so well," Kolber says, "is the days I spent in the hospital waiting for a liver. I had no choice,

I had to stay there, and I complained about the hospital food. From that time on, Eddie [and Peaches] came up around dinner time each night bringing meals from Le Cirque or from one of the great New York steak houses; I was eating like a king, never had to have a hospital dinner after that."

Back in 1987, at the backgammon table, however: "We were just talking that day," Kolber remembers. "and I said, 'Eddie, real estate is cheap. I know from Wall Street what things go for. This is a fantastic opportunity to buy real estate." Gilbert said he had come to the same conclusion. "I saw all kinds of opportunities," Eddie later recalled. "Commercial real estate had been depressed for some time, and the prices were ridiculous. It was like buying dollar bills for fifty cents apiece." They both decided to take advantage of it, forming an informal partnership that day at Park 65.

With the collapse of the savings and loan industry in the mid-1980s, real property values had sharply declined. Because of over-building and speculation in real estate, building occupancy rates were down 25 percent by 1990. Bank foreclosures were commonplace, and properties became available for 40 to 60 percent of what it would cost just to replace those properties. "Fire-sale prices," is the way Eddie Gilbert described it; "One hundred million dollar properties were going for $30 million, a $10 million dollar building could be had for $2 or $3 million." No one was buying, so sellers (banks and insurance companies particularly) were begging investors to take nonperforming properties off their hands.

As Fred Kolber remembers, "At this time, everything was for sale, so finding properties was not hard. There were no buyers. Everyone was a seller. All the institutions [banks, insurance companies, large brokerage houses] were loaded with real estate they had taken back. So much of the property had been repossessed. And it was not in their interest to keep the property. It was not their business [to run real estate investments], so they were looking to sell. Many times they would even offer to lend the money to buy the property they were holding. They'd say, 'Put up 25 percent, and we'll lend you the rest to buy it. Put very simply, the institutions would much rather have had money than real estate. And we were there just at the right time." Part of the reason for the institutions' desire to sell was that a "nonperforming" real estate asset on their books could not be recorded as an asset with any value at all if it was "nonperforming."

The partnership formed between Eddie and Fred Kolber across the backgammon table that day in 1987 led to a real friendship as well. Both were recently remarried, and as they began in earnest to launch their joint venture, they occasionally had dinner together with their wives who seemed to get along together pretty well. "So we began to socialize quite a bit together in New York," Fred Kolber remembers. "And then we traveled together, to Europe, down to St. Barts, and after that we just became pretty good friends."

For their real estate investments, they first thought about hiring someone knowlegeable and experienced in the real estate business—there was an oversupply of them, too, now out of work owing to the devastated market—to seek out optimal properties they might acquire. But Eddie had another idea. For some years Peaches and Eddie had been frequent visitors to Santa Fe, New Mexico (a city Peaches had a special affinity for because of its authentic Southwest art as well as its sophistication), and had vacationed there with friends and family several times a year. Later on, frustrated by the New York residential market, Peaches wanted to make their special home there. Eddie also noted that some very good real estate deals were available in Santa Fe and Albuquerque and some of the surrounding areas. He told Fred Kolber, "I'll do it. I'll find us a property, and we'll get this thing started."

"At the time, I had no idea of the extent of Eddie's talent," Kolber says. "But Eddie was good at doing deals. He always knew what he was doing. So I said, okay, fine. At the time I was thinking of this thing as a little diversion, just something to invest in that was different."

The first deal they made was to buy an R-V park in Santa Fe, a small investment to be sure. But Eddie's philosophy, which had served him well in the years before and would also in the years to come, was to build slowly, carefully, steadily, one property at a time—but crucially to *build*. "After the recreation vehicle park we did a number of other small deals, all things Eddie had found and investigated out there," Kolber explains. "We bought a couple of mini-warehouse centers… storage facilities in Albuquerque. We bought a Taco Bell [in Espanola, New Mexico, just northwest of Santa Fe]—we didn't operate it, just owned the real estate and leased it to the operator—we bought a small shopping center [a 41,201 square-foot strip mall] in Hobbs [New Mexico]."

It was a start. But soon both men had bigger things in mind.

At the same time, Peaches Gilbert was entertaining a grand idea in her own mind. For many years she had loved Santa Fe, the quaint, historic city situated at the foot of the southern extremity of the Sangre de Cristo mountains (Santa Fe lies about 7,000 feet above sea level). New Mexico's capital city, with its 60,000 residents, many of whom lived in adobe haciendas, has a rich heritage—Spanish explorations and settlement, Southwest Indian culture, the terminus of the Santa Fe Trail—but it seemed vibrant and alive to Peaches, blending history with modern cultural diversity and sophistication and interesting people from the West Coast and New York. Santa Fe is also home to one of the most important art colonies in America: The strand of galleries that winds its way up Canyon Road and streets radiating out from the historic town square draw dealers and collectors from all over the world. Fine local silversmiths and ceramic craftsmen display their unique works and offer them for sale in the town's plaza. With warm summers and snowy winters; narrow, winding streets from another age; a spectacular variety of desert and greenery; and a Southwest character all its own, Santa Fe very much appealed to Peaches; it also seemed a perfect place as a second home for *Mabel's*.

And Eddie, ever the New Yorker, suggested in 1988 that maybe they ought to buy a summer home in Santa Fe. Peaches didn't want "a summer home"; if they were to buy a house there it should be for more than just a few weeks in the summer. Over many trips there, they spent a good amount of time looking around, but found nothing. "Peaches is very particular," Eddie says. "She's a perfectionist. What can I tell you, there wasn't anything on the market that she liked enough to buy."

But when Eddie was again in Santa Fe a year later, looking at a prospective real estate venture, he remembers: "I knew she wanted something in Santa Fe, and I was determined to get it for her. I wasn't thinking of settling there. But I wanted to do it for her. So, I looked around myself, and I found this nice place. It looked like what she had been saying she wanted. It was just off Canyon Road, good location, but it needed a little work. So I called her up and said I found the place.

"She said, 'If you like it, it's got to be bad.' She thinks I have no taste."

When he tells that story, Eddie just laughs. Appearances are not all that important to him. The Eddie Gilbert of the post-Allenwood days is a dealmaker to be sure; it's the art of the deal with all its nuances that captures his imagination. On a personal level, he is less absorbed. What clothes he wears, Peaches selects; whether he shaves has little significance to him; what kind of car he drives or is driven in (the man who used to be chauffered around New York in his own Rolls Royce now leaves it to Peaches to do most of the driving) is of little consequence to him.

Peaches had a slightly different take, however. Although understanding Eddie's priorities, she has some of her own as well. She helps him out in the things he doesn't care about. She buys his clothes, she lays them out in the morning or before they go out at night; she makes sure he shaves; she doesn't just look after him, she guides him with an unquestioned hand. And Eddie is fine with it. His three previous wives would not recognize the Eddie Gilbert that emerged in the 1990s. They never cared in that way.

So Eddie did not buy the house then; but some months later when they returned together to Santa Fe, Eddie took Peaches to the house, which was still on the market. It was not as bad as she imagined, she remembers; at least she thought she could, with some work on the rooms and the gardens, make it into the kind of elegant residence she had envisioned for their Santa Fe home. She said she would agree to buying and rehabilitating it *if* Eddie would commit to their spending one week of each month there. Eddie agreed.

Meanwhile, Eddie and Fred Kolber continued to broaden the real estate holdings in their partnership. Another investor named Richard Beatty joined them around this time. In the late 1980s, he was the executive vice president of Ticketron in New York and had been introduced to Eddie by Hy Gordon. Hy's wife Rita worked at the Beacon and knew about Beatty's handling of the theater's Ticketron sales contract. Beatty told Gilbert that he had some independent money that he wanted to invest; Eddie told him what he and Fred Kolber were presently doing and what great opportunities he anticipated in commercial real estate. Gilbert and Kolber welcomed him into the next several deals they were considering. Beatty had earlier bought an interest in Historic Newspaper Archives when offered that business opportunity by Gilbert and Peter Heydon.

The Gilberts' one-week-a-month schedule in Santa Fe soon turned into two weeks a month, and by 1989 they had moved there permanently. They bought a building at the foot of Canyon Road, and Peaches soon opened a *Mabel's* there. Eddie, on the other hand, was working 14-hour days, continuing to trade on Wall Street, talking daily with Beacon Theater manager Andy Feltz about bookings, and laying the strategy for developing the real estate investment business that was soon to become a substantial and lucrative enterprise.

The biggest problem facing the partnership was not in locating an under-performing but good property; it was in securing the necessary mortgaging. Eddie Gilbert had twice been to prison; not surprisingly many bankers, insurance companies, and other lenders were put off when this was revealed in disclosure documents.

One thing Gilbert did have going for himself, however, was his salesmanship. The skill that he had developed during the Empire Millwork days of the early 1950s he now called upon again. Another: he was a consummate deal-maker. For Eddie, it was all just part of the challenge. "He loves every part of making a deal," Fred Kolber later explained. "Selling it, bringing it off; it's sport to him, he thrives on it. But it was difficult. When we were out looking for money and Eddie's name came up, some institutions just passed. J. P. Morgan, they didn't want our account, and I'd been banking there for a long time. I said to the bank officers, 'Look, it's a new company. One of the partners has had some problems in the past, sure, and is sort of well known for them, but we're disclosing that to you.... They just looked at me and said, 'We'd rather not have the account.'" What did help the partnership in other banking relationships, however, was Kolber's spotless name and reputation, which got the institutions at least to listen to the proposed deals and what kind of banking commitment the partnership sought. And Eddie enjoyed certain connections also.

The early investments in their real estate partnerships were funded by Gilbert, Kolber, their families, and friends. Whenever money from banks was needed, the institutions frequently asked for the partners' "personal guarantees." At about this time, Fred Kolber's protegé, Ed Berman, who ran Kolber's Chicago office, was enticed into the deal; he would later become the third partner in the company that would be known as "BGK" (*i.e.,* "Berman, Gilbert, Kolber").

Berman was just 32 years old in 1992 when he joined BGK. He had met Fred Kolber in 1982, shortly after having graduated Phi Beta Kappa from the University of California at Berkeley. A native of Los Angeles (Berman's father was a psychology professor with California State University at Los Angeles), he began working for the Max Factor cosmetics firm in Los Angeles and, on weekends, gave tennis lessons at the Beverly Hills Tennis Club. One of his tennis students was the wealthy Beverly Hills denizen Coco Brown (whose father had been a successful Hollywood movie producer). Brown one day asked Berman if he knew anyone who was good at math. "As a matter of fact, I am," Berman said. "Why?" Brown explained that "a big-time Wall Street trader," an acquaintance of his, was looking for a young man who "was smart with numbers" but knew nothing about the stock market so he could "teach [him] from scratch."

Then Coco Brown introduced Ed Berman to Fred Kolber. "He hired me on the spot," Berman recalls, "and I moved to New York. I was petrified. I was broke. I didn't know anybody in New York. I was 22, and I was very insecure about my knowledge of options and the stock market. Fred trained me in how to trade options, and I worked long hours and studied the rest of the time. As I look back on it now, it was more a drive out of insecurity than a love for it. But it worked out, and after three or four months, he put me on a seat—which was probably unprecedented to be down there that young and that quickly—but he felt the only way to learn was to be 'thrown into the lion's den,' the way he put it."

Berman was exactly the kind of young man Kolber had been looking for: quick to learn, adept at grasping the nuances of the intricate and growing options market, and relentless in his efforts. After a year, Kolber congratulated him and said, "You're doing great. I think you understand this stuff as well as I do. You're ready to go to the big leagues."

"What's that?" Berman asked.

"Chicago," Kolber replied.

As Berman explains, "[Chicago] was the center of the options trading world. At the same time, I had gotten to like New York, and I knew no one in Chicago. I was reluctant." Kolber persisted and Berman finally agreed; it turned out to be mutually advantageous. Berman opened an office for Kolber there, hired several people and soon began trading successfully on the Chicago Board Options Exchange. By the time he was 30, about to be married, Ed Berman was a financial success.

And with the alliance he formed with Kolber and Eddie Gilbert in 1992, he was soon to become an even greater financial success. According to Berman, it happened this way: "Fred was fazing out of the trading business and was spending a good deal of his time traveling or at his home in Santa Fe. I was doing most of the trading and, we used to talk regularly by telephone. One fateful day, he called and said, 'I've got a really good friend out here. He's a wonderful guy, and we're doing some exciting things. Why don't you come out and meet him .... I think maybe there's a fit for eveybody here.'"

Ed Berman had always faithfully listened to Fred Kolber, "his mentor" Berman called him even long after he had made his own mark in the options world. Shortly afterwards, he went to Santa Fe. "I didn't really know very much about Eddie Gilbert when I went out there," Berman recalls. "Fred had told me a little bit about Eddie's problems in the past, but I hadn't really paid a lot of attention to it. I didn't have much of an idea as to what Fred had in mind; I was just going out there to see what he was thinking about."

The first night Berman was there, the three men sat down to talk at Gilbert's house. "I was expecting someone a little different than Eddie turned out to be. I knew he was in his late 60s. I expected he'd be sedate. He was just the opposite: excited, enthusiastic, dynamic although at the same time he exuded a lot of warmth and made me feel very welcome. And he didn't waste any time. He said that first night, right out, 'Why don't the three of us pool some money and do some more deals, some more real estate deals.'"

With Kolber's apparent recommendation and Gilbert's charisma, it might seem that Berman would readily agree to join the partnership. But Ed Berman had some reservations. "I'm a conservative person," Berman explained later, "a conservative investor." He was concerned about Gilbert's past. "I did a little reseach on my own, picked up that book about André Meyer, *Financier*, which had a couple of chapters that focused on Eddie, and I voiced my concerns to Fred. I said: 'He seems like a wonderful guy, but he's been to prison a couple of times. To be frank, I'm a little leery to invest with someone like that, even though he's a great guy socially. I think I may want to research this a little more.'

"Fred came right back at me. 'Look, I've known Ed umpteen years,' he said. 'He's one of the most honest people I've ever known. He's got integrity that exceeds anybody that I've ever been in business with. And he's one of the handful of people in the world that I would do business with on a handshake.'

"As soon as I heard that, for me, there was nothing more to discuss. No more research. I was in."

The arrangement was first for Berman to invest, the three going into a few real estate projects together. Berman, whose business reputation was as immaculate as Kolber's, added further financial credibility to the partnership. Like Kolber, who was well-established in New York financial circles, Berman was similarly well-known in Chicago's. The two might be able to open doors that Gilbert could not (or at least might find it difficult to pass through).

Six months later, Berman remembers getting a call in Chicago from Gilbert. "It was a conference call; he rang up Fred and me. We had done a few small deals at that point, but now he said he had a different idea. He wanted to take it a step further. 'Look,' he said, 'these deals are so compelling. I've never seen anything like this in my life. Why don't we make a real business out of this. Instead of just dabbling with our money, which is fine; we can all make a lot more bucks if we build a business out of it. Tell me, are we on the same page in this?'"

Although both Kolber and Berman were interested, there were some footnotes to the page Eddie was talking about. Fred Kolber was backing away from everyday involvement in the business world. He was wealthy and had no need whatsoever to work more in order to earn more money from his labors. He wanted to invest, yes, but passively. His time commitment was to be personal, making contacts with potential investors and others in the real estate business. "Ed, I'm traveling six to eight months out of the year, these days," Kolber explained. "That's what I want to do, and I have no intention of changing that." And Berman was fully committed to continuing his trading on the options exchange in Chicago: "[I was] an 'upstairs trader,' where you hire personnel for the [trading] floors. I was sitting upstairs and trading with them downstairs. And I'd gotten to love Chicago."

But Gilbert already knew these constraints on his partners' time. "I understand," he said. "That's fine. I'll run the business. I'll find the properties. We'll just be partners... equal partners in it, a third each."

And so they agreed. BGK, the company, was born in 1992 with a telephone call and a handshake.

Gilbert rented office space in a three-story building known as University Plaza on Garfield Street in Santa Fe — a building the company would eventually add to its holdings. He soon hired a secretary, Robin Smith (who would always remain his right hand even after ascending to a vice presidency in the company), and set the business in motion. Eddie's idea was now to go after larger properties, and each would be separately financed through syndication. Other individual investors were to be brought into each deal, each project would be set up as a limited partnership standing on its own merits with BGK serving as the general partner. In the beginning, the first syndications were made up of family and friends. Both Kolber and Berman went first to their families and their close friends and business associates. (They were still a little hesitant to go much beyond that circle with Eddie's past being a possible impediment.) They were comfortable, there was no doubt about that, but the three partners decided that it was in their best interests to establish a successful investment track record before soliciting limited partnership money from outsiders.

Fred Kolber describes the first syndicated deal that BGK did. "It was 1992, and before we had just bought things with our money. Small deals. [This time] we bought a beautiful office building in Albuquerque called the Metro Center [47,044 square feet, four stories]. We bought if for about two and half million dollars... and we had to come up with $650,000 in cash. The brokerage house of Shearson, Hammill and Company [today, part of the investment giant Salomon Smith Barney] leased about 25 percent of the building. I saw that their lease was up in three years, and that worried me. And I expressed that to Eddie. He was not so worried. 'What if they don't renew?' I asked.

"'Then we'll get somebody else,' Eddie said.

"I tell this story because there is a distinct irony in it," Kolber went on, "an irony that is so true of the real estate business at that time. At my insistence we went down to Albuquerque to talk to the people at Shearson, Hammill. I wanted to see if we could get them to extend the lease for another three years. They flew in their leasing agent from California. We had a long talk, and we explained to them that we would keep the rent below the market, or below the expected market, if they would extend their lease. They came back and said they would not. It was just not their policy to negotiate that far in advance. They were simply not in any mood to help us out. Well, we bought the building anyway, despite my nervousness. The irony was that three years later we did not even want them. As it turned out, the manager of that particular office was a terrible problem, a very abusive man to the people we had managing the building. The agent for Shearson, Hammill told us they wanted some kind of a deal if they were going to renew; they wanted some kind of financial incentive from us. By that time the positions had changed. We told them we wouldn't give them a thing below the current market; in fact, we told them we wished they would move, that they were a real pain in the neck. The story ends with them moving, and we leased the space immediately thereafter. The market was that strong by then."

Gilbert's philosphy was to build BGK one property at a time. As there were a great many being offered, Eddie took upon himself the responsibility of finding a candidate and then assessing the property's value. Eddie would look around for a building, shopping center, or similar property, although sometimes brokers came to him as he became better known in the business. If he determined it to be underpriced, as many were in the first half of the 1990s, he would study it and what its potential might be. One key criterion was that the property return 20 percent of the investment from rents and other income annually. If the figures made sense to him, he would make an offer, with closing to occur two to six months later. If the offer was accepted, he would have lawyers draft a limited partnership agreement to bring in investors and simultaneously approach a mortgage lender for 75 percent of the purchase price.

The plan was to return to each investor at least 20 percent per year, paying back the total investment in five years or less. Investors also received one-half of the profit at the time of the property's sale.

Following his philosophy, Gilbert began methodically to acquire property after property, five in 1992 alone, the first year of the business. Mortgage financing was initially difficult, but Gilbert approached that, too, in somewhat the same manner as he was building the business—a step at a time. As Fred Kolber remembers, "It was a problem, with the banks, insurance companies, and investors. In the beginning, when I'd bring up Eddie's background, well, there wouldn't be anything more to talk about."

Eddie, in fact, engineered the small first step, and in his own backyard. Kolber described it this way: "Santa Fe is a peculiar town.... A lot of the people there, I think, had failed one way or another and wanted to get away from the rat race. It's very slow-paced, old-fashioned. And the banks out there had low limits. But Eddie kind of took over. Eddie was exciting to them, these bankers. He is very good at socializing with his business contacts, and he socialized a lot with those bankers. They got to know him personally, and banking is done out there on a very personal basis. And finally they got to saying, 'Well, we can only lend you so much on this....' But they also got to saying, 'But we have very good friends [other, larger banks] we work closely with..., we'll introduce you.'.... It went slowly at first. And when they introduced us to other banks, we occasionally got turned down because of Eddie's background, but as we built a history, that became less and less a factor."

As good as Eddie Gilbert was at selling himself to others, he was equally as adept at building a solid financial track record for his investors. Acquiring building by building, property by property, Eddie was systematic but not conservative. In fact, Fred Kolber had misgivings about how rapidly their venture was growing in the first few years. "I'd sit down with him and say, 'Eddie, what are we missing here? . . . It's too easy . . . . There must be some loophole . . . . We must be overlooking something." Ed Berman shared the same sentiments. "We were moving much faster than I'd ever imagined. We were suddenly making so much money, it was startling. Were we just as suddenly going to crash?" As it turned out, their fears were baseless because the company's acquisitions and operations were rock-solid.

Gilbert began first to acquire properties in New Mexico, but soon moved beyond that market area. From the Metro Center in Albuquerque and others near Santa Fe, Gilbert added a 46,000 square-foot office building in Richmond, Virginia; a research office building in Andover, Massachusetts; an 83,000 square-foot office building in Houston, Texas; a 374-unit apartment complex in Lawrence, Kansas; a 69,544 square-foot distribution facility in Chattanooga, Tennessee; a five-story commercial building in Dunedin, Florida; and other properties in Minnesota, Illinois, Indiana, Oklahoma, Maryland, New Jersey, Iowa, Texas, Louisiana, and Colorado. There were also shopping centers. After that small strip mall in Hobbs, New Mexico, BGK acquired ones in Santa Fe and Albuquerque; Wichita, Kansas; James City County, Virginia; Plymouth, Minnesota; and Bullhead City, Arizona.

The size of the acquisitions grew as well. First there was the 225,988 square-foot, five-building office complex known as Pinetree Corporate Center in Albuquerque; then the 15-story, 194,599 square-foot Midland Office Building in Midland, Texas; a nine-story, 168,017 square-foot office building in Hillard, Ohio; a two-building research facility in Salt Lake City, Utah; a six-building office-showroom complex called Gateway Business Center in El Paso, Texas; a four-building retail aggregate in Wichita, Kansas; the two-building, 374,137 square-foot office complex in Denver, Colorado; the 215,185 square-foot, 12-story 1235 North Loop Building in

Houston, Texas; the 23-story, 352,816 square-foot Borg Warner Building on Chicago's fabled Michigan Avenue; a 12-story, 310,047 square-foot office building on Northwest Freeway in Houston; the 25-story, 333,977 square-foot 666 Walnut Street Building in Des Moines; the 25-story Blaustein Building in Baltimore with 287,068 square feet of office space; and the Sentry Park five-building office complex in Blue Bell, Pennsylvania. Many other buildings or complexes exceeding 100,000 square feet of space followed in cities such as Oklahoma City, Wichita, Cleveland, Hampton (Virginia), Minneapolis, Houston, and New Orleans.

By 1995, three years after Berman, Gilbert, and Kolber had begun BGK, the parent company had real estate holdings in excess of $100 million. Two years later, the figure had grown to $500 million. And finding properties that fell within the BGK parameters was no longer so difficult. Sellers were calling and writing on a daily basis, lining up at BGK's door. Securing financing was no longer a problem, because BGK's financial track record was untarnished, its position enviable. Banks and insurance companies were now *coming* to Gilbert with prospects that they thought he would find attractive; and investors with a return of 20 percent of their initial investment were predictably pleased. Prospective investors abounded.

Joining the families and friends of Berman, Gilbert, and Kolber in BGK limited partnerships were a host of savvy investors, quite diverse in their backgrounds. From Wall Street there was Robert Linton, former board chairman of Drexel Burnham Lambert, and Bruce Carp, former vice chairman of Salomon Brothers; from Broadway (and television, the famous captain of "The Love Boat") Gavin MacLeod; from Soho the respected contemporary artists Ed McGowin and Claudia De Monte; and others from many different walks in life as well as friends from before.

BGK became the corporate umbrella eventually covering a group of affiliated corporations: BGK Properties, Inc.; BGK Realty, Inc.; BGK Equities, Inc.; BGK Equities II, LLC; BGK Equities III LLC; and G & P Resorts, Incorporated.

A typical example of why investors and bankers were pleased can be found in the 1993 partnership for the property known as Plaza at Paseo del Norte, located in Albuquerque. A 300,000 square-foot shopping center with an additional 30 acres for expansion, the original purchase price to BGK was $5.95 million. Eddie raised $1.8 million from limited partners and borrowed $4.3 million in the form of a mortgage from the seller. Within a short time, he sold off 23 of the 30 expansion acres, leaving a seven-acre parcel of land, and soon thereafter refinanced the remaining income-producing property for $2 million more than the original mortgage, thus enabling BGK to repay the investors in full after only three years. In June 1998, BGK sold the Plaza shopping center to a San Diego, California, real estate trust for $17.8 million, with the $11.4 million profit divided equally among BGK and the limited partners.

Another enormously successful deal started off when BGK bought the Borg Warner Building in Chicago in 1995. A prime piece of commercial real estate on the city's most luxurious street, Michigan Avenue, it became available through the mortgage holder. Gilbert did the paperwork and figured the building to be worth $49 a square foot, or a little more than $17 million in total. He offered much less and finally settled on a purchase price of $13.75 million for the 23-story building. After raising $5 million from his growing list of enthusiastic limited partners, he mortgaged the remaining $8.75 million. Eddie anticipated that in five years the building would be valued at $80 a square foot, or approximately $28 million total. Five years later, in fact, the limited partners having been repaid by then their total investment of $5 million, BGK sold the property to the Berwind Property Group of Philadelphia for *exactly* $28 million, netting a profit of $14.25 million equally divided among the general partner, BGK, and the participating limited partners.

Only once in the first ten years of BGK's existence had a deal performed poorly: A strip mall in Petersburgh, Virginia, for which the company paid $2.1 million in 1993, lost its anchor tenant to bankruptcy a year and a half later. Gilbert had provided in the purchase documents that, in the event of such a circumstance, the seller would take back the property. There was, nevertheless, a net loss of $600,000. The limited partners' deficit would have been $360,000 in this particular deal, but because it was an anomaly, the three partners—Berman, Gilbert, and Kolber—agreed to cover the investors' loss from the BGK treasury so that the limited partners at least recovered their invested dollars.

Meanwhile, Eddie Gilbert and Peaches had settled into life in Santa Fe, many miles and cultures away from New York City. They sold their first house after Peaches found and fell in love with a much more elegant one, a gated, five-acre estate just off Canyon Road with a spectacular view, swimming pool, tennis court, donkey paddock, and dog kennel. It was one of the oldest houses in Santa Fe but badly in need of restoration; and she looked upon it as a great challenge, which indeed it was before she turned it into a showplace. They also decided to build a family of their own, adopting six-year-old Sasha in 1996, seven-year-old Bee the following year, and eight-year-old Zoe in 1999, all from orphanages in the former Soviet Union.

In late 1997, to celebrate Eddie's 75th birthday, Peaches threw a grand party. On the night of December 16, twelve days before his actual birthday, she engaged the Café Carlyle in New York's Carlyle Hotel (where Eddie's parents years before had had their co-op apartment). The surprise party — although it is doubtful Eddie was surprised — was a black-tie dinner for 100 of Eddie's closest friends and family. The party in fact began the day before in New Orleans, where Peaches had taken Eddie to meet with 36 friends and family members to make the overnight train ride in several private rail cars (an echo perhaps of the Orient Express) to Penn Station in New York. At the Carlyle party, the celebrated cabaret pianist Bobby Short entertained with his orchestra; Beluga caviar, fois gras, and truffles pleased the palates of those on hand to help Eddie celebrate; champagne and vintage wines flowed. Eddie's daughters recited poetry, Gene Wolkoff roasted and paid tribute to him; many were touched when Eddie himself spoke of how lucky he had been in his life, "blessed" as he was with friends who believed in him and stood by him. It was quite an occasion.

Elsa Maxwell was long gone from the New York party scene, Cholley Knickerbocker had closed up his typewriter many years earlier, El Morocco was only a distant memory, but the Carlyle evening brought back memories to many there of the social world that Eddie Gilbert had known in the 1950s and early 60s. Many in attendance that night had been there with Eddie decades before.

It was a return in a way, a triumphant one, because Eddie was back on top. His company was a smashing success; he was once again a wealthy man; he now enjoyed the respect and admiration of many friends and business associates alike. And he was clearly touched by it all.

After the party, Eddie went back to Santa Fe; it was his home now. New York was just a remembrance. Back to the 14-hour days he often put in to maintain the company that he had built with his own initiative and had grown to love. Moving into the 21st century, he knew he had launched BGK on a 15-year ascent. Ignited by a conversation at a backgammon table in

New York in 1987, the company had climbed to a point where it controlled 180 properties in 25 states worth $1.5 billion; a company that once struggled to lure a single outside investor could now claim more than 1,700. From the day when there was just Eddie and a secretary, there were now hundreds of BGK employees all over the country carefully managing the company's assets; and in Santa Fe a team of top-level lawyers, architects, former bankers, businessmen, and real estate experts were on board to make sure that the future of the company would remain as bright as the vision Eddie had for it.

Still, there was his past, relentlessly inescapable and still cast darkly even with the illumination of his recent successes. A *Forbes* magazine article in 1999 about Gilbert and the meteoric rise of BGK began with the lead sentence: "Convicted embezzler and stock manipulator Edward M. Gilbert is back in business." Peppered with uncomplimentary observations such as, "Gilbert's rise from disgrace has been a long time coming..." or "To meet margin calls, he took $2 million from the till at E.L. Bruce...," the *Forbes* article was far less a paean to BGK's success than a resurrection of Eddie's past sins, continuing to paint an unflattering portrait of him as a businessman. The article unleashed a flood of angry letters to the editor of *Forbes* (some of which were later published in the magazine) from Eddie's friends and BGK investors alike. Although hurt and feeling betrayed again—he had cooperated fully with the *Forbes* writer—Eddie took it as he had the many similar, painful treatments by the press in the past, without breaking stride.

His old high school chum, Jack Kerouac, best observed Eddie's style: "Eddie used to come breezing and bouncing down the hall by himself with a wicked little pale grin and rush by as everybody yelled at him to stop... He rushed down the hall all the way." He is still rushing, maybe not in the headlong way that characterized his youth, but ahead, or in Kerouac's words, all the way.

Eddie Gilbert's often wild, surely erratic roller-coaster ride of a life had finally leveled off. Unlike the conventional, amusement-park roller coasters, however, which glide to a stop at the bottom, his continues to roll along at the top. But then there never was very much conventional about Eddie Gilbert.

♦♦♦

# *Notes*

### PROLOGUE

p.10 HAD HE GLANCED: *New York Times*, 12 June 1962, p. 1, etc.

12 ONE OF WALL STREET'S BOY WONDERS: *Time*, 22 June 1962, p. 85.

13 I WASN'T THINKING CLEARLY: Author interview, Eddie Gilbert, 1997.

13 FREE-SPENDING MILLIONAIRE: *New York Times*, 24 June 1962, p. 56.

15 MY MAJOR BLUNDER: *New York Times*, 24 June 1962, p. 56.

16 I WAS DESPERATE: Author interview, Eddie Gilbert, 1997.

17 I WOULD STILL BE IN TROUBLE: Author interview, Eddie Gilbert, 1997.

17 I GOT PAUL ON THE LINE: Author interview, Eddie Gilbert, 1998.

18 I REALLY DON'T REMEMBER ANYTHING: Author interview, Eddie Gilbert, 1997.

19 THE WAY I LET THAT: Author interview, Eddie Gilbert, 1998.

19 SOME BOARD MEMBERS: *New York Times*, 24 June 1962, p. 56.

20 YOU KNOW I'M NOT PLEASED: Author interview, Eddie Gilbert, 1997.

21 LET'S JUST GIVE EDDIE: Harry Gilbert testimony before the Securities and Exchange Commission, 14 June 1962.

21 BOOK A RESERVATION: Author interview, Eddie Gilbert, 1997.

### CHAPTER ONE

25 CAPTURED IN BLACK AND WHITE: Halberstam, *The Fifties*, Preface pp. ix–x.

26 MONEY, AS HE LATER OBSERVED: Eddie Gilbert, interviewed on CBS-TV, Eye-

witness Reports, "Refuge in Rio," 28 July 1962.

28 IT JUST CAME UP ONE DAY: Interview with Yolan Gilbert, 1981, transcript provided by Eddie Gilbert.

28 IN FACT, THE FAMILY NAME: Author interview, Enid Smiley, 1998.

28 YOU MUST REMEMBER: Author interview, Enid Smiley, 1998.

29 I WAS NEVER IN REAL TROUBLE: Heller, *Now and Then*, p. 86.

30 IT NEVER WORKED WITH ME: Interview with Yolan Gilbert, 1981, transcript provided by Eddie Gilbert.

31 PEOPLE FROM THE HUNGARIAN GROUP: Author interview, Enid Smiley, 1998.

32 A FIERCE COMPETITOR: Author interview, Enid Smiley, 1998.

32 WHEN HE WAS FIVE YEARS OLD: Interview with Yolan Gilbert, 1981, transcript provided by Eddie Gilbert.

33 WE HAD A BEAUTIFUL LIFE: Interview with Yolan Gilbert, 1981, transcript provided by Eddie Gilbert.

34 EDDIE WAS THE ABSOLUTE IDOL: Author interview, Enid Smiley, 1998.

34 A STAR ... ALWAYS A STAR: Author interview, Enid Smiley, 1998.

34 WHEN WE WERE VERY YOUNG: Author interview, Enid Smiley, 1998.

36 HE WROTE ON A TYPEWRITER: *New York Times*, 19 August 1999, p. 9.

37 RIDE THE RATTLING SUBWAY: Miles, *Jack Kerouac, King of the Beats*, p. 22.

38 I USED TO DO HIS MATH HOMEWORK: Author interview, Eddie Gilbert, 1998.

38 AMONG THE FANTASTIC WITS: Jack
Kerouac, *Life*, 29 June 1962, p. 22.
38 WE WERE VERY GOOD: Author interview,
Eddie Gilbert, 1999.
39 IN THE 1940 HORACE MANN YEARBOOK:
Jack Kerouac, *Life*, 29 June 1962, p. 22.
39 HE COULD NOT AFFORD TO BUY: Miles,
p. 26.

CHAPTER TWO

44 IT WASN'T BECAUSE OF ANY PROBLEM:
Author interview, Eddie Gilbert, 1999.
45 SHOT IN THE ASS MY FIRST DAY: Author
interview, Eddie Gilbert, 1999.
46 IT MUST HAVE BEEN USED FOR SHIPPING:
Author interview, Eddie Gilbert, 1999.
48 THE COLONEL WAS NOT GOOD: Author
interview, Eddie Gilbert, 2000.
50 BUT WE SURE KNEW IT WAS: Author interview, Gordon Dick, 2000.
50 ARMY OF TERRIFIED CIVILIANS: Author
interview, Gordon Dick, 2000.
50 IT WAS A BIG PROMINENT SQUARE: Author
interview, Eddie Gilbert, 2000.
52 WE DECIDED TO GO ANYWAY: Author
interview, Eddie Gilbert, 2000.
57 I DIDN'T REALLY INTERVIEW HIM: Author
interview, Eddie Gilbert, 2001.
58 THE "WE" GENERATION OF WORLD WAR II:
Ambrose, *Citizen Soldiers*, p. 472.

CHAPTER THREE

60 WHEN I GOT THERE, TO THE PLANT:
Author interview, Eddie Gilbert, 1998.
62 ROYALTY, RICH, BEAUTIFUL, SMART:
Author interview, Eddie Gilbert, 2000.
64 WELL, WHY DON'T WE JUST PRODUCE:
Author interview, Eddie Gilbert, 1998.
65 HE WAS VERY DRAMATIC: Author interview, Eddie Gilbert, 1998.
67 MISS JAMES HAS HAD: *The Playbill*, "How
Long Till Summer," 1949, p. 20.
68 I WENT UP THERE WITH SOME ANXIETY:
Author interview, Eddie Gilbert, 2000.
68 ARTIE, WHAT DO YOU THINK: Author
interview, Eddie Gilbert, 2000.
69 QUITE DIGNIFIED, AFFABLE, AND
CHARMING: Simon, *Neil Simon Rewrites*,
p. 49.
70 THE HERMAN SHUMLIN: Simon, p. 46.
70 I COULD TAKE IT DOWN: Author interview, Eddie Gilbert, 2000.

72 HOW LONG TILL SUMMER . . . SEVEN DAYS:
*New York World-Telegram*, 28 December
1949, Theater page.
72 ALTHOUGH THE THEME IS VITAL: *New York
Times*, 28 December 1949, p. 30.
73 TO CLOSE THE SHOW: Author interview,
Eddie Gilbert, 2000.
73 ALL RIGHT, SEND SOME STUFF OVER:
Author interview, Eddie Gilbert, 1998.
78 TALK TO PETER LAWRENCE: Author interview, Eddie Gilbert, 1999.
80 ALTHOUGH THE WORLD MAY HAVE GROWN
OLD: *New York Times*, 25 April 1950, p. 27.

CHAPTER FOUR

83 IN HIS HEART HE WANTED TO BUILD
HOUSES: Author interview, Eddie
Gilbert, 1998.
84 I'LL PAY YOU THE $50,000: Author inter-
view, Eddie Gilbert, 1998.
85 STRONG AND MODERATELY SUCCESSFUL:
*Business Week*, 5 July 1958, p. 23.
86 IT CAUGHT MY IMAGINATION: Author
interview, Eddie Gilbert, 1998.
87 I'D CONVINCED THEM AT EMPIRE: Author
interview, Eddie Gilbert, 1998.
88 THIS UNWANTED HOSTILE INTRUSION: E.L.
Bruce Company letter to stockholders,
1958.
89 MOST OF THE CLASSIC CORNERS: *Business
Week*, 5 July 1958, p. 22.
89 GILBERT HAD NO INTENTION: *Business
Week*, 5 July 1958, p. 23.
91 I AM A LUMBERMAN: *Business Week*, 5 July
1958, p. 23.
91 THE TIFFANY OF THE FLOORING INDUSTRY:
*Business Week*, 5 July 1958, p. 23.
92 THIS PUTS CONTROL OF THE COMPANY:
*New York Times*, 22 August 1958,
Business section, p. 1.
92 THIS DOES NOT COME AS A SURPRISE:
Benjamin Javits, news release, 1958.
93 AN ILLEGAL VIOLATION: Javits, news
release, 1958.
93 IT WAS AN ACCOMPLISHMENT: Author
interview, Tom Field, 1997.
94 THE DRAMA SURROUNDING THIS ACTION:
Author interview, Tom Field, 1997.
95 A HORRIFYING PROSPECT: Author interview, Tom Field, 1997.
95 IT WAS STATED IN SUCH AN OMINOUS:
Author interview, Tom Field, 1997.

97 MR. GILBERT SAID YESTERDAY: Benjamin Javits, press conference, 12 September 1958.

97 [JAVITS] SAID 17,255 SHARES: *New York Times*, 16 September 1958, p. 37.

98 LOOK, WHAT'S THE USE OF WASTING: Author interview, Eddie Gilbert, 1997.

98 YESTERDAY, 1,000 MILES FROM MEMPHIS: *New York World-Telegram*, 23 September 1958, p. 51.

99 THE EXISTING POLICIES OF THE BRUCE COMPANY: E.L. Bruce Company press release, 28 October 1958.

CHAPTER FIVE

101 PARIS CAME TO NEW YORK LAST NIGHT: *New York Journal-American*, 27 April 1960, p. 18.

102 EDDIE GILBERT... WHAT A VIBRANT: *Long Island Press*, 18 May 1969, p. 17.

103 THERE, ONE GUEST RECALLS: *Saturday Evening Post*, 19 October 1963, p. 44.

104 SOMETIMES HE LIVED: Brooks, *The Go-Go Years*, p. 66.

104 EDDIE WAS ALWAYS THE MAESTRO: Brooks, p. 66.

104 NEVER! TO INDULGE HIM?: Author interview, Eddie Gilbert, 1998.

104 ADJOURNED THE PARTY TO LE PIRATE: *Life*, 29 June 1962, p. 19.

105 COQUELIN HAD ALSO BEEN A WW II: Author interview, Gene Wolkoff, 2001.

106 EDDIE AND RHODA WERE STAYING: Author interview, Enid Smiley, 1998.

107 A RAKISH MILLIONAIRE: *London Times*, 30 June 2000, Obituary.

107 IDLE AND REBELLIOUS: *London Times*, 30 June 2000, Obituary.

108 THE SUCCESS HE HAD IN FLEECING: *New York Times*, 1 July 2000, Section A, p. 11.

108 SHE WAS ABSOLUTELY BEAUTIFUL: Author interview, Eddie Gilbert, 1998.

108 HOW COULD ONE FORGET: Author interview, John Aspinall, 1998.

109 EDDIE... DID NOT EMBARRASS HIS FRIEND: Masters, *The Passion of John Aspinall*, p. 103.

110 IT WAS IN FEBRUARY AND EDDIE: Author interview, John Aspinall, 1998.

111 ON THE GROUND THAT THE COMPANY: *Business Week*, 12 March 1960, p. 58.

112 IN LOPPING OFF LUMBER: *Business Week*, 12 March 1960, p. 58.

112 MORE IMPORTANT: *Business Week*, 12 March 1960, p. 58.

114 WE WOULD LIKE TO PURSUE THIS: Author interview, Eddie Gilbert, 1998.

114 LYNDON JOHNSON WOULD OFTEN SEEK: Reich, *Financier—The Biography of André Meyer*, p. 15.

115 I SPOKE WITH MR. MEYER: Author interview, Eddie Gilbert, 1998.

115 MEYER WAS ENTHUSIASTIC: Reich, p. 16.

116 EDWARD M. GILBERT, PRESIDENT OF THE E.L. BRUCE: *New York Times*, 11 April 1962, p. 66.

116 IN MY VIEW [CELOTEX]: *New York Times*, 18 April 1962, p. 49.

CHAPTER SIX

118 I'VE BEEN TRYING TO GET YOU: Author interview, Eddie Gilbert, 1997.

119 THE VALUE OF ALL LISTED STOCKS: Sobel, *Panic on Wall Street*, p. 415.

119 I COULD SENSE THINGS: Author interview, Eddie Gilbert, 1997.

119 IS THIS A MERE FORECAST: *New York Times*, 27 May 1962, p. 1.

120 ONE ENCOURAGING ASPECT: *New York Times*, 30 May 1962, Business section, p. 3.

120 INVESTORS ARE NOT PANICKING: *New York Times*, 30 May 1962, Business section, p. 3.

120 FOR MANY AMERICANS, THE DECLINE: Sobel, p. 417.

120 SHOULD THE INDUSTRIAL AVERAGE: *Dow-Jones News Service*, press release, 25 May 1962.

121 YET THE ATMOSPHERE OF PANIC: Sobel, p. 417.

121 IT'S AS BIG A CRASH AS THE ONE: Author interview, Eddie Gilbert, 1997.

121 I THOUGHT HE MUST BE JOKING: Eddie Gilbert, deposition filed with the U.S. District Court, Southern District of New York, 23 February 1967.

122 SHARES ON THE NEW YORK STOCK EXCHANGE: *New York Times*, 29 May 1962, p. 1.

123 REPORTS OF MARGIN CALLS ECHOED: *New York Times*, 29 May 1962, p. 1.

123 SOMEWHERE IN THE VICINITY OF THREE MILLION: Author interview, Eddie Gilbert, 1997.

123 I TOLD HIM THAT WE MUST: Eddie Gilbert, deposition filed with the U.S. District Court, Southern District of New York, 23 February 1967.

123 WHEN I GOT BACK [TO NEW YORK]: Author interview, Eddie Gilbert, 1997.

124 I REMEMBER SAYING TO HIM: Author interview, Eddie Gilbert, 1997.

125 I WOULD LIKE TO PUT ON THE RECORD: Eddie Gilbert, deposition filed with the U.S. District Court, Southern District of New York, 23 February 1967.

125 JACK, WHAT DO YOU THINK: Author interview, Eddie Gilbert, 1997.

126 ALL DURING MY STAY: *New York Times*, 6 October 1962, Business section, p. 1.

127 ZILKHA CALLED A NUMBER OF TIMES: Author interview, Eddie Gilbert, 1997.

128 THERE WERE SOME OPTIMISTS: *New York Times*, 29 May 1962, p. 37.

129 THREE OF THE LARGEST BROKERAGE HOUSES: *New York Times*, 30 May 1962, p. 1.

129 THE STOCKS CAME BACK TO $28: Eddie Gilbert, deposition filed with the U.S. District Court, Southern District of New York, 23 February 1967.

131 WELL, IF YOU CAN'T HELP ME: Author interview, Eddie Gilbert, 1997.

132 BROODED UPON THE UNFAIRNESS: Reich, *Financier—The Biography of André Meyer*, p. 14.

132 A PARADE OF ALL THE BANKERS: Eddie Gilbert, deposition filed with the U.S. District Court, Southern District of New York, 23 February 1967.

133 HAD I NOT COVERED THESE MARGINS: Eddie Gilbert, deposition filed with the U.S. District Court, Southern District of New York, 23 February 1967.

134 [EDDIE] CAME TO ME AND HE SAID: Harry Gilbert testimony before the Securities and Exchange Commission, 14 June 1962.

134 BY HEARSAY, WEST EXPLAINED: Harry Gilbert testimony before the Securities and Exchange Commission, 14 June 1962.

135 THE PRICE WAS SET AT $36: Harry Gilbert testimony before the Securities and Exchange Commission, 14 June 1962.

135 MY DEAR BOY: Reich, p. 17.

136 CALM ABOUT THE MATTER: Harry Gilbert testimony before the Securities and Exchange Commission, 14 June 1962.

141 I DIDN'T WANT TO GO TO MY APARTMENT: Author interview, Eddie Gilbert, 1997.

141 THERE WAS A LOT OF TENSION: Author interview, Enid Smiley, 1998.

142 IF YOU NEED MONEY: Author interview, Turid Holtan Gilbert, 1997.

142 WHERE'S GILBERT NOW: Harry Gilbert testimony before the Securities and Exchange Commission, 14 June 1962.

CHAPTER SEVEN

144 I REALLY COULDN'T THINK STRAIGHT: Author interview, Eddie Gilbert, 1997.

153 LIKE A CAGED ANIMAL: Tony Stratton Smith, personal journal, 1962.

153 YOU'D LOOK UPSET, TOO: Author interview, Eddie Gilbert, 1997.

154 I THINK THIS MAN MAY BE COMMITTING: Tony Stratton Smith, personal journal, 1962.

155 THEY WERE JUST THE NICEST PEOPLE: Author interview, Eddie Gilbert, 1997.

155 HE WOULD JUST GET TO TALKING: Tony Stratton Smith, personal journal, 1962.

156 DEVELOPMENTS IN THE FAST-MOVING SITUATION: *New York Times*, 15 June 1962, p. 33.

157 HE MISSED HIS FRIENDS BADLY: Tony Stratton Smith, personal journal, 1962.

157 IN FLEEING, MR. GILBERT LEFT: *New York Times*, 24 June 1962, p. 56.

158 HOW THEY FOUND ME: Author interview, Eddie Gilbert, 1998.

159 BUILT AND WRECKED: *Business Week*, 30 June 1962, p. 55.

159 WHEN EDDIE PICKED UP THE PHONE: Author interview, Eddie Gilbert, 1998.

164 A PROFITABLE SIDELINE: *Business Week*, 30 June 1962, p. 56.

165 EDWARD M. GILBERT IS CONSIDERING TAKING UP: *New York Times*, 15 June 1962, p. 33.

165 SENHOR CHALOUPE SAID MR. GILBERT: *Associated Press Wire Service* report, 15 June 1962.

166 WE'RE TRYING TO RECONSTRUCT THE SITUATION: William Moran, Securities and Exchange Commission press conference, 14 June 1962.

166 SINCE BLUE MONDAY ON WALL STREET: *Brazil Herald*, 16 June 1962, p. 1.

168 JUNE BEING THE START OF WINTER: *Life*, 29 June 1962, p. 18.

168 I KNOW THEY THINK I BROUGHT: *Life*, 29 June 1962, p. 18.

169 EDWARD M. GILBERT, THE FUGITIVE FINANCIER: *Life*, 29 June 1962, p. 16.

169 SURE I DID SOME WRONG THINGS: *Life*, June 29, 1962, p. 18.

170 AS A KID, I CAN REMEMBER HIM WALKING: *Life*, 29 June 1962, p. 18.

170 HE WAS TERRIBLY EAGER: *Life*, 29 June 1962, p. 19.

170 AN HABITUÉ OF MONTE CARLO: *Life*, 29 June 1962, p. 18.

171 AMONG THE FANTASTIC WITS: Jack Kerouac, *Life*, 29 June 1962, p. 22.

173 DOWN HERE, IN A WAY, IT MAY BE: *Life*, 29 June 1962, p. 18.

174 AT HIS VILLA AT CAP MARTIN: *Life*, 29 June 1962, p. 19.

174 HE ALSO ACQUIRED A 35-ROOM: *Life*, 29 June 1962, p. 19.

174 ALTHOUGH EDDIE LIKED TO SPEND: *Life*, 29 June 1962, p. 19.

175 HE STARTED OUT AS EDWARD GINSBERG: *Life*, 29 June 1962, p. 19.

175 AWARE THAT HIS GLOOM: *Life*, 29 June 1962, p. 21.

175 HE WAS NAÏVE: *Life*, 29 June 1962, p. 21.

CHAPTER EIGHT

177 HE WAS BRUSQUE: Author interview, Eddie Gilbert, 1997.

179 THERE'S NO CRIME HERE: Author interview, Eddie Gilbert, 1997.

179 THE DECISION ON THAT IS HIS: Arnold Bauman, press conference at Idlewild Airport, June 1962.

182 GILBERT'S STORY: AN OPERATOR'S FALL: *New York Times*, 24 June 1962, p. 1.

183 TRANSFER A NUMBER OF THE FUNCTIONS: *New York Times*, 27 June 1962, p. 49.

184 IN BAGGY BLUE SHORTS: Tony Stratton Smith, personal journal, 1962.

185 FILLED WITH SADNESS AND SELF-ACCUSATION: Tony Stratton Smith, personal journal, 1962.

185 I'D DONE A LOT OF BUSINESS WITH THEM: Author interview, Eddie Gilbert, 1998.

186 AFTER ALL, I DIDN'T FEEL: Author interview, Eddie Gilbert, 1997.

187 ON A BEACHFRONT PROMENADE IN RIO: CBS-TV, Eyewitness Reports, "Refuge in Rio," 28 July 1962.

191 I HAVE COME TO SEE ZAT EDDIE: *Time*, 13 July 1962, p. 79.

191 HE WAS VERY SUPPORTIVE: Author interview, Eddie Gilbert, 1998.

191 HERE, USE THIS FOR WHATEVER: Author interview, Eddie Gilbert, 1998.

192 EDDIE CALLED ME IN LONDON: Author interview, Richard Parkes, 1998.

193 IT WAS A DISASTER: Author interview, John Aspinall, 1998.

194 HE [ASPINALL] DID NOT ONCE CONSIDER: Masters, *The Passion of John Aspinall*, p. 113.

195 I ALWAYS KNEW THERE WAS AN INHERENT RISK: Author interview, John Aspinall, 1998.

196 I WAS HORRIFIED AT FIRST: Author interview, Richard Parkes, 1998.

196 RICHARD, I'M GOING OUT WITH JANE: Author interview, Richard Parkes, 1998.

196 HE SOUNDED FINE ON THE TELEPHONE: Author interview, John Aspinall, 1998.

196 ALTHOUGH I'D NOT KNOWN EDDIE: Author interview, Richard Parkes, 1998.

196 HE HAD A SMILE, SO DELIGHTED: Author interview, John Aspinall, 1999.

196 IT WAS ALL THEY COULD MUSTER: Author interview, Eddie Gilbert, 1999.

196 HE TOLD ME HE HAD A LOT OF CASH: Author interview, Eddie Gilbert, 1997.

197 [ASPINALL ENGAGED] IN AN ELABORATE CHARADE: Masters, p. 114.

197 A RATHER UNINSPIRED PICNIC: Author interview, John Aspinall, 1998.

197 THE BOAT WAS NAMED: Author interview, Richard Parkes, 1998.

197 A LONG, FRUITLESS AFTERNOON: Author interview, Eddie Gilbert, 1999.

197 FROM A PURVEYOR OF COLORED STONES: H. Stern Company corporate brochure, 2000.

197 IT WAS A DISTRESSED SALE: Author interview, John Aspinall, 1998.

198 HE NOSED AROUND IN EACH: Author interview, Eddie Gilbert, 1999.

199 I DIDN'T KNOW WHAT WAS GOING ON: Author interview, Turid Holtan Gilbert, 1997.

200 SHE LOOKED FABULOUS: Author interview, Eddie Gilbert, 1997.

200 OLD-FASHIONED SCANDINAVIAN WOMAN: Author interview, Turid Holtan Gilbert, 1997.

CHAPTER NINE

204 IN THE UNITED STATES YOU'VE GOT THREE: Author interview, Eddie Gilbert, 1998.

204 WELL-WORN JEEP: Tony Stratton Smith, personal journal, 1962.

205 SICKENED HIS LUMBERMAN'S SOUL: Tony Stratton Smith, personal journal, 1962.

205 YOU'RE THE EDDIE GILBERT: Author interview, Eddie Gilbert, 1998.

212 HE WROTE ALMOST EVERY DAY: Author interview, Turid Holtan Gilbert, 1997.

212 IT'S AT DINNERTIME THAT: Tony Stratton Smith, personal journal, 1962.

213 WE HAD SEVERAL DINNERS TOGETHER: Tony Stratton Smith, personal journal, 1962.

214 TONY AND I HAVE BEEN PROGRESSING: Eddie Gilbert letter to John Dos Passos, October 1962.

216 MY FATHER ESPECIALLY WAS OPPOSED: Author interview, Turid Holtan Gilbert, 1997.

217 IT WAS A WONDERFUL TIME: Author interview, Turid Holtan Gilbert, 1997.

218 BRAZIL DENIES GILBERT PERMANENT RESIDENCE: New York Times, 3 October 1962, p. 55.

220 THE FEAR I LIVE WITH: Tony Stratton Smith, personal journal, 1962.

220 TIGHTEN THE COMPANY'S OPERATIONS: Wall Street Journal, 29 October 1962, p. 8.

220 MAKE YOUR ARRANGEMENTS TO COME BACK: Author interview, Eddie Gilbert, 1998.

222 I'M RETURNING OF MY OWN FREE WILL: New York Times, 27 October 1962, p. 11.

224 ARE YOU GLAD TO BE BACK: New York Times, 30 October 1962, p. 1.

224 MR. GILBERT FLED TO BRAZIL: New York Journal-American, 29 October 1962, p. 11.

225 AT THE ARRAIGNMENT, I HEARD MR. GILBERT: Wall Street Journal, 30 October 1962, p. 9.

225 I ORIGINALLY LEFT, HE SAID: New York Times, 30 October 1962, p. 23.

225 THERE HAS BEEN NO DEAL WHATSOEVER: Wall Street Journal, 30 October 1962, p. 9.

225 WE INTEND TO MOVE ALONG: Wall Street Journal, 30 October 1962, p. 9.

226 TANNED AND APPARENTLY REFRESHED: New York World-Telegram, 29 October 1962, p. 1.

226 LOOKING LIKE A WELL-TANNED TOURIST: New York Journal-American, 29 October 29 1962, p. 1.

226 TO FACE MUSIC: New York Mirror, 30 October 1962, p. 1.

CHAPTER TEN

227 THE DARING YOUNG MAN: Tony Stratton Smith, personal journal, 1962.

232 WHY TAKE THE CHANCE: Author interview, Eddie Gilbert, 1998.

232 A NUMBER OF EXTRAORDINARY ITEMS: E.L. Bruce Company audit report, 1962.

233 FOR ALL PRACTICAL PURPOSES, [GILBERT]: New York Times, 10 November 1962, p. 53.

235 PLANNING TO PAY BACK EVERY CENT: Saturday Evening Post, 19 October 1963, p. 45.

235 SMALL AND CLUTTERED: New York Times, 21 February 1967, p. 67.

235 I USED TO ORDER $500,000 WORTH OF LUMBER: Saturday Evening Post, 19 October 1963, p. 45.

236 FRIENDS SAY THAT ALMOST ALL OF GILBERT'S: New York Times, 21 February 1967, p. 75.

237 TO THE SURPRISE OF CYNICS: Saturday Evening Post, 19 October 1963, p. 45.

238 EDWARD M. GILBERT, THE 40-YEAR-OLD NEW YORK: New York Times, 15 April 1963, p. 66.

242 THE DAY, WHAT A DAY: Author interview, Turid Holtan Gilbert, 1997.

243 THE PUBLICITY WAS TERRIBLE: Author interview, Eddie Gilbert, 1999.

243 WE DID NOT IN ANY WAY WANT: Author interview, Turid Holtan Gilbert, 1997.

243 THE REASON FOR SO MANY ADJUSTMENTS: *New York Journal-American*, 24 July 1964, p. 29.

244 I GUESS I WAS AS CLOSE TO HIM: Author interview, Red Chandor, 1997.

244 I HEARD THEY ARE RECOMMENDING: Author interview, Tom Field, 1997.

244 I WAS SITTING IN HIS APARTMENT: Author interview, Red Chandor, 1997.

245 THE SLIGHTLY-BUILT, DAPPERLY DRESSED: *New York World-Telegram*, 25 September 1964, p. 7.

245 NODDED SOLEMNLY TO HIS LAWYER: *New York Times*, 25 September 1964, p. 1.

250 HIS PLEA CAME AS A SURPRISE: *New York Times*, 25 September 1964, p. 1.

## CHAPTER ELEVEN

256 I DON'T THINK ANYTHING THAT WAS SAID: Author interview, Eddie Gilbert, 1999.

256 I WAS NOT A NERVOUS WRECK: Author interview, Eddie Gilbert, 1999.

257 I'LL TREAT YOU PROPERLY: Author interview, Eddie Gilbert, 1999.

258 I . . . BECAME APPREHENSIVE: Author interview, Eddie Gilbert, 2000.

258 I WENT TO A FRIEND OF MINE: Eddie Gilbert, U.S. Grand Jury testimony, 1970.

258 HE [CHANDOR] CAME BACK TO ME: Eddie Gilbert, U.S. Grand Jury testimony, 1970.

259 HAD A LOT OF POLITICAL CONNECTIONS: Eddie Gilbert, U.S. Grand Jury testimony, 1970.

259 I WENT ALONE: Eddie Gilbert, U.S. Grand Jury testimony, 1970.

260 FINALLY I WAS ESCORTED INTO HIS OFFICE: Eddie Gilbert, U.S. Grand Jury testimony, 1970.

260 OH, NOT MUCH TIME: Eddie Gilbert, U.S. Grand Jury testimony, 1970.

261 DON'T WORRY ABOUT IT: Eddie Gilbert, U.S. Grand Jury testimony, 1970.

261 I WAS WORRIED: Eddie Gilbert, U.S. Grand Jury testimony, 1970.

262 THINGS WERE IN THE WORKS: Author interview, Eddie Gilbert, 1999.

262 I INTRODUCED MY LAWYER: Author interview, Eddie Gilbert, 1999.

266 GILBERT, WEARING A DARK SUIT: *New York Times*, 9 May 1967, p. 69.

## CHAPTER TWELVE

268 A SHOCKING PERFORMANCE: Author interview, Eddie Gilbert, 1998.

268 A SCATHING ARTICLE: *Life*, 31 October 1969, pp. 52–56.

269 ANOTHER ARTICLE AROUND THE SAME TIME: *Time*, 31 October 1969, pp. 19–20.

270 MARTIN SWEIG PHONED: *Life*, 31 October 1969, p. 55.

271 AFTER WHAT SEEMED A LIFETIME: Eddie Gilbert's prison journal, 1967–68.

271 [THE DOCTOR] WAS A COLD: Eddie Gilbert's prison journal, 1967–68.

271 I WENT DOWN THERE: Author interview, Turid Holtan Gilbert, 1997.

272 AS STRANGE AS IT MAY SEEM: Eddie Gilbert's prison journal, 1967–68.

272 OUT ON THE STREET: Eddie Gilbert's prison journal, 1967–68.

272 HEY, JOE . . . SAM, HOW YOU DOIN': Author interview, Eddie Gilbert, 1998.

273 GENTLY AND FRIENDLY: Author interview, Eddie Gilbert, 1998.

277 EDWARD M. GILBERT, THE FORMER BOY WONDER: *New York Times*, 17 June 1969, p. 36.

277 WE'LL GET THIS THING STRAIGHTENED OUT: Author interview, Eddie Gilbert, 1998.

277 I WAS ASKING FOR MY PLEA BACK: Eddie Gilbert, U.S. Grand Jury testimony, 1969.

286 FOR HIS ADVICE AND HELP: Yolan Gilbert, U.S Grand Jury testimony, 1969.

286 MOM [YOLAN GILBERT] AND I: Author interview, Turid Holtan Gilbert, 1997.

287 RUSSELL G. OSWALD, NEW YORK STATE: *Life*, 31 October 1969, p. 56.

287 IT IS WELL KNOWN IN WASHINGTON: *Time*, 31 October 1969, p. 20.

287 I NEVER SPOKE WITH MR. OSWALD: *New York Times*, 24 October 1969, p. 1.

288 NATHAN VOLOSHEN'S MOST NOTABLE: *Life*, 31 October 1969, p. 55.

288 EDWARD M. GILBERT, THE ONETIME MULTI-MILLIONAIRE: *New York Times*, 24 October 1969, p. 1.

288 A CONVICTED CORPORATE SWINDLER: *Time*, 31 October 1969, p. 20.

288 ONETIME WALL STREET WONDER: *Newsweek*, 26 January 1970, p. 16.

289 Q. DID YOU HAVE ANY CONVERSATION: Eddie Gilbert, U.S. Grand Jury testimony, 1969.

291 I CAN NEVER FORGET IT: Author interview, John Aspinall, 1998.

292 ONE NEVER REALIZES HOW VALUABLE: Eddie Gilbert's prison journal, 1967–68.

293 PROBABLY ONE OF THE MOST PAINFUL THINGS: Eddie Gilbert's prison journal, 1967–68.

294 I WANT TO LEAVE HERE IN STYLE: Author interview, Turid Holtan Gilbert, 1997.

CHAPTER THIRTEEN

296 WITHOUT A TRACE OF CHARM: Author interview, Eddie Gilbert, 2000.

296 IN MANY WAYS, ANDRÉ MEYER: Reich, *Financier—The Biography of André Meyer*, p. 18.

296 MY DEAR BOY: Reich, p. 17.

305 THAT SON OF A BITCH: Reich, p. 17.

310 EVEN IF HE WAS THE AGGRIEVED PARTY: Reich, p. 288.

310 LOATHSOME! HE IS LOATHSOME: Reich, p. 287.

312 MANY YEARS AFTERWARD: Reich, p. 293.

313 WHEN I REALLY LIKE A STOCK: *New York Times*, 5 October 1980, Section 3, p. 4.

315 GEE, WHAT A NICE FELLA: Author interview, Turid Holtan Gilbert, 1997.

316 HE USED TO WRITE ME: Author interview, Eddie Gilbert, 1999.

317 I THINK IT WAS SELLING FOR: Author interview, Eddie Gilbert, 1999.

318 I THINK THEY HAD A BUDGET: Author interview, Eddie Gilbert, 1999.

318 MAYBE ABOUT 50,000 SHARES: Author interview, Eddie Gilbert, 1999.

319 UNKNOWN TO ME, HOWEVER: Author interview, Eddie Gilbert, 1999.

319 I SOLD MINE BETWEEN $25 AND $28: Author interview, Eddie Gilbert, 1999.

320 EDWARD M. GILBERT ISN'T REALLY A CROOK: *Wall Street Journal*, 6 April 1977, p. 26.

324 SPECIFICALLY, THE APPEALS PANEL: *Wall Street Journal*, 6 April 1977, p. 26.

324 HOW DO I FEEL?: *Wall Street Journal*, 6 April 1977, p. 26.

CHAPTER FOURTEEN

326 UNKNOWN TO ME . . . : Eddie Gilbert, written statement, 1975.

330 IT'S THE SEC'S CONTENTION: *Barron's*, 10 July 1978, p. 20.

331 IT WAS A COMFORTABLE MEETING: Author interview, Linda Watkins, 2002.

332 NO SMOKING GUN: *Barron's*, 10 July 1978, p. 4.

333 AND JOHN REVSON IS STILL: *Barron's*, 10 July 1978, p. 22.

333 MR. GILBERT HAS DENIED: Stanley Reiben, press statement on behalf of Eddie Gilbert, 1978.

333 THERE WAS A HUGE COLLECTION: Author interview, Jeffrey Livingston, 1997.

334 THE FUGITIVE FINANCIER: *Fortune*, 28 July1980, p. 64.

335 BEFORE HE WAS 39, EDDIE GILBERT: Stanley Reiben, letter to *Fortune*, 1980.

335 EDDIE GILBERT: THE HIGHS AND LOWS: *New York Times*, 5 October 1980, Section 3, p. 4.

335 MR. GILBERT STARTS HIS DAY: *New York Times*, 5 October 1980, Section 3, p. 5.

338 WE ASSERT THAT MR. GILBERT: *Wall Street Journal*, 20 August 1980, p. 24.

339 FOR THE FIRST TIME IN ABOUT TWO YEARS: *Wall Street Journal*, 24 September 1980, p. 20.

339 GENERALLY WHAT IS DONE: Author interview, Gene Wolkoff, 2000.

341 THERE IS NO WAY: Author interview, Herald Fahringer, 1997.

342 THE GOVERNMENT'S OBSESSION: Author interview, Eddie Gilbert, 2001.

342 EDDIE VERY MUCH: Author interview, Herald Fahringer, 1997.

343 I DON'T THINK ANYONE: Author interview, Jeffrey Livingston, 1997.

345 HE WORKED FOR A COMPANY: Author interview, Eddie Gilbert, 2001.

345 ASK HIM THIS ONE QUESTION: Author interview, Eddie Gilbert, 1999.

346 THE SCENE AT THE TRIAL: Author interview, Gene Wolkoff, 2000.

346 IT WAS VERY FRUSTRATING: Author interview, Gene Wolkoff, 2000.

347 COURI WAS A LIAR: Author interview, Eddie Gilbert, 1999.

347 EDWARD M. GILBERT WAS CONVICTED: *New York Times*, 26 February 1981, p. 1.

348 A COOPERATING WITNESS: Letter from Jeffrey Livingston to Henry Putzel and Henry H. Korn, 18 March 1981.

349 THE AGGREGATE OVERSTATEMENT: Letter from Jeffrey Livingston to Henry Putzel and Henry H. Korn, 18 March 1981.

CHAPTER FIFTEEN

352 WELL, THE VERY SIMPLE ANSWER: Author interview, Jeffrey Livingston, 1997.

352 I THINK, NO: Author interview, Jeffrey Livingston, 1997.

360 HE [EDDIE] MADE A NICE IMPRESSION: Author interview, fellow-inmate of Eddie Gilbert at Allenwood prison, 1997.

361 BRAGGING STUFF, SOB STORIES: Author interview, fellow-inmate of Eddie Gilbert at Allenwood prison, 1997.

365 AS YOU ALREADY KNOW: Eddie Gilbert letter to Kenneth Geist, 26 August 1982.

366 DEAR ED, THERE ARE MANY THINGS: Kenneth Geist letter to Eddie Gilbert, 15 April 1983.

367 AS EVERY PHONE CALL: Kenneth Geist letter to Eddie Gilbert, 27 August 1984.

CHAPTER SIXTEEN

370 MY FIRST THOUGHT: Author interview, Eddie Gilbert, 2000.

370 IT'S AMAZING TO ME: author interview Peaches Gilbert, 1998.

370 A MENAGERIE REALLY: author interview Peaches Gilbert, 1998.

375 THE MAN NEEDED A JOB: Author interview, Eddie Gilbert, 2001.

376 SHE KEPT HIM IN FOCUS: Author interview, Peter Heydon, 1997.

377 HE WAS IN BAD SHAPE: Author interview, Eddie Gilbert, 2001.

377 BUT I WANTED TO DO: Author interview, Eddie Gilbert, 2001.

378 THERE WERE A LOT OF PROBLEMS: Author interview, Andy Feltz, 1997.

379 LOOK, I'LL BACK THE FIRST MONTH: Author interview, Peter Heydon, 2000.

CHAPTER SEVENTEEN

387 AFTER A FEW YEARS OF TRADING: Author interview, Fred Kolber, 1998.

387 IT WAS 1989: Author interview, Fred Kolber, 1998.

388 I SAW ALL KINDS OF OPPORTUNITIES: Author interview, Eddie Gilbert, 2001.

388 FIRE-SALE PRICES: Author interview, Eddie Gilbert, 2001.

388 AT THIS TIME, EVERYTHING WAS FOR SALE: Author interview, Fred Kolber, 1998.

389 SO WE BEGAN TO SOCIALIZE: Author interview, Fred Kolber, 1998.

389 I'LL DO IT: Author interview, Eddie Gilbert, 1997.

389 AT THE TIME, I HAD NO IDEA: Author interview, Fred Kolber, 1998.

389 AFTER THE RECREATION VEHICLE PARK: Author interview, Fred Kolber, 1998.

390 A SUMMER HOME: Author interview, Eddie Gilbert, 2001.

392 HE LOVES EVERY PART: Author interview, Fred Kolber, 1998.

393 AS A MATTER OF FACT, I AM: Author interview, Ed Berman, 1997.

393 HE HIRED ME ON THE SPOT: Author interview, Ed Berman, 1997.

393 YOU'RE DOING GREAT: Author interview, Fred Kolber, 1998.

393 [CHICAGO] WAS THE CENTER: Author interview, Ed Berman, 1997.

393 FRED WAS FAZING OUT: Author interview, Ed Berman, 1997.

394 I DIDN'T REALLY KNOW: Author interview, Ed Berman, 1997.

394 I WAS EXPECTING SOMEONE: Author interview, Ed Berman, 1997.

394 I'M A CONSERVATIVE PERSON: Author interview, Ed Berman, 1997.

395 IT WAS A CONFERENCE CALL: Author interview, Ed Berman, 1997.

395 ED, I'M TRAVELING: Author interview, Fred Kolber, 1998.

396 IT WAS 1992 AND BEFORE: Author interview, Fred Kolber, 1998.

397 IT WAS A PROBLEM: Author interview, Fred Kolber, 1998.

397 SANTA FE IS A PECULIAR TOWN: Author interview, Fred Kolber, 1998.

398 I'D SIT DOWN WITH HIM: Author interview, Fred Kolber, 1998.

402 CONVICTED EMBEZZLER AND STOCK MANIPULATOR: *Forbes*, 3 May 1999, p. 98.

402 EDDIE USED TO COME BREEZING: Jack Kerouac, *Life*, 29 June 1962, p. 22.

◆◆◆

# Bibliography

## BOOKS, JOURNALS, AND NEWSPAPERS

Adams, Walter. *Dangerous Pursuits: Mergers and Acquisitions in the Age of Wall Street.* New York: Pantheon, 1989.

*Albuquerque Journal.* 10 April 1995.

Ambrose, Stephen E. *Citizen Soldiers.* New York: Simon & Schuster, 1997.

*Barron's.* 10 July 1978; 2 March 1981.

Blume. Marshall. *Revolution on Wall Street: The Rise and Decline of the New York Stock Exchange.* New York: W.W. Norton, 1993.

*Brazil Herald.* 19 June 1962; 23 June 1962; 24 June 1962; 27 June 1962; 29 June 1962; 17 July 1962; 23 October 1962.

Brooks, John. *The Go-Go Years.* New York: Weybright and Talley, 1973.

*Business Week.* 5 July 1958; 12 March, 1960; 14 April, 1962; 16 June 1962; 30 June 1962.

*Chicago Tribune.* 26 September 1999.

*Forbes.* 15 September 1958; 15 August 1962; 3 May 1999.

*Fortune.* July 1962; December 1962; 28 July 1980.

Frey, Stephen W. *The Inner Sanctum.* New York: E.P Dutton, 1997.

Fridson, Martin S. *It Was a Very Good Year: Extraordinary Moments in Stock Market History.* New York: John Wiley & Sons, 1998.

Geisst, Charles R. *Wall Street: A History.* New York: Oxford University Press, 1997.

————. *100 Years of Wall Street.* New York: McGraw-Hill, 2000.

Halberstam, David. *The Fifties.* New York: Villard Books, 1993.

Heller, Joseph. *Now and Then.* New York: Alfred A. Knopf, 1998.

*Life.* 3 February 1958; 29 June 1962; 31 October 1969.

*Long Island Press.* 18 May 1969.

Masters, Brian. *The Passion of John Aspinall.* London: Jonathan Cape, Ltd., 1988.

*Memphis Commercial Appeal.* 29 October 1958.

Miles, Barry. *Jack Kerouac, King of the Beats: A Portrait.* New York: Henry Holt and Co., 1998.

*Nashville Tennessean.* 23 June 1962.

*National Law Journal.* 20 August 1980; 6 July 1981.

*New York Daily News.* 21 August 1962; 30 October 1962; 3 July 1977; 6 February 1984; 29 December 1989.

*New York Herald-Tribune.* 26 July 1962

*New York Journal-American.* 24 April 1960; 10 July 1962; 29 October 1962; 23 July 1964; 24 July 1964; 1 April 1966.

*New York Mirror.* 30 October 1962

*New York Observer.* 19–26 July 1993.

*New York Post.* 14 June 1962; 25 September 1964; 22 February 1989.

*New York Times.* 3 December 1948; 28 December 1948; 26 January 1958; 25 April 1958; 13 June 1958; 18 June 1958; 23 June 1958; 18 July 1958; 2 August 1958; 16 August 1958; 19–22 August 1958; 24–25 August 1958; 28–29 August 1958; 3–5 September 1958; 9 September 1958; 12–13 September 1958; 15–18 September 1958; 23 September 1958; 26 September 1958; 28 September 1958; 16 October 1959; 23 November 1959; 28 November 1959; 8 April 1960; 26 May 1960; 3 November 1960; 5 November 1960; 19 December 1960; 21 January 1961; 30 June 1961; 29 August 1961; 15 September 1961; 20 September 1961; 11–12 April 1962; 18 April 1962; 27 May 1962; 29–30 May 1962; 11–16 June 1962; 18–29 June 1962; 2 July 1962; 6 July 1962; 12–14 July 1962; 21 July 1962; 3 August 1962; 21 August 1962; 25 August 1962; 3 October 1962; 5–6 October 1962; 13 October 1962; 23 October 1962; 27 October 1962; 30 October 1962; 9–10 November 1962; 16 January 1963; 20 February 1963; 15 April 1963; 12 May 1963; 19 May 1963; 26 September 1964; 10 December 1964; 11 October 1966; 21 January 1967; 21 February 1967; 3 March 1967; 31 March 1967; 28 April 1967; 2 May 1967; 9 May 1967; 17 June 1967; 23–25 October 1969; 28 October 1969; 13 January 1970; 24–25 June 1970; 3 July 1970; 25 November 1970; 25 August 1971; 5 October 1980; 13 January 1981; 1 August 1981

*New York Times Magazine.* 24 November 1968; 5 October 1980.

*New York World-Telegram & Sun.* 26 November 1960; 9 April 1962; 10 May 1962; 15–16 June 1962; 29–30 August 1962; 29 October 1962; 13 November 1962; 25 September 1964.

*Newsday.* 27 August 1989; 31 August 1989; 1 September 1989; 29 December 1989; 29 August 1999.

*Newsweek.* 25 June 1962; 23 July 1962; 13 August 1962; 12 November 1962; 26 January 1970; 6 September 1971.

*Paris Match.* 18 August 1962.

*The Playbill.* "How Long Till Summer," 1949.

*Quest.* September 1987.

Reich, Cary. *Financier: The Biography of André Meyer.* New York: William Morrow and Co., 1983.

*Rio de Janeiro Diario de Noticias.* 27 June 1962.

*Santa Fe Reporter.* 7–13 July 1999.

*Saturday Evening Post.* 19 October 1963.

Sharp, Robert M. *The Lore and Legends of Wall Street.* Homewood, Ill.: Dow Jones-Irwin, 1989.

Simon, Neil. *Neil Simon Rewrites: A Memoir.* New York: Simon & Schuster, 1996.

Sobel, Robert. *Inside Wall Street: Continuity and Change in the Financial District.* New York: W.W. Norton, 1977.

———. *Panic on Wall Street: A Classic History of America's Financial Disasters.* New York: E.P Dutton, 1988.

*Time.* 22 June 1962; 6 July 1962; 13 July 1962; 20 July 1962; 9 November 1962; 24 October 1969; 31 October 1969; 26 January 1970.

*True.* November 1962.

*Wall Street Journal.* 13 June 1962; 29–30 October 1962; 27 January 1971; 26 January 1976;14 April 1976; 6 April 1977; 20 August 1979; 26 February 1980; 20 August 1980; 5 September 1980; 24 September 1980; 3 August 1981; 22 February 1989; 27 February 1989; 30 January 1990.

## COURT DOCUMENTS

Court of Appeals of the State of New York. Edward M. Gilbert vs. André Meyer and Lazard Frères: 1972. Brief for defendants-respondents.

Edward M. Gilbert vs. André Meyer and Lazard Frères, Supreme Court of the State of New York, 1970. Defendant's memorandum of law in support of motion for summary judgment.

Edward M. Gilbert vs. André Meyer and Lazard Frères, Supreme Court of the State of New York, 1970. Plaintiff's memorandum of law in opposition to motion for summary judgment.

Edward M. Gilbert vs. André Meyer and Lazard Frères, Supreme Court of the State of New York, May 1, 1970. Judgment against defendants.

Edward M. Gilbert vs. André Meyer and Lazard Frères, Supreme Court of the State of New York, December 21, 1970. Testimony of Thomas F. X. Mullarkey.

E.L. Bruce Co., Inc., vs. McDonnell & Co., Inc., vs. Turid Holton (interpleaded defendant-claimant). 1965. Claims.

James C. Couri vs. Edward M. Gilbert, John C. Revson, et. al. Supreme Court of State of New York, County of New York. October 12, 1982, Index # 8021/82. Transcript of court proceedings.

National Association of Securities Dealers Arbitration Division, New York. Kenneth L. Geist vs. Bear Stearns & Co., Inc., et. al. July 1988. Demand for arbitration and statement of claims.

New York Supreme Court, Appellate Division, First Department, Edward M. Gilbert vs. André Meyer and Lazard Frères. 1971. Brief for plaintiff-appellant.

People of the State of New York vs. Edward M. Gilbert. 1962. Grand jury indictment, indictment charges.

People of the State of New York vs. Edward M. Gilbert. January 1967. Memorandum of law, Coramnobis writ to vacate guilty plea.

People of the State of New York vs. Edward M. Gilbert. 1967. Reply memorandum of law, Coramnobis writ to vacate guilty plea.

People of the State of New York vs. Edward M. Gilbert. 1967. Memorandum in opposition to defendant's motion to dismiss indictment on grounds of double jeopardy.

People of the State of New York vs. Edward M. Gilbert, Supreme Court of the State of New York. January 1968. Memorandum of law, writ to vacate guilty plea in state court.

Securities and Exchange Commission, New York. In the matter of Celotex Corporation, Harry Gilbert, and Edward M. Gilbert. June 14, 1962. Testimony of Harry Gilbert.

*USA vs. Edward M. Gilbert. June 28,1962. Grand Jury indictment, 62 Cr664, indictment charges.

USA vs. Edward M. Gilbert, Rhoda Gilbert, et.al. November 23, 1964. Complaint 64 Civ. 3558. IRS claim.

USA vs. E.L. Bruce Co., Inc., McDonnell & Co., Inc., Edward M. Gilbert, et.al. January 22, 1965. Deposition of Thomas Harvey Creech, vice president, E.L. Bruce Co., Inc.

USA vs. Edward M. Gilbert, Rhoda Gilbert, Wildenstein & Co., Inc., et. al. January 20, 1965. Deposition of Clyde M. Newhouse.

USA vs. Edward M. Gilbert, Rhoda Gilbert, Wildenstein & Co., Inc. November 24, 1965. Deposition of Daniel Wildenstein.

USA vs. Edward M. Gilbert, Rhoda Gilbert, Wildenstein & Co., Inc., et.al. January 16, 1967, Deposition of Edward M. Gilbert.

USA vs. Edward M. Gilbert. February 23, 1967, 66 Civ. 3358, 62 Civ. 4001. Transcript of deposition of Edward M. Gilbert.

USA vs. Edward M. Gilbert. April 27, 1967, 62 Cr 664. Filing of charges.

USA vs. Edward M. Gilbert. April 27, 1967. Pre-sentencing arguments.

USA vs. Edward M. Gilbert. May 8, 1967. Sentencing proceedings.

USA vs. Edward M. Gilbert. June 16, 1967, 62 Cr 664. Petition to reduce federal sentence.

USA vs. Edward M. Gilbert, Rhoda Gilbert, Wildenstein & Co., Inc., et.al. June 24, 1969, 64 Civ. 3558. Stipulation.

USA vs. Edward M. Gilbert, John C. Revson and Ludwig Cserhat. December 24, 1980. Memorandum opinion and order, severance of trials.

USA vs. Edward M. Gilbert. January 12, 1981 – February 25, 1981, S 80 Cr 493 (CSH). Court transcript of trial.

USA vs. Edward M. Gilbert. Commencing January 22, 1981, S 80 Cr 493 (CSH). Testimony of James Couri.

USA vs. Edward M. Gilbert. July 23, 1981. Court rulings on defense motions.

USA vs. Edward M. Gilbert. July 31, 1981. Pre-sentencing and bail proceedings.

---

* All U.S. government judicial proceedings, identified as USA vs. Edward M. Gilbert, were conducted under the auspices of the United States District Court for the Southern District of New York, unless otherwise cited.

USA vs. Edward M. Gilbert. 1981, S 80 Cr 493 (CSH). Motion for a new trial.

USA vs. Jost C. Fleck, Edward M. Gilbert, et. al. January 3, 1985, Civil Action # CV83-1381. Trial brief.

USA vs. Edward M. Gilbert. July 11, 1989, S80 Cr 493 (CSH). Memorandum opinion and order regarding probation violations.

USA vs. Edward M. Gilbert. August 30, 1989, S80 Cr 493 (CSH). Transcript of court proceedings regarding probation violations.

USA vs. Edward M. Gilbert. October 19, 1989. Defendant's post-hearing memorandum, defendant's statement of facts.

USA vs. Edward M. Gilbert. April 4, 1990, S80 Cr 493 (CSH). Memorandum opinion and order, sentencing proceedings.

U.S. Court of Appeals, Edward M. Gilbert vs. Commissioner of Internal Revenue. April 4, 1977. Appeal decision.

U.S. Court of Appeals for the Second Circuit, USA vs. Edward M. Gilbert, on appeal from the U. S. District Court, Southern District of New York. October 3, 1981, Docket # 81-1323. Brief and addendum for the USA.

U.S. Grand Jury proceedings against Nathan Voloshen. 1969. U. S. District Court, Southern District of New York. Testimony of Edward M. Gilbert.

U.S. Tax Court, Edward M. vs. Commissioner of Internal Revenue. April 21, 1975, Docket # 76-4170. General document/stipulation.

U.S. Tax Court, Edward M. Gilbert vs. Commissioner of Internal Revenue. April 1, 1976. Petition and findings of fact and opinion, T.C. Memorandum 1976-104, Docket # 6426-72.

♦♦♦

# Index

# O

O'Connor, Frank 97–99, 135, 137
Ossining State Correctional Facility "Sing
  Sing" 272–93

# P

Paley, William 102, 114
Palmieri, Judge Edmund L. 251, 253–57, 273,
  276–77
Papert, Fred 8
Papock, Herb 337, 374, 375
Parkes, Richard 104, 192, 195–96
parole violation issues 272–74, 381
Peat, Marwick, Mitchell and Company 140
  Bruce Co. audit 219, 232
Pele 215, 238
Peltz, Bob 378
*Peter Pan* 78–81
Plazagal International Corporation 334,
  348–49, 351, 353
Polivy, Irwin 123–24, 127, 129–30, 132, 137,
  140, 156, 166, 252
Pollack, Irving 200
Postel, Judge George 280, 284, 288
Putzel, Henry 348, 353–54, 372
Pynchon, Thomas 41

# R

Ratner, Albert 185–86, 204
Reeve, Christopher 41
Reiben, Stanley 305, 307, 313, 335, 336, 346
Reich, Carey 114, 135, 296, 310, 312
Reinach, Tony 73–77
Reinach, Udo "The Baron" 73, 75, 76,
  234–35
Revson, John 314–15, 318, 320, 327–29, 332,
  333, 336, 340–41, 342, 351
Rhodes Enterprises 129, 229, 230
Rhodes Flooring Company 83–84
Rifkind, Simon 309–10, 312
Robbins, Irwin 317
Romatowski, Peter J. 383, 348, 355
Rose, Fred 38
Rossant, Murray 182–83, 237, 238
Ruberoid Company 133–39
Rudley, Herbert and Sarett 64–68, 72

# S

Salathe, Trevor 127, 131
Santayana, George 57–58
Sarlie, Jacques 125–26, 130, 132, 178, 249
Schaap, Dick 41
Schlesinger, James 35
Schweitzer, Judge Mitchell D. 268, 270
Securities and Exchange Commission 92,
  166, 140, 156, 211, 219, 233, 332
  Bruce-Celotex investigation 134, 138, 166,
    200–01
  Commodore International investigation
    340–41
  Conrac investigation 319–20, 325–27, 329
  lawsuit 327–31
  insiders' report 224, 228, 229
Shearman and Sterling 97, 133, 134–35, 137
Shargel, Gerald L. 350, 351, 353, 355, 356,
  359
Sheffield, Frederick 137
Sherman, Matt 38
Shumlin, Herman 69–70, 72
Simon, Al 337
Simon, Neil 69–70
Sing Sing *see* Ossining State Correctional
  Facility
Slucker, Rudy 378
Smiley, Leonard 141
Smith, Robin 395
Smith, Tony Stratton 157, 176, 183–85,
  204–06, 208, 210, 212–16, 220, 237, 238
  photo 299
Sobel, Robert 119–21
Societe Anonyme Financier Ficomer 125,
  132
Sonnenblick, Jack 38
Sosler, Stuart 368, 372
Stern, Hans 196–97
Stern, Jerry 70, 127, 176, 209, 236, 378–79
Stork Club 61
Strausberg, Marc 339–41
Streicher, Judson 330, 332
Streit, Judge Saul S. 224
Sugarman, Judge Sidney 245
Sulzberger, Arthur Hays 35
Supreme Court, U.S. 248
Sweig, Martin 268, 270, 287, 288–90

COLOPHON

*The text of* Boy Wonder of Wall Street: The Life and Times of
Financier Eddie Gilbert *was composed in Dante, a typeface designed by the
scholar-printer and archtypographer, Giovanni Mardersteig. Originally
hand-engraved (cut) by Charles Malin of Paris in 1952 for private use, it was also
one of the last fonts cast by the Monotype Corporation for trade use.
The 1991 digitized version by Ron Carpenter used in this book consists of
roman and italics with expert and titling characters. Dante continues to be
admired as one of the best classic book faces.*

*The book was designed and typeset by Marc Alain Meadows on a
MacIntosh Powerbook G3 in QuarkXpress and carefully crafted using ligatures,
ranging numerals, and other expert characters throughout the text.*

*Printed and bound in Canada by Friesens printing company, the text pages are
acid-free "Superfine" by Mohawk Paper Mills. The endleaves are "MegaMoola
Greenbacks" by CTI Paper USA, an acid-free paper made with 30 percent
post-consumer waste and flecked with shredded authentic U.S.currency.
The binding cloth is "Pearl Linen" cotton fabric by ICG Holliston.*

❧